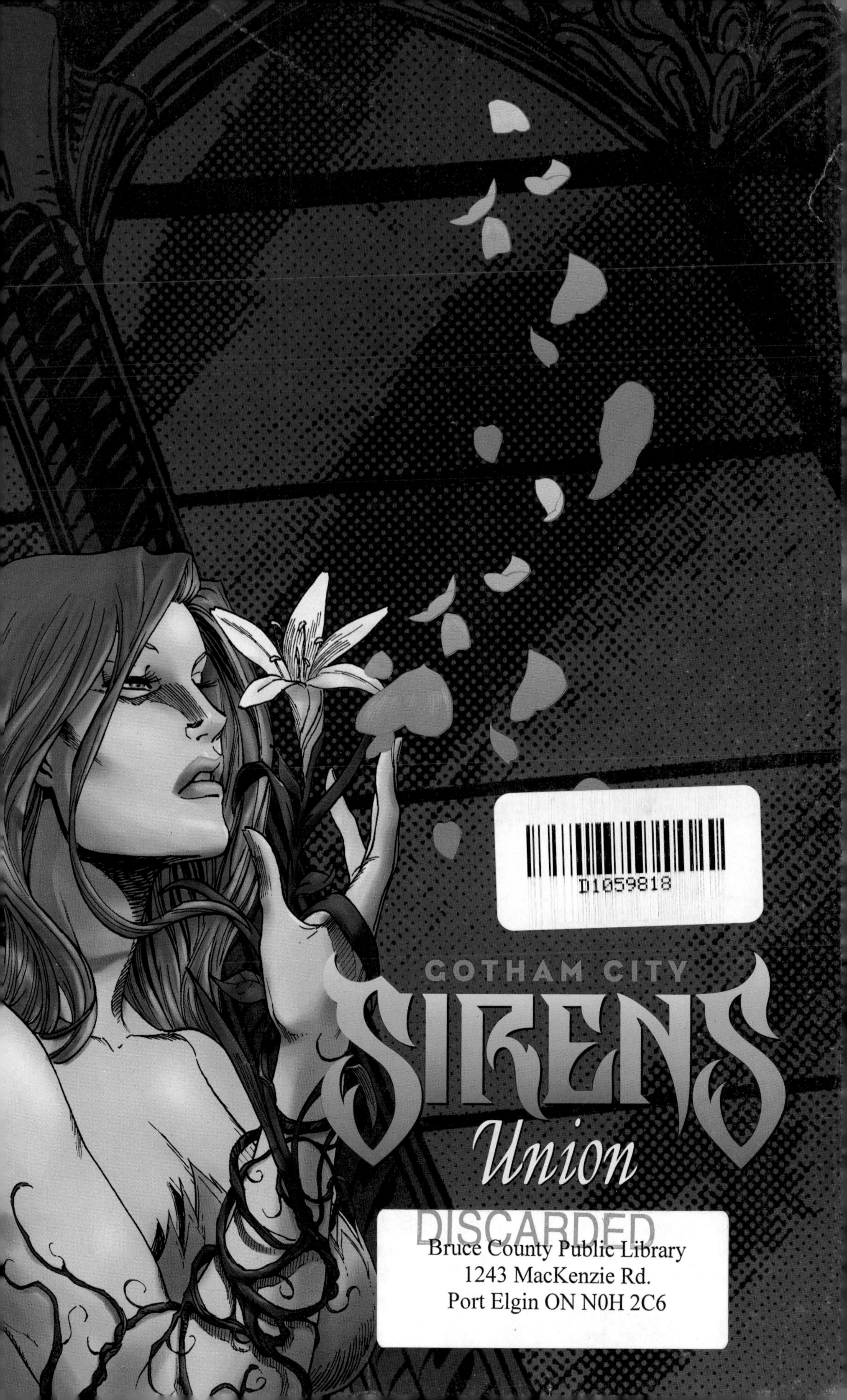
GOTHAM CITY
SIRENS
Union

**PAUL DINI** *writer* **GUILLEM MARCH** *artist & covers*

**SCOTT LOBDELL** *writer on issue #3*

**DAVID LOPEZ & ALVARO LOPEZ** *artists on issue #7*

**JOSE VILLARRUBIA** **TOMEU MOREY** **GUILLEM MARCH** *colorists*

**STEVE WANDS** **TRAVIS LANHAM** *letterers*

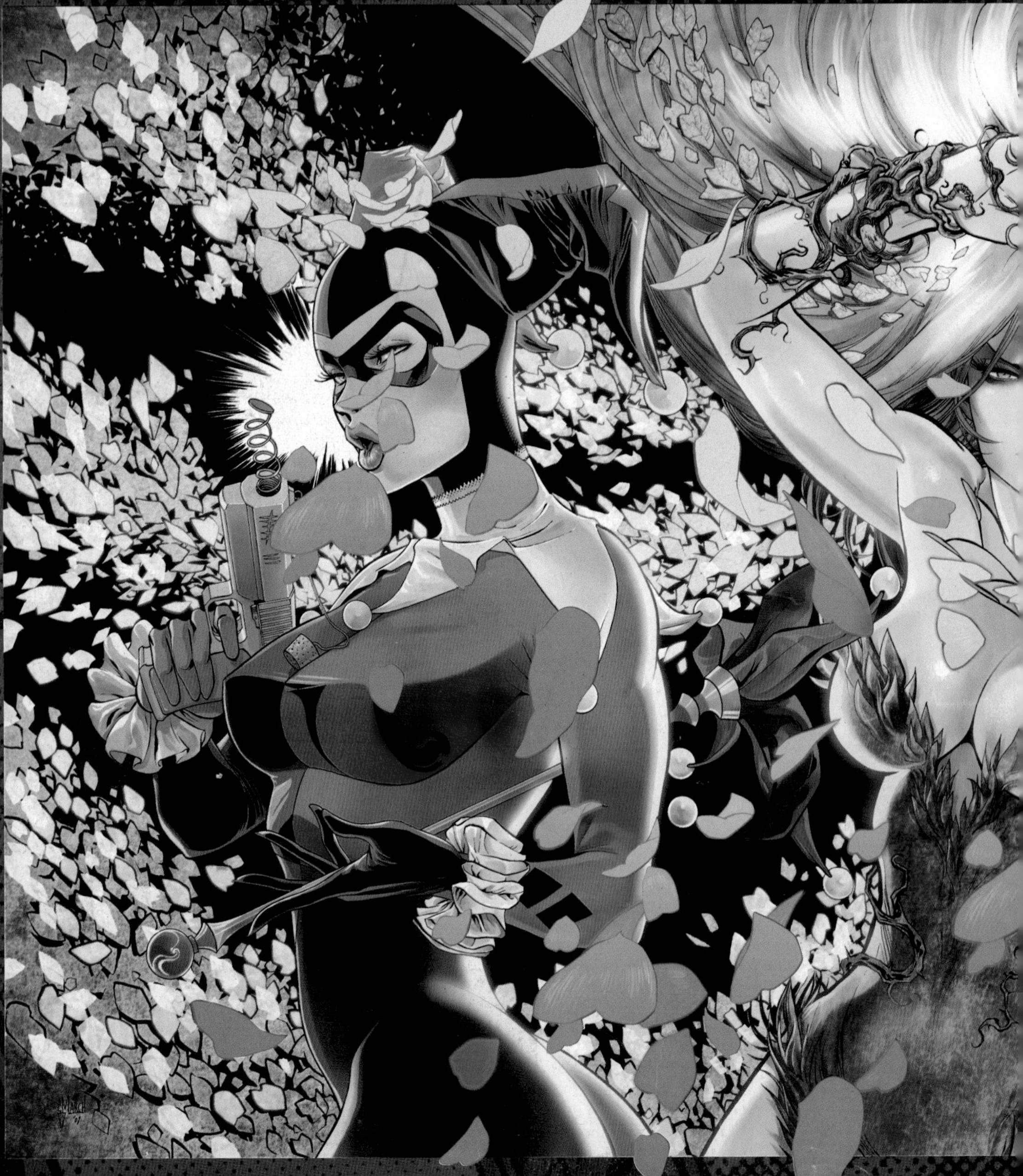

# GOTHAM CITY SIRENS

## *Union*

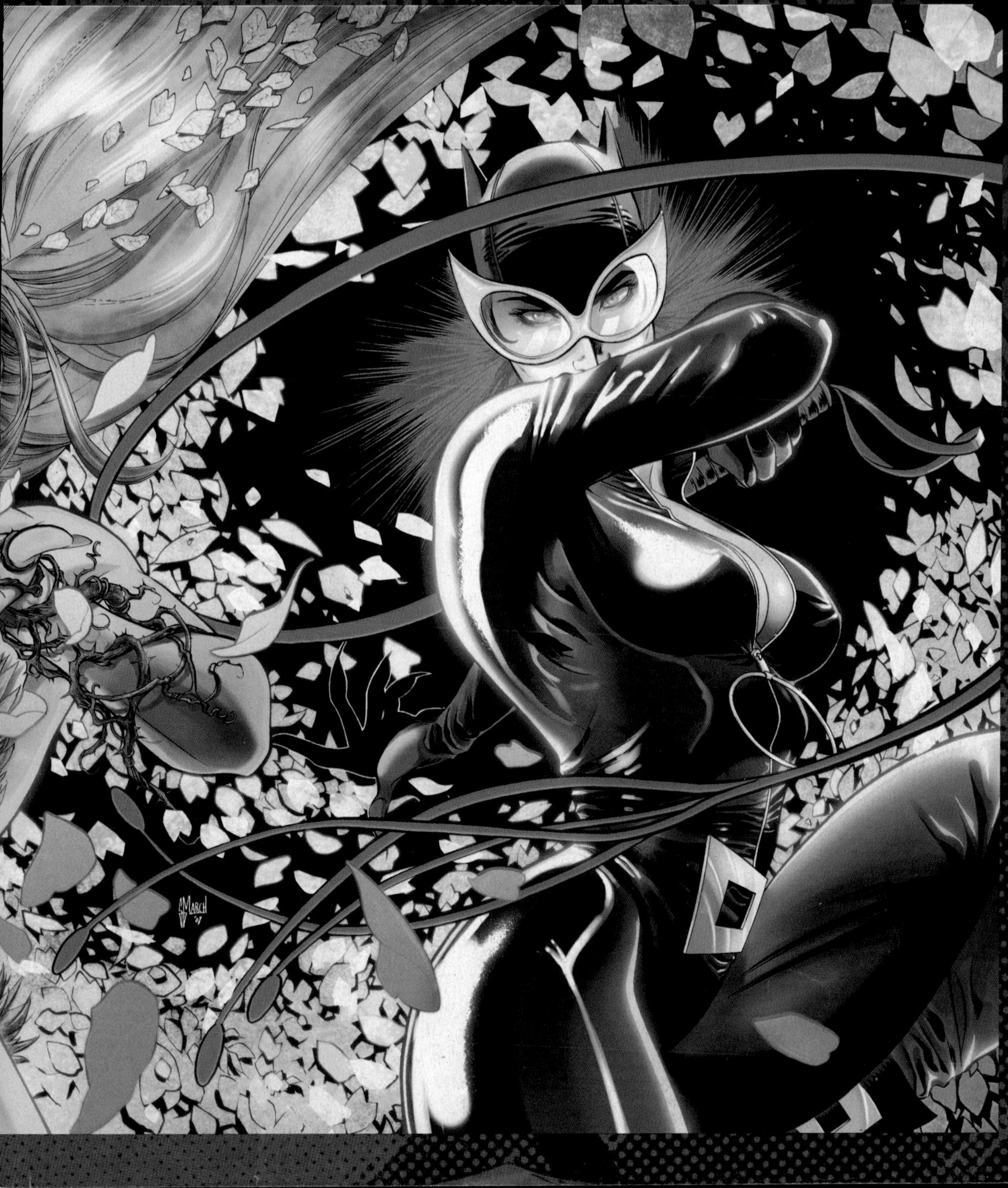

**Dan DiDio** SVP-Executive Editor
**Mike Marts** Editor-original series
**Janelle Siegel** Assistant Editor-original series
**Georg Brewer** VP-Design & DC Direct Creative
**Bob Harras** Group Editor-Collected Editions
**Anton Kawasaki** Editor
**Robbin Brosterman** Design Director-Books

**DC COMICS**
**Paul Levitz** President & Publisher
**Richard Bruning** SVP-Creative Director
**Patrick Caldon** EVP-Finance & Operations
**Amy Genkins** SVP-Business & Legal Affairs
**Jim Lee** Editorial Director-WildStorm
**Gregory Noveck** SVP-Creative Affairs
**Steve Rotterdam** SVP-Sales & Marketing
**Cheryl Rubin** SVP-Brand Management

Cover by **Guillem March**

**GOTHAM CITY SIRENS: UNION**
Published by DC Comics.
Cover, text and compilation Copyright © 2010 DC Comics.
All Rights Reserved.

Originally published in single magazine form in GOTHAM CITY
SIRENS #1-7. Copyright © 2009, 2010 DC Comics.
All Rights Reserved. All characters, their distinctive likenesses
and related elements featured in this publication are trademarks
of DC Comics. The stories, characters and incidents featured in
this publication are entirely fictional. DC Comics does not read or
accept unsolicited submissions of ideas, stories or artwork.

DC Comics, 1700 Broadway, New York, NY 10019
A Warner Bros. Entertainment Company
Printed by RR Donnelley, Salem, VA, USA
3/11/11. First Printing.
SC ISBN: 978-1-4012-2571-1

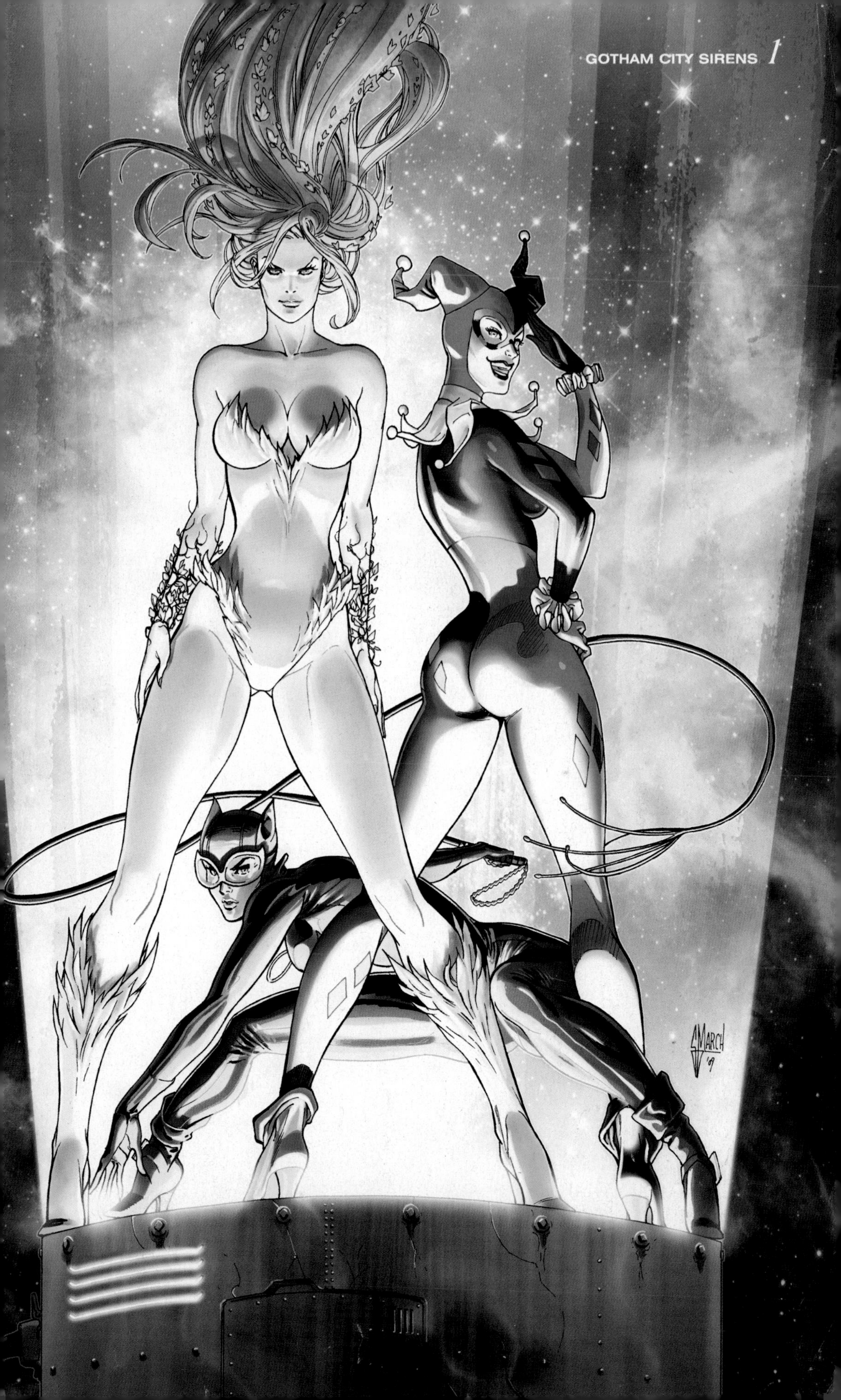
GOTHAM CITY SIRENS 1
GMARCH '09

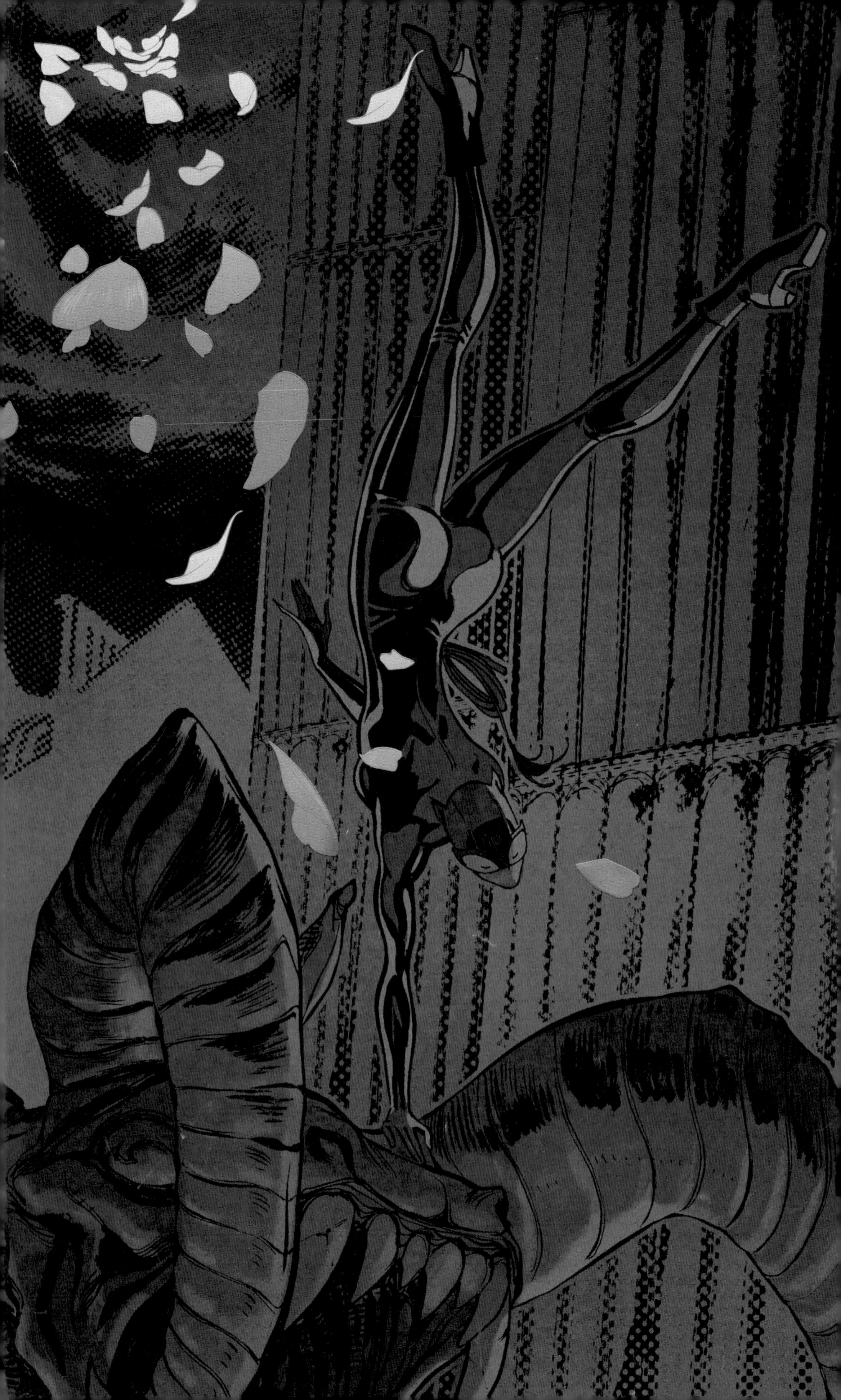

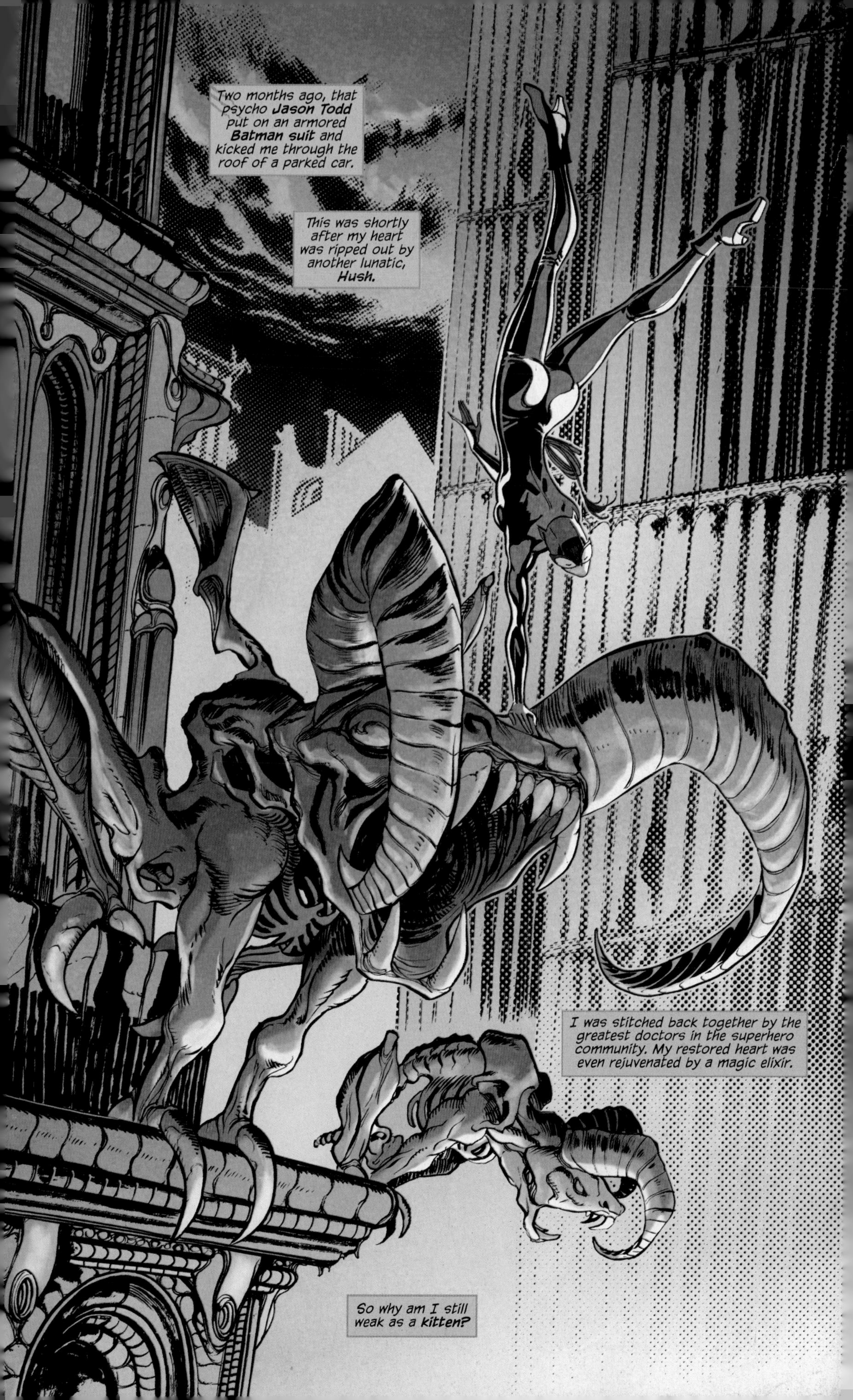
Two months ago, that psycho **Jason Todd** put on an armored **Batman suit** and kicked me through the roof of a parked car.
This was shortly after my heart was ripped out by another lunatic, **Hush.**
I was stitched back together by the greatest doctors in the superhero community. My restored heart was even rejuvenated by a magic elixir.
So why am I still weak as a **kitten?**

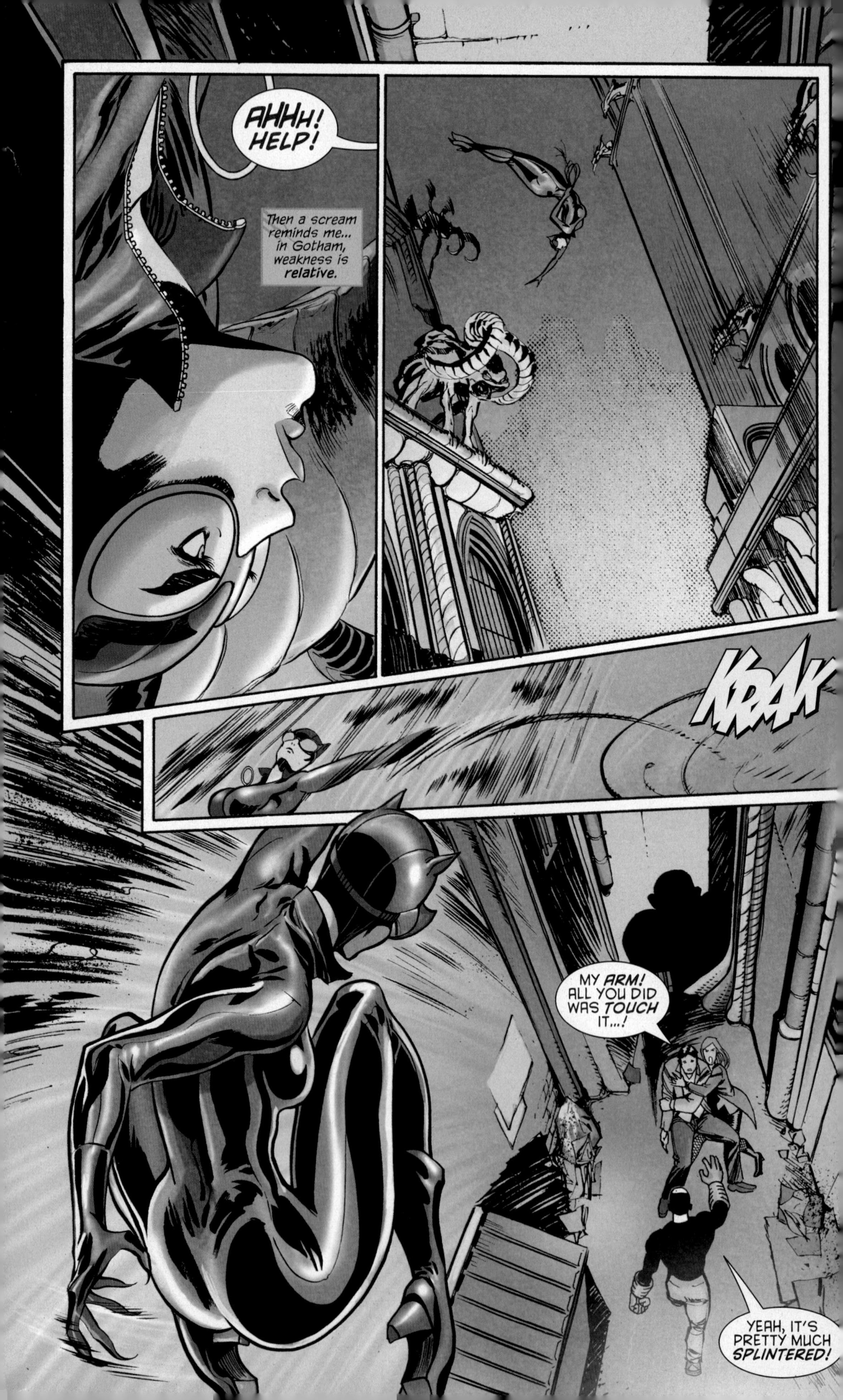
AHHH! HELP!
Then a scream reminds me... in Gotham, weakness is relative.
KRAK
MY ARM! ALL YOU DID WAS TOUCH IT...!
YEAH, IT'S PRETTY MUCH SPLINTERED!

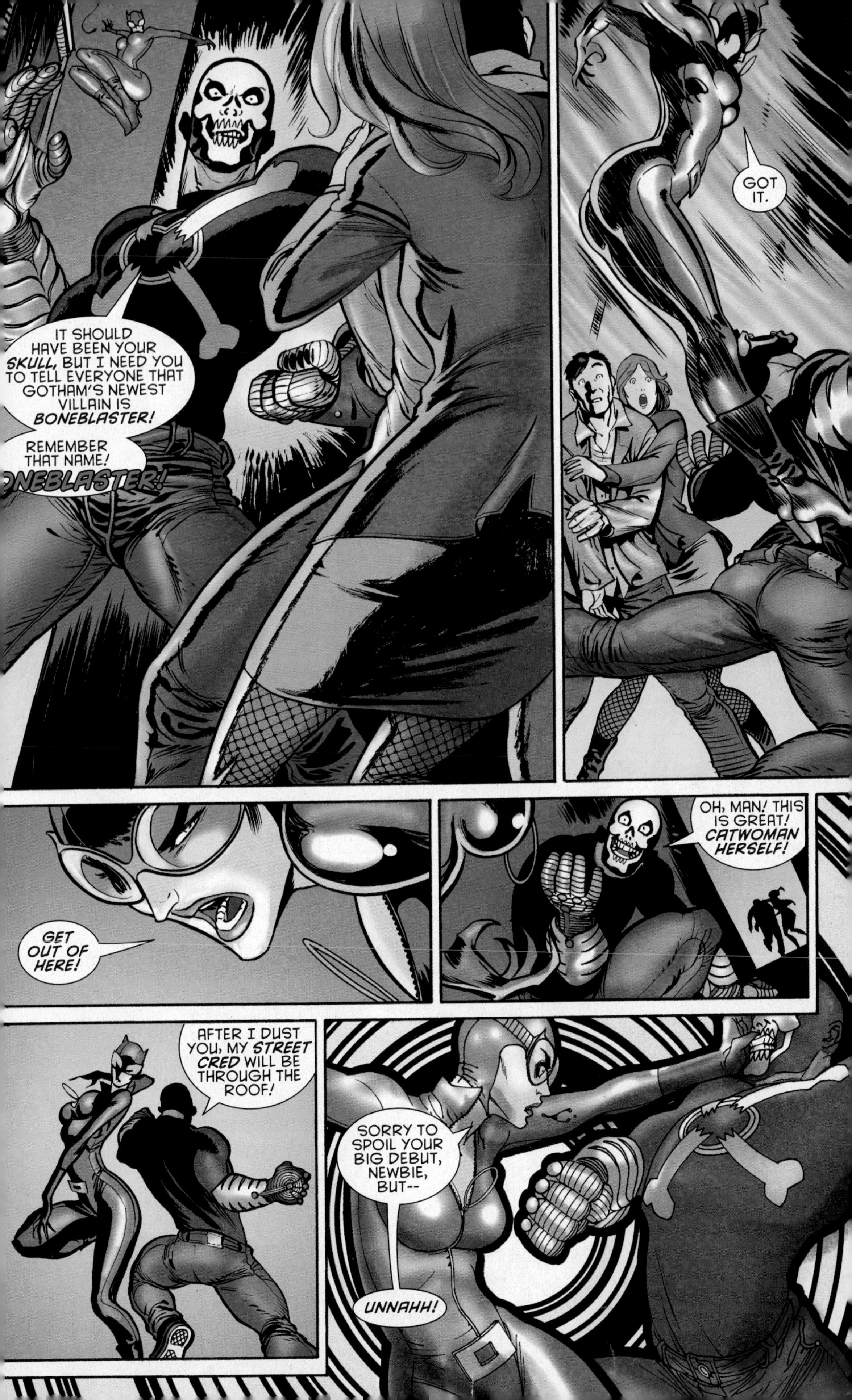
IT SHOULD HAVE BEEN YOUR SKULL, BUT I NEED YOU TO TELL EVERYONE THAT GOTHAM'S NEWEST VILLAIN IS BONEBLASTER!
REMEMBER THAT NAME!
ONEBLASTER!
GOT IT.
GET OUT OF HERE!
OH, MAN! THIS IS GREAT! CATWOMAN HERSELF!
AFTER I DUST YOU, MY STREET CRED WILL BE THROUGH THE ROOF!
SORRY TO SPOIL YOUR BIG DEBUT, NEWBIE, BUT--
UNNAHH!

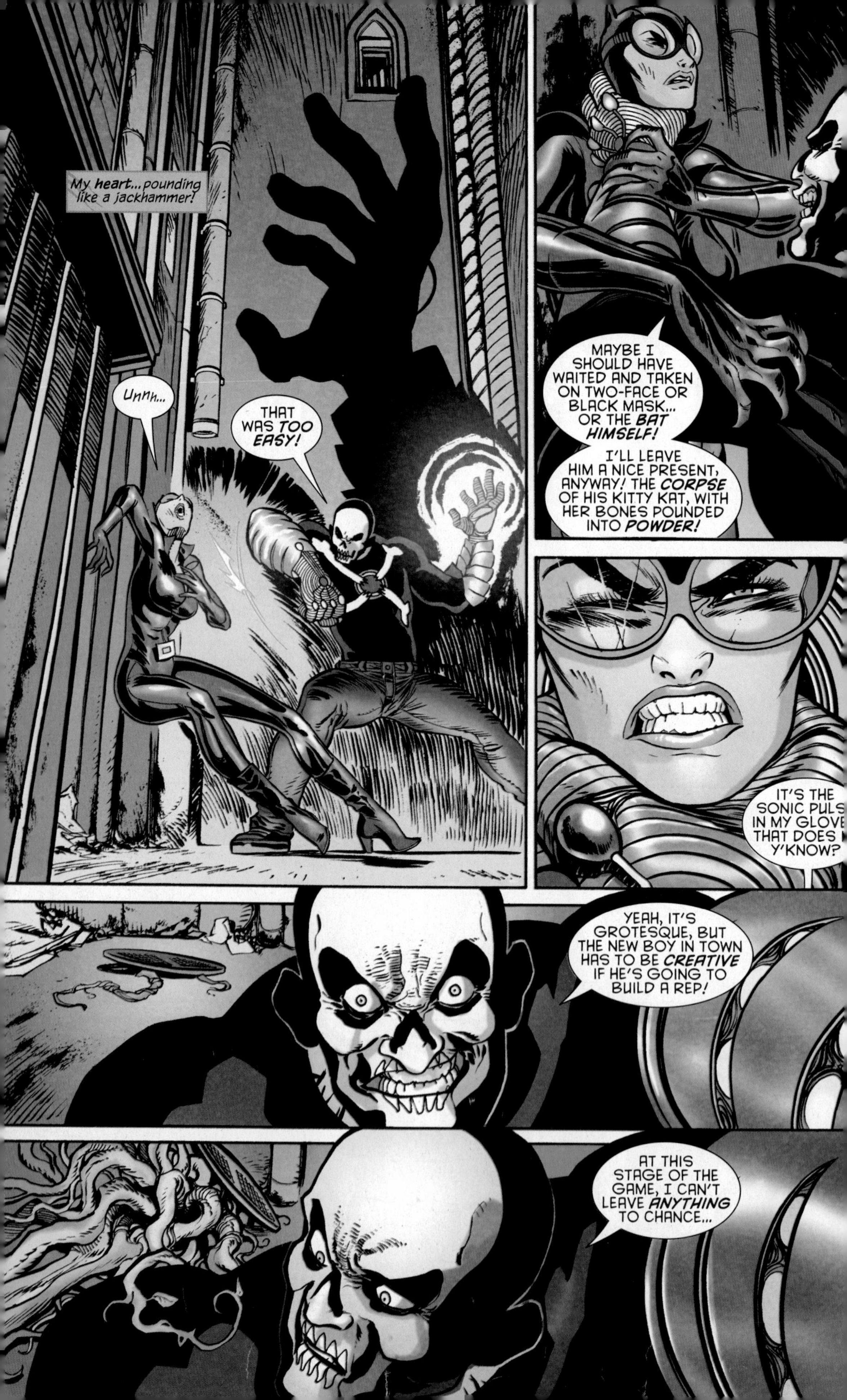
My heart...pounding like a jackhammer!
Unnh...
THAT WAS TOO EASY!
MAYBE I SHOULD HAVE WAITED AND TAKEN ON TWO-FACE OR BLACK MASK... OR THE BAT HIMSELF!
I'LL LEAVE HIM A NICE PRESENT, ANYWAY! THE CORPSE OF HIS KITTY KAT, WITH HER BONES POUNDED INTO POWDER!
IT'S THE SONIC PULS IN MY GLOVE THAT DOES Y'KNOW?
YEAH, IT'S GROTESQUE, BUT THE NEW BOY IN TOWN HAS TO BE CREATIVE IF HE'S GOING TO BUILD A REP!
AT THIS STAGE OF THE GAME, I CAN'T LEAVE ANYTHING TO CHANCE...

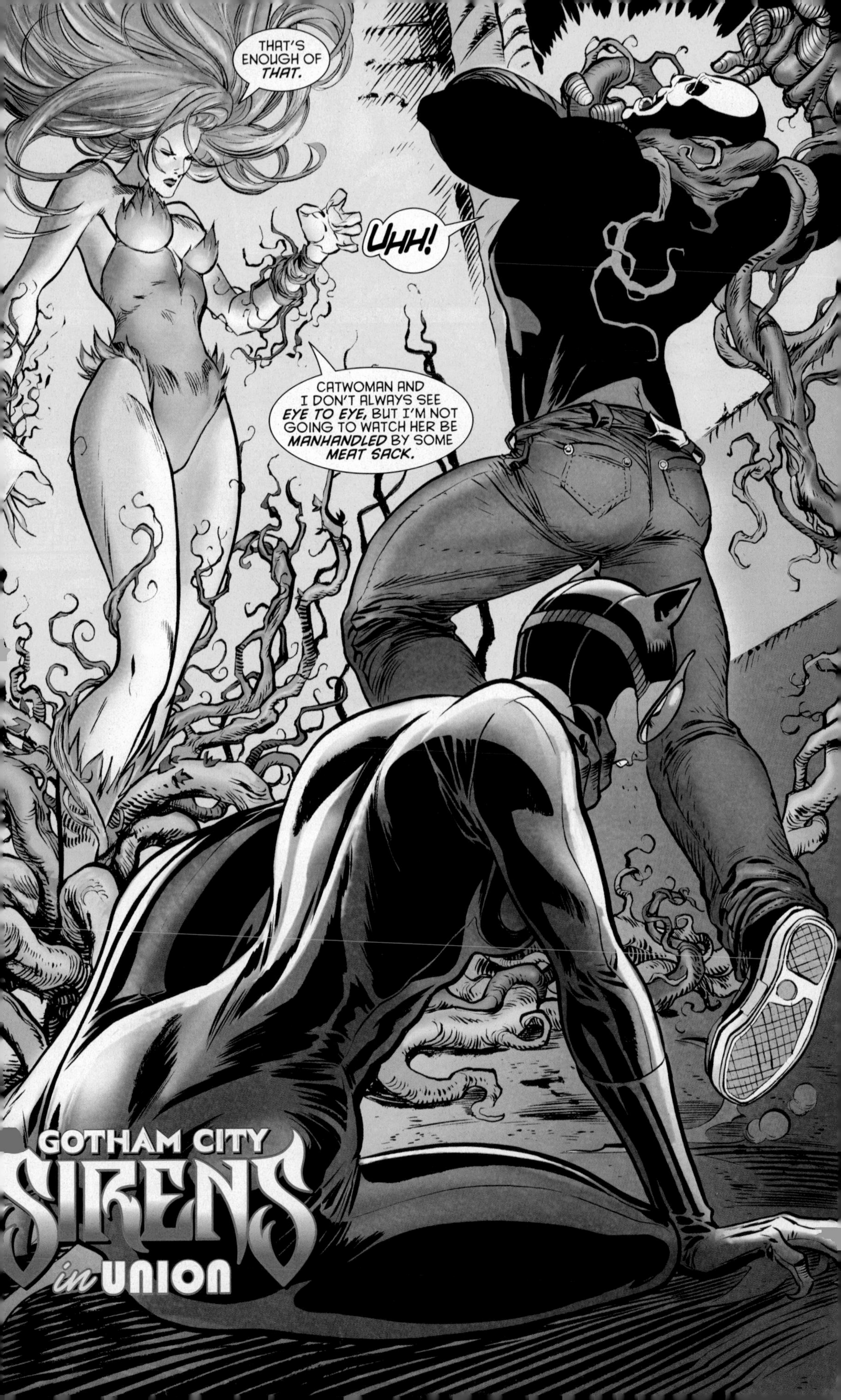

THAT'S ENOUGH OF *THAT.*
UHH!
CATWOMAN AND I DON'T ALWAYS SEE *EYE TO EYE,* BUT I'M NOT GOING TO WATCH HER BE *MANHANDLED* BY SOME *MEAT SACK.*
GOTHAM CITY SIRENS
in UNION

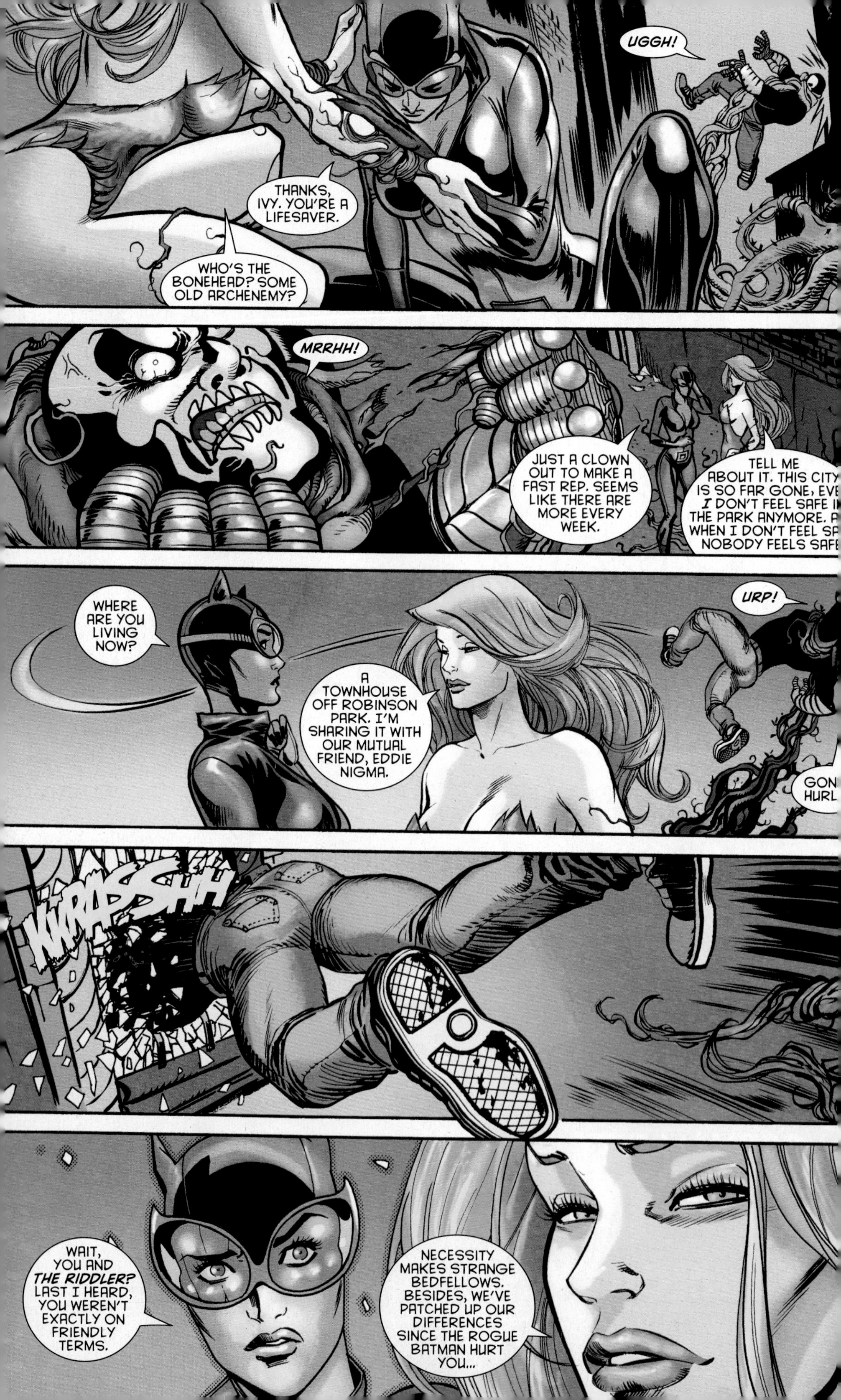
UGGH!
THANKS, IVY. YOU'RE A LIFESAVER.
WHO'S THE BONEHEAD? SOME OLD ARCHENEMY?
MRRHH!
JUST A CLOWN OUT TO MAKE A FAST REP. SEEMS LIKE THERE ARE MORE EVERY WEEK.
WHERE ARE YOU LIVING NOW?
A TOWNHOUSE OFF ROBINSON PARK. I'M SHARING IT WITH OUR MUTUAL FRIEND, EDDIE NIGMA.
URP!
KKRASHH
WAIT, YOU AND THE RIDDLER? LAST I HEARD, YOU WEREN'T EXACTLY ON FRIENDLY TERMS.
NECESSITY MAKES STRANGE BEDFELLOWS. BESIDES, WE'VE PATCHED UP OUR DIFFERENCES SINCE THE ROGUE BATMAN HURT YOU...

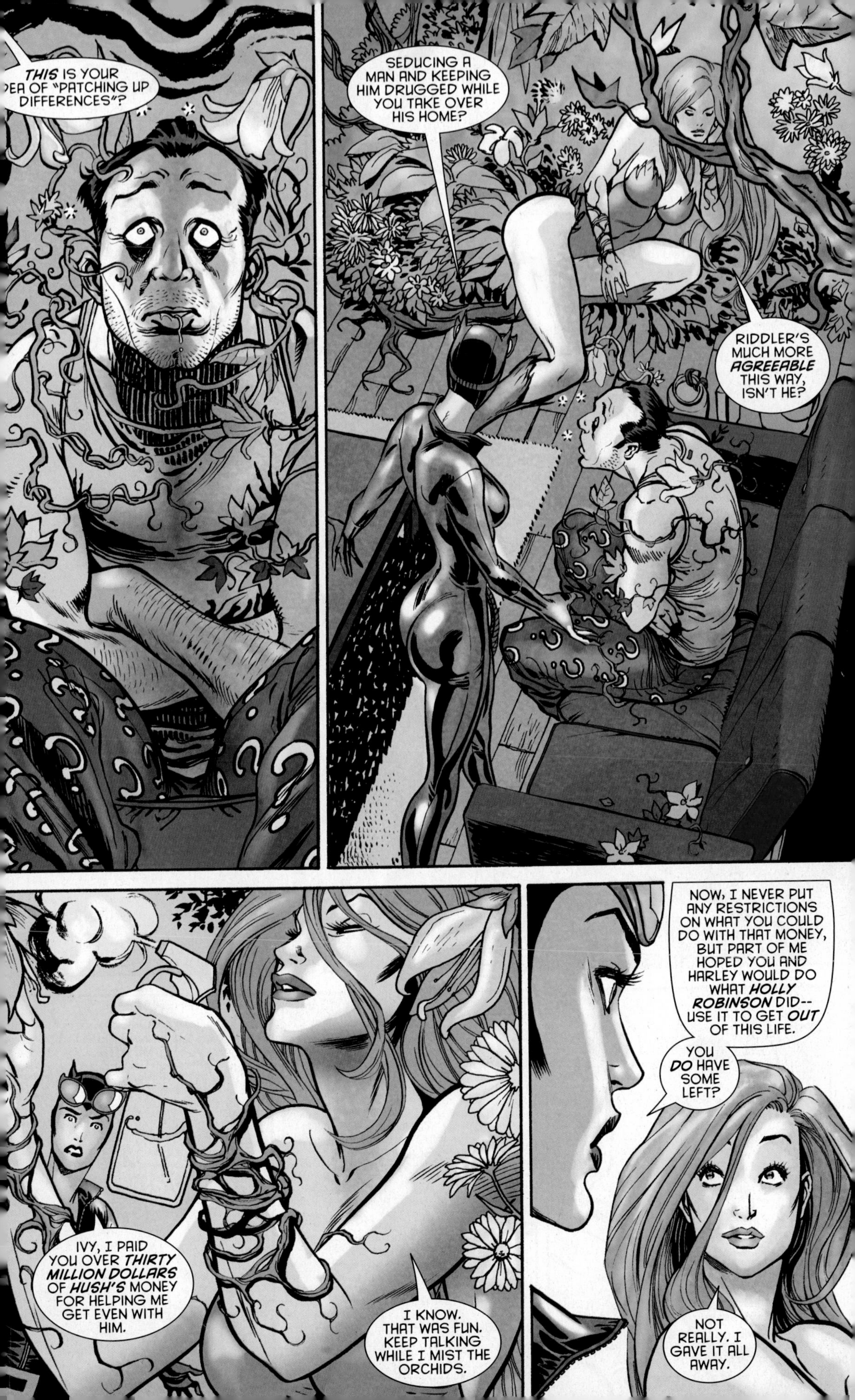
THIS IS YOUR DEA OF "PATCHING UP DIFFERENCES"?
SEDUCING A MAN AND KEEPING HIM DRUGGED WHILE YOU TAKE OVER HIS HOME?
RIDDLER'S MUCH MORE AGREEABLE THIS WAY, ISN'T HE?
IVY, I PAID YOU OVER THIRTY MILLION DOLLARS OF HUSH'S MONEY FOR HELPING ME GET EVEN WITH HIM.
I KNOW. THAT WAS FUN. KEEP TALKING WHILE I MIST THE ORCHIDS.
NOW, I NEVER PUT ANY RESTRICTIONS ON WHAT YOU COULD DO WITH THAT MONEY, BUT PART OF ME HOPED YOU AND HARLEY WOULD DO WHAT HOLLY ROBINSON DID-- USE IT TO GET OUT OF THIS LIFE.
YOU DO HAVE SOME LEFT?
NOT REALLY. I GAVE IT ALL AWAY.

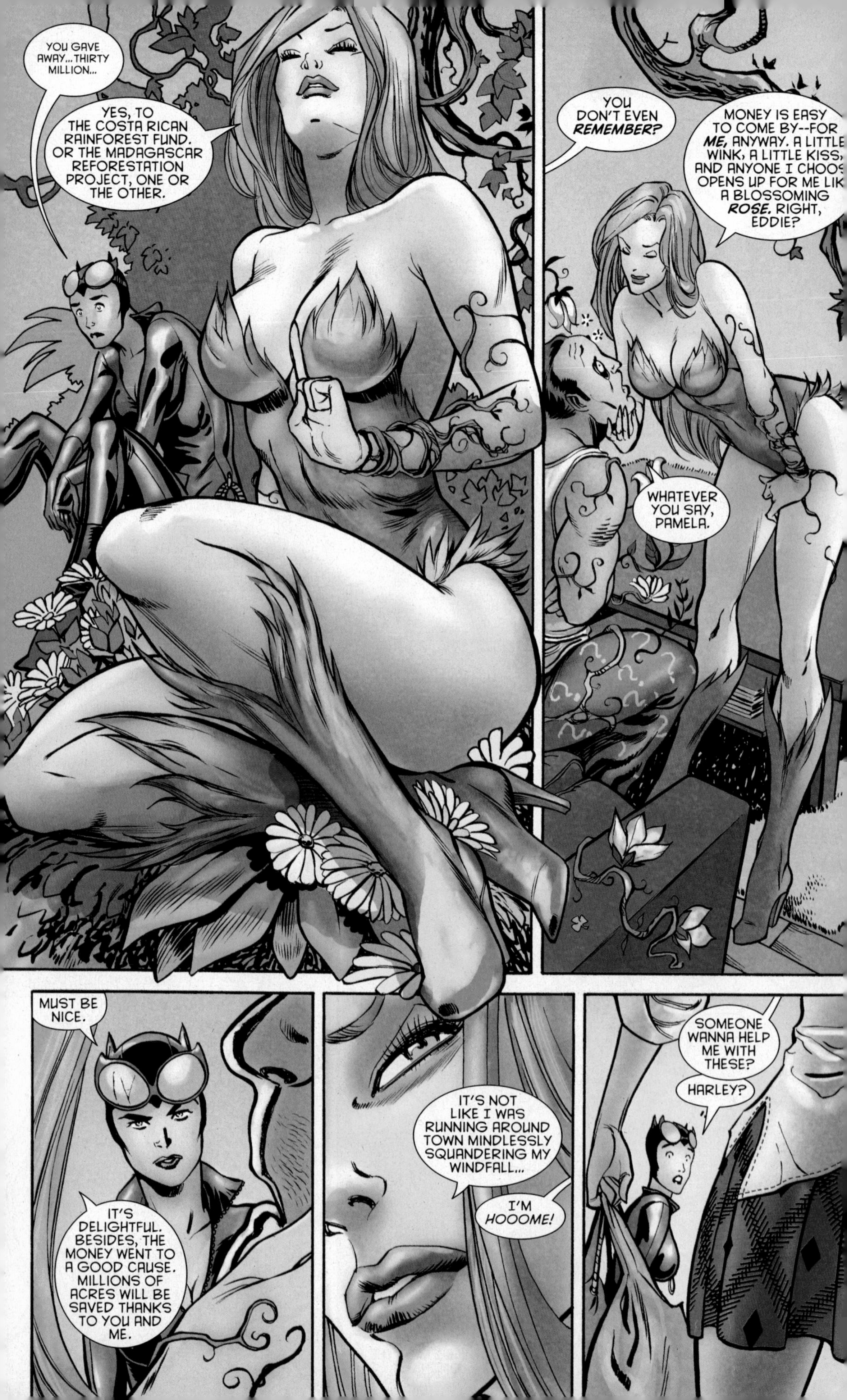
YOU GAVE AWAY...THIRTY MILLION...
YES, TO THE COSTA RICAN RAINFOREST FUND. OR THE MADAGASCAR REFORESTATION PROJECT, ONE OR THE OTHER.
YOU DON'T EVEN *REMEMBER?*
MONEY IS EASY TO COME BY--FOR *ME,* ANYWAY. A LITTLE WINK, A LITTLE KISS, AND ANYONE I CHOOS OPENS UP FOR ME LIK A BLOSSOMING *ROSE.* RIGHT, EDDIE?
WHATEVER YOU SAY, PAMELA.
MUST BE NICE.
IT'S DELIGHTFUL. BESIDES, THE MONEY WENT TO A GOOD CAUSE. MILLIONS OF ACRES WILL BE SAVED THANKS TO YOU AND ME.
IT'S NOT LIKE I WAS RUNNING AROUND TOWN MINDLESSLY SQUANDERING MY WINDFALL...
I'M *HOOOME!*
SOMEONE WANNA HELP ME WITH THESE?
HARLEY?

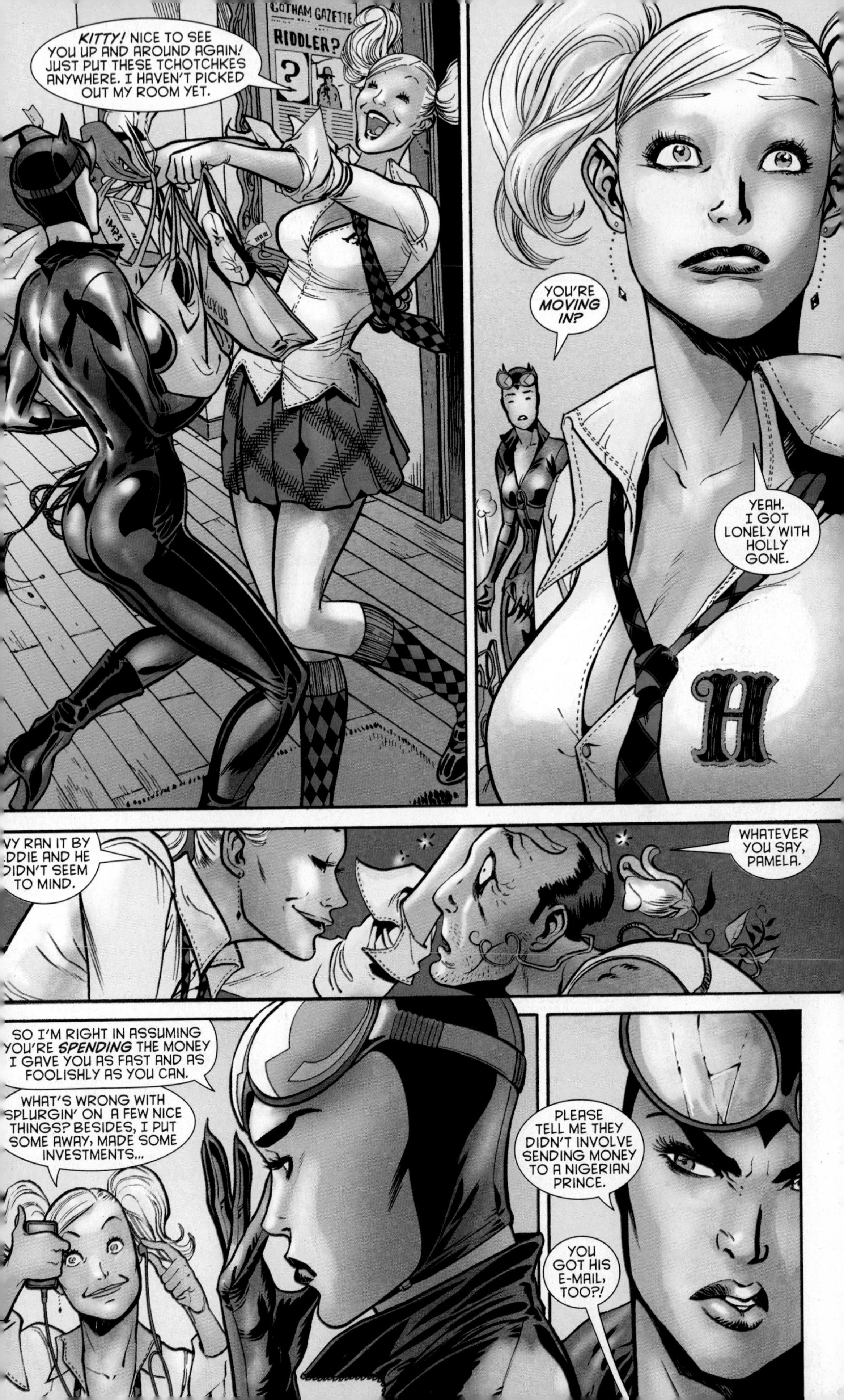
GOTHAM GAZETTE
RIDDLER?
KITTY! NICE TO SEE YOU UP AND AROUND AGAIN! JUST PUT THESE TCHOTCHKES ANYWHERE. I HAVEN'T PICKED OUT MY ROOM YET.
YOU'RE MOVING IN?
YEAH. I GOT LONELY WITH HOLLY GONE.
VY RAN IT BY DDIE AND HE DIDN'T SEEM TO MIND.
WHATEVER YOU SAY, PAMELA.
SO I'M RIGHT IN ASSUMING YOU'RE SPENDING THE MONEY I GAVE YOU AS FAST AND AS FOOLISHLY AS YOU CAN.
WHAT'S WRONG WITH SPLURGIN' ON A FEW NICE THINGS? BESIDES, I PUT SOME AWAY, MADE SOME INVESTMENTS...
PLEASE TELL ME THEY DIDN'T INVOLVE SENDING MONEY TO A NIGERIAN PRINCE.
YOU GOT HIS E-MAIL, TOO?!

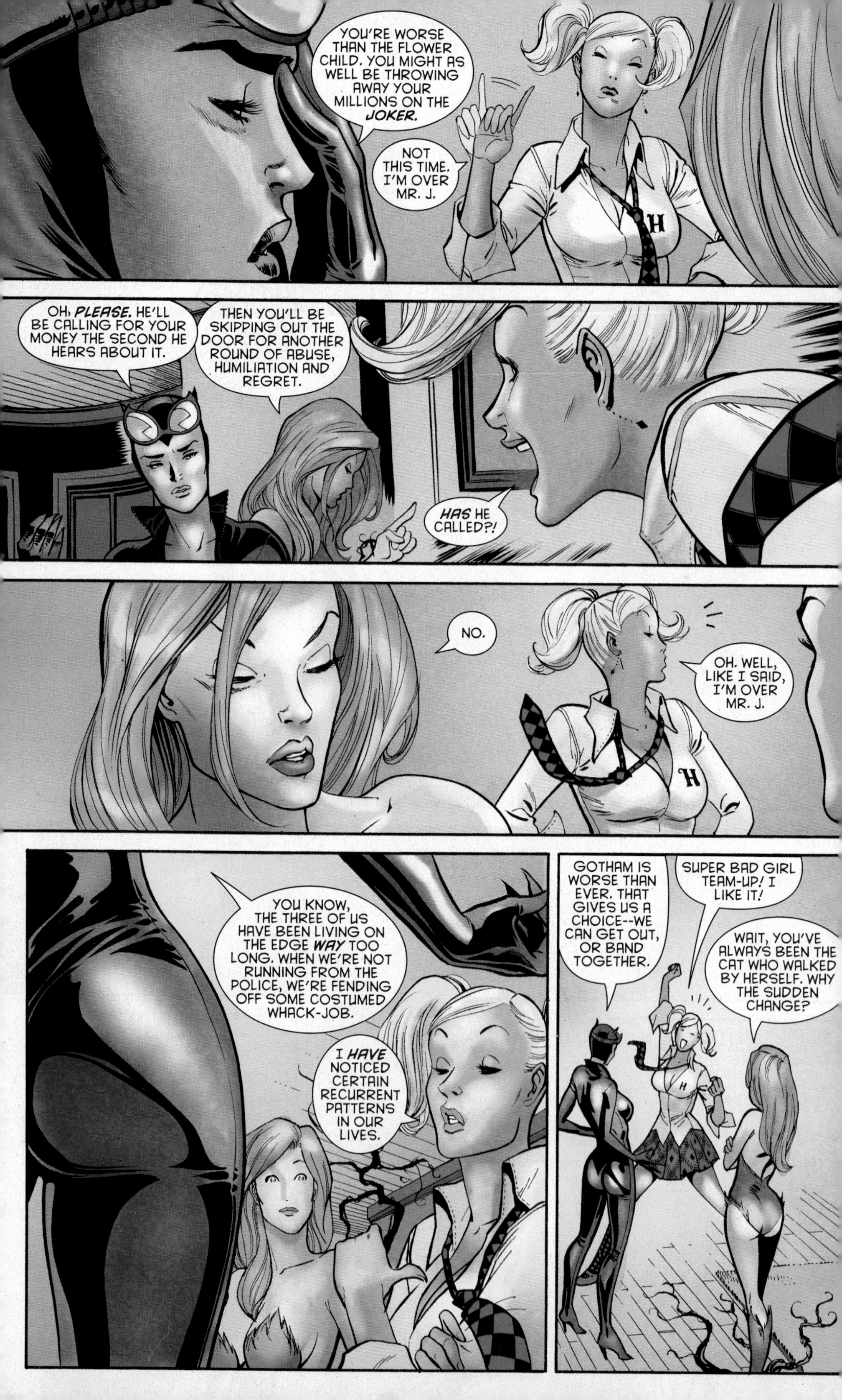
YOU'RE WORSE THAN THE FLOWER CHILD. YOU MIGHT AS WELL BE THROWING AWAY YOUR MILLIONS ON THE JOKER.
NOT THIS TIME. I'M OVER MR. J.
OH, PLEASE. HE'LL BE CALLING FOR YOUR MONEY THE SECOND HE HEARS ABOUT IT.
THEN YOU'LL BE SKIPPING OUT THE DOOR FOR ANOTHER ROUND OF ABUSE, HUMILIATION AND REGRET.
HAS HE CALLED?!
NO.
OH. WELL, LIKE I SAID, I'M OVER MR. J.
YOU KNOW, THE THREE OF US HAVE BEEN LIVING ON THE EDGE WAY TOO LONG. WHEN WE'RE NOT RUNNING FROM THE POLICE, WE'RE FENDING OFF SOME COSTUMED WHACK-JOB.
I HAVE NOTICED CERTAIN RECURRENT PATTERNS IN OUR LIVES.
GOTHAM IS WORSE THAN EVER. THAT GIVES US A CHOICE--WE CAN GET OUT, OR BAND TOGETHER.
SUPER BAD GIRL TEAM-UP! I LIKE IT!
WAIT, YOU'VE ALWAYS BEEN THE CAT WHO WALKED BY HERSELF. WHY THE SUDDEN CHANGE?

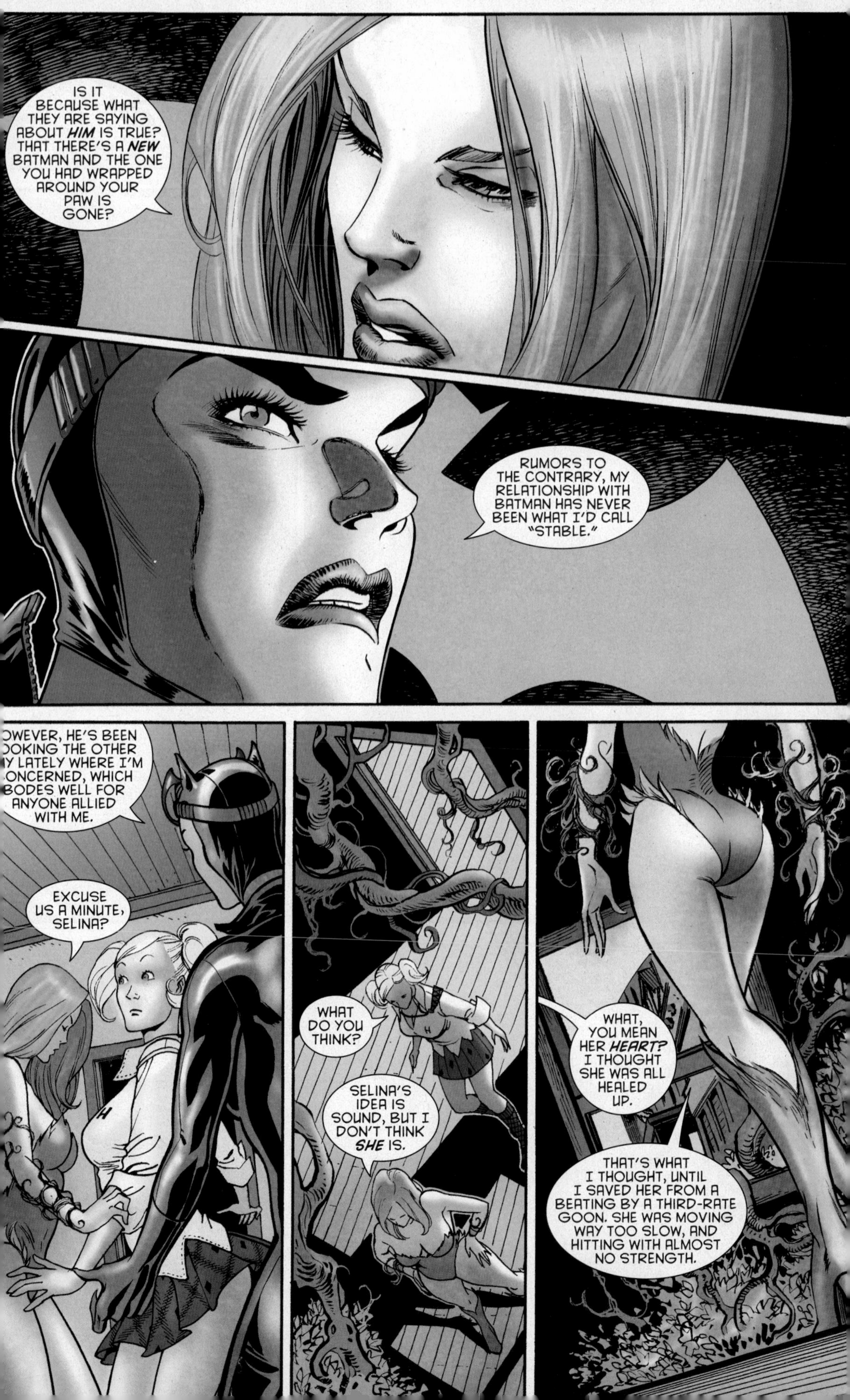
IS IT BECAUSE WHAT THEY ARE SAYING ABOUT *HIM* IS TRUE? THAT THERE'S A *NEW* BATMAN AND THE ONE YOU HAD WRAPPED AROUND YOUR PAW IS GONE?
RUMORS TO THE CONTRARY, MY RELATIONSHIP WITH BATMAN HAS NEVER BEEN WHAT I'D CALL "STABLE."
OWEVER, HE'S BEEN OOKING THE OTHER Y LATELY WHERE I'M ONCERNED, WHICH BODES WELL FOR ANYONE ALLIED WITH ME.
EXCUSE US A MINUTE, SELINA?
WHAT DO YOU THINK?
SELINA'S IDEA IS SOUND, BUT I DON'T THINK *SHE* IS.
WHAT, YOU MEAN HER *HEART?* I THOUGHT SHE WAS ALL HEALED UP.
THAT'S WHAT I THOUGHT, UNTIL I SAVED HER FROM A BEATING BY A THIRD-RATE GOON. SHE WAS MOVING WAY TOO SLOW, AND HITTING WITH ALMOST NO STRENGTH.

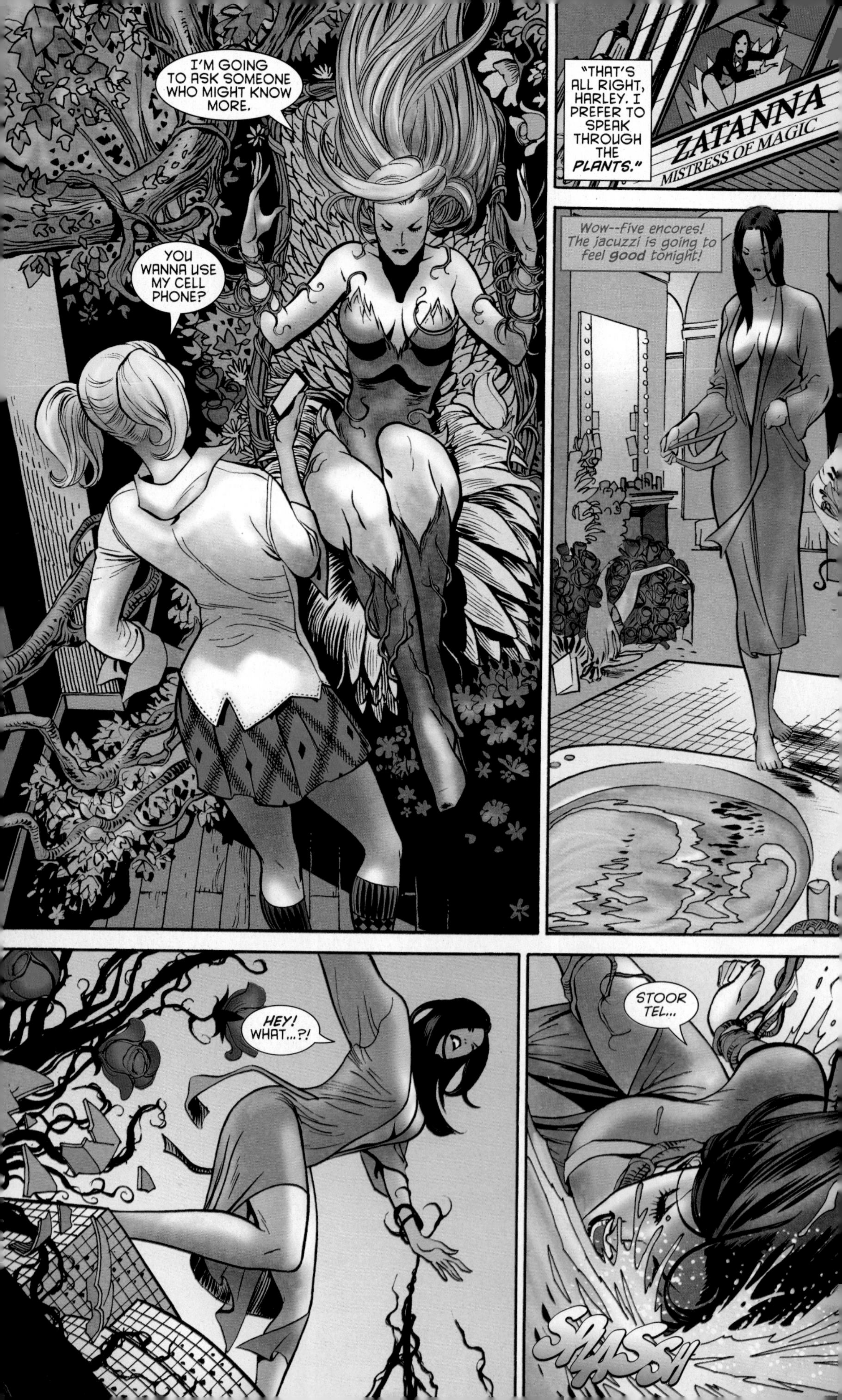
I'M GOING TO ASK SOMEONE WHO MIGHT KNOW MORE.
YOU WANNA USE MY CELL PHONE?
"THAT'S ALL RIGHT, HARLEY. I PREFER TO SPEAK THROUGH THE PLANTS."
ZATANNA
MISTRESS OF MAGIC
Wow--five encores! The jacuzzi is going to feel good tonight!
HEY! WHAT...?!
STOOR TEL...
SPLASSH

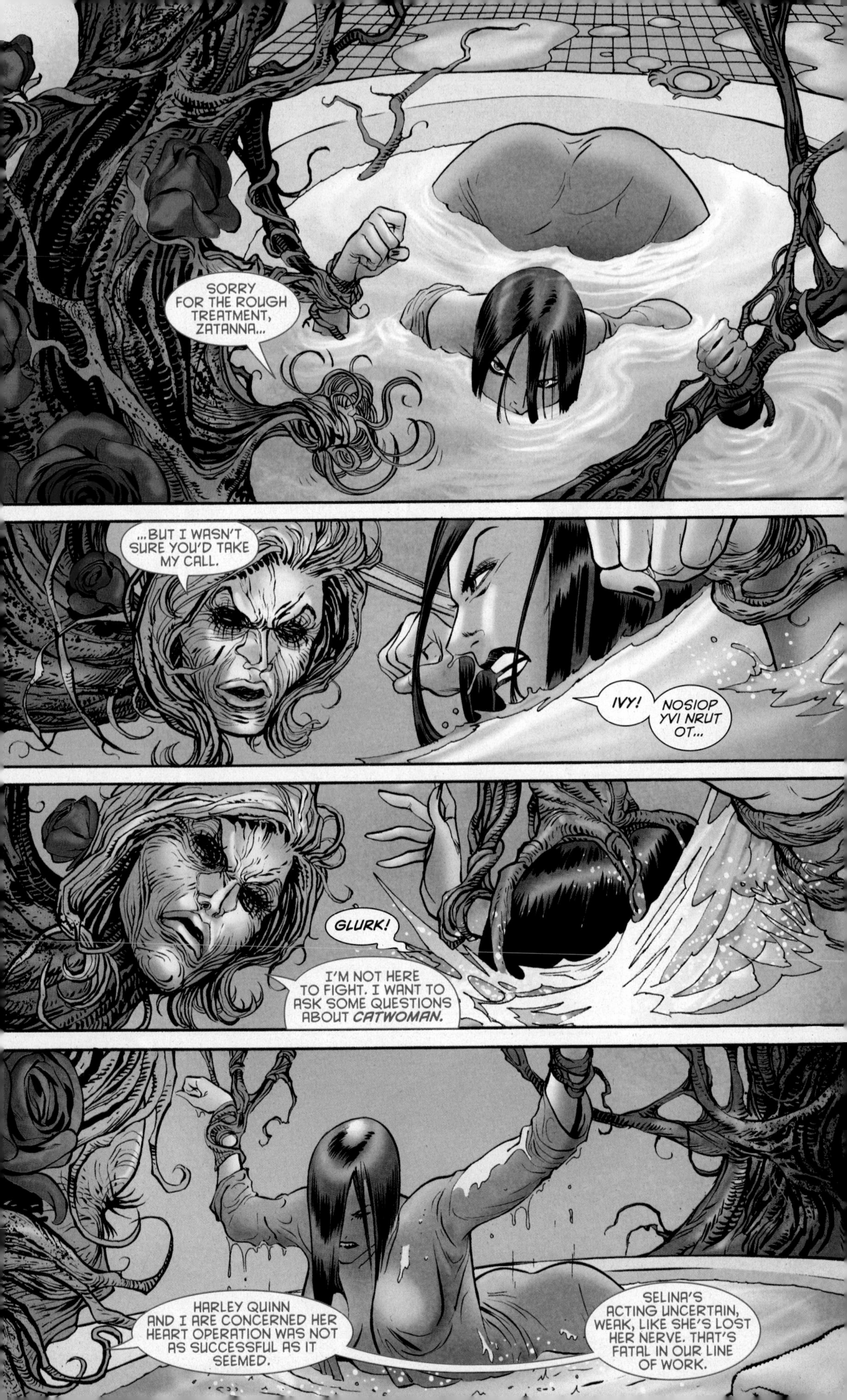
SORRY FOR THE ROUGH TREATMENT, ZATANNA...
...BUT I WASN'T SURE YOU'D TAKE MY CALL.
IVY!
NOSIOP YVI NRUT OT...
GLURK!
I'M NOT HERE TO FIGHT. I WANT TO ASK SOME QUESTIONS ABOUT CATWOMAN.
HARLEY QUINN AND I ARE CONCERNED HER HEART OPERATION WAS NOT AS SUCCESSFUL AS IT SEEMED.
SELINA'S ACTING UNCERTAIN, WEAK, LIKE SHE'S LOST HER NERVE. THAT'S FATAL IN OUR LINE OF WORK.

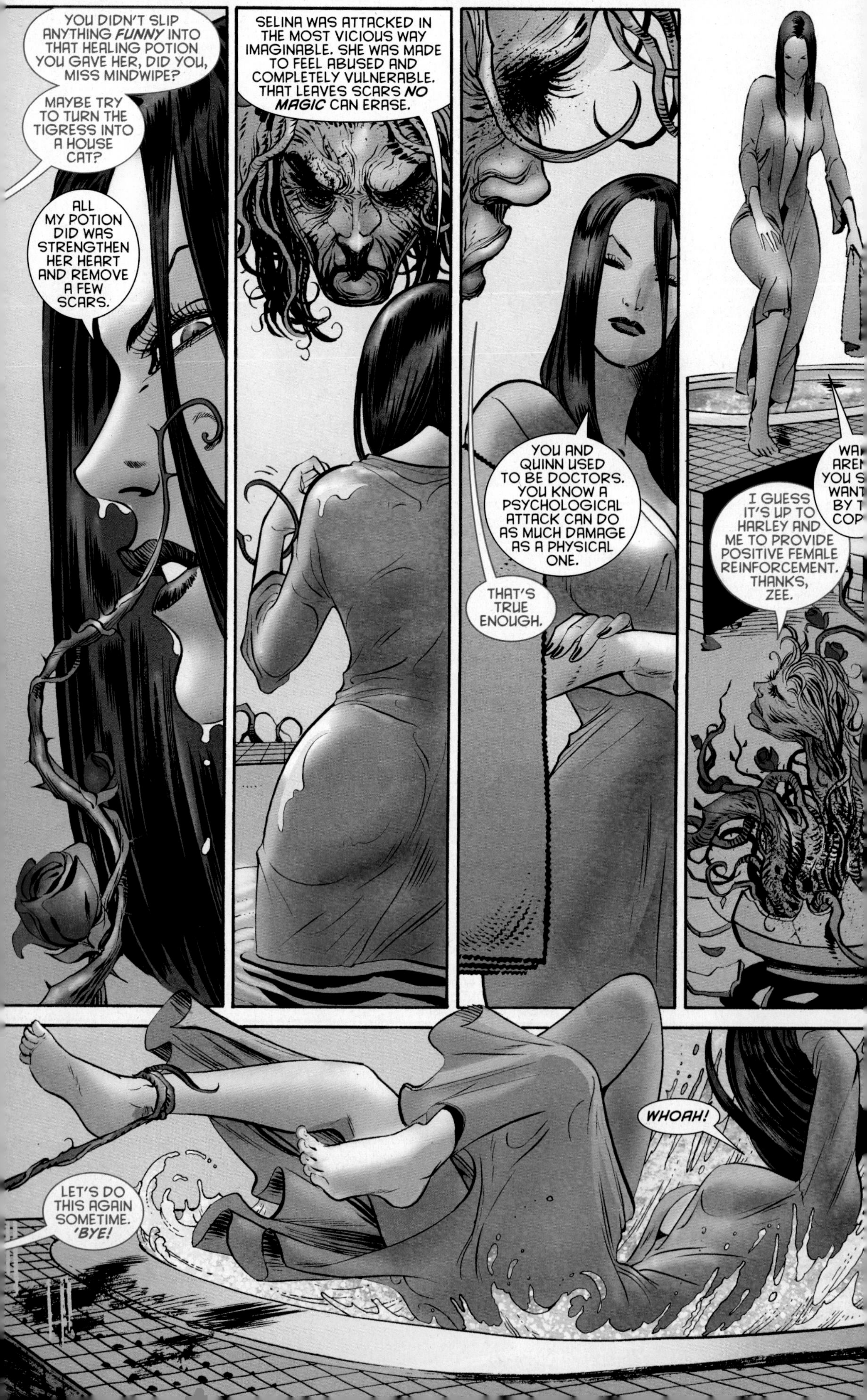
YOU DIDN'T SLIP ANYTHING *FUNNY* INTO THAT HEALING POTION YOU GAVE HER, DID YOU, MISS MINDWIPE?
MAYBE TRY TO TURN THE TIGRESS INTO A HOUSE CAT?
ALL MY POTION DID WAS STRENGTHEN HER HEART AND REMOVE A FEW SCARS.
SELINA WAS ATTACKED IN THE MOST VICIOUS WAY IMAGINABLE. SHE WAS MADE TO FEEL ABUSED AND COMPLETELY VULNERABLE. THAT LEAVES SCARS *NO MAGIC* CAN ERASE.
YOU AND QUINN USED TO BE DOCTORS. YOU KNOW A PSYCHOLOGICAL ATTACK CAN DO AS MUCH DAMAGE AS A PHYSICAL ONE.
THAT'S TRUE ENOUGH.
I GUESS IT'S UP TO HARLEY AND ME TO PROVIDE POSITIVE FEMALE REINFORCEMENT. THANKS, ZEE.
*WHOAH!*
LET'S DO THIS AGAIN SOMETIME. *'BYE!*

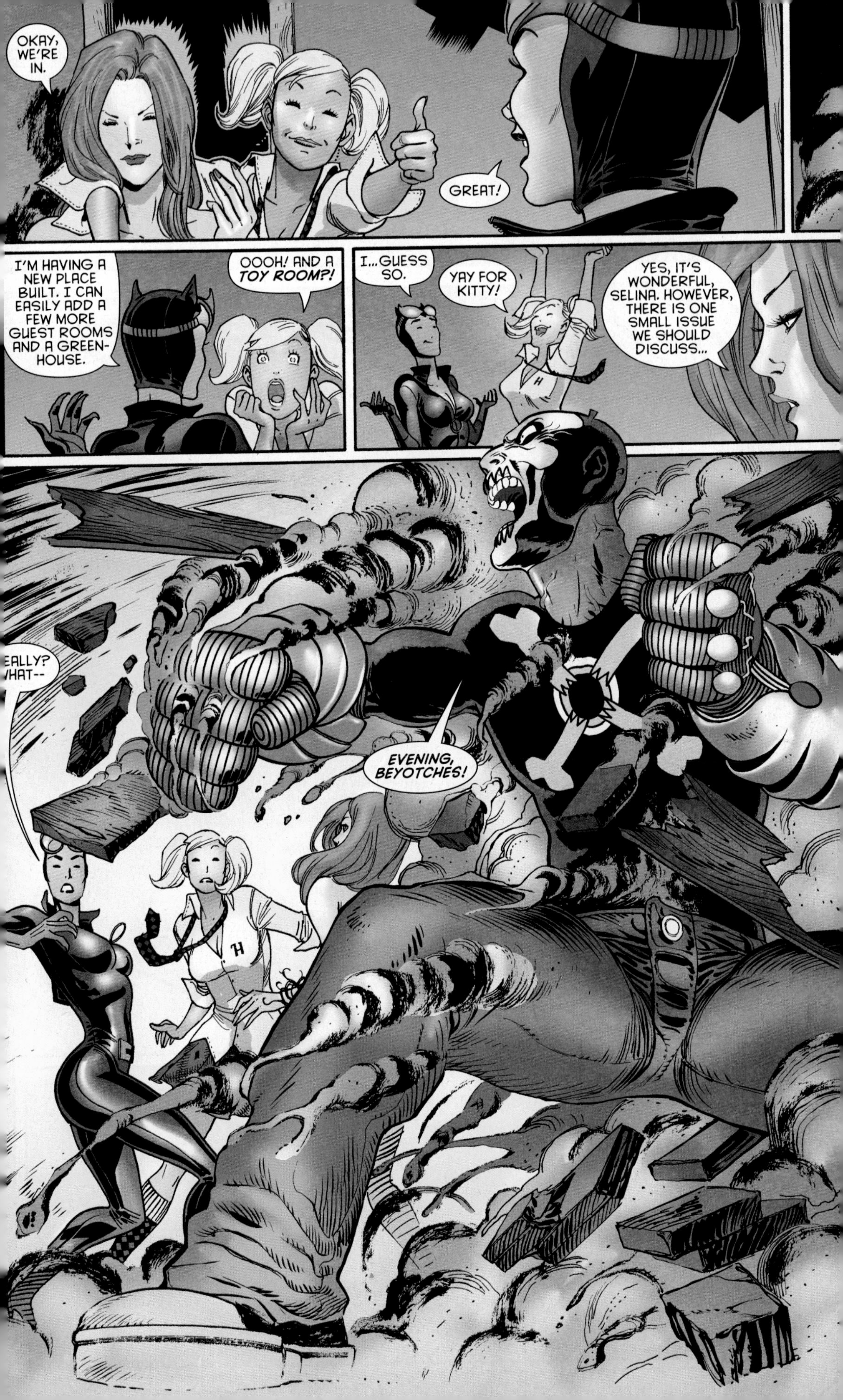
OKAY, WE'RE IN.
GREAT!
I'M HAVING A NEW PLACE BUILT. I CAN EASILY ADD A FEW MORE GUEST ROOMS AND A GREEN-HOUSE.
OOOH! AND A *TOY ROOM?!*
I... GUESS SO.
YAY FOR KITTY!
YES, IT'S WONDERFUL, SELINA. HOWEVER, THERE IS ONE SMALL ISSUE WE SHOULD DISCUSS...
EALLY? HAT--
*EVENING, BEYOTCHES!*

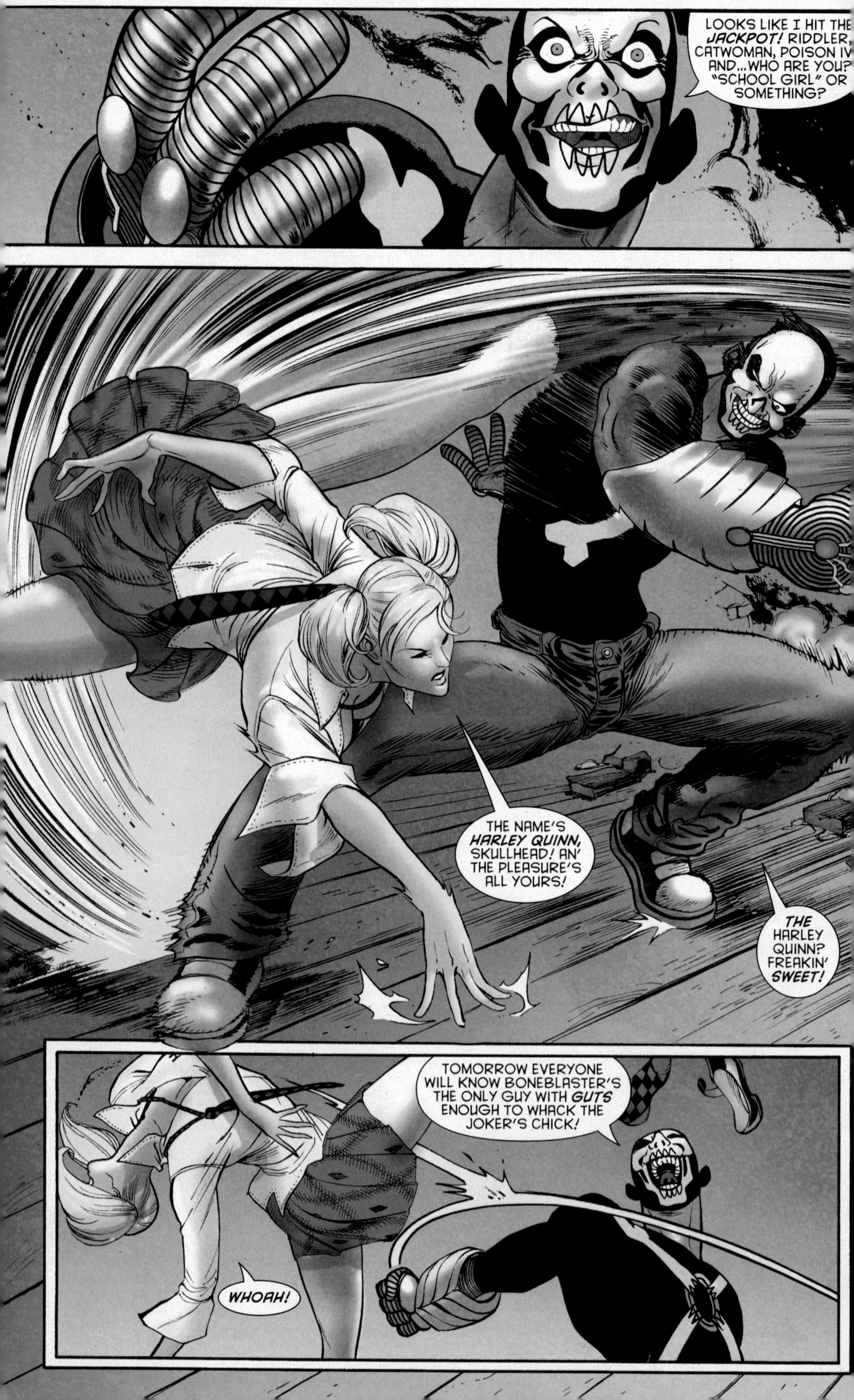
LOOKS LIKE I HIT THE JACKPOT! RIDDLER, CATWOMAN, POISON IVY AND...WHO ARE YOU? "SCHOOL GIRL" OR SOMETHING?
THE NAME'S HARLEY QUINN, SKULLHEAD! AN' THE PLEASURE'S ALL YOURS!
THE HARLEY QUINN? FREAKIN' SWEET!
TOMORROW EVERYONE WILL KNOW BONEBLASTER'S THE ONLY GUY WITH GUTS ENOUGH TO WHACK THE JOKER'S CHICK!
WHOAH!

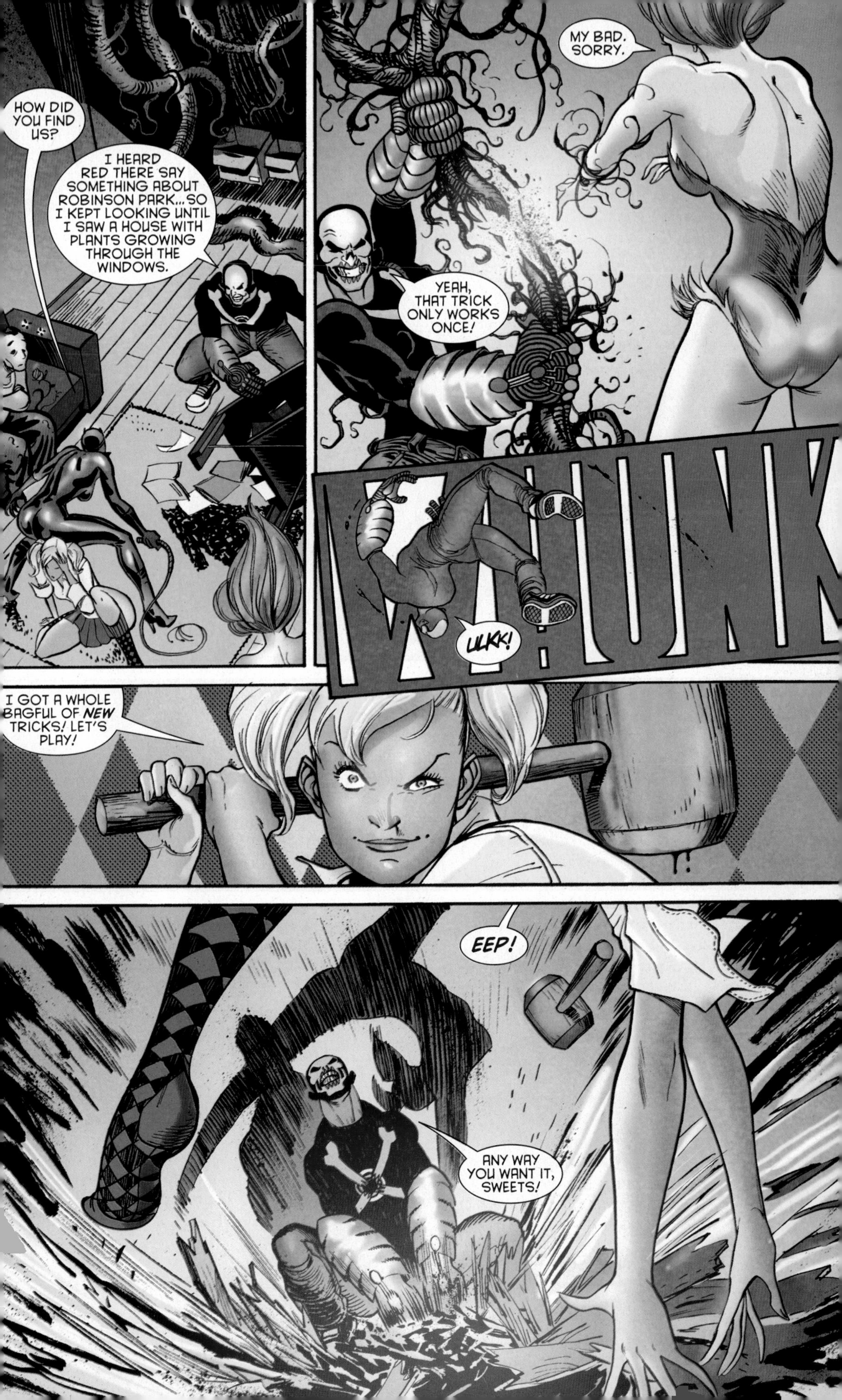
HOW DID YOU FIND US?
I HEARD RED THERE SAY SOMETHING ABOUT ROBINSON PARK... SO I KEPT LOOKING UNTIL I SAW A HOUSE WITH PLANTS GROWING THROUGH THE WINDOWS.
MY BAD. SORRY.
YEAH, THAT TRICK ONLY WORKS ONCE!
WHUNK
ULKK!
I GOT A WHOLE BAGFUL OF NEW TRICKS! LET'S PLAY!
EEP!
ANY WAY YOU WANT IT, SWEETS!

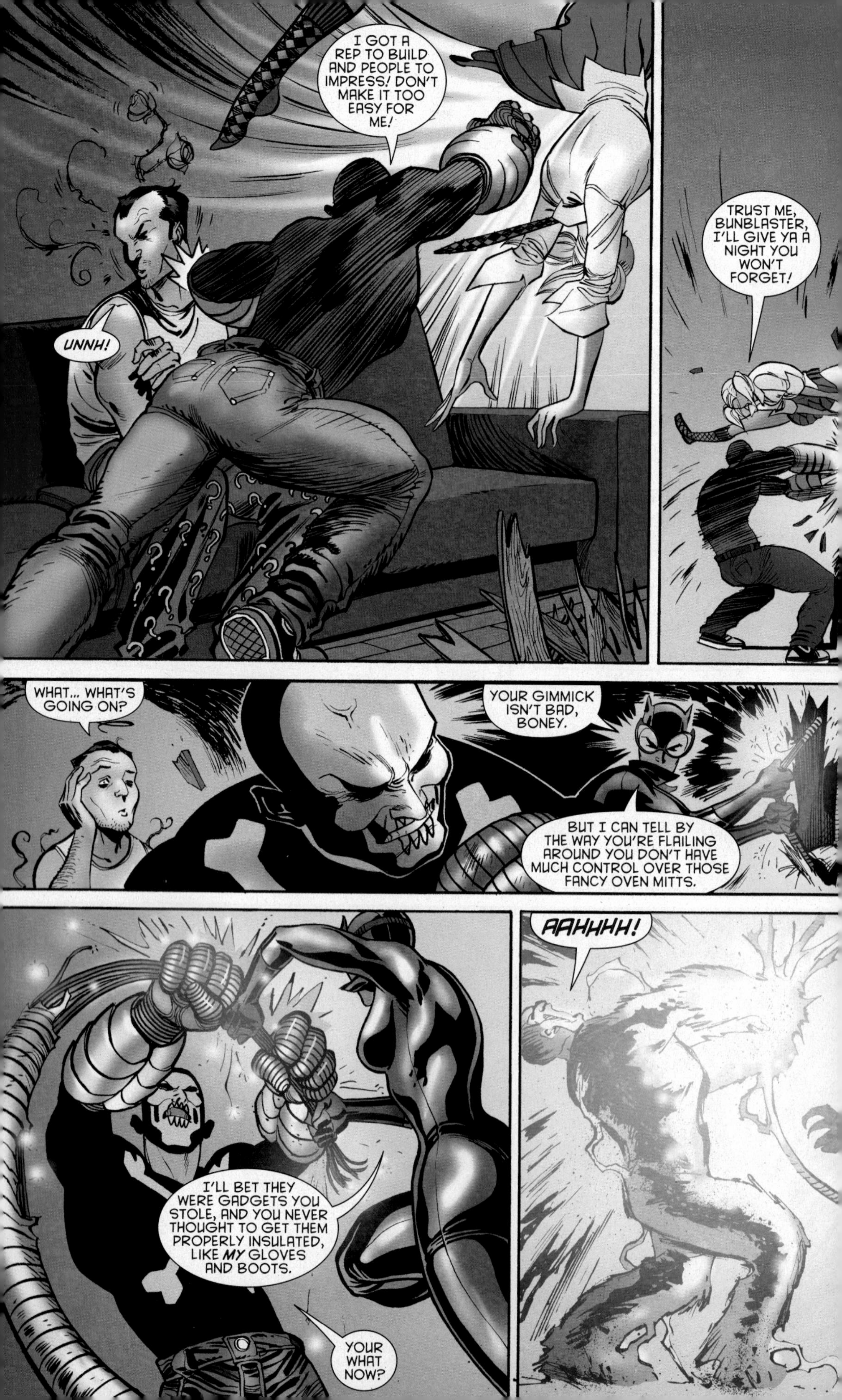

I GOT A REP TO BUILD AND PEOPLE TO IMPRESS! DON'T MAKE IT TOO EASY FOR ME!
UNNH!
TRUST ME, BUNBLASTER, I'LL GIVE YA A NIGHT YOU WON'T FORGET!
WHAT... WHAT'S GOING ON?
YOUR GIMMICK ISN'T BAD, BONEY.
BUT I CAN TELL BY THE WAY YOU'RE FLAILING AROUND YOU DON'T HAVE MUCH CONTROL OVER THOSE FANCY OVEN MITTS.
I'LL BET THEY WERE GADGETS YOU STOLE, AND YOU NEVER THOUGHT TO GET THEM PROPERLY INSULATED, LIKE *MY* GLOVES AND BOOTS.
YOUR WHAT NOW?
AAHHHH!

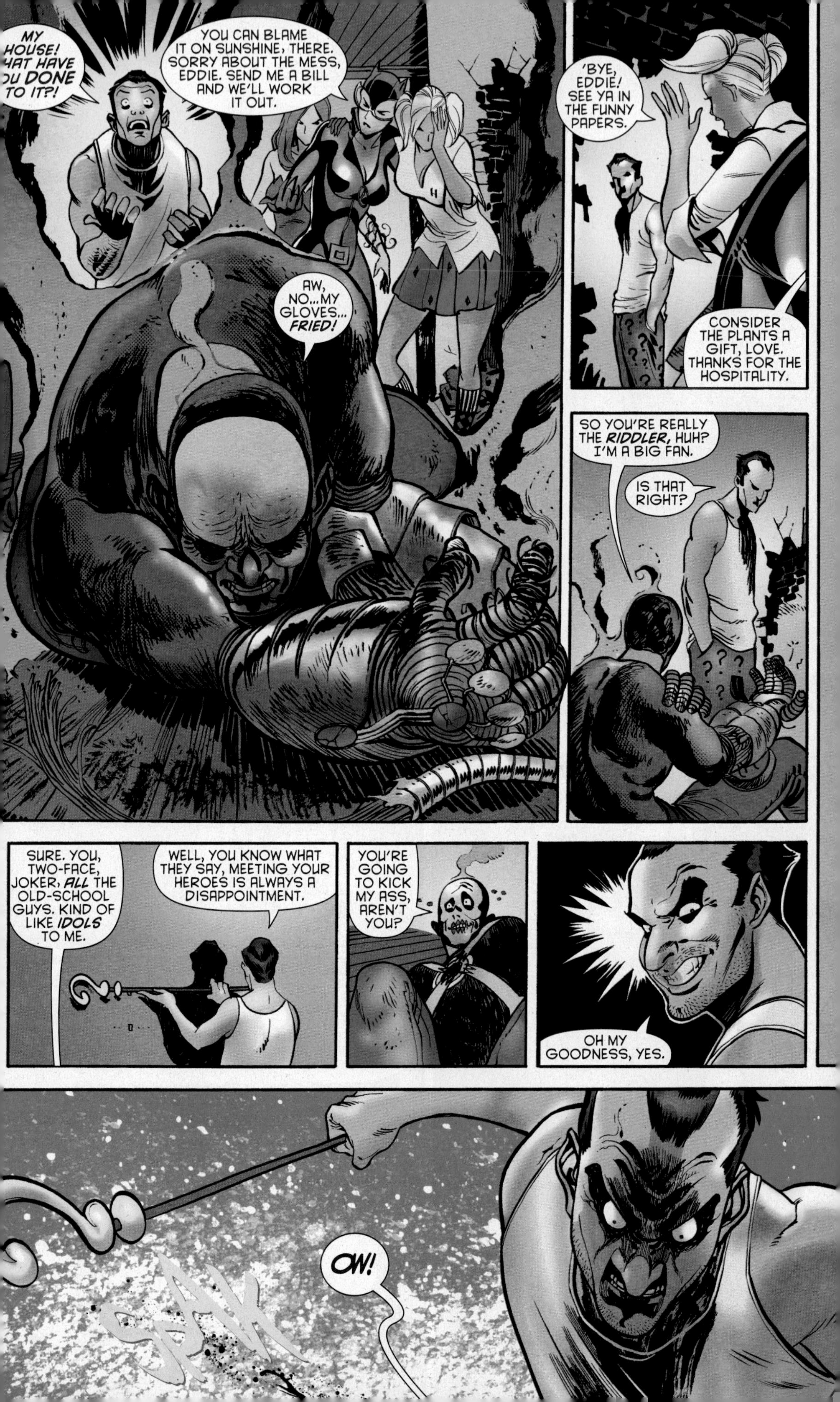
MY HOUSE! HAT HAVE OU DONE TO IT?!
YOU CAN BLAME IT ON SUNSHINE, THERE. SORRY ABOUT THE MESS, EDDIE. SEND ME A BILL AND WE'LL WORK IT OUT.
AW, NO...MY GLOVES... FRIED!
'BYE, EDDIE! SEE YA IN THE FUNNY PAPERS.
CONSIDER THE PLANTS A GIFT, LOVE. THANKS FOR THE HOSPITALITY.
SO YOU'RE REALLY THE RIDDLER, HUH? I'M A BIG FAN.
IS THAT RIGHT?
SURE. YOU, TWO-FACE, JOKER, ALL THE OLD-SCHOOL GUYS. KIND OF LIKE IDOLS TO ME.
WELL, YOU KNOW WHAT THEY SAY, MEETING YOUR HEROES IS ALWAYS A DISAPPOINTMENT.
YOU'RE GOING TO KICK MY ASS, AREN'T YOU?
OH MY GOODNESS, YES.
OW!

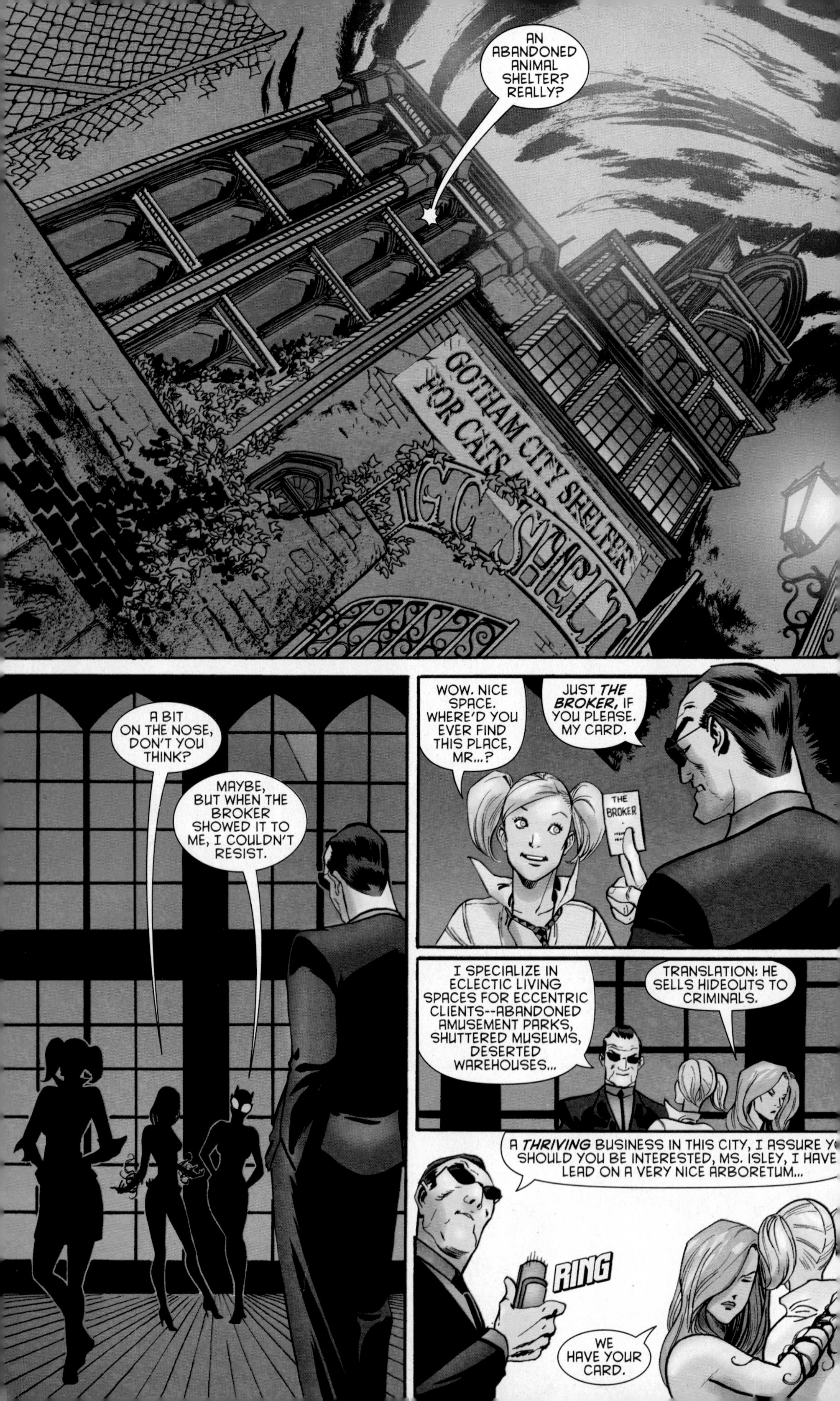
AN ABANDONED ANIMAL SHELTER? REALLY?
GOTHAM CITY SHELTER FOR CATS
A BIT ON THE NOSE, DON'T YOU THINK?
MAYBE, BUT WHEN THE BROKER SHOWED IT TO ME, I COULDN'T RESIST.
WOW. NICE SPACE. WHERE'D YOU EVER FIND THIS PLACE, MR...?
JUST THE BROKER, IF YOU PLEASE. MY CARD.
THE BROKER
I SPECIALIZE IN ECLECTIC LIVING SPACES FOR ECCENTRIC CLIENTS--ABANDONED AMUSEMENT PARKS, SHUTTERED MUSEUMS, DESERTED WAREHOUSES...
TRANSLATION: HE SELLS HIDEOUTS TO CRIMINALS.
A THRIVING BUSINESS IN THIS CITY, I ASSURE Y SHOULD YOU BE INTERESTED, MS. ISLEY, I HAVE LEAD ON A VERY NICE ARBORETUM...
RING
WE HAVE YOUR CARD.

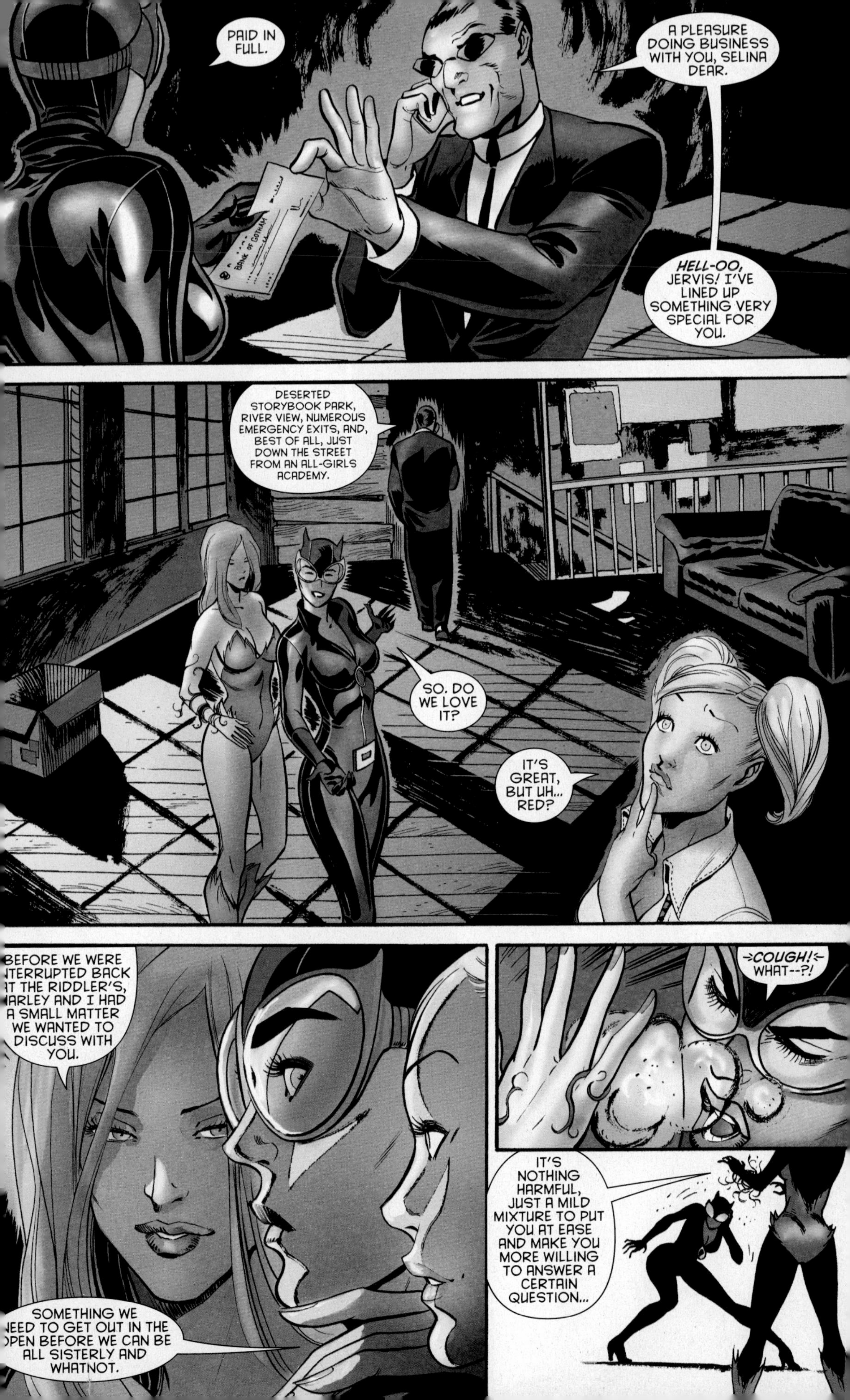
PAID IN FULL.
A PLEASURE DOING BUSINESS WITH YOU, SELINA DEAR.
BANK OF GOTHAM
*HELL-OO,* JERVIS! I'VE LINED UP SOMETHING VERY SPECIAL FOR YOU.
DESERTED STORYBOOK PARK, RIVER VIEW, NUMEROUS EMERGENCY EXITS, AND, BEST OF ALL, JUST DOWN THE STREET FROM AN ALL-GIRLS ACADEMY.
SO. DO WE LOVE IT?
IT'S GREAT, BUT UH... RED?
BEFORE WE WERE NTERRUPTED BACK AT THE RIDDLER'S, ARLEY AND I HAD A SMALL MATTER WE WANTED TO DISCUSS WITH YOU.
SOMETHING WE EED TO GET OUT IN THE OPEN BEFORE WE CAN BE ALL SISTERLY AND WHATNOT.
*COUGH!* WHAT--?!
IT'S NOTHING HARMFUL, JUST A MILD MIXTURE TO PUT YOU AT EASE AND MAKE YOU MORE WILLING TO ANSWER A CERTAIN QUESTION...

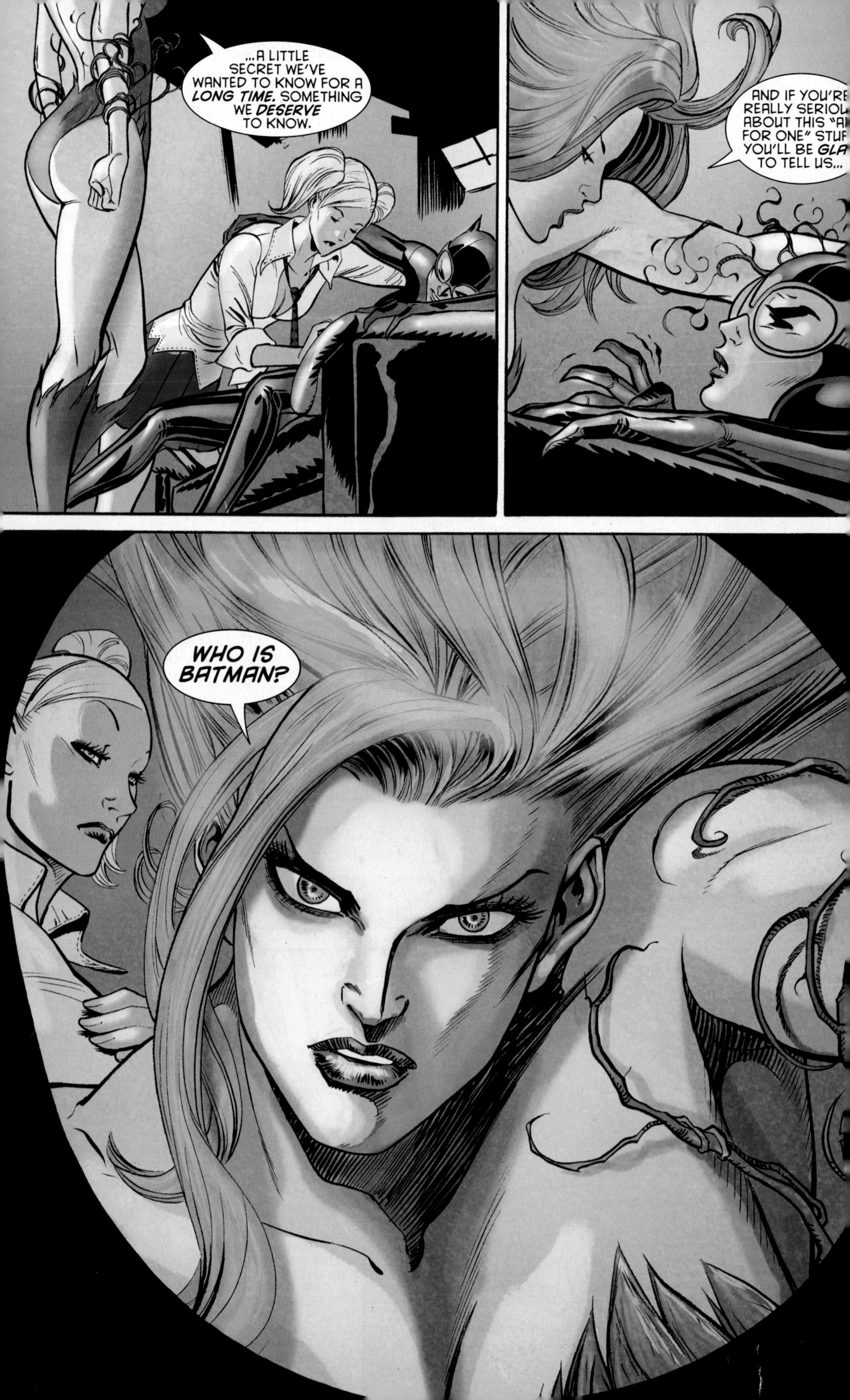
...A LITTLE SECRET WE'VE WANTED TO KNOW FOR A LONG TIME. SOMETHING WE DESERVE TO KNOW.
AND IF YOU'RE REALLY SERIOU ABOUT THIS "A FOR ONE" STUF YOU'LL BE GLA TO TELL US...
WHO IS BATMAN?

# GOTHAM CITY SIRENS 2

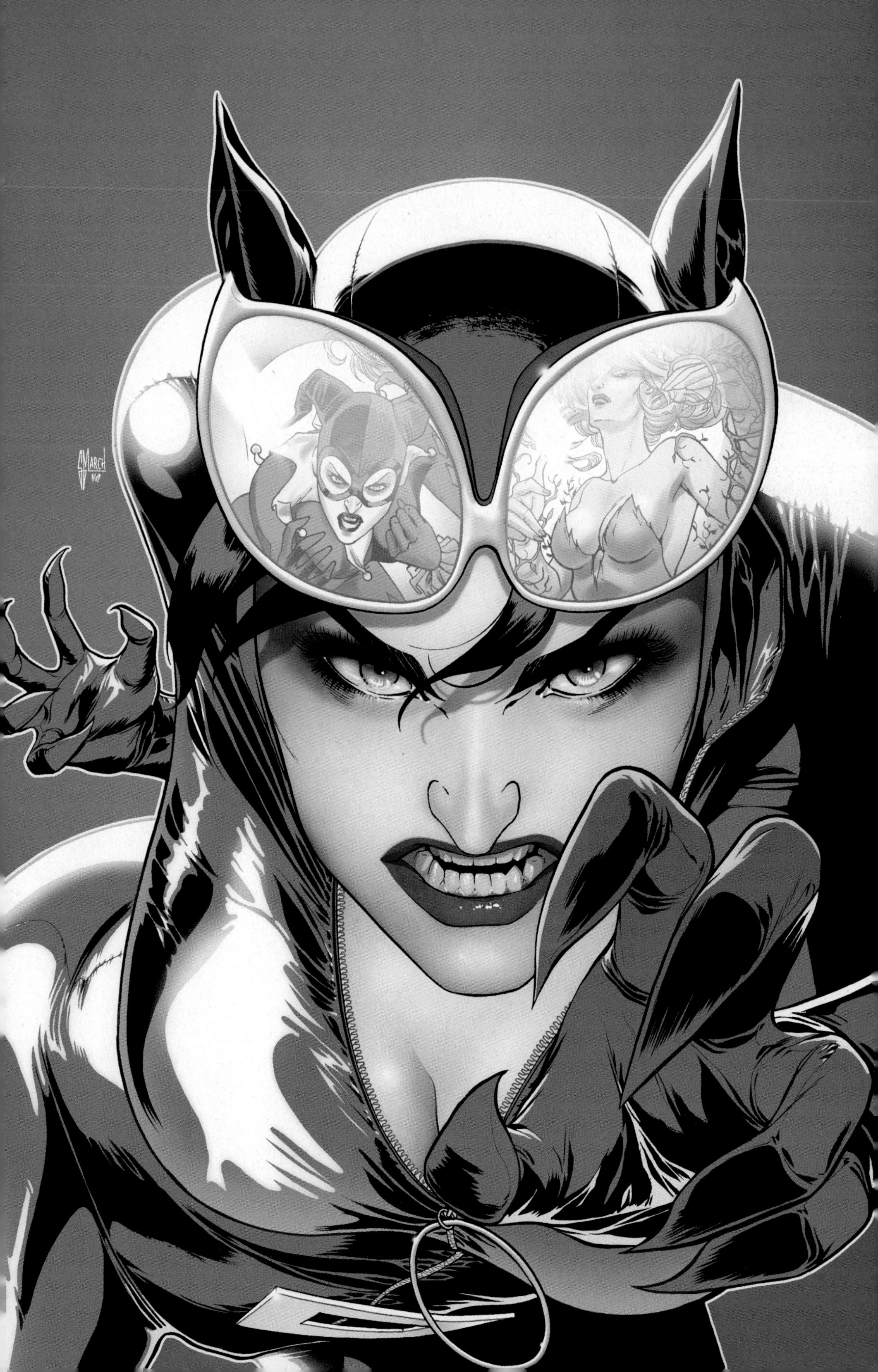

SHELTER

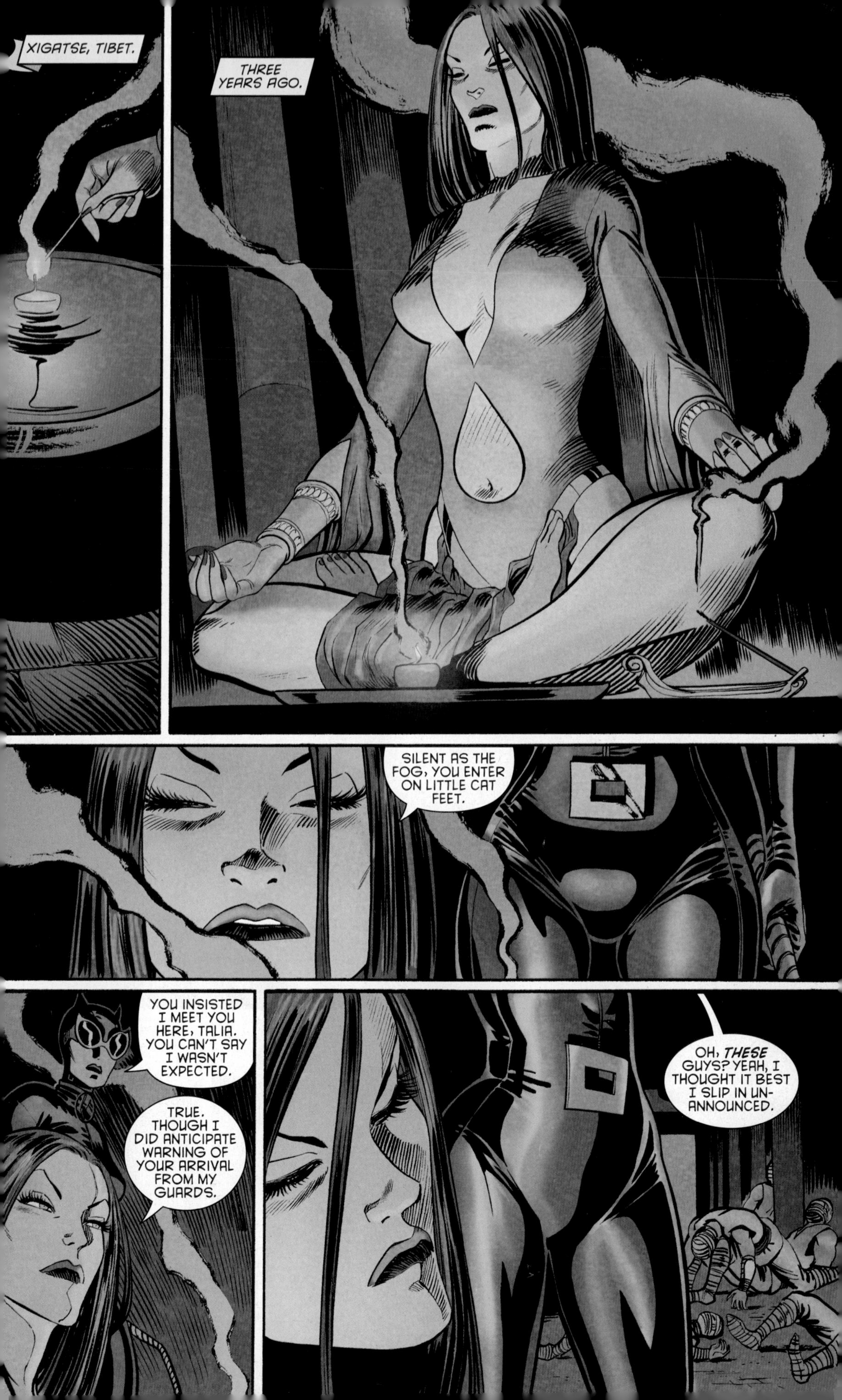
XIGATSE, TIBET.
THREE YEARS AGO.
SILENT AS THE FOG, YOU ENTER ON LITTLE CAT FEET.
YOU INSISTED I MEET YOU HERE, TALIA. YOU CAN'T SAY I WASN'T EXPECTED.
TRUE. THOUGH I DID ANTICIPATE WARNING OF YOUR ARRIVAL FROM MY GUARDS.
OH, *THESE* GUYS? YEAH, I THOUGHT IT BEST I SLIP IN UN-ANNOUNCED.

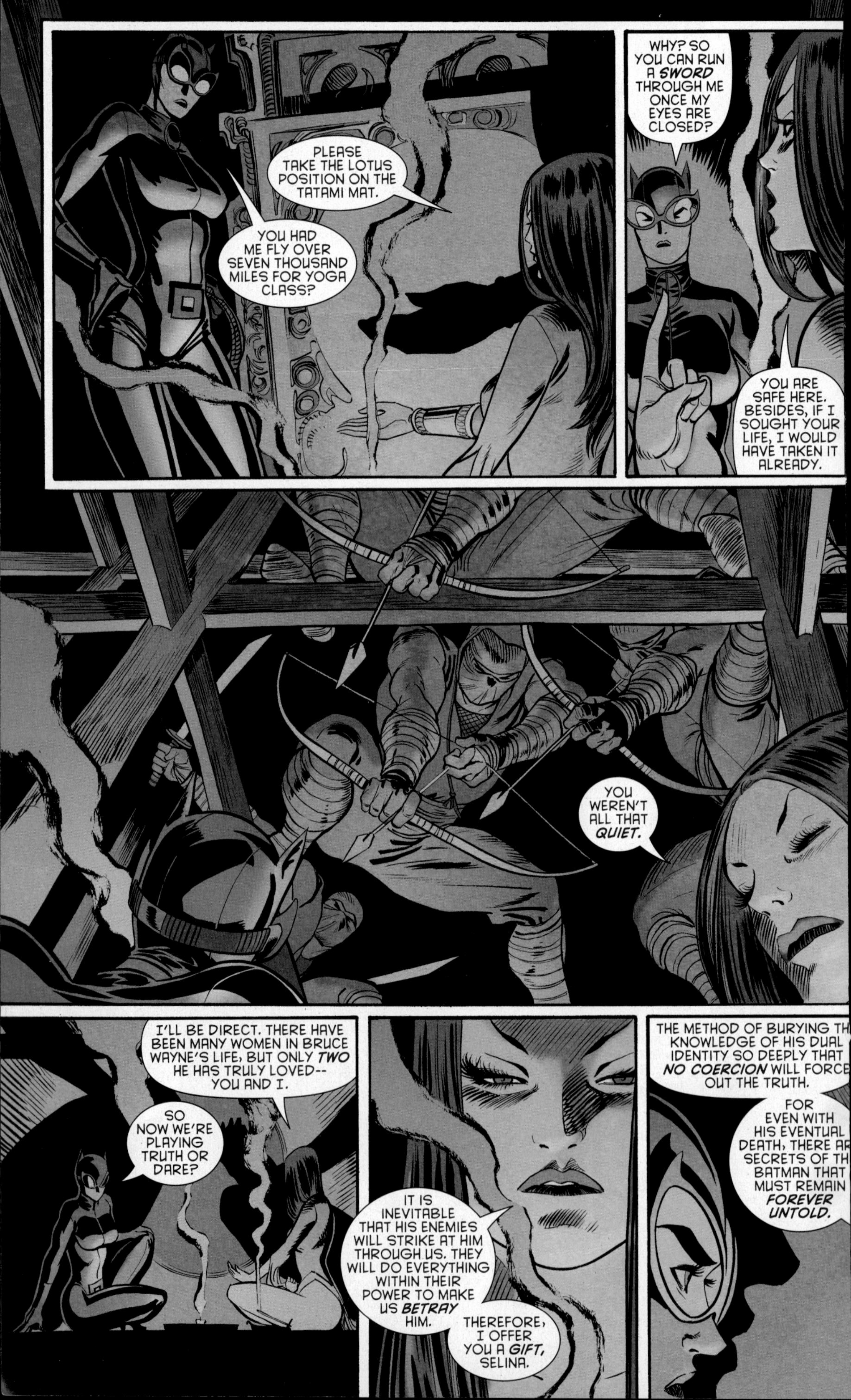
PLEASE TAKE THE LOTUS POSITION ON THE TATAMI MAT.
YOU HAD ME FLY OVER SEVEN THOUSAND MILES FOR YOGA CLASS?
WHY? SO YOU CAN RUN A **SWORD** THROUGH ME ONCE MY EYES ARE CLOSED?
YOU ARE SAFE HERE. BESIDES, IF I SOUGHT YOUR LIFE, I WOULD HAVE TAKEN IT ALREADY.
YOU WEREN'T ALL THAT **QUIET.**
I'LL BE DIRECT. THERE HAVE BEEN MANY WOMEN IN BRUCE WAYNE'S LIFE, BUT ONLY **TWO** HE HAS TRULY LOVED-- YOU AND I.
SO NOW WE'RE PLAYING TRUTH OR DARE?
IT IS INEVITABLE THAT HIS ENEMIES WILL STRIKE AT HIM THROUGH US. THEY WILL DO EVERYTHING WITHIN THEIR POWER TO MAKE US **BETRAY** HIM.
THEREFORE, I OFFER YOU A **GIFT,** SELINA.
THE METHOD OF BURYING THE KNOWLEDGE OF HIS DUAL IDENTITY SO DEEPLY THAT **NO COERCION** WILL FORCE OUT THE TRUTH.
FOR EVEN WITH HIS EVENTUAL DEATH, THERE ARE SECRETS OF THE BATMAN THAT MUST REMAIN **FOREVER UNTOLD.**

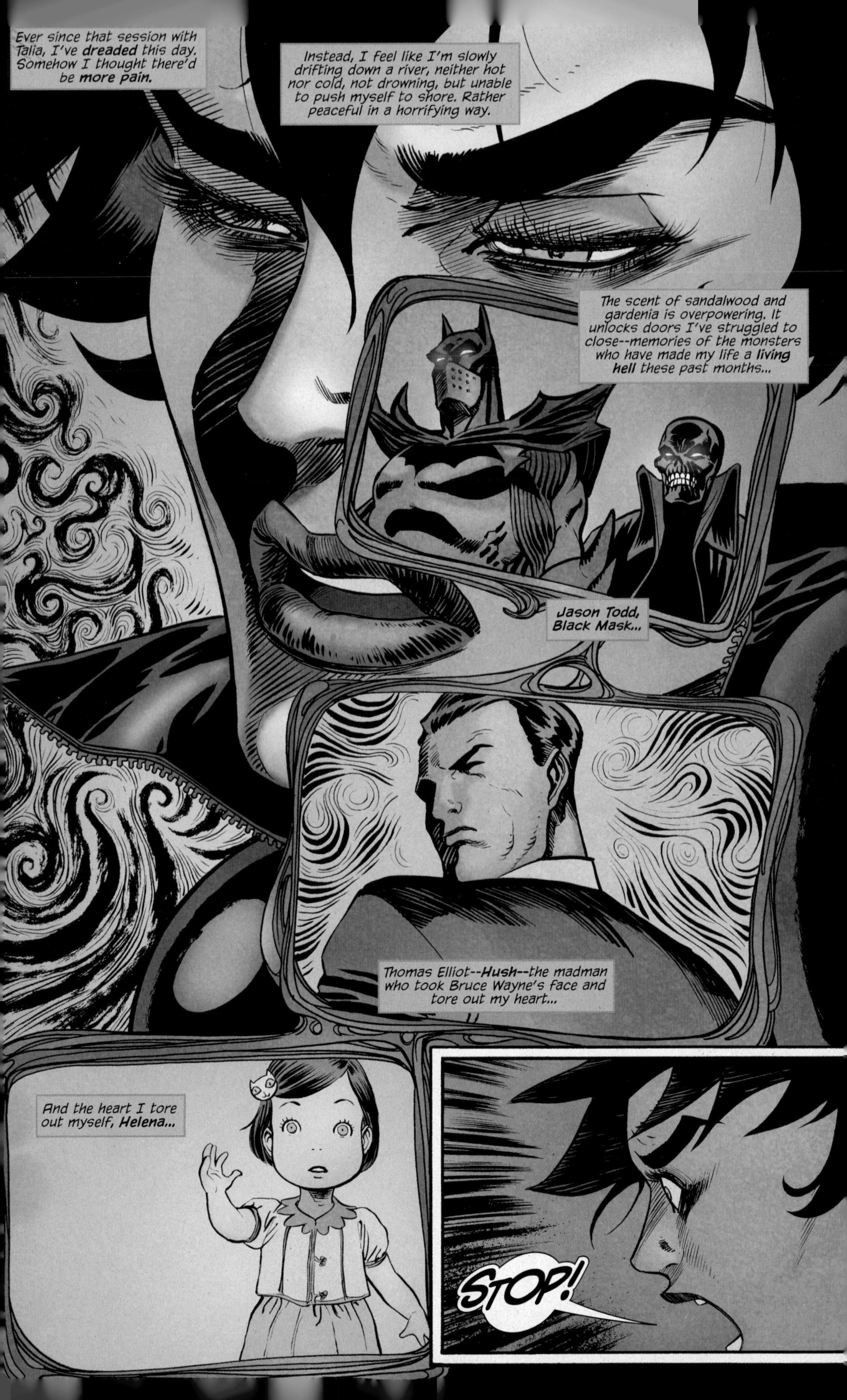
Ever since that session with Talia, I've **dreaded** this day. Somehow I thought there'd be **more pain.**
Instead, I feel like I'm slowly drifting down a river, neither hot nor cold, not drowning, but unable to push myself to shore. Rather peaceful in a horrifying way.
The scent of sandalwood and gardenia is overpowering. It unlocks doors I've struggled to close--memories of the monsters who have made my life a **living hell** these past months...
Jason Todd, Black Mask...
Thomas Elliot--**Hush**--the madman who took Bruce Wayne's face and tore out my heart...
And the heart I tore out myself, **Helena**...
STOP!

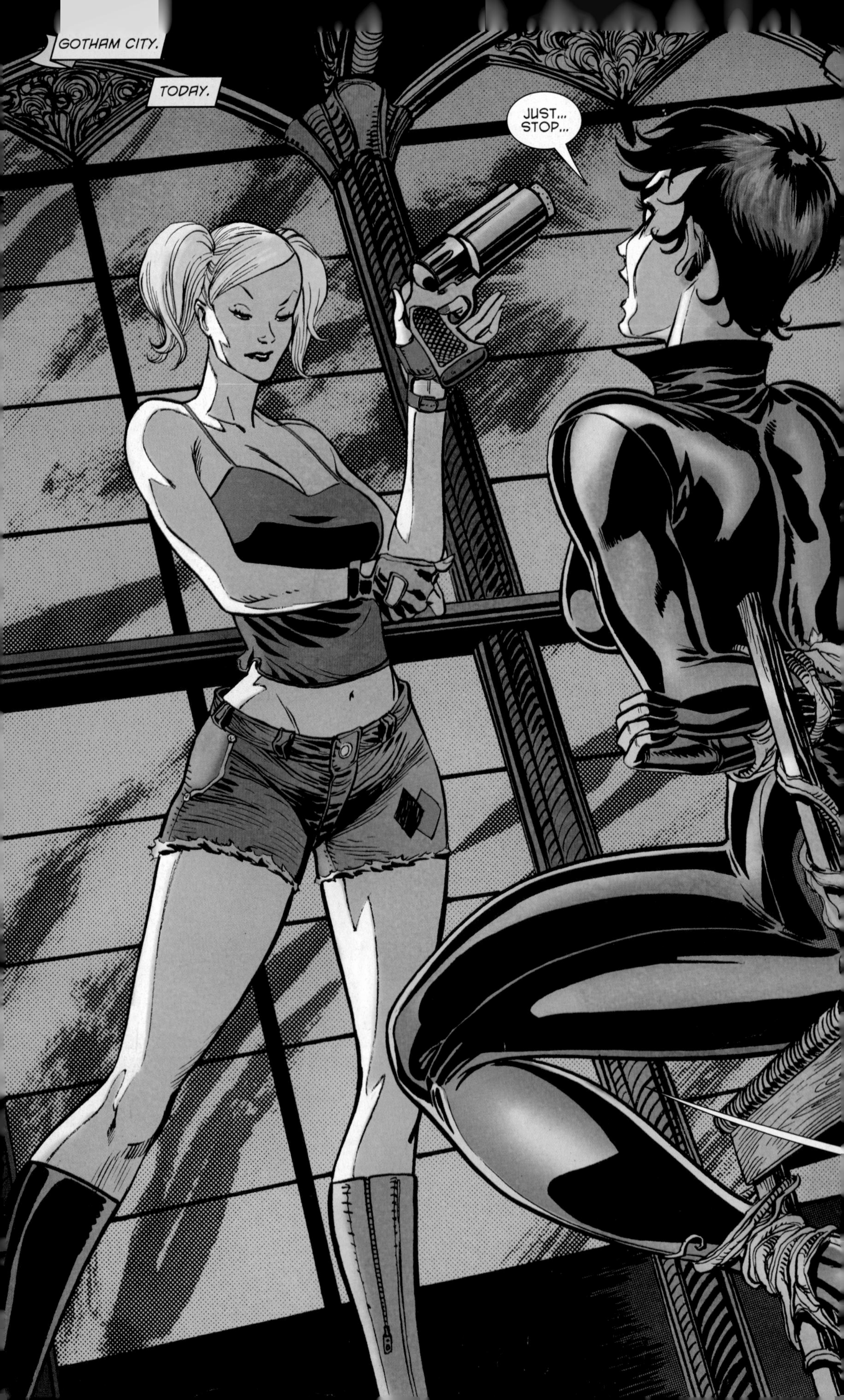
GOTHAM CITY.
TODAY.
JUST... STOP...

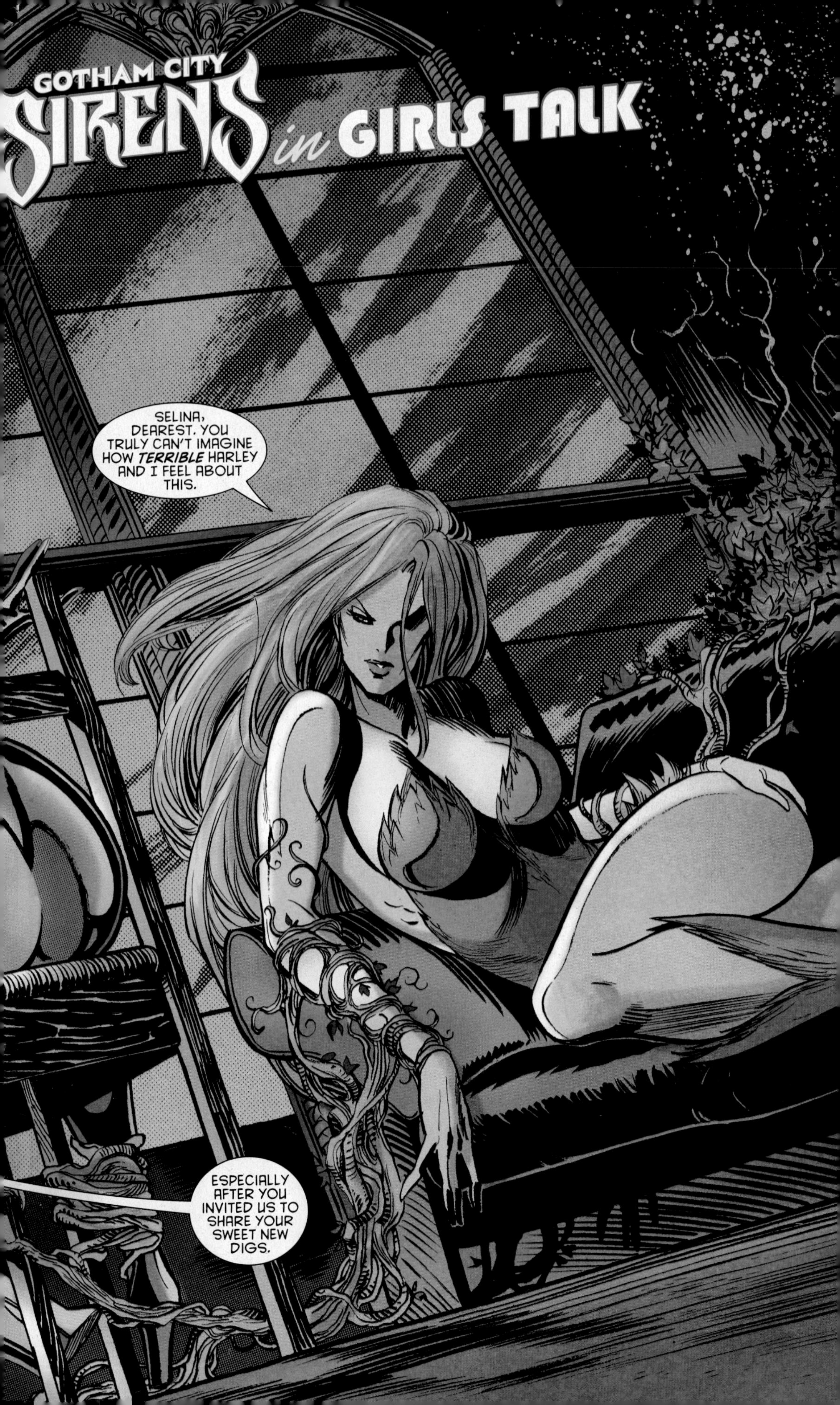
GOTHAM CITY SIRENS in GIRLS TALK
SELINA, DEAREST. YOU TRULY CAN'T IMAGINE HOW TERRIBLE HARLEY AND I FEEL ABOUT THIS.
ESPECIALLY AFTER YOU INVITED US TO SHARE YOUR SWEET NEW DIGS.

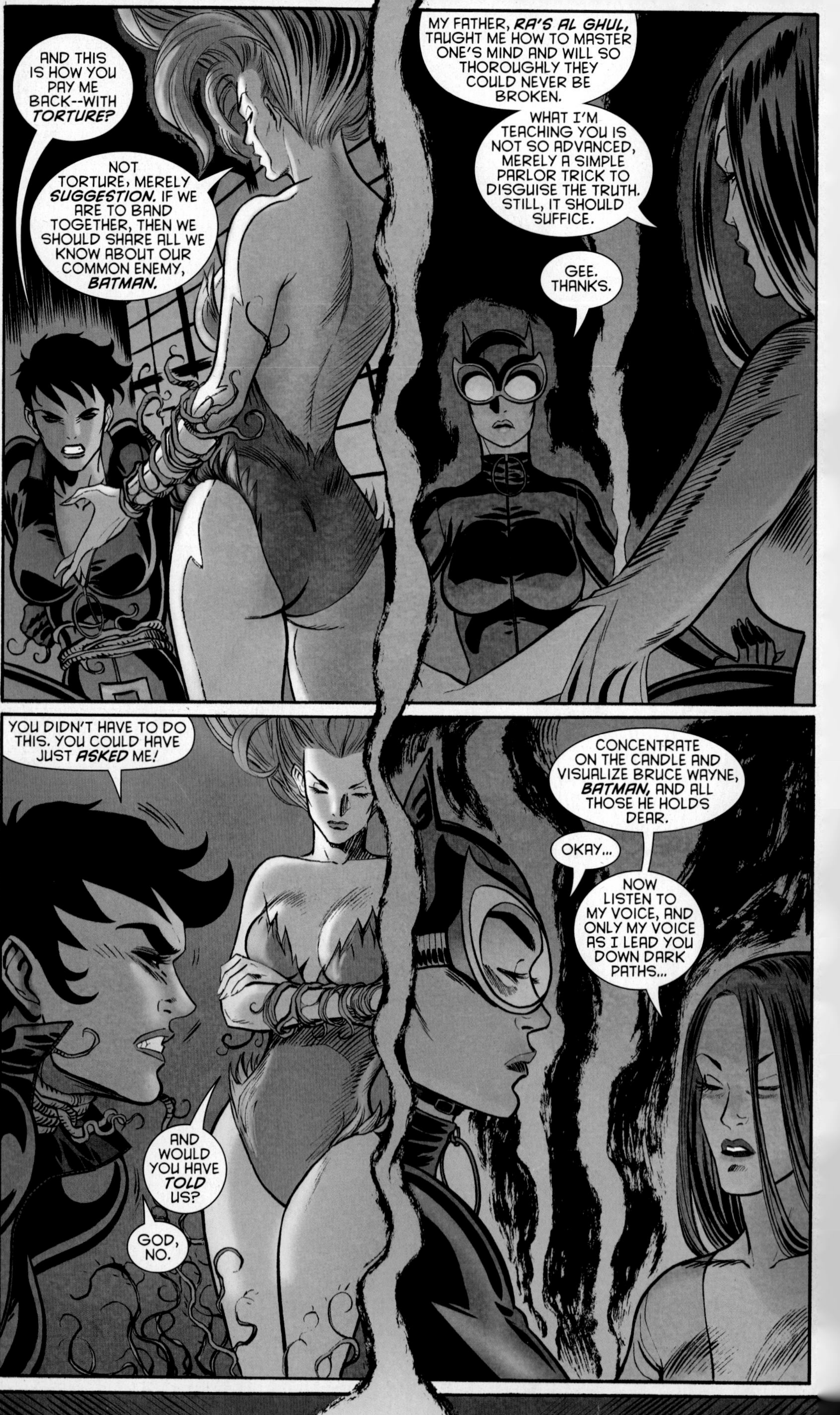

AND THIS IS HOW YOU PAY ME BACK--WITH *TORTURE?*
NOT TORTURE, MERELY *SUGGESTION.* IF WE ARE TO BAND TOGETHER, THEN WE SHOULD SHARE ALL WE KNOW ABOUT OUR COMMON ENEMY, *BATMAN.*
MY FATHER, *RA'S AL GHUL,* TAUGHT ME HOW TO MASTER ONE'S MIND AND WILL SO THOROUGHLY THEY COULD NEVER BE BROKEN.
WHAT I'M TEACHING YOU IS NOT SO ADVANCED, MERELY A SIMPLE PARLOR TRICK TO DISGUISE THE TRUTH. STILL, IT SHOULD SUFFICE.
GEE. THANKS.
YOU DIDN'T HAVE TO DO THIS. YOU COULD HAVE JUST *ASKED* ME!
AND WOULD YOU HAVE *TOLD* US?
GOD, NO.
CONCENTRATE ON THE CANDLE AND VISUALIZE BRUCE WAYNE, *BATMAN,* AND ALL THOSE HE HOLDS DEAR.
OKAY...
NOW LISTEN TO MY VOICE, AND ONLY MY VOICE AS I LEAD YOU DOWN DARK PATHS...

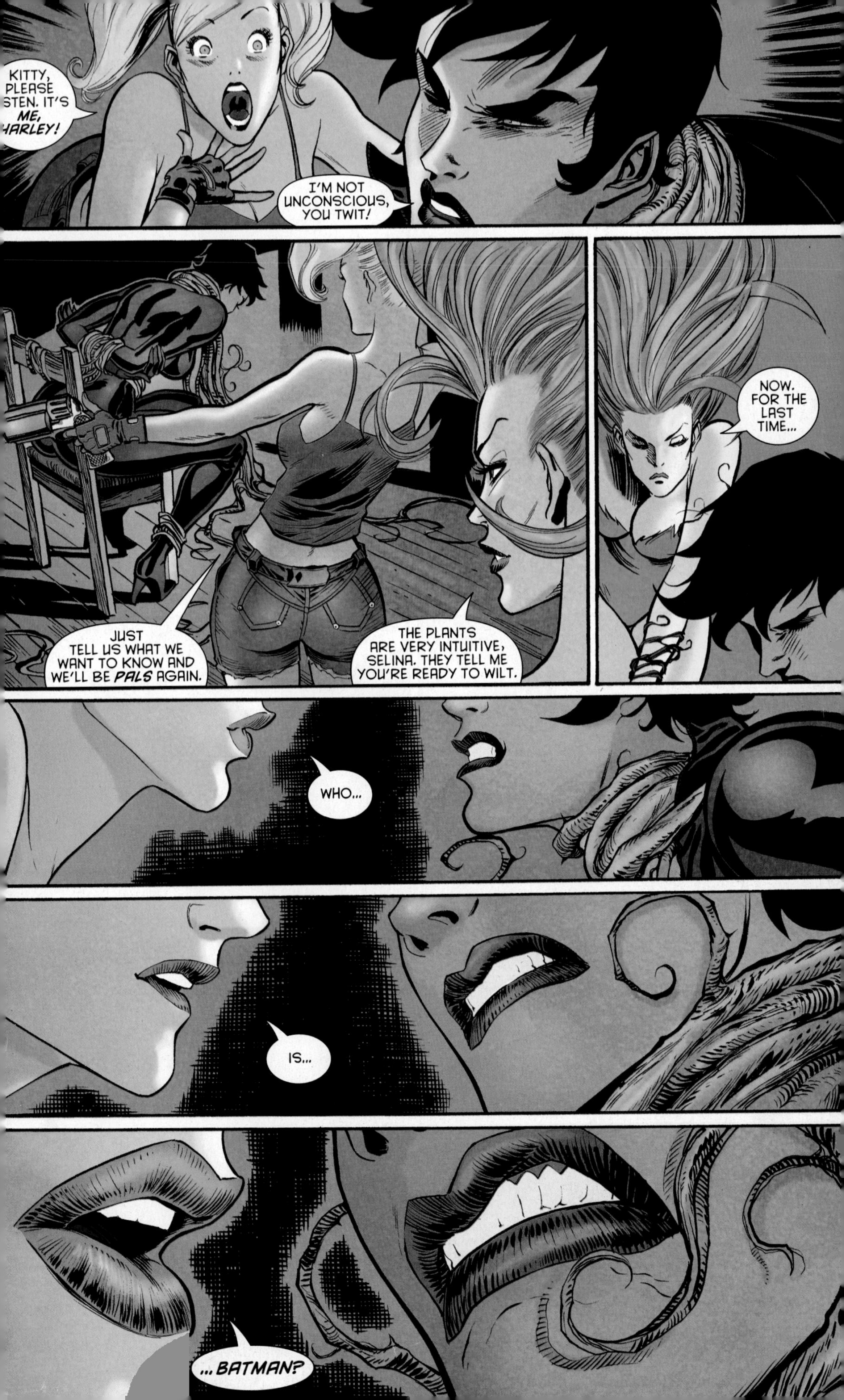
KITTY, PLEASE STEN. IT'S ME, HARLEY!
I'M NOT UNCONSCIOUS, YOU TWIT!
JUST TELL US WHAT WE WANT TO KNOW AND WE'LL BE PALS AGAIN.
THE PLANTS ARE VERY INTUITIVE, SELINA. THEY TELL ME YOU'RE READY TO WILT.
NOW. FOR THE LAST TIME...
WHO...
IS...
...BATMAN?

THE DOOR IS LOCKED.

BRUCE WAYNE.

AW, COME ON...!

SHE'S FIGHTING BA I'LL THROW SOM THORNS IN.

JIM GORDON...

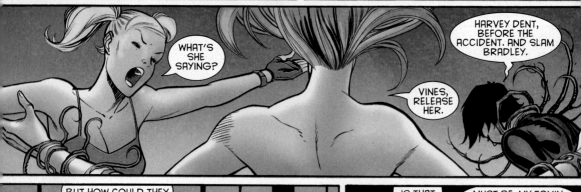

WHAT'S SHE SAYING?

HARVEY DENT, BEFORE THE ACCIDENT. AND SLAM BRADLEY.

VINES, RELEASE HER.

BUT HOW COULD THEY ALL BE--

DON'T YOU GET IT? THERE HAS BEEN A LEGION OF DO-GOODERS WHO HAVE PUT ON THE SUIT ONE TIME OR ANOTHER.

SOME ONLY FOR A MINUTE OR TWO, FOR A PR STUNT OR CHARITY EVENT, WHILE OTHERS HAVE OPERATED IN THE FIELD AS BATMAN FOR MONTHS.

IS THAT RIGHT?

MUST BE. MY TOXIN FORCES THE TRUTH OUT EVENTUALLY.

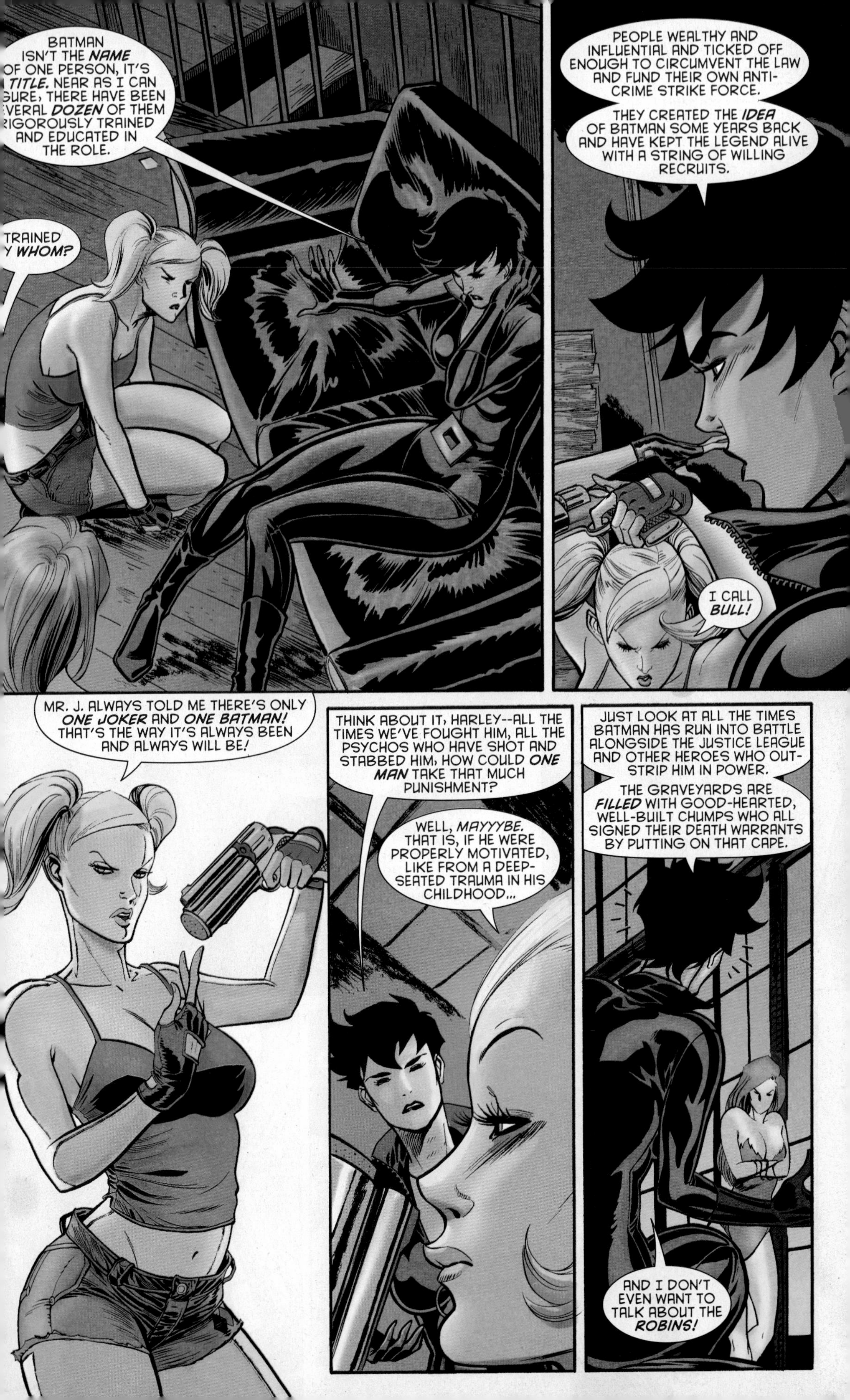
BATMAN ISN'T THE NAME OF ONE PERSON, IT'S A TITLE. NEAR AS I CAN FIGURE, THERE HAVE BEEN SEVERAL DOZEN OF THEM RIGOROUSLY TRAINED AND EDUCATED IN THE ROLE.
TRAINED BY WHOM?
PEOPLE WEALTHY AND INFLUENTIAL AND TICKED OFF ENOUGH TO CIRCUMVENT THE LAW AND FUND THEIR OWN ANTI-CRIME STRIKE FORCE.
THEY CREATED THE IDEA OF BATMAN SOME YEARS BACK AND HAVE KEPT THE LEGEND ALIVE WITH A STRING OF WILLING RECRUITS.
I CALL BULL!
MR. J. ALWAYS TOLD ME THERE'S ONLY ONE JOKER AND ONE BATMAN! THAT'S THE WAY IT'S ALWAYS BEEN AND ALWAYS WILL BE!
THINK ABOUT IT, HARLEY--ALL THE TIMES WE'VE FOUGHT HIM, ALL THE PSYCHOS WHO HAVE SHOT AND STABBED HIM, HOW COULD ONE MAN TAKE THAT MUCH PUNISHMENT?
WELL, MAYYYBE. THAT IS, IF HE WERE PROPERLY MOTIVATED, LIKE FROM A DEEP-SEATED TRAUMA IN HIS CHILDHOOD...
JUST LOOK AT ALL THE TIMES BATMAN HAS RUN INTO BATTLE ALONGSIDE THE JUSTICE LEAGUE AND OTHER HEROES WHO OUT-STRIP HIM IN POWER.
THE GRAVEYARDS ARE FILLED WITH GOOD-HEARTED, WELL-BUILT CHUMPS WHO ALL SIGNED THEIR DEATH WARRANTS BY PUTTING ON THAT CAPE.
AND I DON'T EVEN WANT TO TALK ABOUT THE ROBINS!

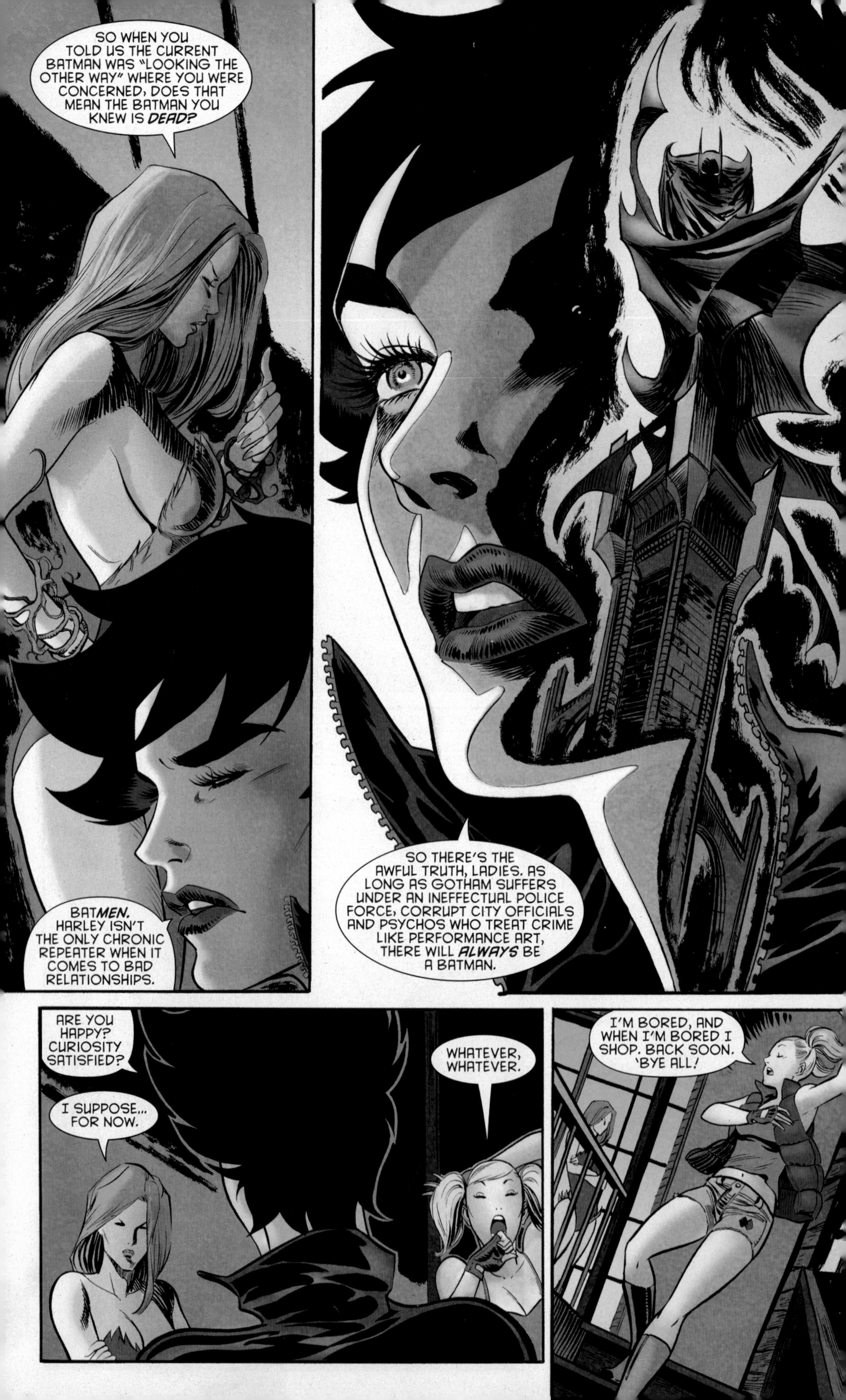
SO WHEN YOU TOLD US THE CURRENT BATMAN WAS "LOOKING THE OTHER WAY" WHERE YOU WERE CONCERNED, DOES THAT MEAN THE BATMAN YOU KNEW IS *DEAD?*
BAT*MEN.* HARLEY ISN'T THE ONLY CHRONIC REPEATER WHEN IT COMES TO BAD RELATIONSHIPS.
SO THERE'S THE AWFUL TRUTH, LADIES. AS LONG AS GOTHAM SUFFERS UNDER AN INEFFECTUAL POLICE FORCE, CORRUPT CITY OFFICIALS AND PSYCHOS WHO TREAT CRIME LIKE PERFORMANCE ART, THERE WILL *ALWAYS* BE A BATMAN.
ARE YOU HAPPY? CURIOSITY SATISFIED?
I SUPPOSE... FOR NOW.
WHATEVER, WHATEVER.
I'M BORED, AND WHEN I'M BORED I SHOP. BACK SOON. 'BYE ALL!

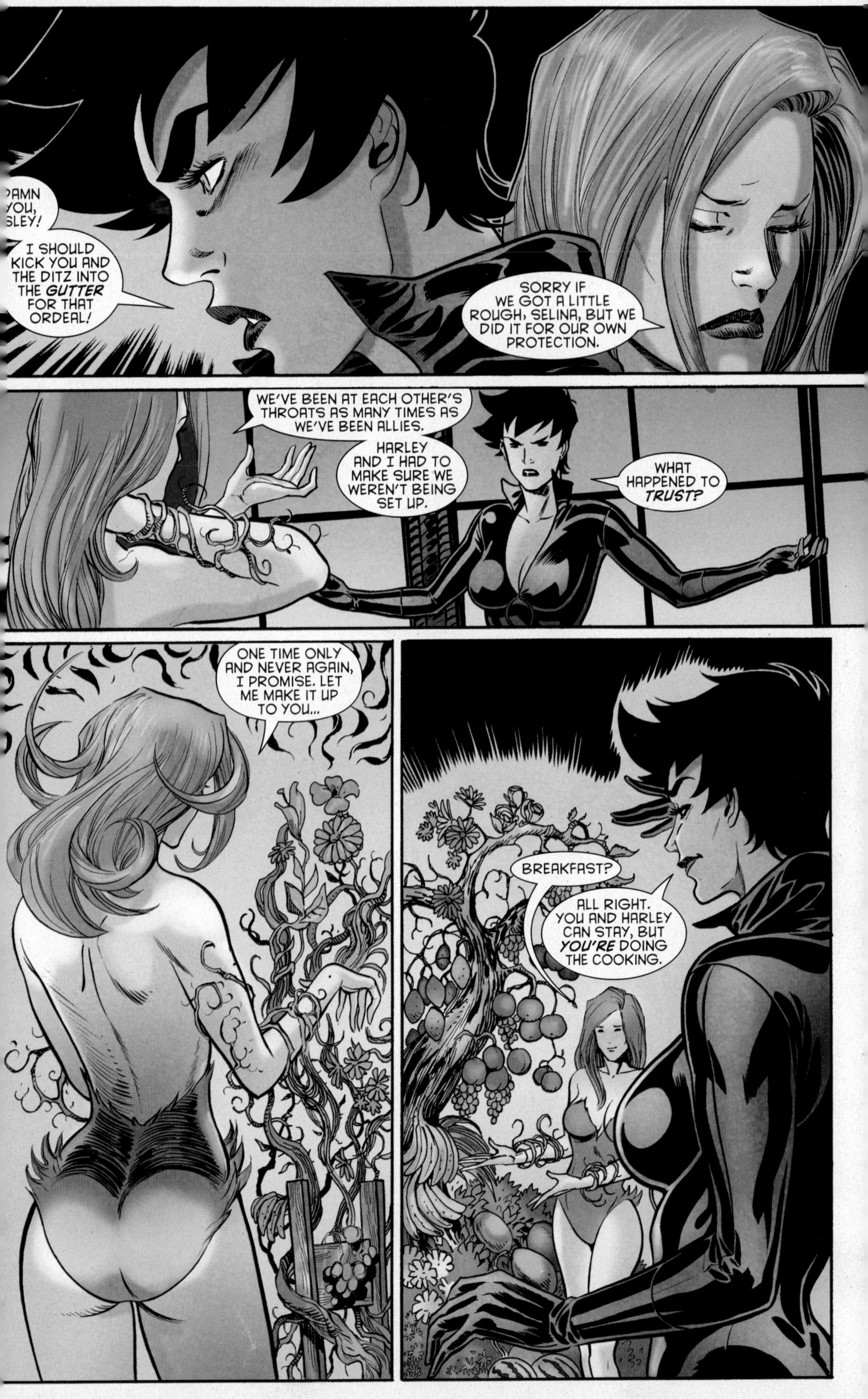

DAMN YOU, ISLEY!
I SHOULD KICK YOU AND THE DITZ INTO THE GUTTER FOR THAT ORDEAL!
SORRY IF WE GOT A LITTLE ROUGH, SELINA, BUT WE DID IT FOR OUR OWN PROTECTION.
WE'VE BEEN AT EACH OTHER'S THROATS AS MANY TIMES AS WE'VE BEEN ALLIES.
HARLEY AND I HAD TO MAKE SURE WE WEREN'T BEING SET UP.
WHAT HAPPENED TO TRUST?
ONE TIME ONLY AND NEVER AGAIN, I PROMISE. LET ME MAKE IT UP TO YOU...
BREAKFAST?
ALL RIGHT. YOU AND HARLEY CAN STAY, BUT YOU'RE DOING THE COOKING.

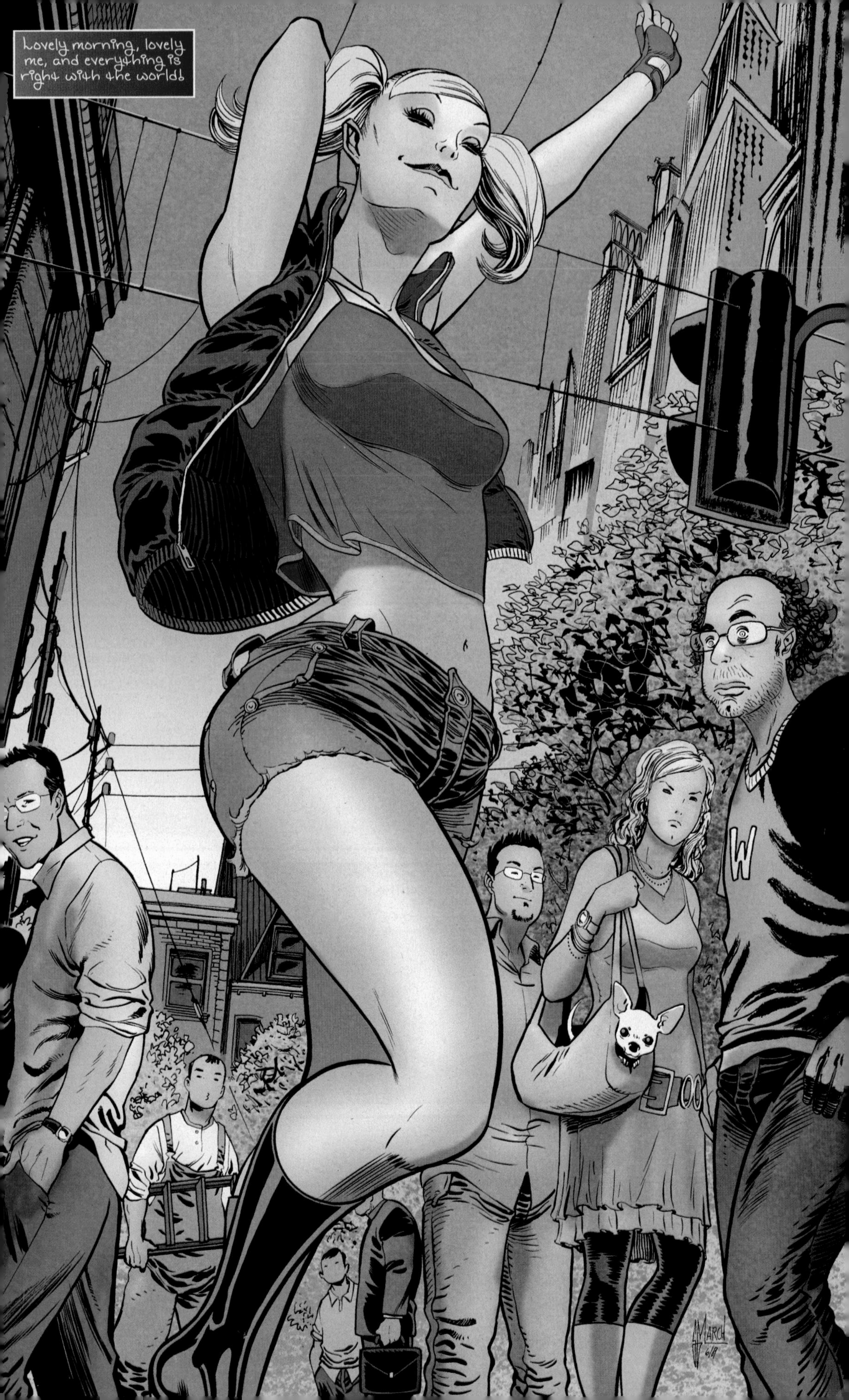
Lovely morning, lovely me, and everything is right with the world!
MARCH 6/8

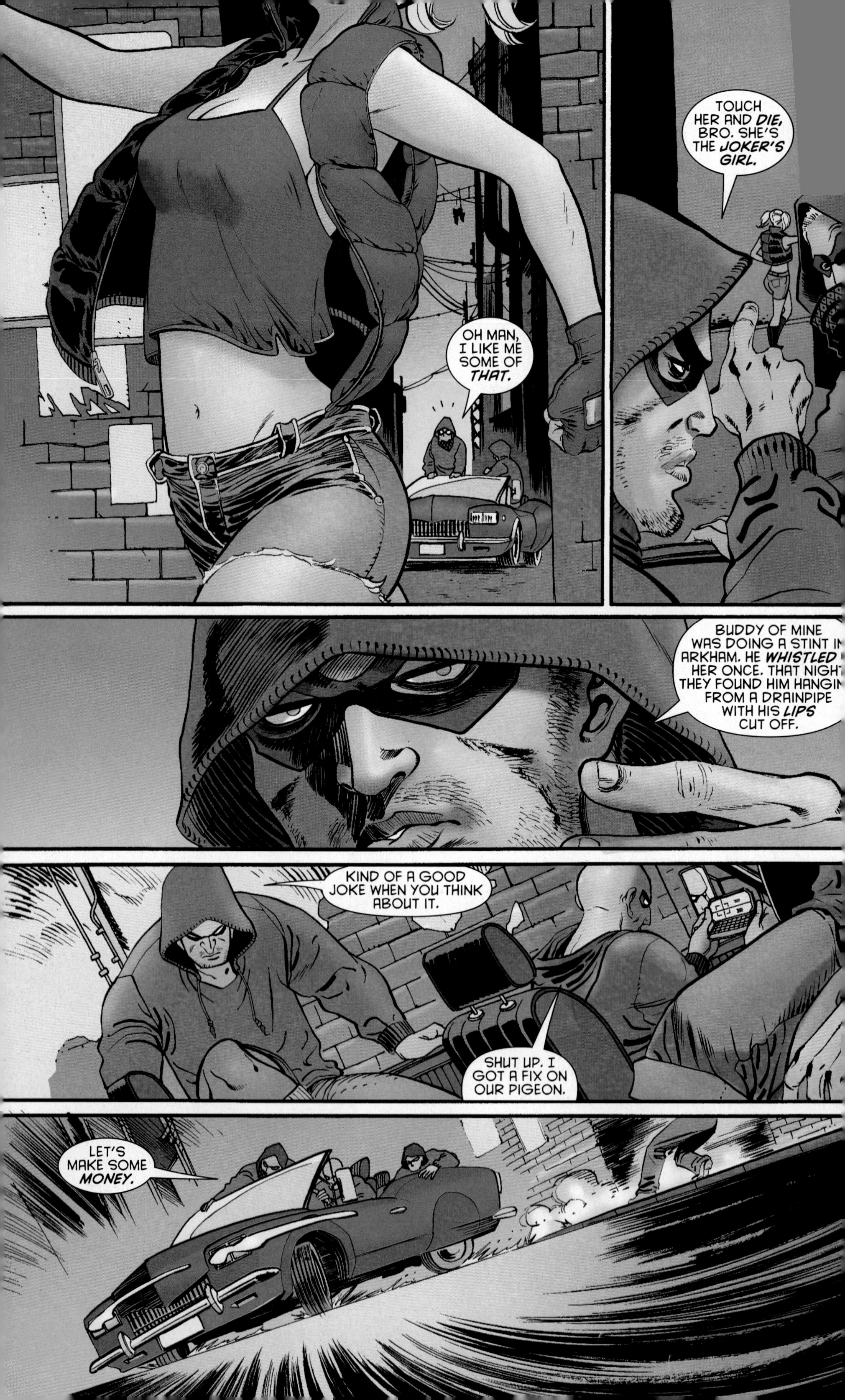
OH MAN, I LIKE ME SOME OF *THAT.*
TOUCH HER AND *DIE,* BRO. SHE'S THE *JOKER'S GIRL.*
BUDDY OF MINE WAS DOING A STINT IN ARKHAM. HE *WHISTLED* AT HER ONCE. THAT NIGHT THEY FOUND HIM HANGING FROM A DRAINPIPE WITH HIS *LIPS* CUT OFF.
KIND OF A GOOD JOKE WHEN YOU THINK ABOUT IT.
SHUT UP. I GOT A FIX ON OUR PIGEON.
LET'S MAKE SOME *MONEY.*

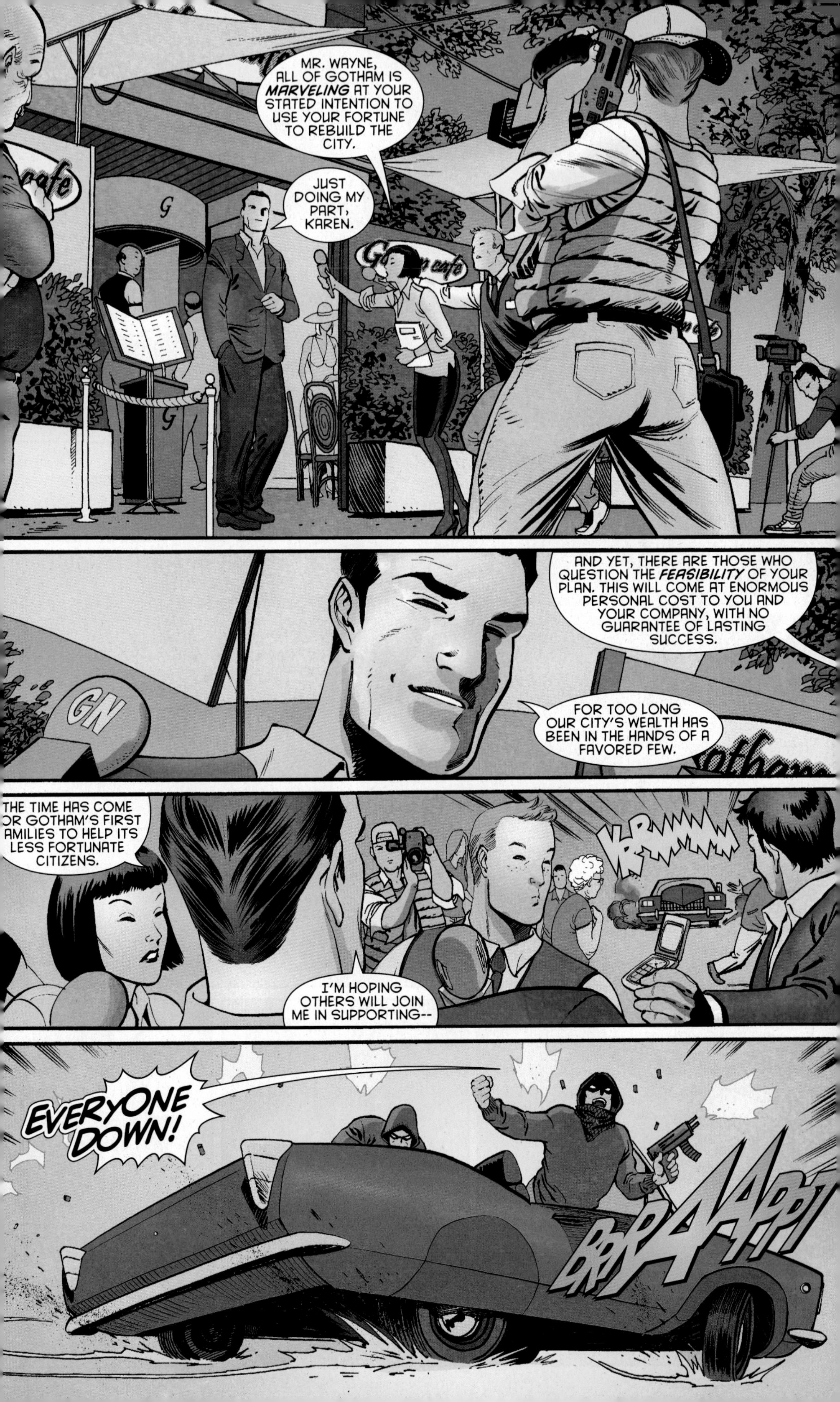
MR. WAYNE, ALL OF GOTHAM IS MARVELING AT YOUR STATED INTENTION TO USE YOUR FORTUNE TO REBUILD THE CITY.
JUST DOING MY PART, KAREN.
AND YET, THERE ARE THOSE WHO QUESTION THE FEASIBILITY OF YOUR PLAN. THIS WILL COME AT ENORMOUS PERSONAL COST TO YOU AND YOUR COMPANY, WITH NO GUARANTEE OF LASTING SUCCESS.
FOR TOO LONG OUR CITY'S WEALTH HAS BEEN IN THE HANDS OF A FAVORED FEW.
THE TIME HAS COME OR GOTHAM'S FIRST AMILIES TO HELP ITS LESS FORTUNATE CITIZENS.
VRRMMMMMM
I'M HOPING OTHERS WILL JOIN ME IN SUPPORTING--
EVERYONE DOWN!
BRRAAPP!

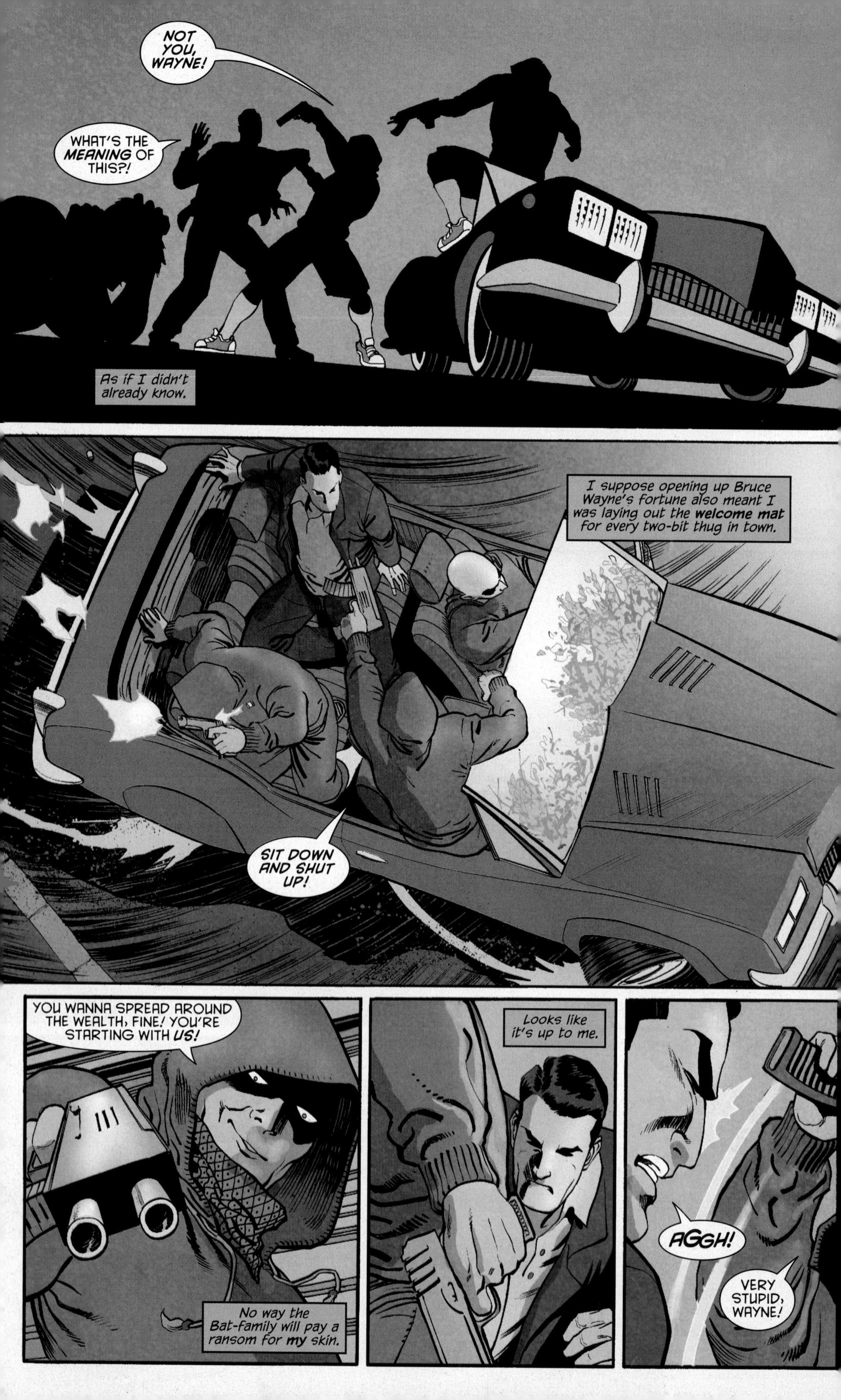
NOT YOU, WAYNE!
WHAT'S THE MEANING OF THIS?!
As if I didn't already know.
I suppose opening up Bruce Wayne's fortune also meant I was laying out the welcome mat for every two-bit thug in town.
SIT DOWN AND SHUT UP!
YOU WANNA SPREAD AROUND THE WEALTH, FINE! YOU'RE STARTING WITH US!
No way the Bat-family will pay a ransom for my skin.
Looks like it's up to me.
AGGH!
VERY STUPID, WAYNE!

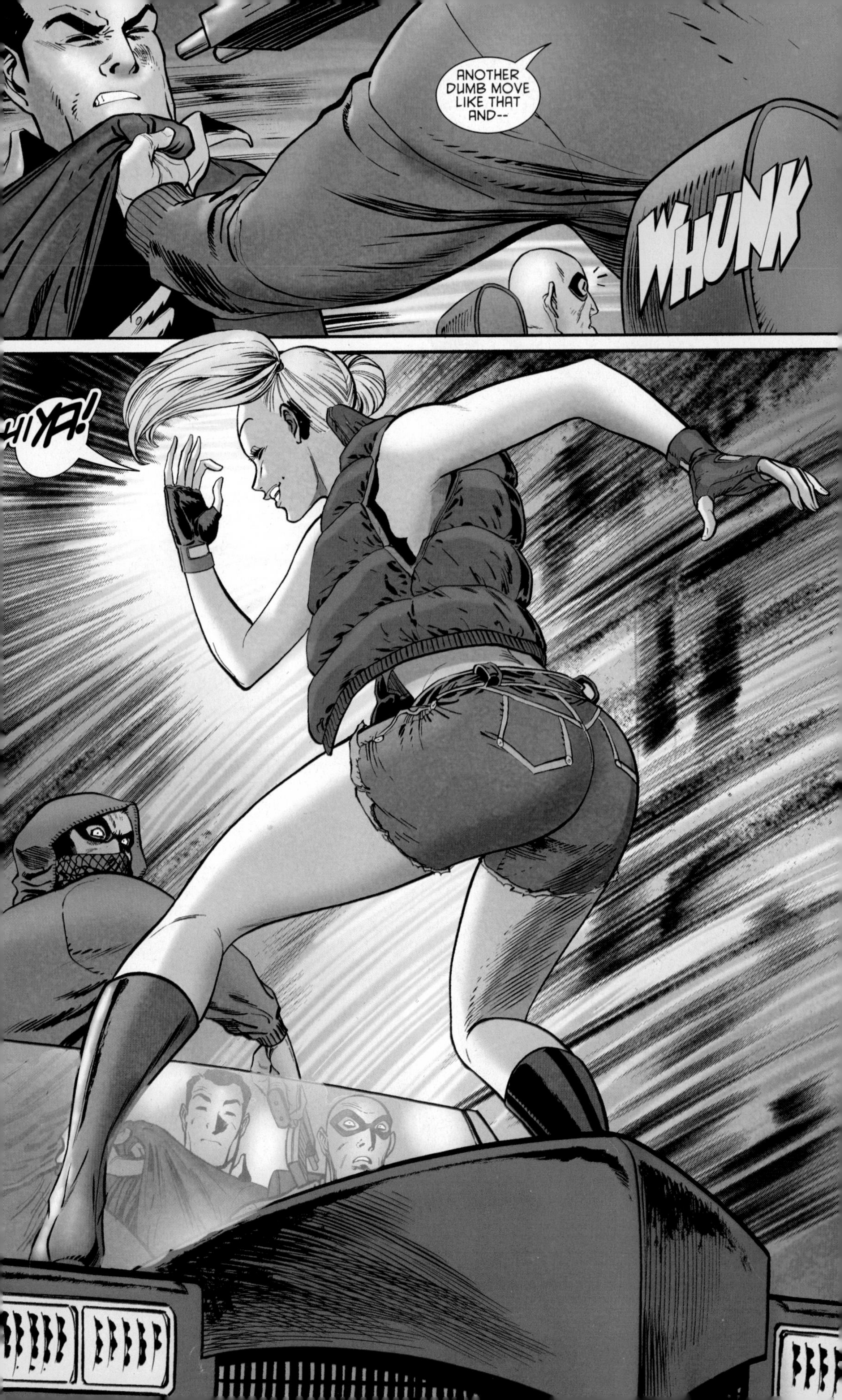
ANOTHER DUMB MOVE LIKE THAT AND--
WHUNK
HIIYA!

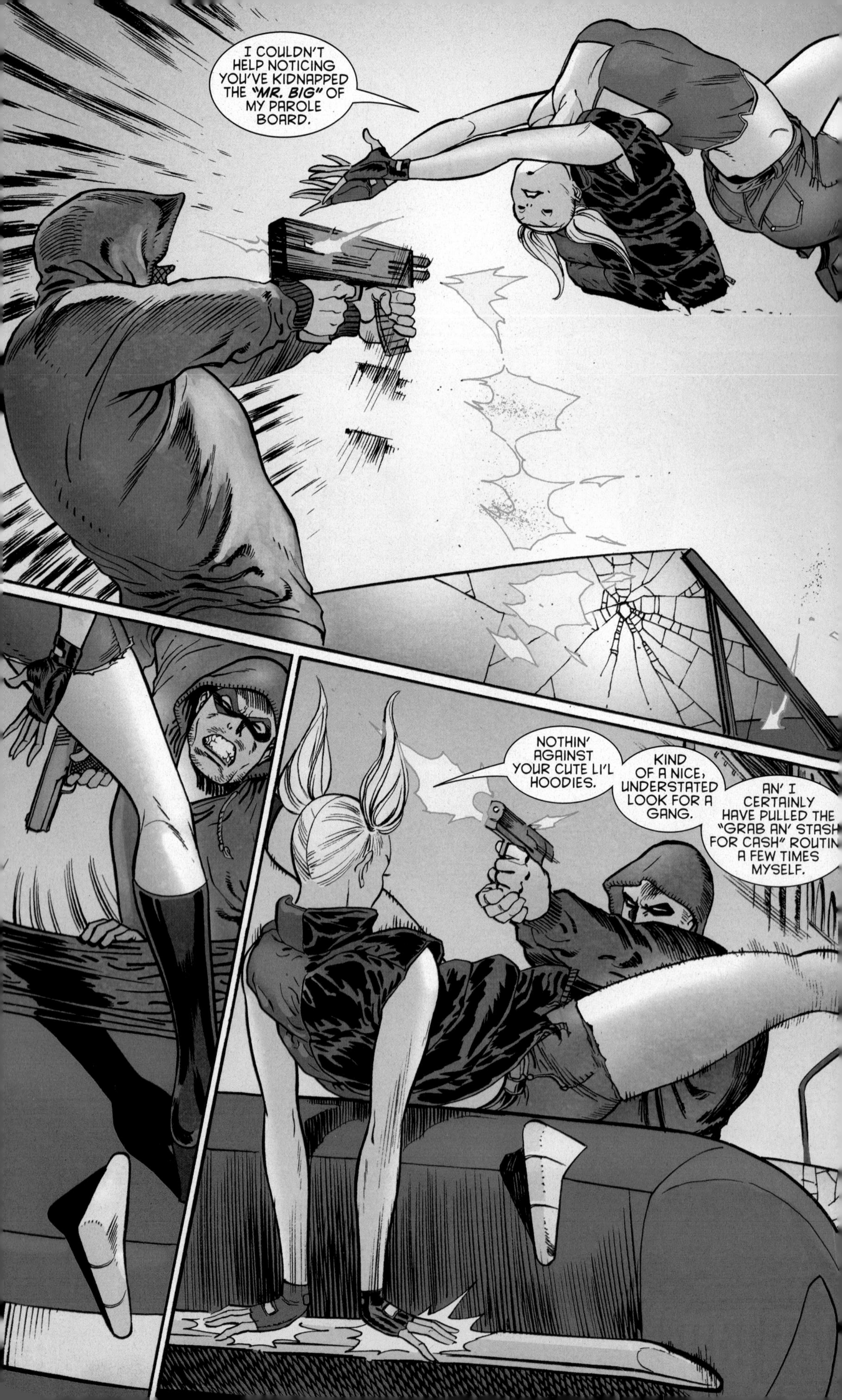

I COULDN'T HELP NOTICING YOU'VE KIDNAPPED THE "MR. BIG" OF MY PAROLE BOARD.
NOTHIN' AGAINST YOUR CUTE LI'L HOODIES.
KIND OF A NICE, UNDERSTATED LOOK FOR A GANG.
AN' I CERTAINLY HAVE PULLED THE "GRAB AN' STASH FOR CASH" ROUTIN A FEW TIMES MYSELF.

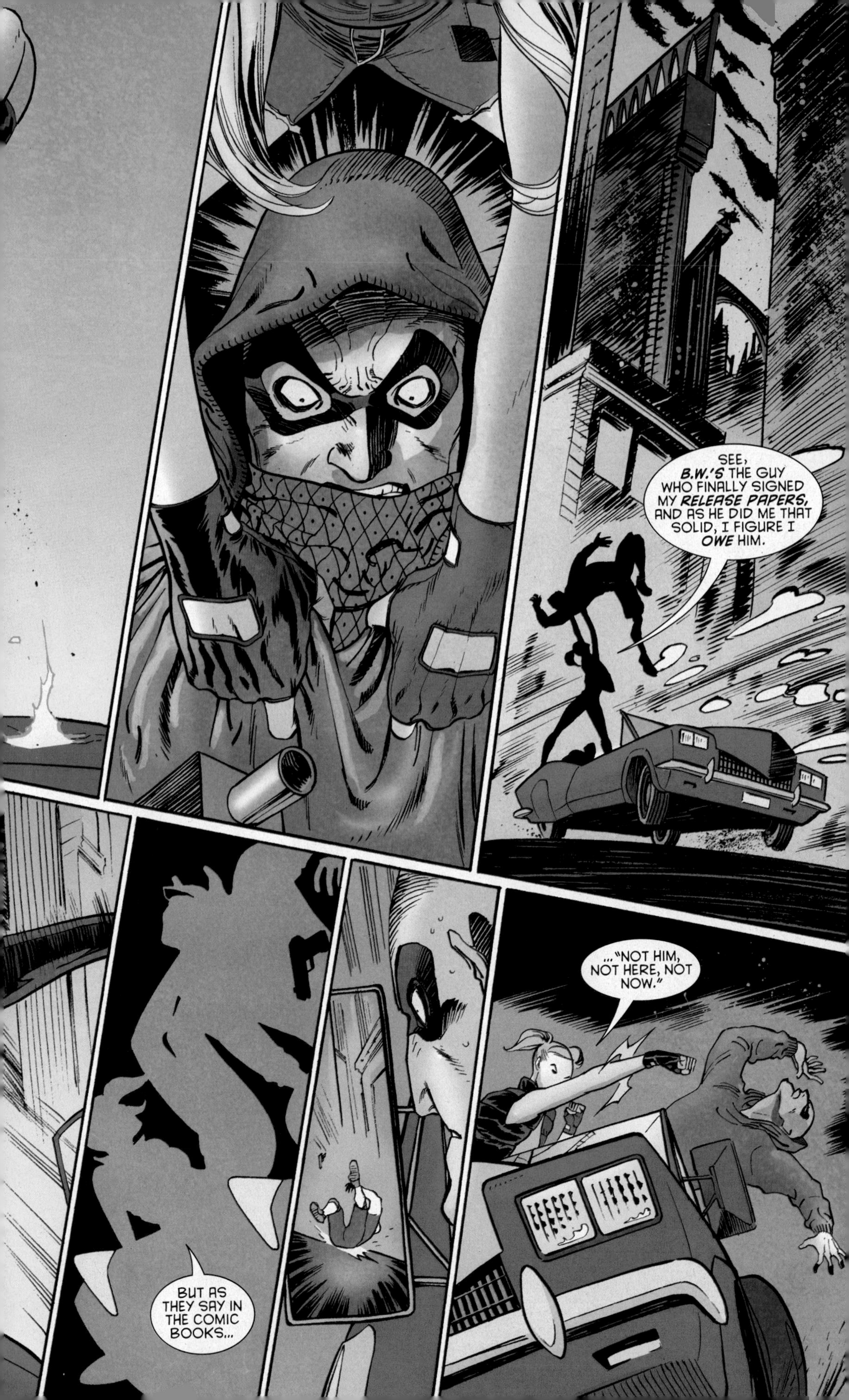
SEE, B.W.'S THE GUY WHO FINALLY SIGNED MY RELEASE PAPERS, AND AS HE DID ME THAT SOLID, I FIGURE I OWE HIM.
BUT AS THEY SAY IN THE COMIC BOOKS...
..."NOT HIM, NOT HERE, NOT NOW."

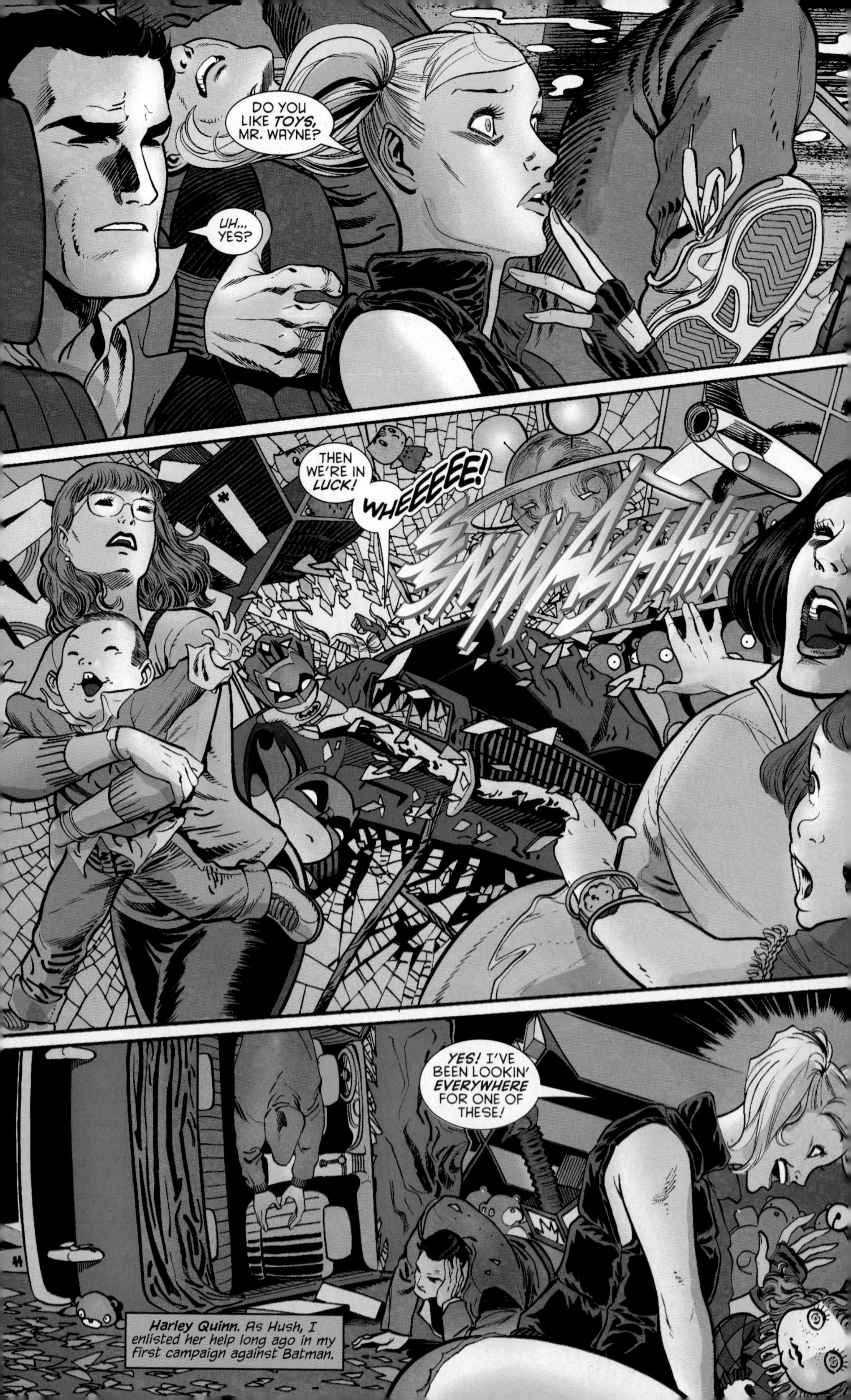
DO YOU LIKE *TOYS*, MR. WAYNE?
UH... YES?
THEN WE'RE IN *LUCK*!
WHEEEEEE!
SMMASHHH
*YES!* I'VE BEEN LOOKIN' *EVERYWHERE* FOR ONE OF THESE!
*Harley Quinn*. As Hush, I enlisted her help long ago in my first campaign against Batman.

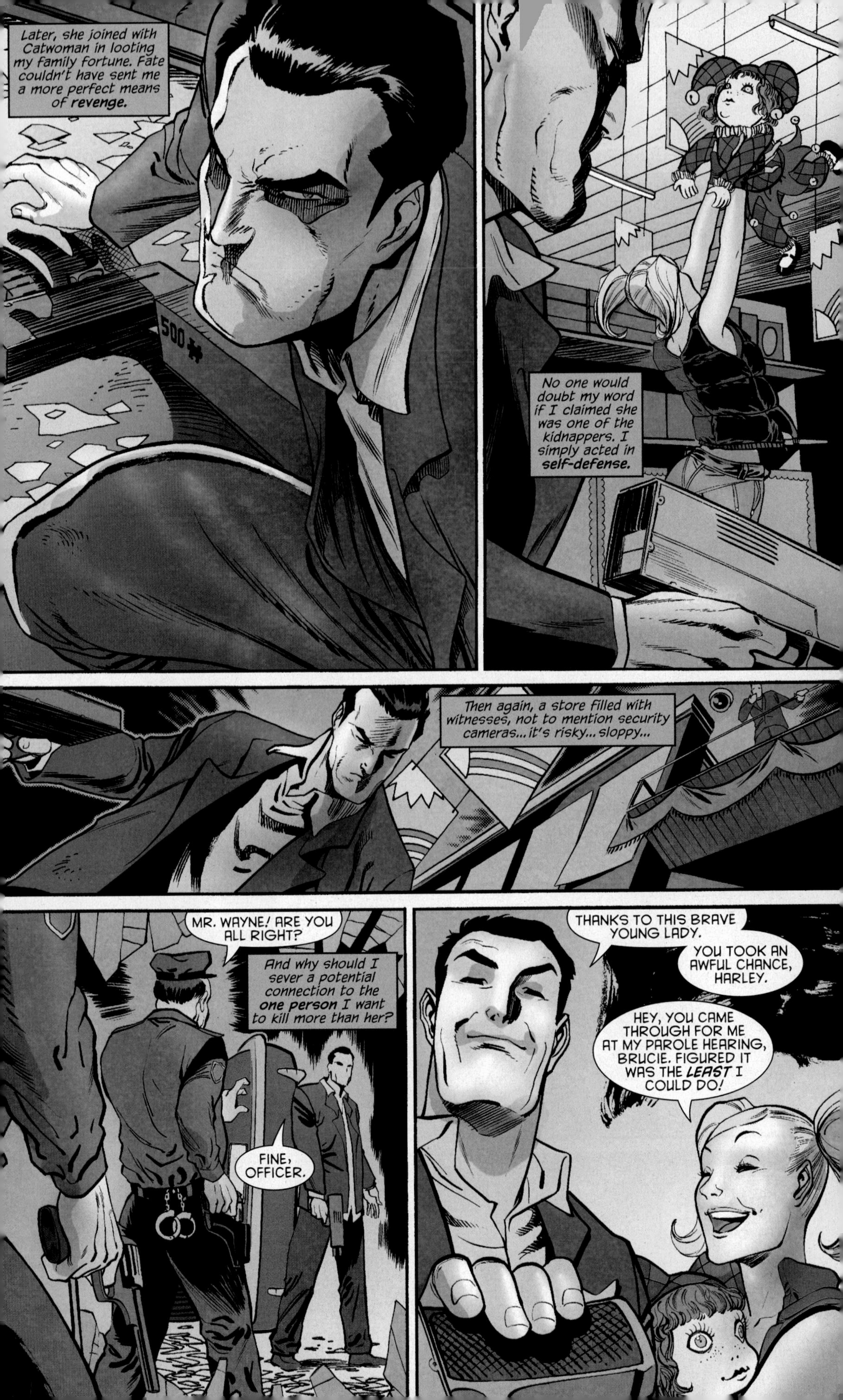

Later, she joined with Catwoman in looting my family fortune. Fate couldn't have sent me a more perfect means of revenge.
500
No one would doubt my word if I claimed she was one of the kidnappers. I simply acted in self-defense.
Then again, a store filled with witnesses, not to mention security cameras... it's risky... sloppy...
MR. WAYNE! ARE YOU ALL RIGHT?
And why should I sever a potential connection to the one person I want to kill more than her?
FINE, OFFICER.
THANKS TO THIS BRAVE YOUNG LADY.
YOU TOOK AN AWFUL CHANCE, HARLEY.
HEY, YOU CAME THROUGH FOR ME AT MY PAROLE HEARING, BRUCIE. FIGURED IT WAS THE LEAST I COULD DO!

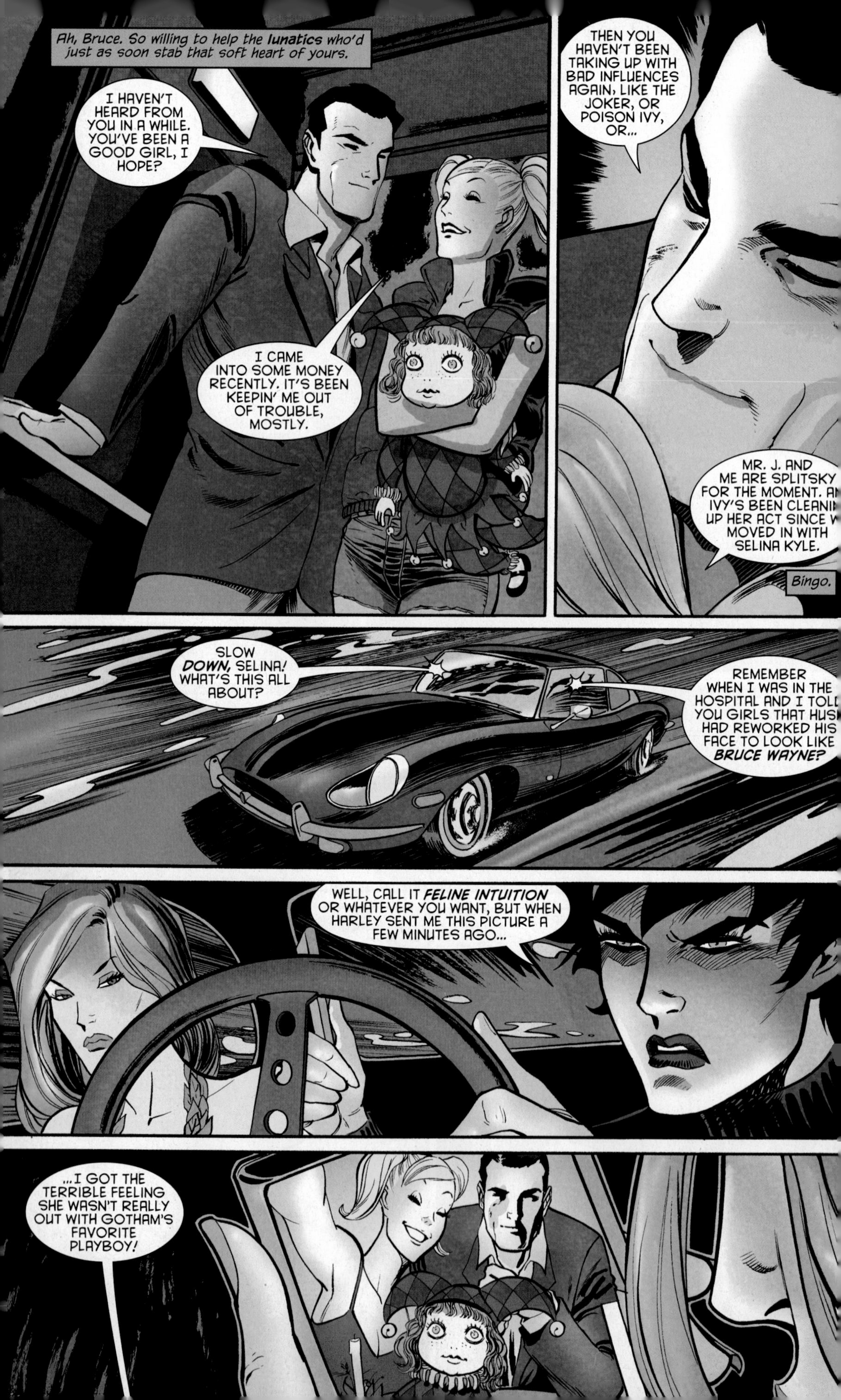
Ah, Bruce. So willing to help the **lunatics** who'd just as soon stab that soft heart of yours.
I HAVEN'T HEARD FROM YOU IN A WHILE. YOU'VE BEEN A GOOD GIRL, I HOPE?
I CAME INTO SOME MONEY RECENTLY. IT'S BEEN KEEPIN' ME OUT OF TROUBLE, MOSTLY.
THEN YOU HAVEN'T BEEN TAKING UP WITH BAD INFLUENCES AGAIN, LIKE THE JOKER, OR POISON IVY, OR...
MR. J. AND ME ARE SPLITSKY FOR THE MOMENT. A IVY'S BEEN CLEANI UP HER ACT SINCE MOVED IN WITH SELINA KYLE.
Bingo.
SLOW ***DOWN,*** SELINA! WHAT'S THIS ALL ABOUT?
REMEMBER WHEN I WAS IN THE HOSPITAL AND I TOL YOU GIRLS THAT HUS HAD REWORKED HIS FACE TO LOOK LIKE ***BRUCE WAYNE?***
WELL, CALL IT ***FELINE INTUITION*** OR WHATEVER YOU WANT, BUT WHEN HARLEY SENT ME THIS PICTURE A FEW MINUTES AGO...
...I GOT THE TERRIBLE FEELING SHE WASN'T REALLY OUT WITH GOTHAM'S FAVORITE PLAYBOY!

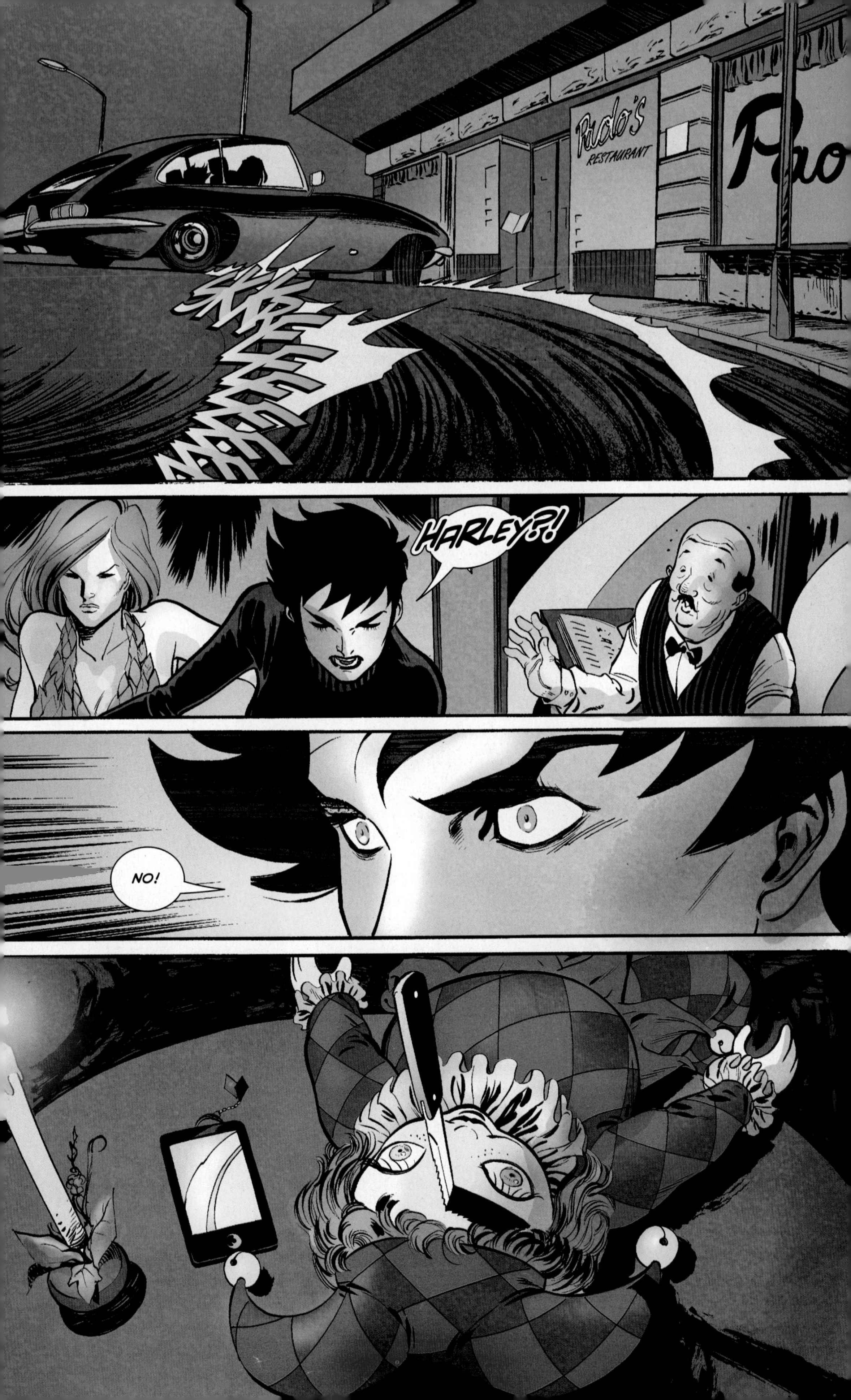
Paolo's
RESTAURANT
Pao
SKREEEEEE
HARLEY?!
NO!

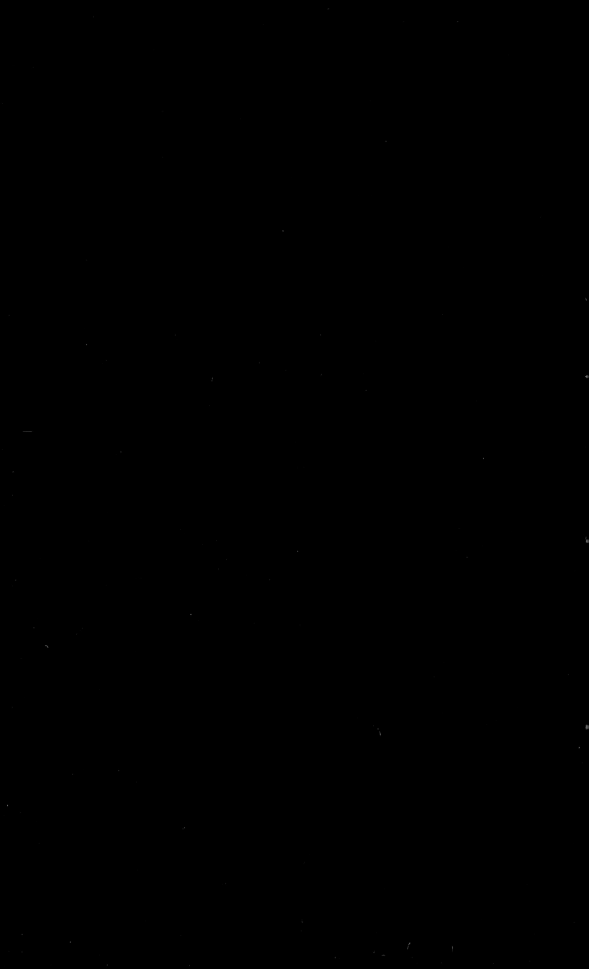

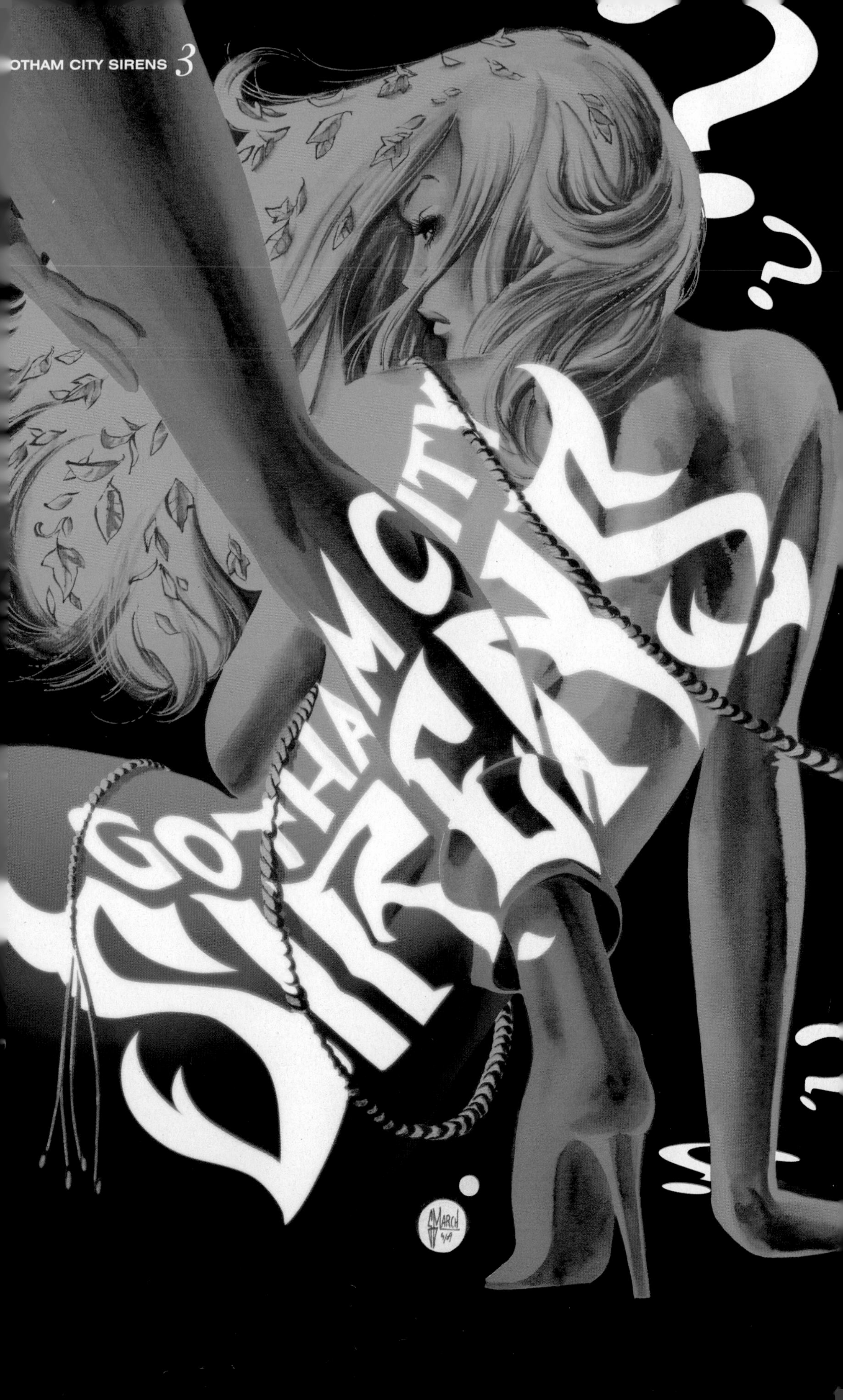
OTHAM CITY SIRENS 3
GOTHAM CITY SIRENS
MARCH

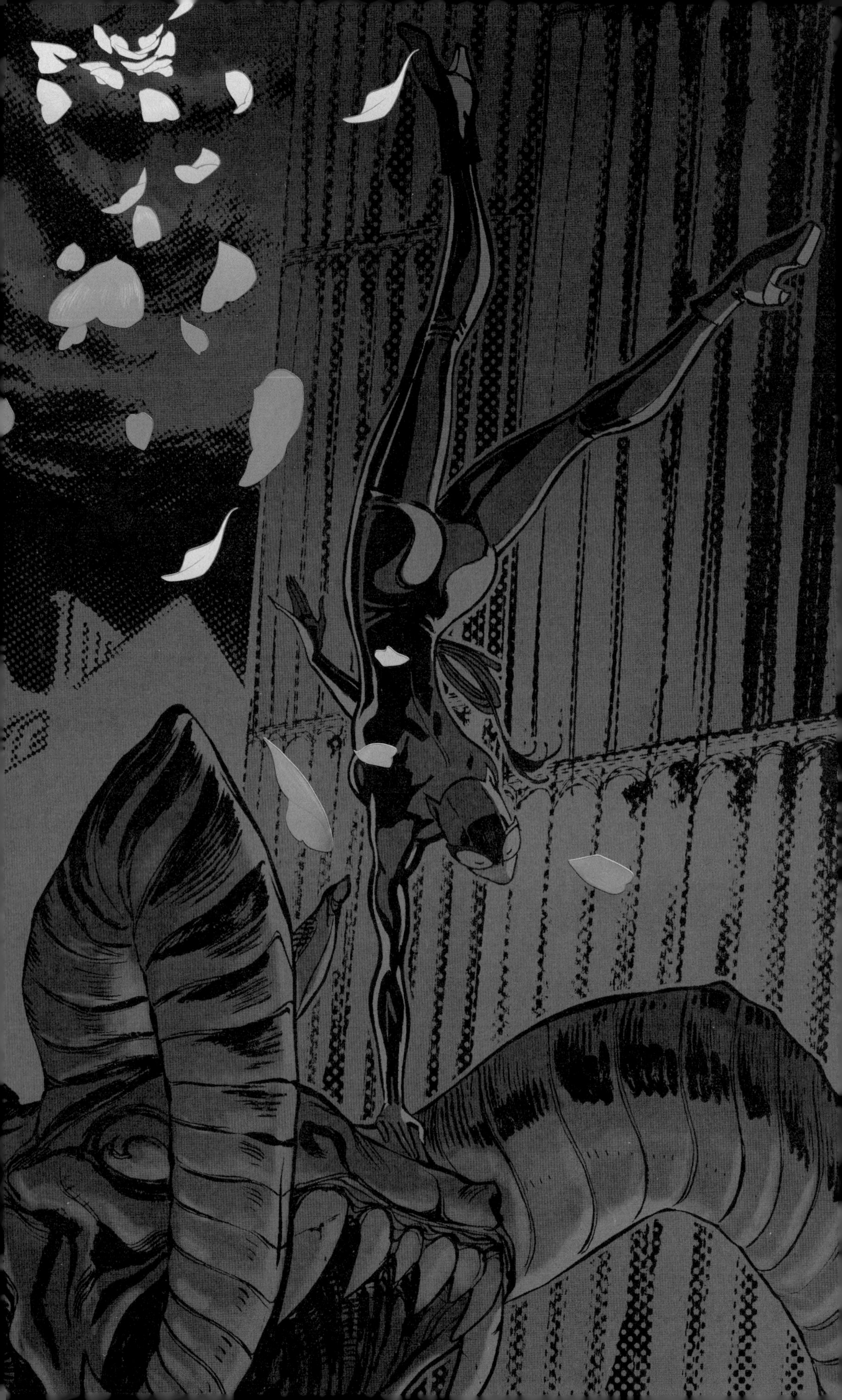

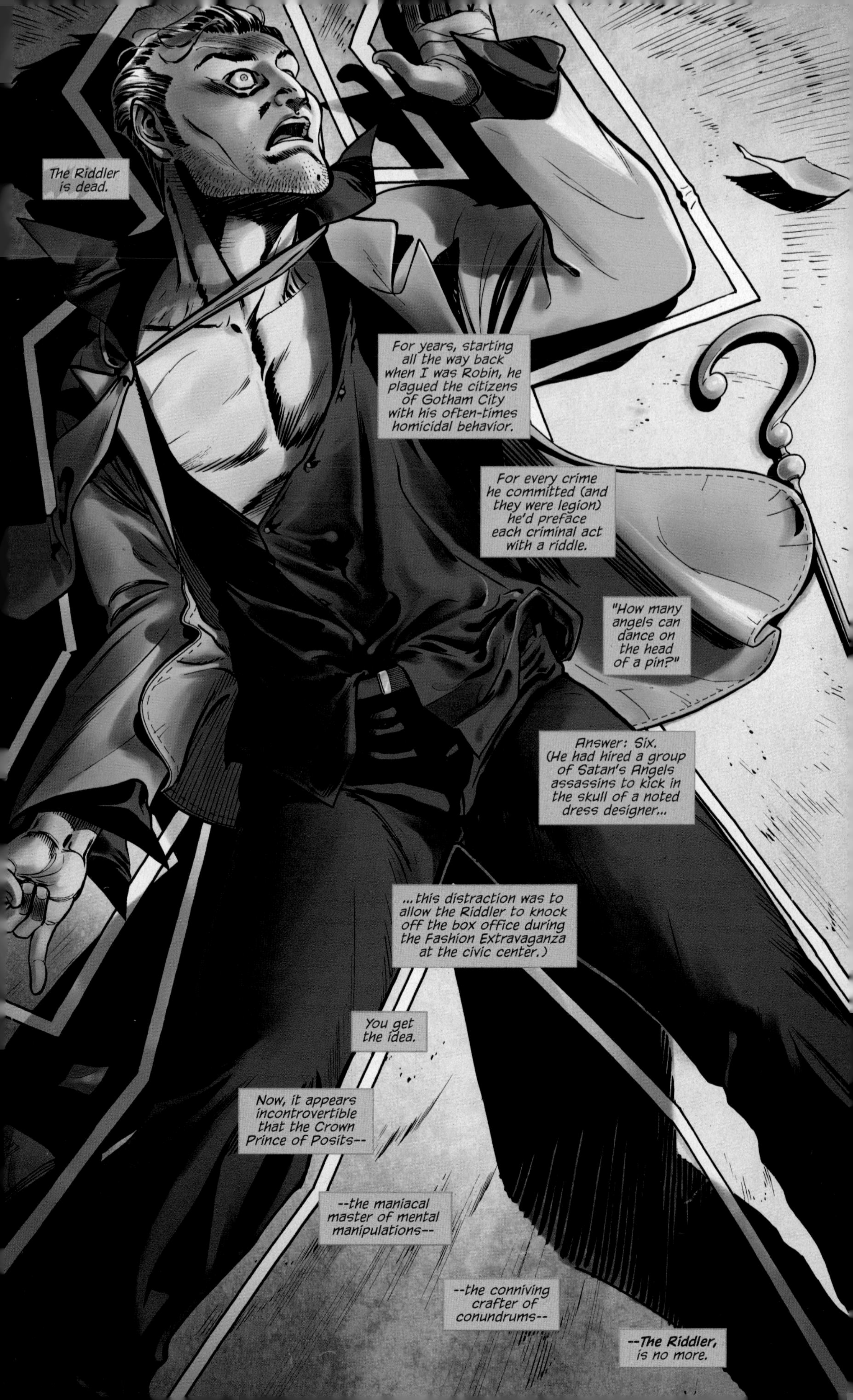

The Riddler is dead.
For years, starting all the way back when I was Robin, he plagued the citizens of Gotham City with his often-times homicidal behavior.
For every crime he committed (and they were legion) he'd preface each criminal act with a riddle.
"How many angels can dance on the head of a pin?"
Answer: Six. (He had hired a group of Satan's Angels assassins to kick in the skull of a noted dress designer...
...this distraction was to allow the Riddler to knock off the box office during the Fashion Extravaganza at the civic center.)
You get the idea.
Now, it appears incontrovertible that the Crown Prince of Posits--
--the maniacal master of mental manipulations--
--the conniving crafter of conundrums--
--The Riddler, is no more.

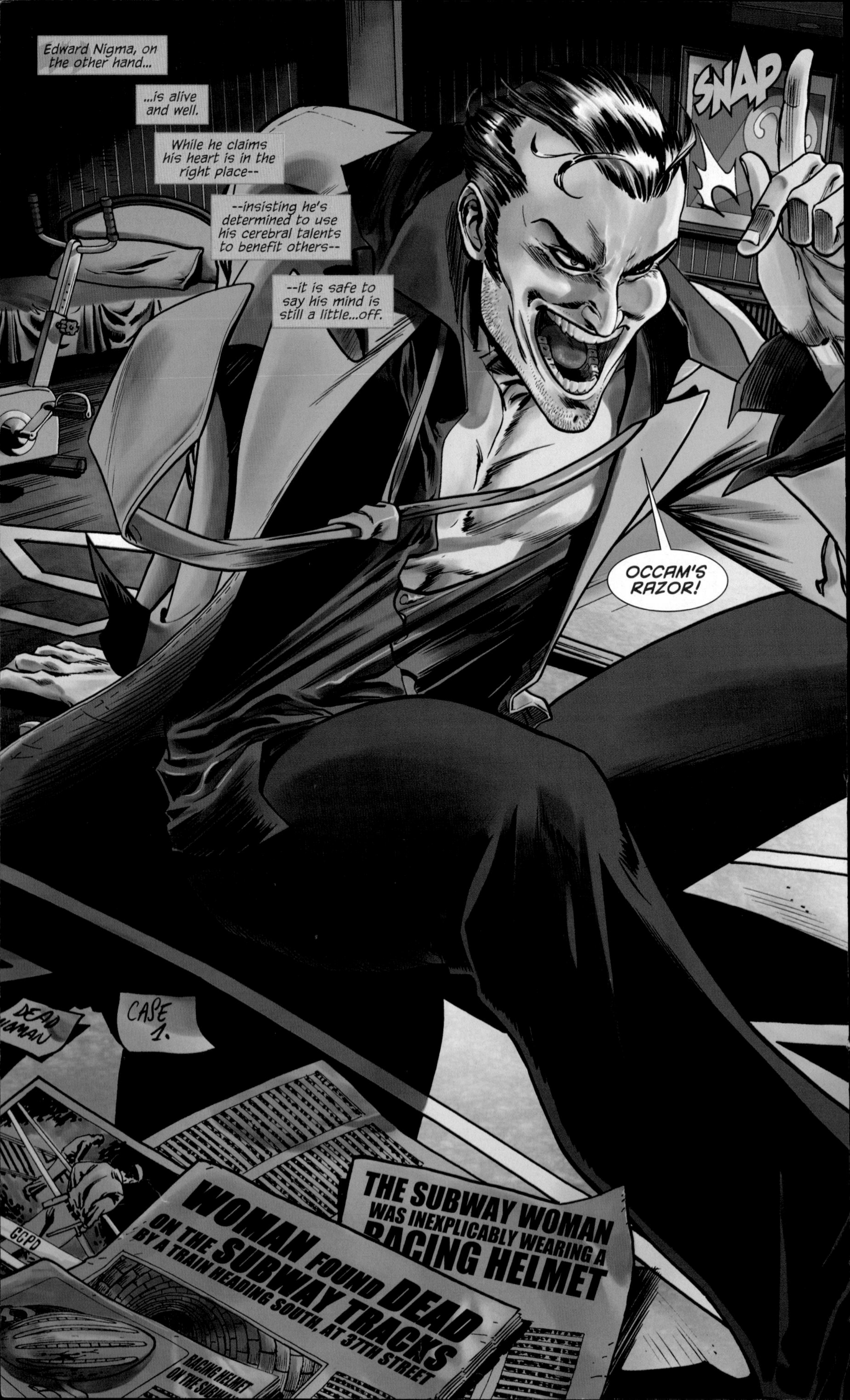
Edward Nigma, on the other hand...
...is alive and well.
While he claims his heart is in the right place--
--insisting he's determined to use his cerebral talents to benefit others--
--it is safe to say his mind is still a little...off.
SNAP
OCCAM'S RAZOR!
DEAD WOMAN
CASE 1.
GCPD
WOMAN FOUND DEAD ON THE SUBWAY TRACKS BY A TRAIN HEADING SOUTH, AT 37TH STREET
THE SUBWAY WOMAN WAS INEXPLICABLY WEARING A RACING HELMET

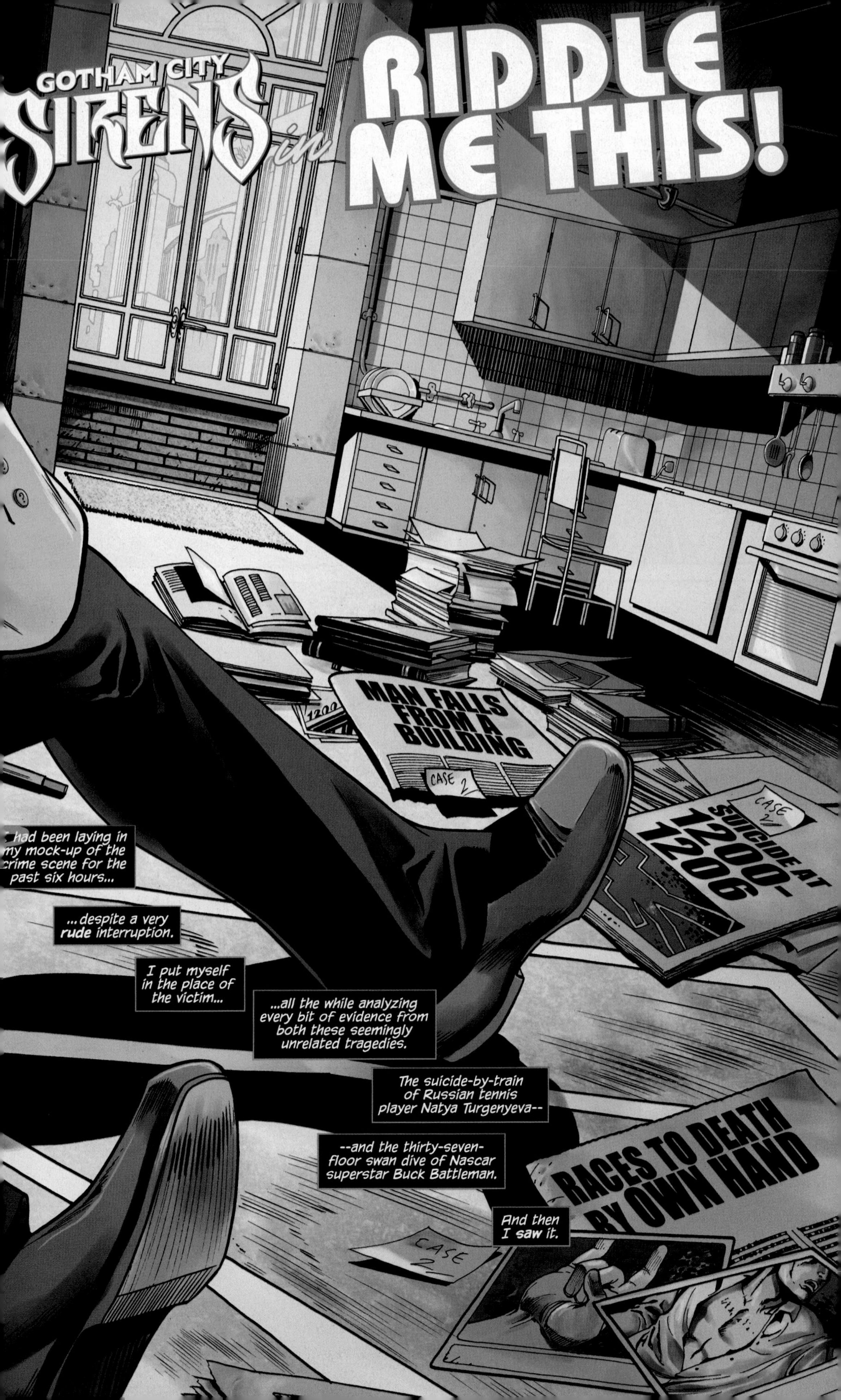
GOTHAM CITY SIRENS in RIDDLE ME THIS!
MAN FALLS FROM A BUILDING
CASE 2
SUICIDE AT 1200-1206
CASE 2
I had been laying in my mock-up of the crime scene for the past six hours...
...despite a very rude interruption.
I put myself in the place of the victim...
...all the while analyzing every bit of evidence from both these seemingly unrelated tragedies.
The suicide-by-train of Russian tennis player Natya Turgenyeva--
--and the thirty-seven-floor swan dive of Nascar superstar Buck Battleman.
RACES TO DEATH BY OWN HAND
And then I saw it.
CASE 2

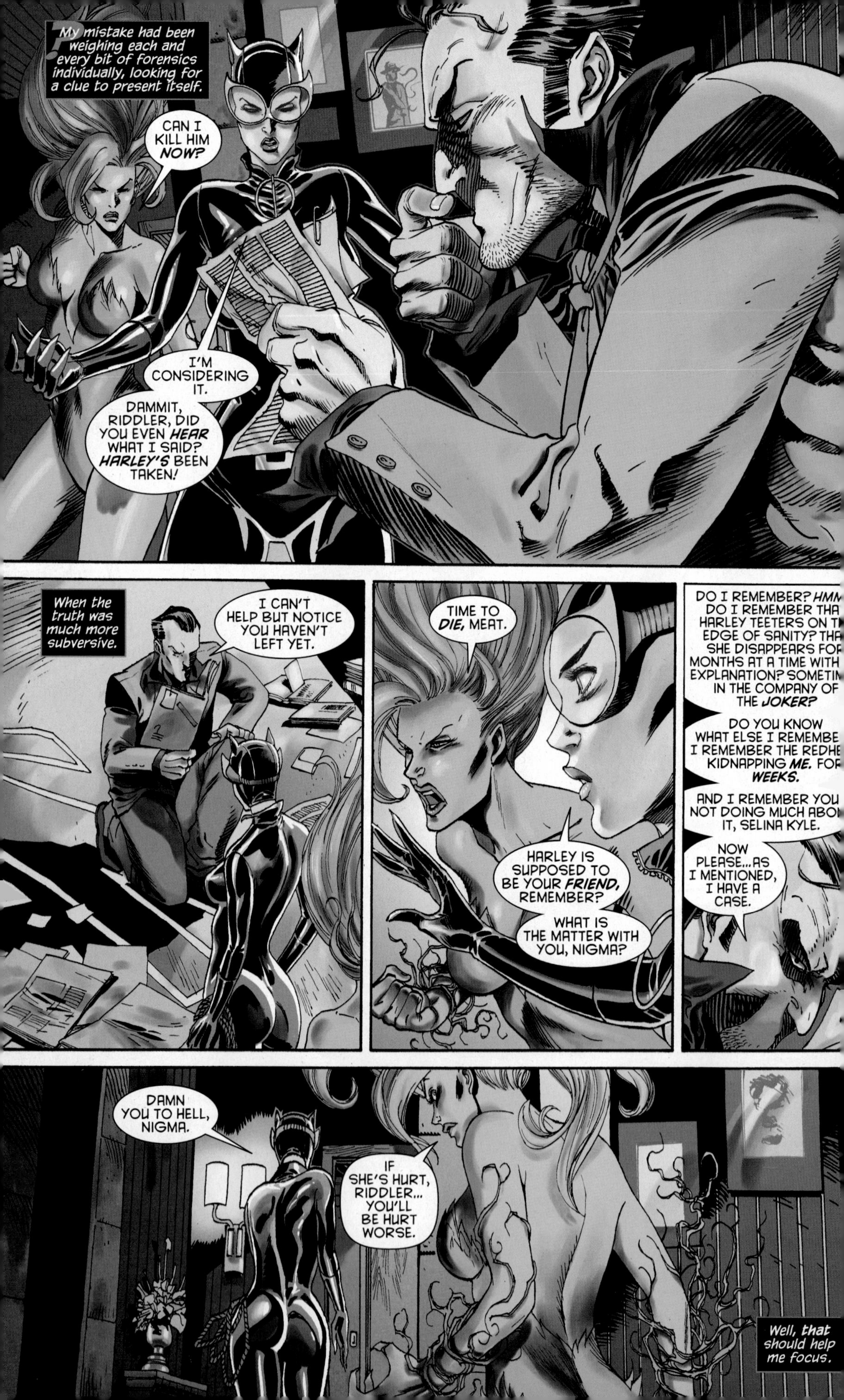
My mistake had been weighing each and every bit of forensics individually, looking for a clue to present itself.
CAN I KILL HIM NOW?
I'M CONSIDERING IT.
DAMMIT, RIDDLER, DID YOU EVEN HEAR WHAT I SAID? HARLEY'S BEEN TAKEN!
When the truth was much more subversive.
I CAN'T HELP BUT NOTICE YOU HAVEN'T LEFT YET.
TIME TO DIE, MEAT.
HARLEY IS SUPPOSED TO BE YOUR FRIEND, REMEMBER?
WHAT IS THE MATTER WITH YOU, NIGMA?
DO I REMEMBER? HMM DO I REMEMBER THA HARLEY TEETERS ON T EDGE OF SANITY? THA SHE DISAPPEARS FOR MONTHS AT A TIME WITH EXPLANATION? SOMETIM IN THE COMPANY OF THE JOKER?
DO YOU KNOW WHAT ELSE I REMEMBE I REMEMBER THE REDHE KIDNAPPING ME. FOR WEEKS.
AND I REMEMBER YOU NOT DOING MUCH ABO IT, SELINA KYLE.
NOW PLEASE...AS I MENTIONED, I HAVE A CASE.
DAMN YOU TO HELL, NIGMA.
IF SHE'S HURT, RIDDLER... YOU'LL BE HURT WORSE.
Well, that should help me focus.

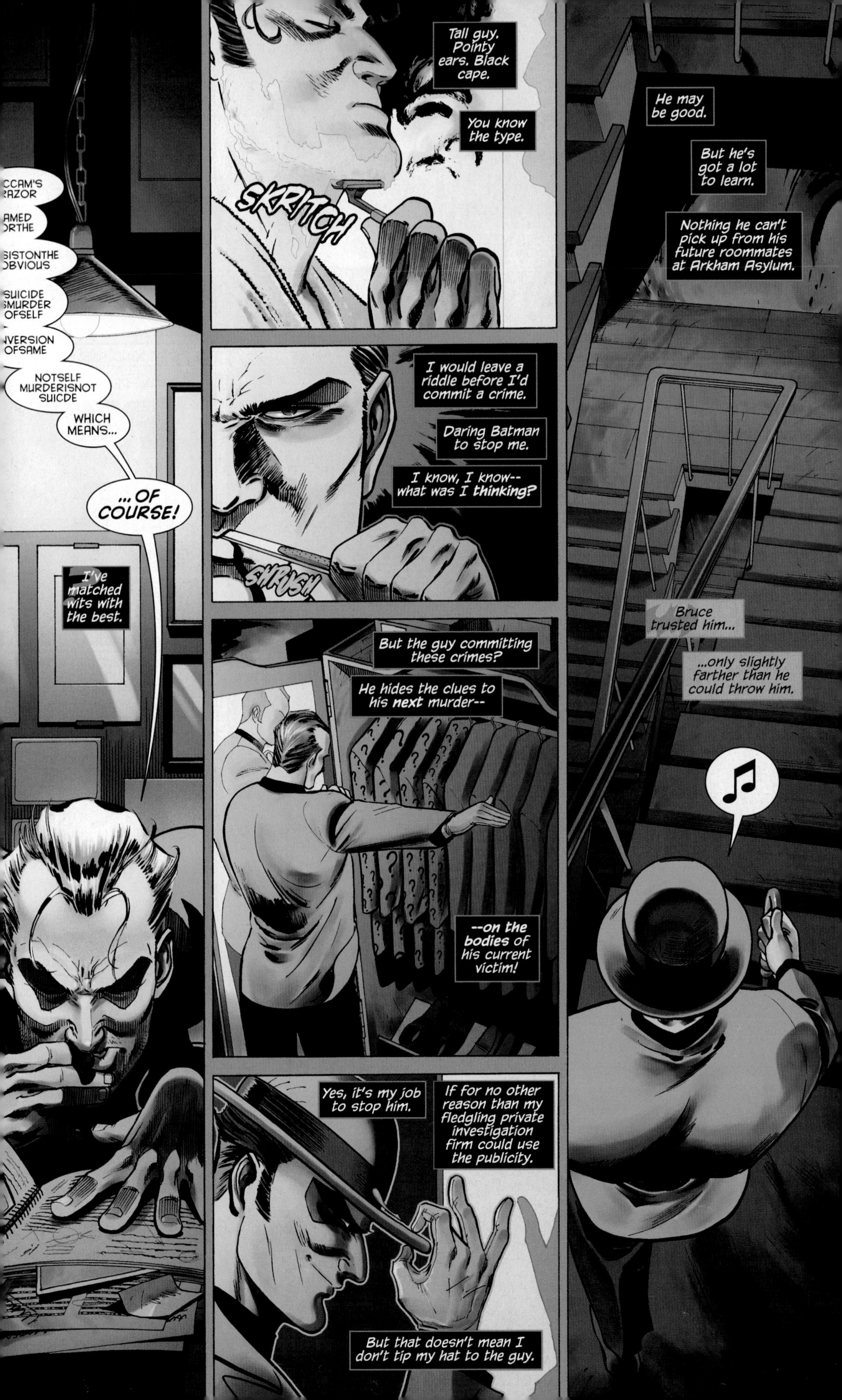

CCAM'S AZOR
AMED ORTHE
SISTONTHE OBVIOUS
SUICIDE SMURDER OFSELF
VERSION OFSAME
NOTSELF MURDERISNOT SUICDE
WHICH MEANS...
...OF COURSE!
I've matched wits with the best.
Tall guy. Pointy ears. Black cape.
You know the type.
SKRITCH
I would leave a riddle before I'd commit a crime.
Daring Batman to stop me.
I know, I know--what was I thinking?
SHRUSH
But the guy committing these crimes?
He hides the clues to his next murder--
--on the bodies of his current victim!
Yes, it's my job to stop him.
If for no other reason than my fledgling private investigation firm could use the publicity.
But that doesn't mean I don't tip my hat to the guy.
He may be good.
But he's got a lot to learn.
Nothing he can't pick up from his future roommates at Arkham Asylum.
Bruce trusted him...
...only slightly farther than he could throw him.
♫

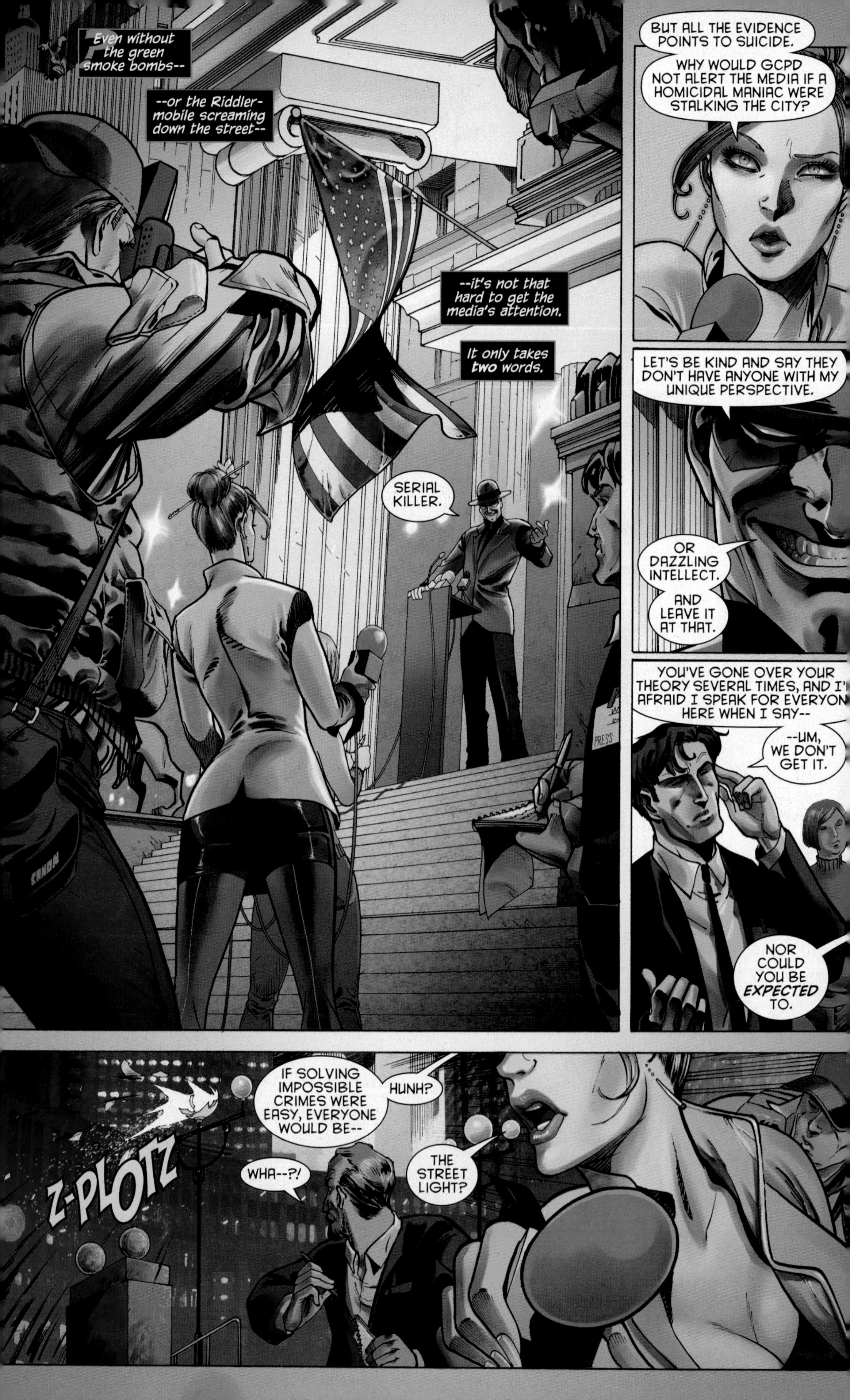

Even without the green smoke bombs--
--or the Riddler-mobile screaming down the street--
--it's not that hard to get the media's attention.
It only takes **two** words.
SERIAL KILLER.
BUT ALL THE EVIDENCE POINTS TO SUICIDE.
WHY WOULD GCPD NOT ALERT THE MEDIA IF A HOMICIDAL MANIAC WERE STALKING THE CITY?
LET'S BE KIND AND SAY THEY DON'T HAVE ANYONE WITH MY UNIQUE PERSPECTIVE.
OR DAZZLING INTELLECT.
AND LEAVE IT AT THAT.
YOU'VE GONE OVER YOUR THEORY SEVERAL TIMES, AND I' AFRAID I SPEAK FOR EVERYON HERE WHEN I SAY--
--UM, WE DON'T GET IT.
NOR COULD YOU BE *EXPECTED* TO.
IF SOLVING IMPOSSIBLE CRIMES WERE EASY, EVERYONE WOULD BE--
Z-PLOTZ
HUNH?
WHA--?!
THE STREET LIGHT?

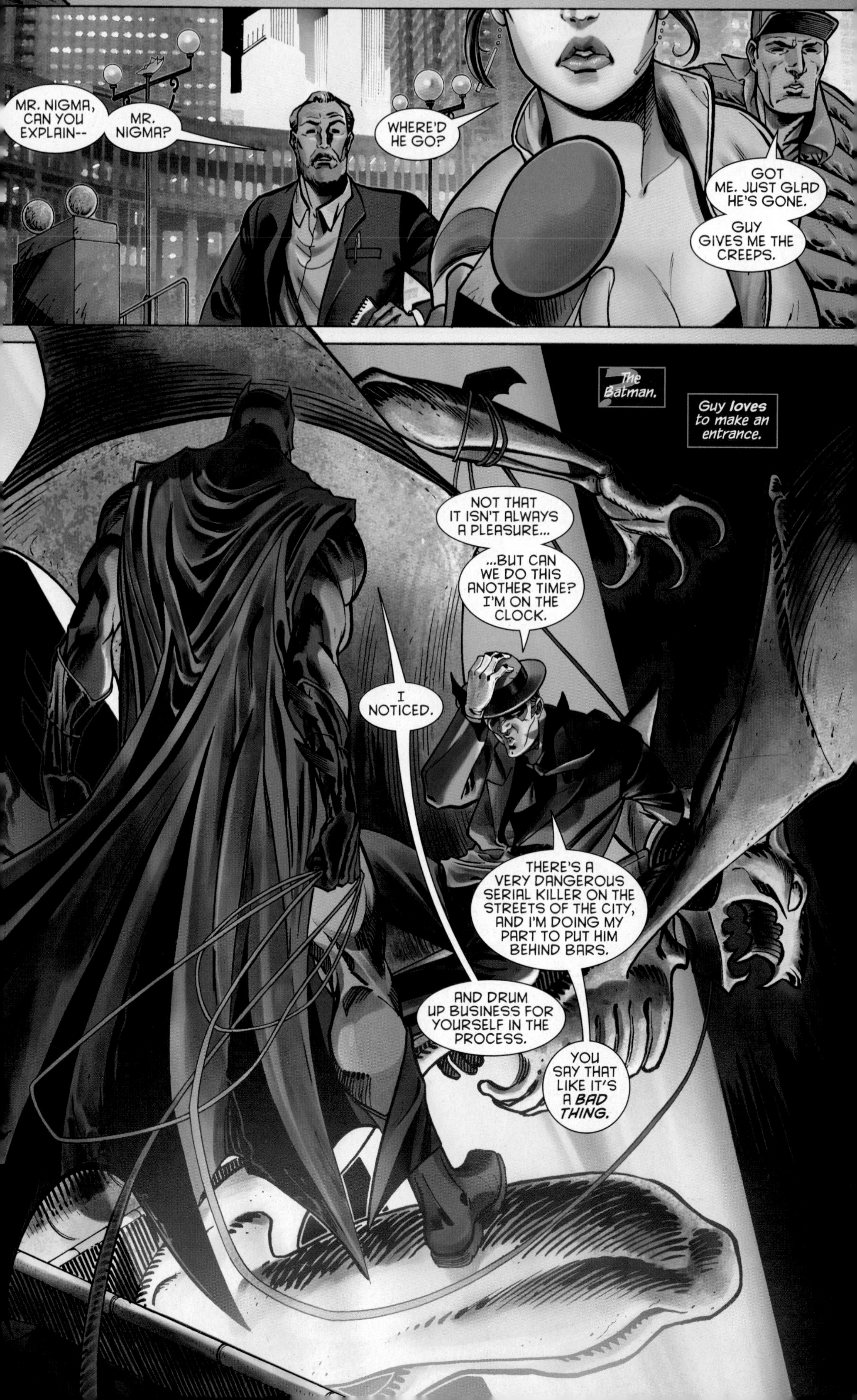
MR. NIGMA, CAN YOU EXPLAIN--
MR. NIGMA?
WHERE'D HE GO?
GOT ME. JUST GLAD HE'S GONE.
GUY GIVES ME THE CREEPS.
The Batman.
Guy *loves* to make an entrance.
NOT THAT IT ISN'T ALWAYS A PLEASURE...
...BUT CAN WE DO THIS ANOTHER TIME? I'M ON THE CLOCK.
I NOTICED.
THERE'S A VERY DANGEROUS SERIAL KILLER ON THE STREETS OF THE CITY, AND I'M DOING MY PART TO PUT HIM BEHIND BARS.
AND DRUM UP BUSINESS FOR YOURSELF IN THE PROCESS.
YOU SAY THAT LIKE IT'S A *BAD THING.*

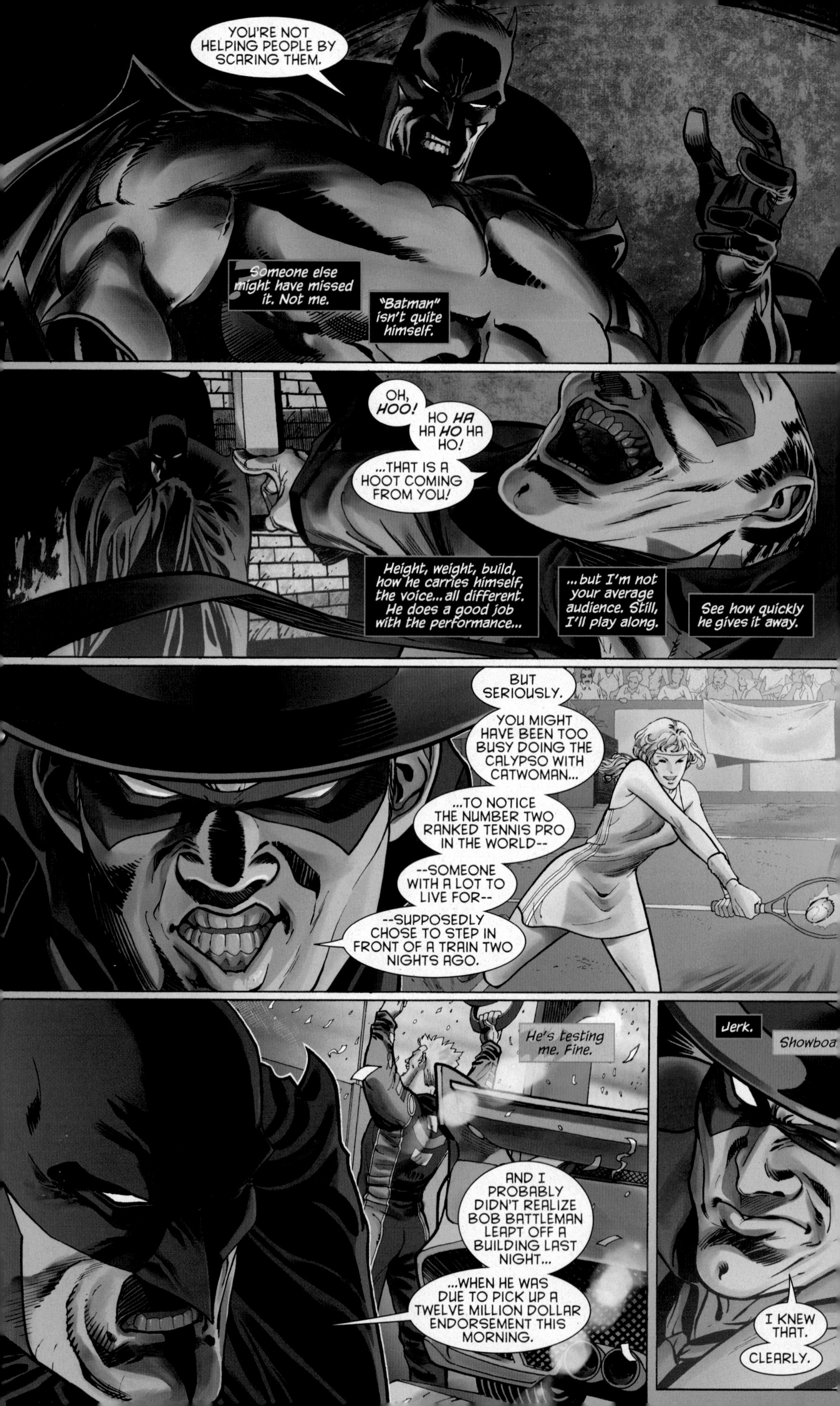

YOU'RE NOT HELPING PEOPLE BY SCARING THEM.
Someone else might have missed it. Not me.
"Batman" isn't quite himself.
OH, HOO!
HO HA HA HO HA HO!
...THAT IS A HOOT COMING FROM YOU!
Height, weight, build, how he carries himself, the voice... all different. He does a good job with the performance...
...but I'm not your average audience. Still, I'll play along.
See how quickly he gives it away.
BUT SERIOUSLY.
YOU MIGHT HAVE BEEN TOO BUSY DOING THE CALYPSO WITH CATWOMAN...
...TO NOTICE THE NUMBER TWO RANKED TENNIS PRO IN THE WORLD--
--SOMEONE WITH A LOT TO LIVE FOR--
--SUPPOSEDLY CHOSE TO STEP IN FRONT OF A TRAIN TWO NIGHTS AGO.
He's testing me. Fine.
AND I PROBABLY DIDN'T REALIZE BOB BATTLEMAN LEAPT OFF A BUILDING LAST NIGHT...
...WHEN HE WAS DUE TO PICK UP A TWELVE MILLION DOLLAR ENDORSEMENT THIS MORNING.
Jerk.
Showboa
I KNEW THAT.
CLEARLY.

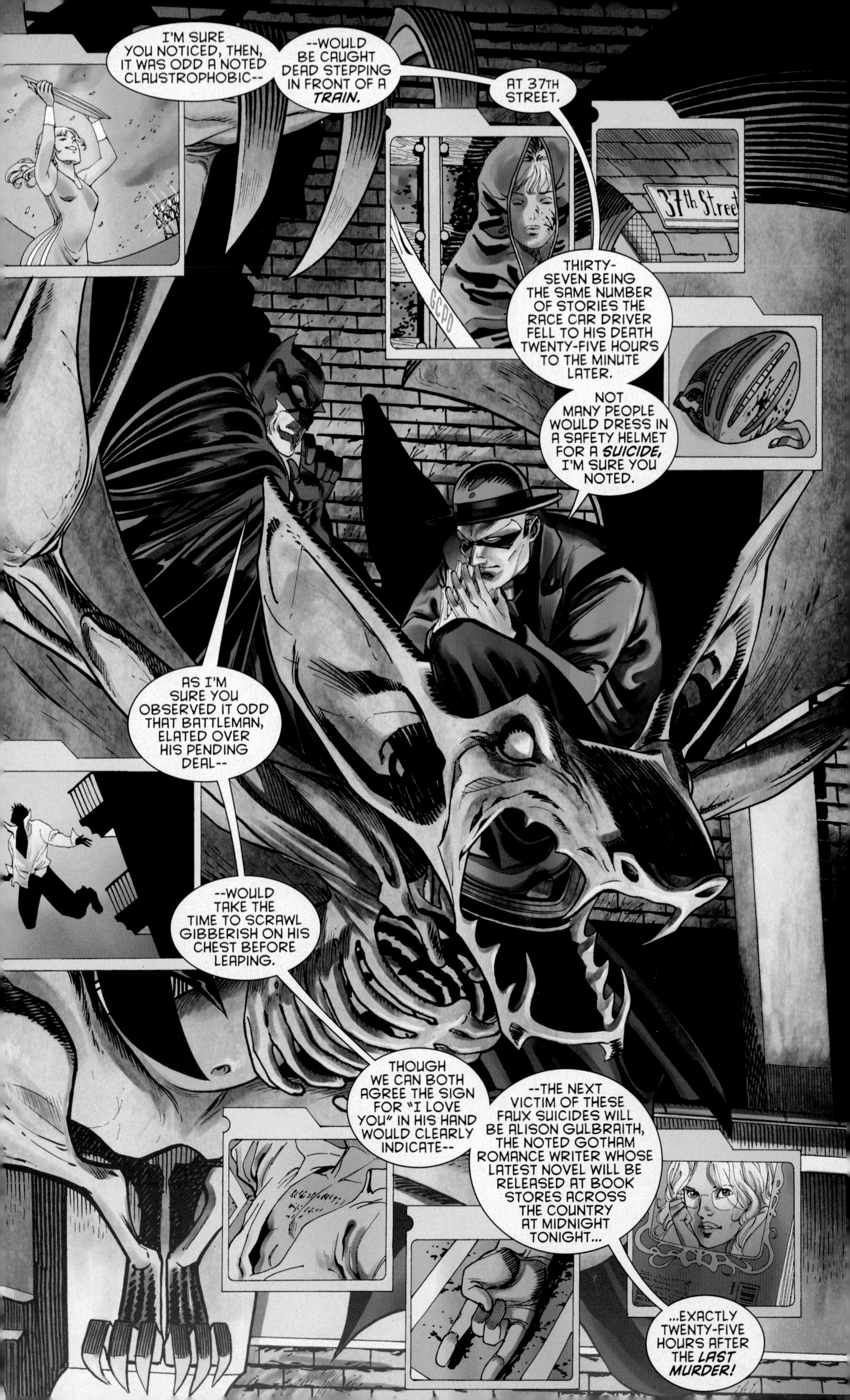
I'M SURE YOU NOTICED, THEN, IT WAS ODD A NOTED CLAUSTROPHOBIC--
--WOULD BE CAUGHT DEAD STEPPING IN FRONT OF A *TRAIN.*
AT 37TH STREET.
37th Street
THIRTY-SEVEN BEING THE SAME NUMBER OF STORIES THE RACE CAR DRIVER FELL TO HIS DEATH TWENTY-FIVE HOURS TO THE MINUTE LATER.
GCPD
NOT MANY PEOPLE WOULD DRESS IN A SAFETY HELMET FOR A *SUICIDE,* I'M SURE YOU NOTED.
AS I'M SURE YOU OBSERVED IT ODD THAT BATTLEMAN, ELATED OVER HIS PENDING DEAL--
--WOULD TAKE THE TIME TO SCRAWL GIBBERISH ON HIS CHEST BEFORE LEAPING.
THOUGH WE CAN BOTH AGREE THE SIGN FOR "I LOVE YOU" IN HIS HAND WOULD CLEARLY INDICATE--
--THE NEXT VICTIM OF THESE FAUX SUICIDES WILL BE ALISON GULBRAITH, THE NOTED GOTHAM ROMANCE WRITER WHOSE LATEST NOVEL WILL BE RELEASED AT BOOK STORES ACROSS THE COUNTRY AT MIDNIGHT TONIGHT...
...EXACTLY TWENTY-FIVE HOURS AFTER THE *LAST MURDER!*

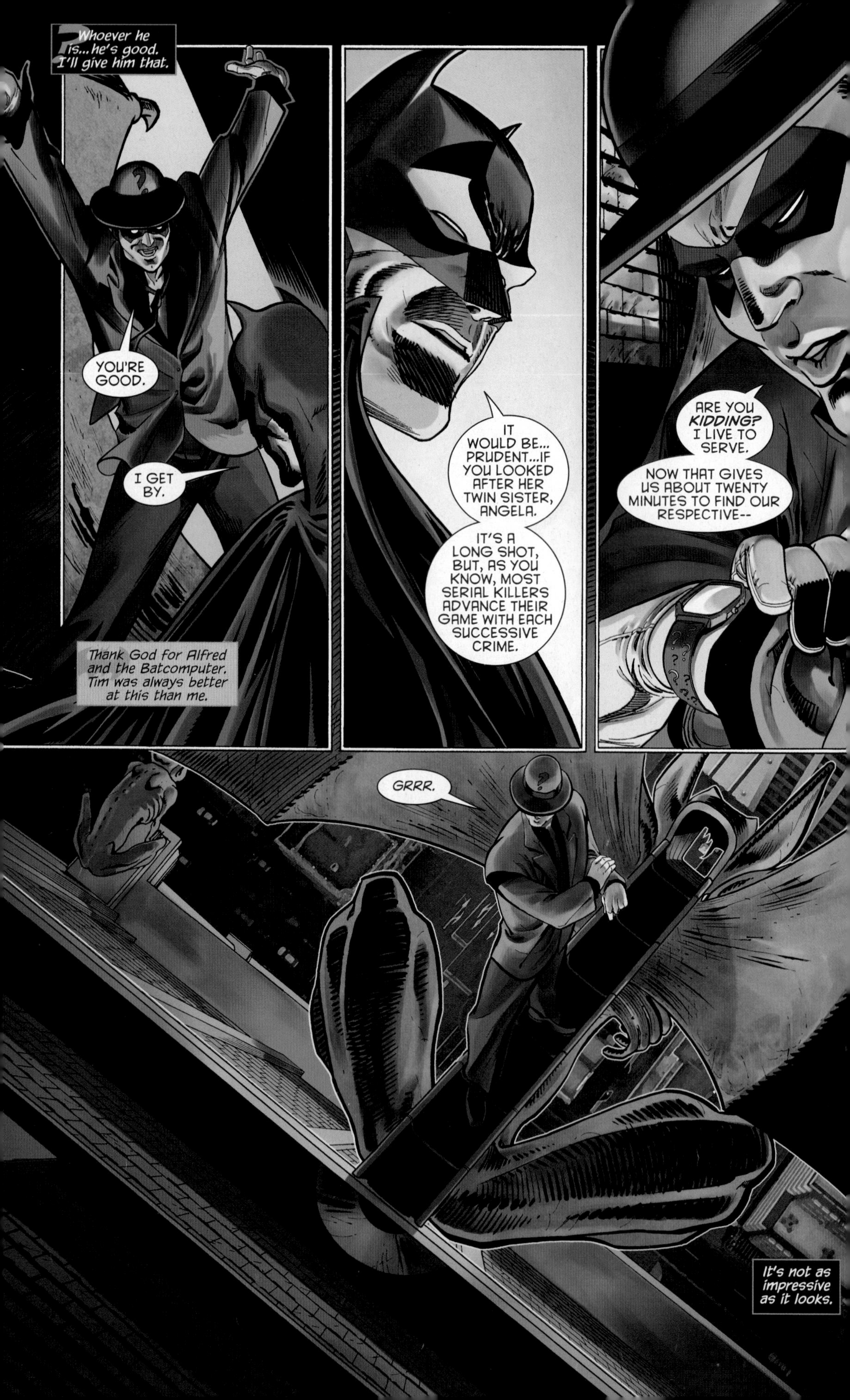
Whoever he is...he's good. I'll give him that.
YOU'RE GOOD.
I GET BY.
Thank God for Alfred and the Batcomputer. Tim was always better at this than me.
IT WOULD BE... PRUDENT...IF YOU LOOKED AFTER HER TWIN SISTER, ANGELA.
IT'S A LONG SHOT, BUT, AS YOU KNOW, MOST SERIAL KILLERS ADVANCE THEIR GAME WITH EACH SUCCESSIVE CRIME.
ARE YOU KIDDING? I LIVE TO SERVE.
NOW THAT GIVES US ABOUT TWENTY MINUTES TO FIND OUR RESPECTIVE--
GRRR.
It's not as impressive as it looks.

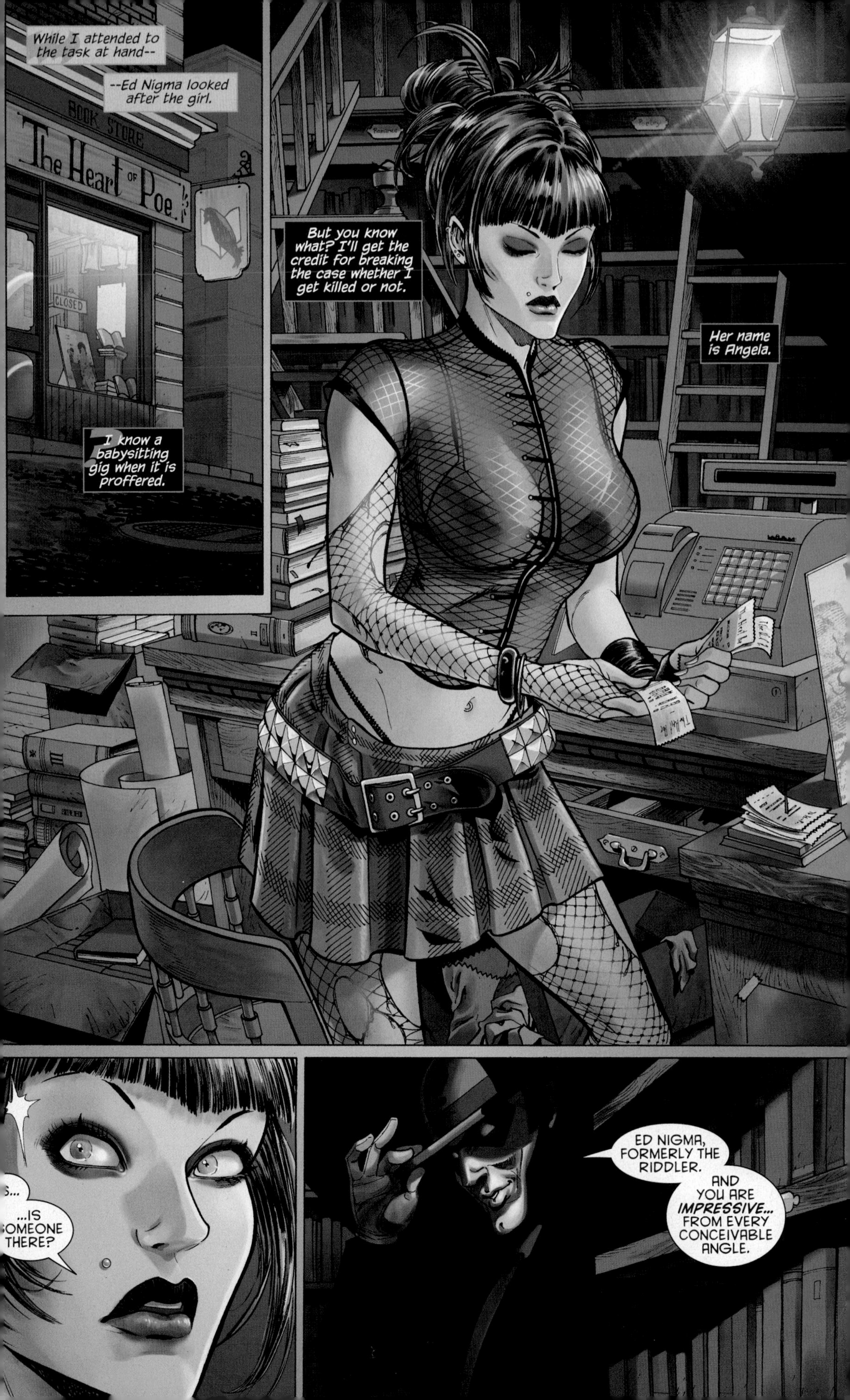
While I attended to the task at hand--
--Ed Nigma looked after the girl.
BOOK STORE
The Heart of Poe
CLOSED
I know a babysitting gig when it is proffered.
But you know what? I'll get the credit for breaking the case whether I get killed or not.
Her name is Angela.
...IS
SOMEONE THERE?
ED NIGMA, FORMERLY THE RIDDLER.
AND YOU ARE IMPRESSIVE... FROM EVERY CONCEIVABLE ANGLE.

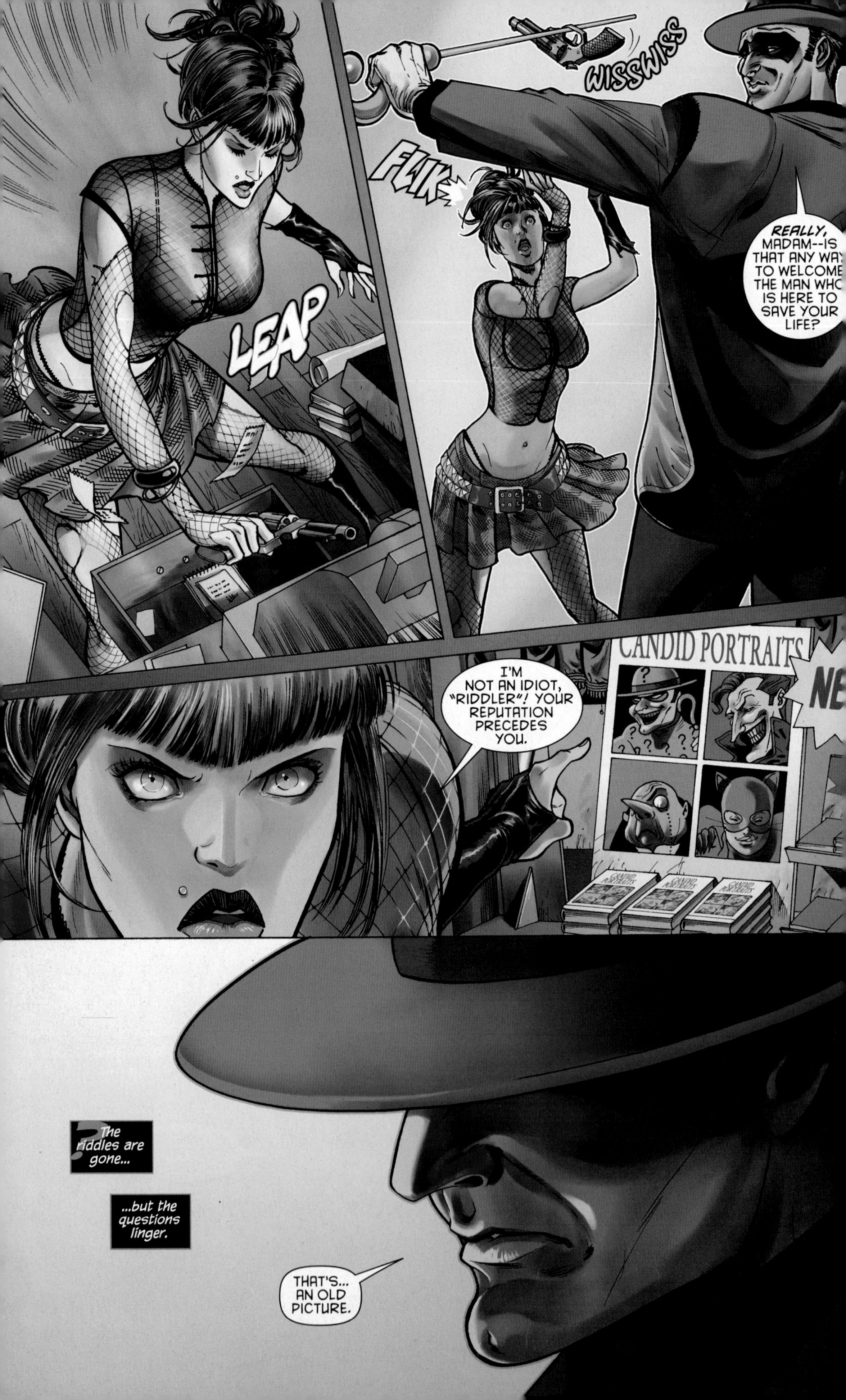
LEAP
WISSWISS
FLIK
REALLY, MADAM--IS THAT ANY WAY TO WELCOME THE MAN WHO IS HERE TO SAVE YOUR LIFE?
I'M NOT AN IDIOT, "RIDDLER"! YOUR REPUTATION PRECEDES YOU.
CANDID PORTRAITS
The riddles are gone...
...but the questions linger.
THAT'S... AN OLD PICTURE.

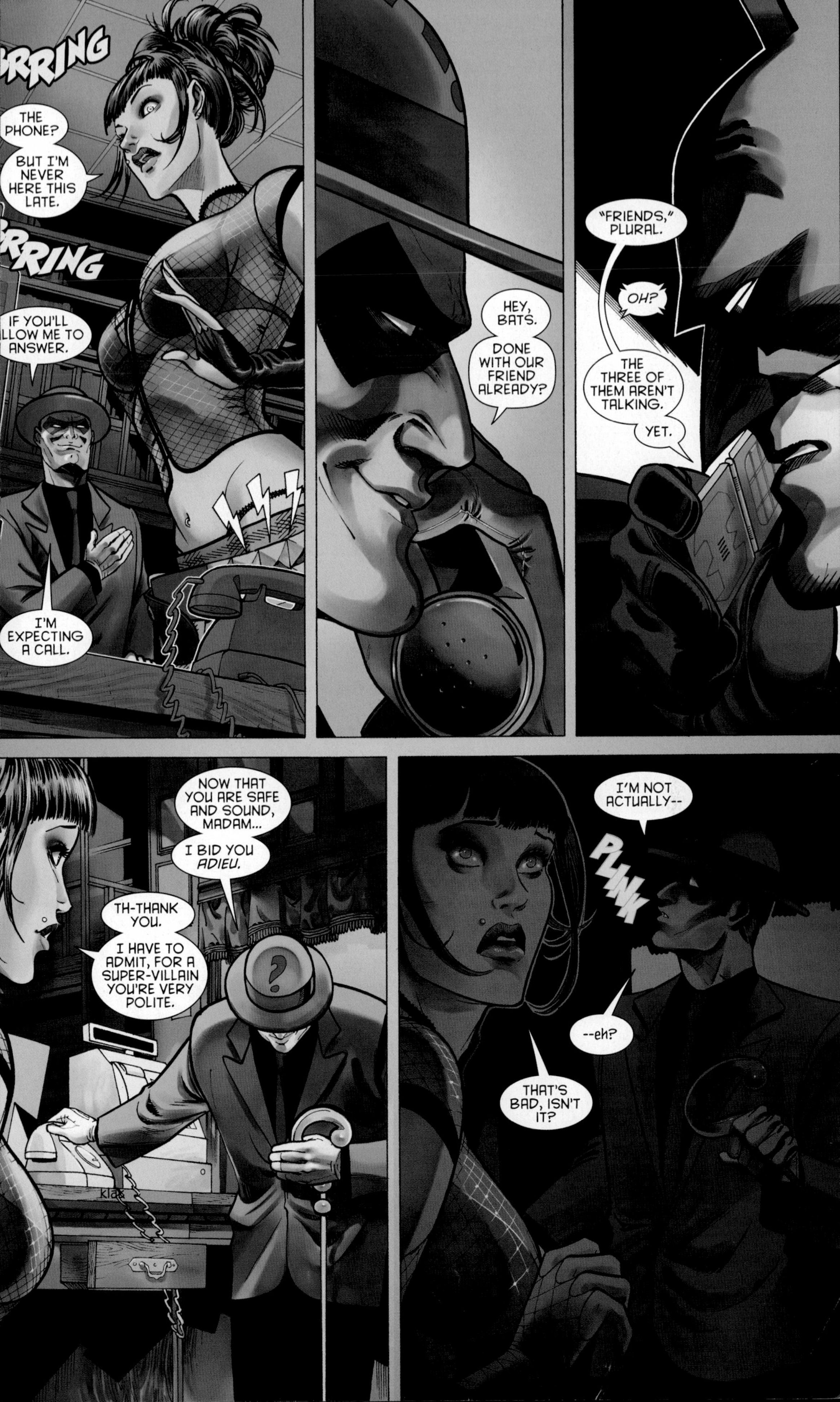

RRRING
THE PHONE?
BUT I'M NEVER HERE THIS LATE.
RRRING
IF YOU'LL ALLOW ME TO ANSWER.
I'M EXPECTING A CALL.
HEY, BATS.
DONE WITH OUR FRIEND ALREADY?
"FRIENDS," PLURAL.
OH?
THE THREE OF THEM AREN'T TALKING.
YET.
NOW THAT YOU ARE SAFE AND SOUND, MADAM...
I BID YOU ADIEU.
TH-THANK YOU.
I HAVE TO ADMIT, FOR A SUPER-VILLAIN YOU'RE VERY POLITE.
I'M NOT ACTUALLY--
PLINK
--eh?
THAT'S BAD, ISN'T IT?

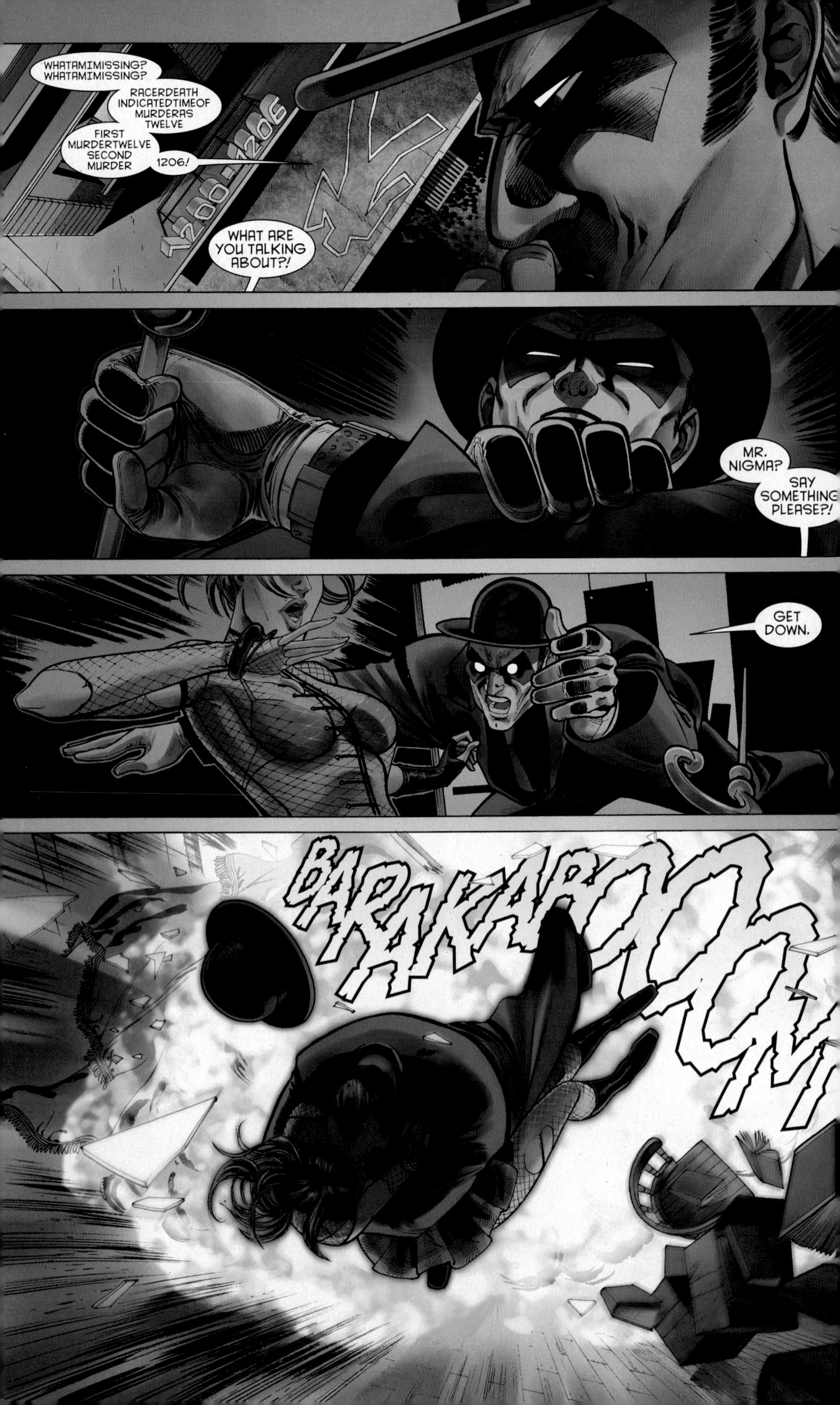

WHATAMIMISSING? WHATAMIMISSING?
RACERDEATH INDICATEDTIMEOF MURDERAS TWELVE
FIRST MURDERTWELVE SECOND MURDER
1206!
1200-1206
WHAT ARE YOU TALKING ABOUT?!
MR. NIGMA?
SAY SOMETHING PLEASE?!
GET DOWN.
BARAKAROOOOM

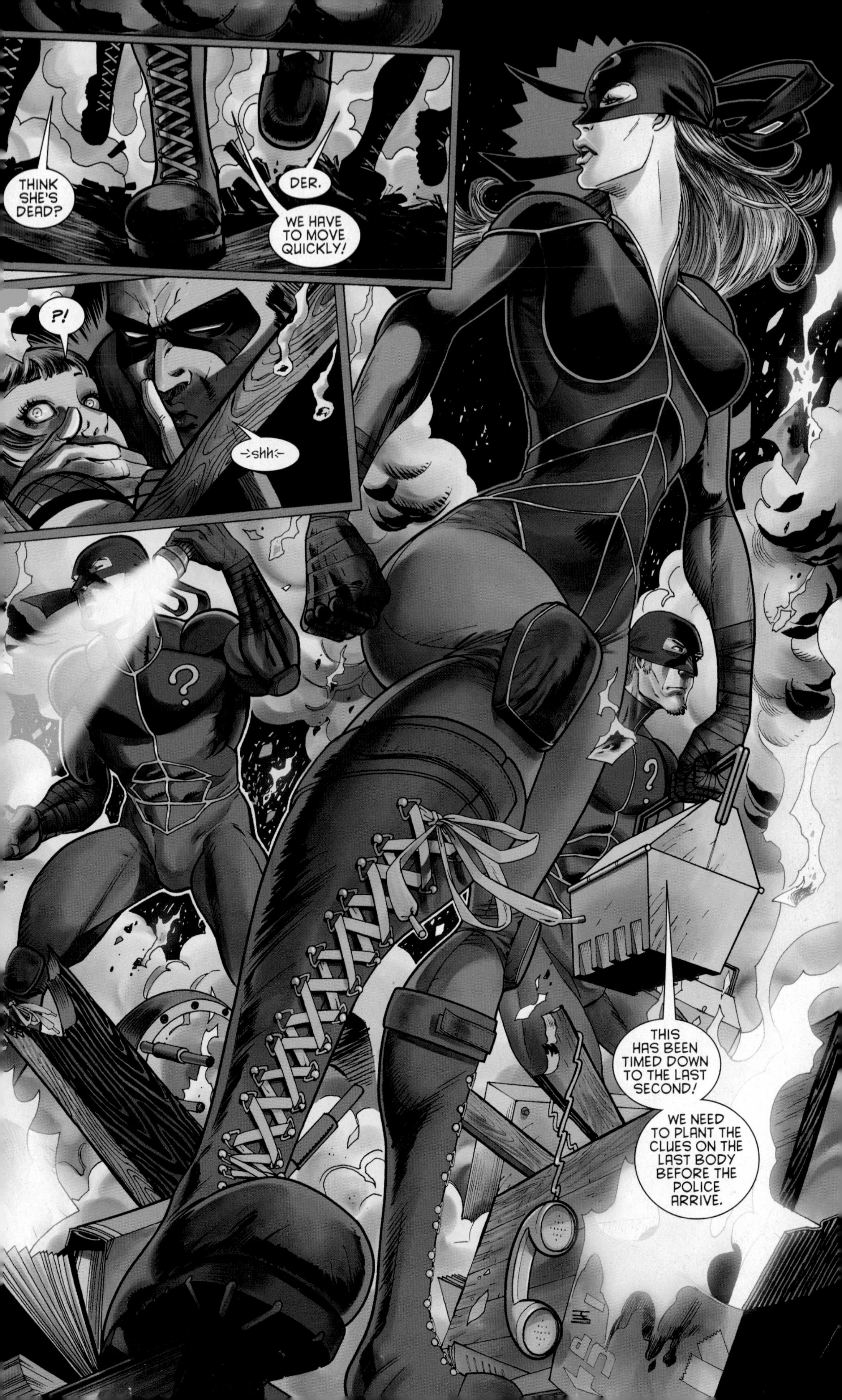
THINK SHE'S DEAD?
DER.
WE HAVE TO MOVE QUICKLY!
?!
-shh-
THIS HAS BEEN TIMED DOWN TO THE LAST SECOND!
WE NEED TO PLANT THE CLUES ON THE LAST BODY BEFORE THE POLICE ARRIVE.

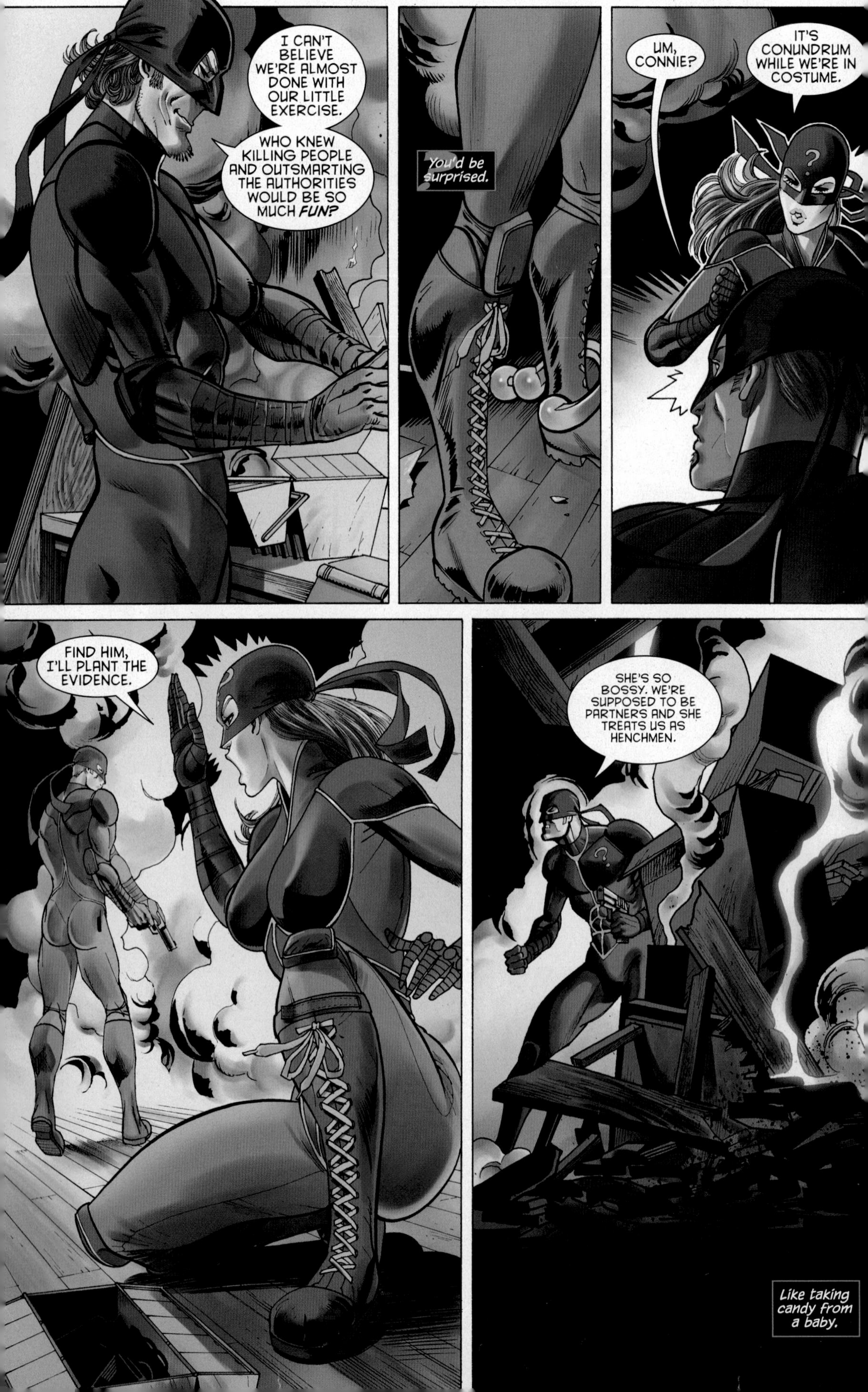
I CAN'T BELIEVE WE'RE ALMOST DONE WITH OUR LITTLE EXERCISE.
WHO KNEW KILLING PEOPLE AND OUTSMARTING THE AUTHORITIES WOULD BE SO MUCH *FUN?*
*You'd be surprised.*
UM, CONNIE?
IT'S CONUNDRUM WHILE WE'RE IN COSTUME.
FIND HIM, I'LL PLANT THE EVIDENCE.
SHE'S SO BOSSY. WE'RE SUPPOSED TO BE PARTNERS AND SHE TREATS US AS HENCHMEN.
*Like taking candy from a baby.*

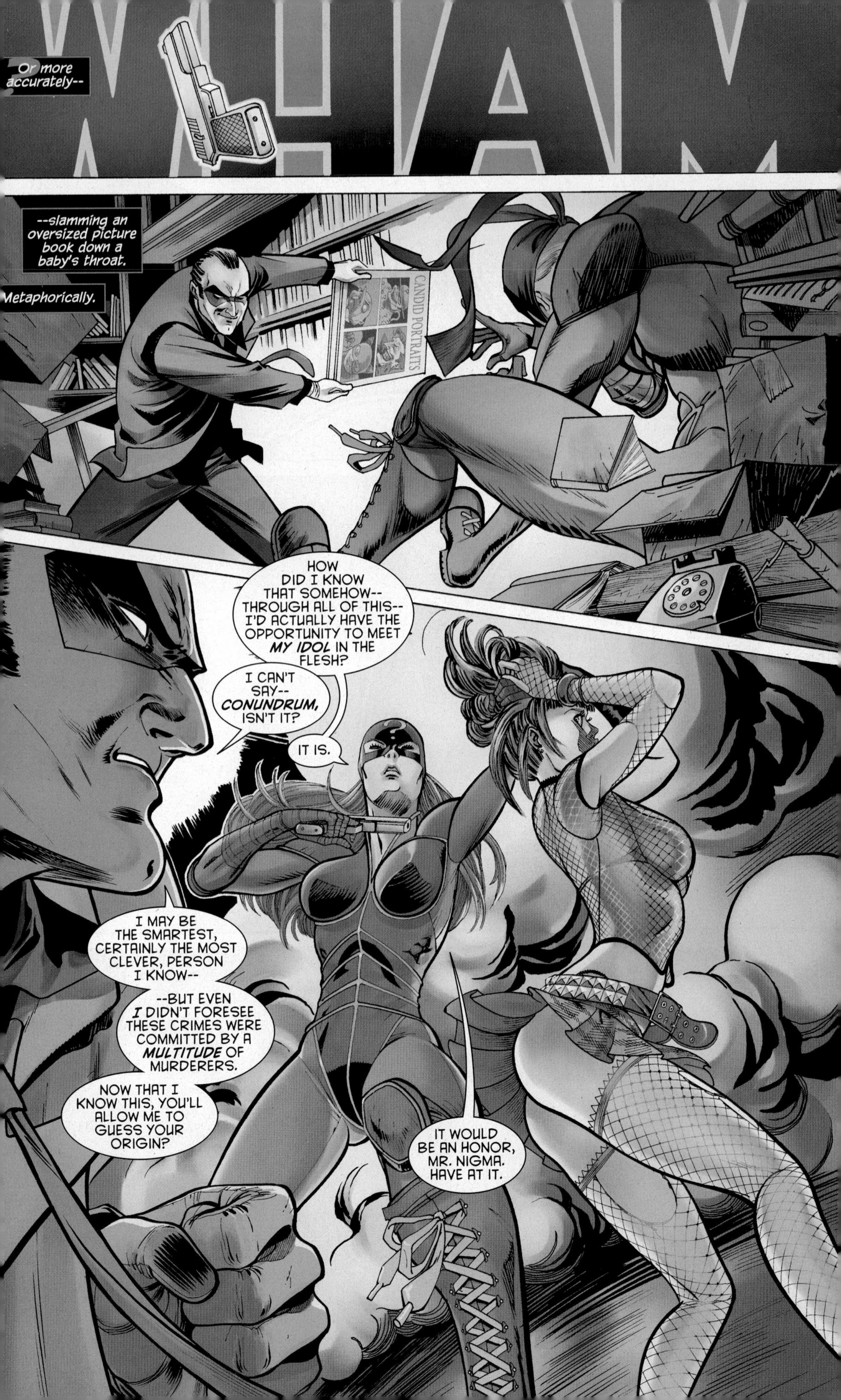
Or more accurately--
--slamming an oversized picture book down a baby's throat.
Metaphorically.
CANDID PORTRAITS
HOW DID I KNOW THAT SOMEHOW-- THROUGH ALL OF THIS-- I'D ACTUALLY HAVE THE OPPORTUNITY TO MEET MY IDOL IN THE FLESH?
I CAN'T SAY-- CONUNDRUM, ISN'T IT?
IT IS.
I MAY BE THE SMARTEST, CERTAINLY THE MOST CLEVER, PERSON I KNOW--
--BUT EVEN I DIDN'T FORESEE THESE CRIMES WERE COMMITTED BY A MULTITUDE OF MURDERERS.
NOW THAT I KNOW THIS, YOU'LL ALLOW ME TO GUESS YOUR ORIGIN?
IT WOULD BE AN HONOR, MR. NIGMA. HAVE AT IT.

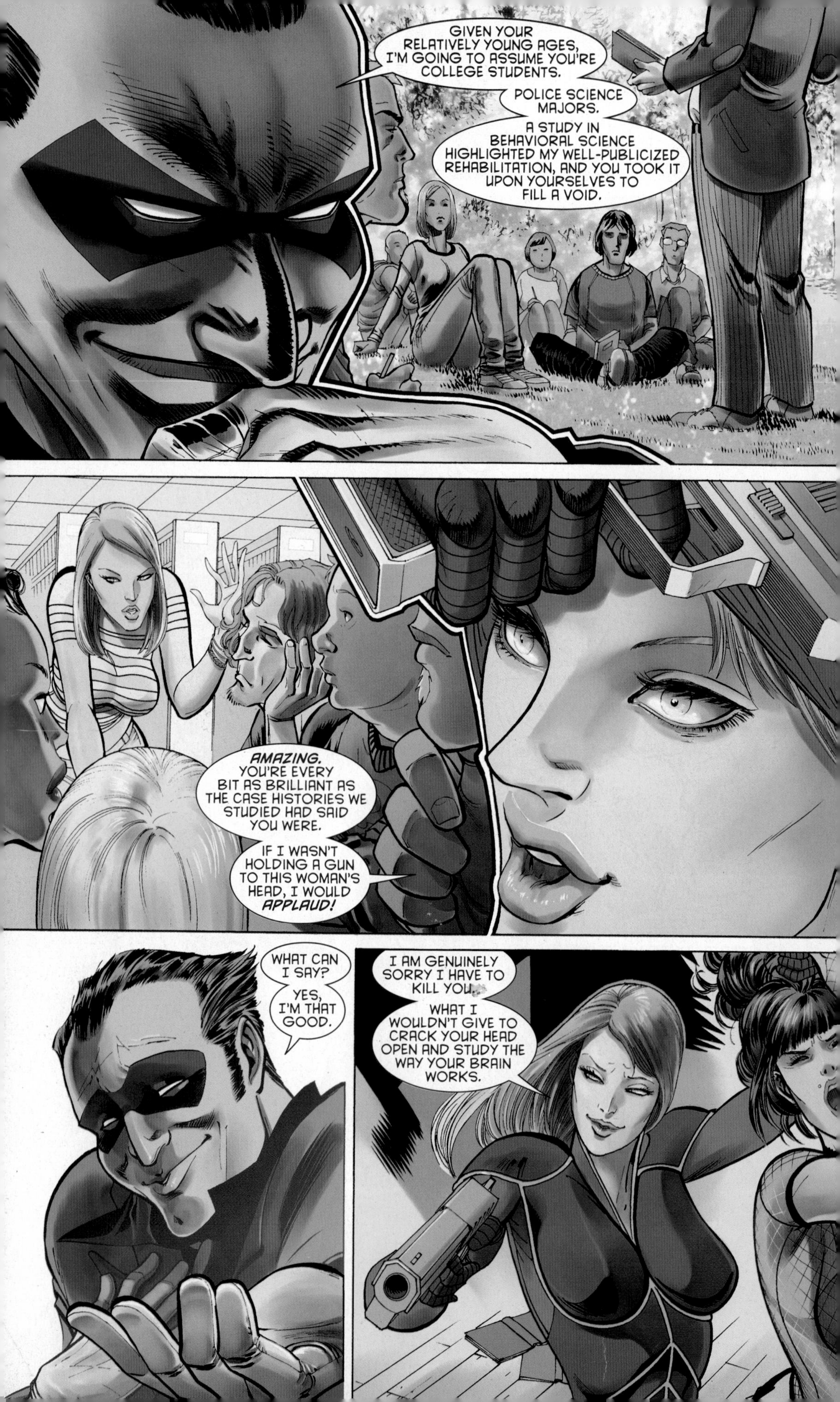
GIVEN YOUR RELATIVELY YOUNG AGES, I'M GOING TO ASSUME YOU'RE COLLEGE STUDENTS.
POLICE SCIENCE MAJORS.
A STUDY IN BEHAVIORAL SCIENCE HIGHLIGHTED MY WELL-PUBLICIZED REHABILITATION, AND YOU TOOK IT UPON YOURSELVES TO FILL A VOID.
*AMAZING.* YOU'RE EVERY BIT AS BRILLIANT AS THE CASE HISTORIES WE STUDIED HAD SAID YOU WERE.
IF I WASN'T HOLDING A GUN TO THIS WOMAN'S HEAD, I WOULD ***APPLAUD!***
WHAT CAN I SAY?
YES, I'M THAT GOOD.
I AM GENUINELY SORRY I HAVE TO KILL YOU.
WHAT I WOULDN'T GIVE TO CRACK YOUR HEAD OPEN AND STUDY THE WAY YOUR BRAIN WORKS.

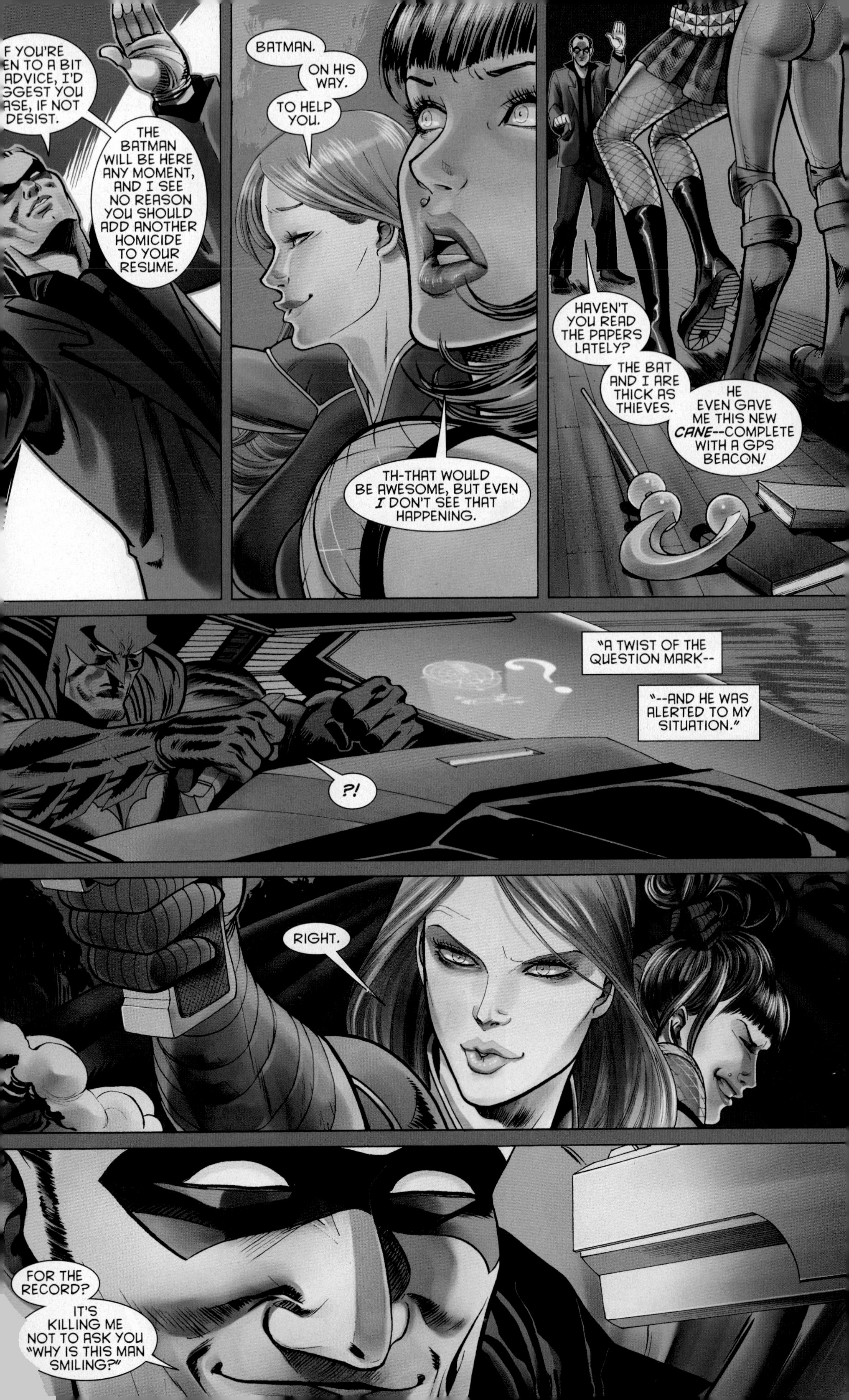
F YOU'RE
EN TO A BIT
ADVICE, I'D
GGEST YOU
ASE, IF NOT
DESIST.
THE BATMAN WILL BE HERE ANY MOMENT, AND I SEE NO REASON YOU SHOULD ADD ANOTHER HOMICIDE TO YOUR RESUME.
BATMAN.
ON HIS WAY.
TO HELP YOU.
TH-THAT WOULD BE AWESOME, BUT EVEN I DON'T SEE THAT HAPPENING.
HAVEN'T YOU READ THE PAPERS LATELY?
THE BAT AND I ARE THICK AS THIEVES.
HE EVEN GAVE ME THIS NEW CANE--COMPLETE WITH A GPS BEACON!
"A TWIST OF THE QUESTION MARK--
"--AND HE WAS ALERTED TO MY SITUATION."
?!
RIGHT.
FOR THE RECORD?
IT'S KILLING ME NOT TO ASK YOU "WHY IS THIS MAN SMILING?"

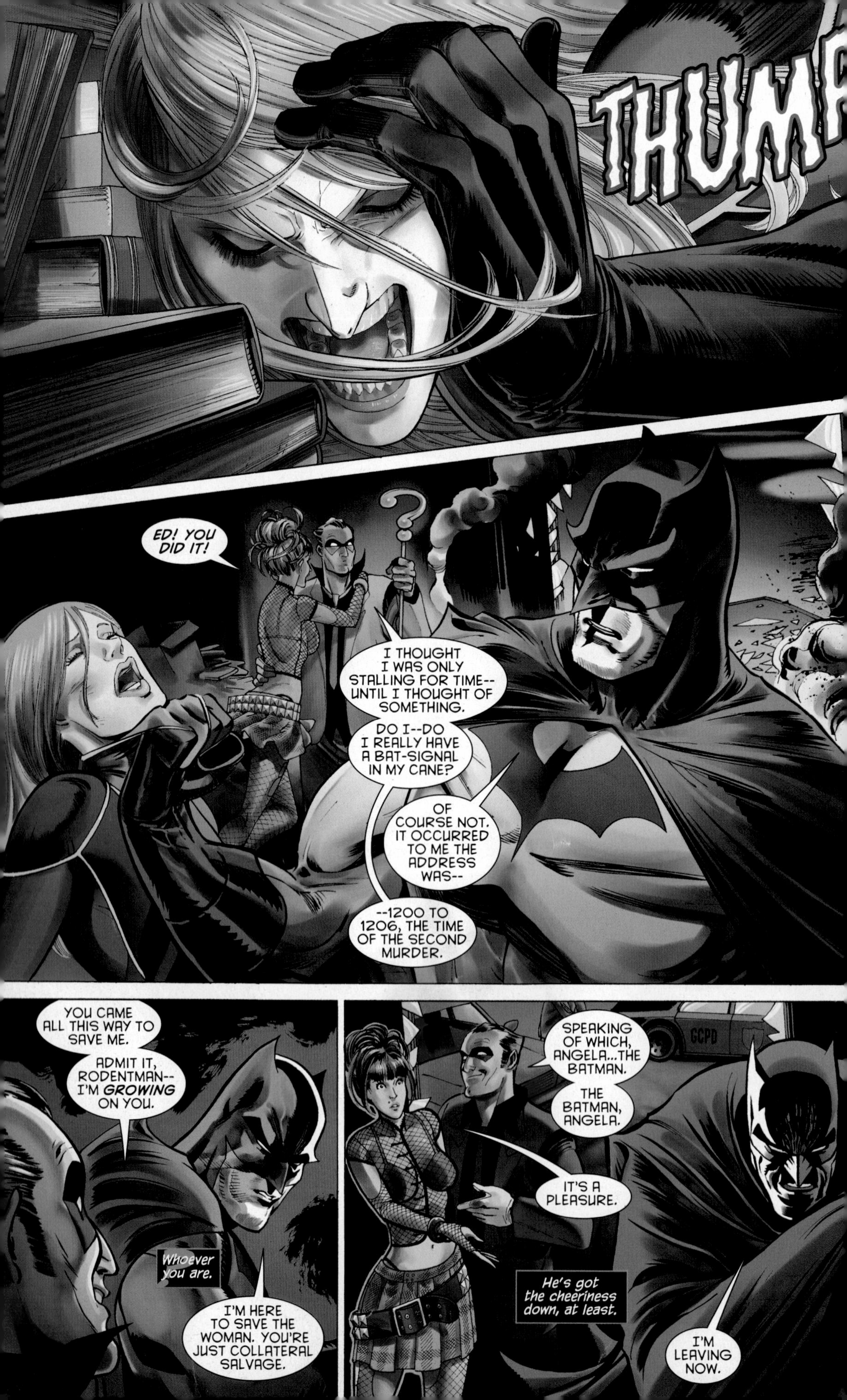
THUMP
ED! YOU DID IT!
I THOUGHT I WAS ONLY STALLING FOR TIME-- UNTIL I THOUGHT OF SOMETHING.
DO I--DO I REALLY HAVE A BAT-SIGNAL IN MY CANE?
OF COURSE NOT. IT OCCURRED TO ME THE ADDRESS WAS--
--1200 TO 1206, THE TIME OF THE SECOND MURDER.
YOU CAME ALL THIS WAY TO SAVE ME.
ADMIT IT, RODENTMAN-- I'M *GROWING* ON YOU.
*Whoever you are.*
I'M HERE TO SAVE THE WOMAN. YOU'RE JUST COLLATERAL SALVAGE.
GCPD
SPEAKING OF WHICH, ANGELA...THE BATMAN.
THE BATMAN, ANGELA.
IT'S A PLEASURE.
*He's got the cheeriness down, at least.*
I'M LEAVING NOW.

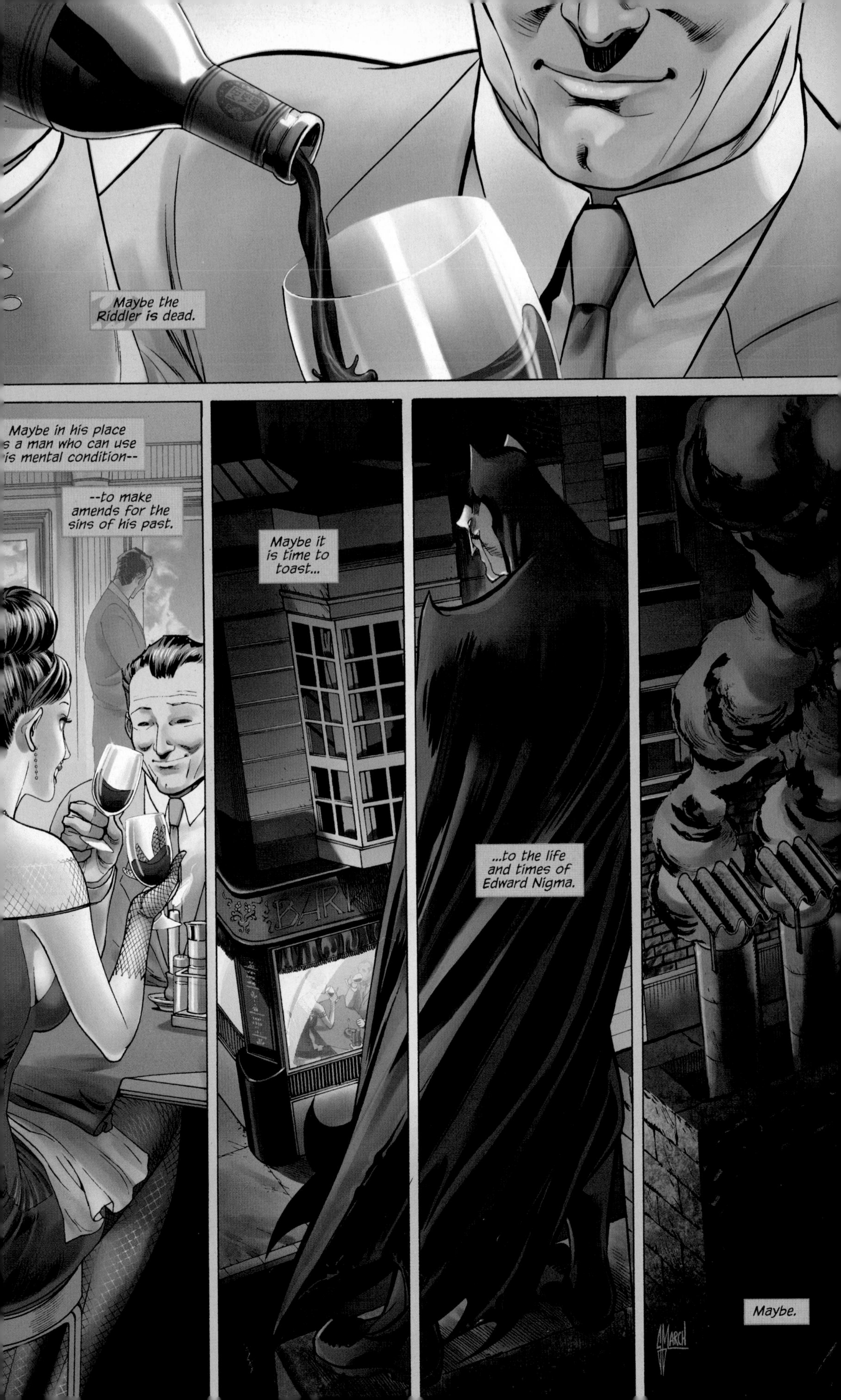
Maybe the Riddler is dead.
Maybe in his place
s a man who can use
is mental condition--
--to make amends for the sins of his past.
Maybe it is time to toast...
...to the life and times of Edward Nigma.
Maybe.

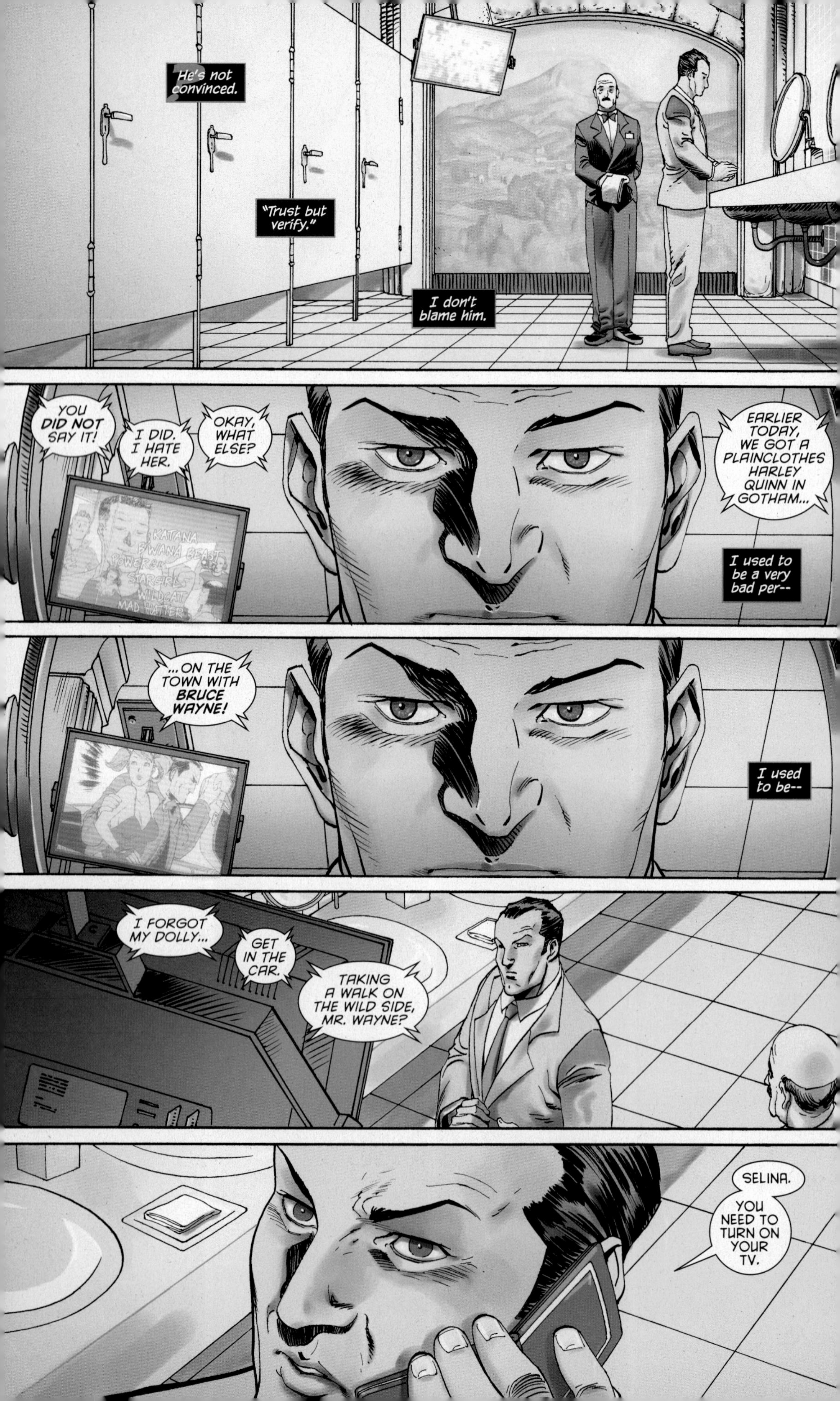

He's not convinced.
"Trust but verify."
I don't blame him.
YOU DID NOT SAY IT!
I DID. I HATE HER.
OKAY, WHAT ELSE?
EARLIER TODAY, WE GOT A PLAINCLOTHES HARLEY QUINN IN GOTHAM...
I used to be a very bad per--
KATANA
B'WANA BEAST
POWERGIRL
STARGIRL
WILDCAT
MAD HATTER
...ON THE TOWN WITH BRUCE WAYNE!
I used to be--
I FORGOT MY DOLLY...
GET IN THE CAR.
TAKING A WALK ON THE WILD SIDE, MR. WAYNE?
SELINA.
YOU NEED TO TURN ON YOUR TV.

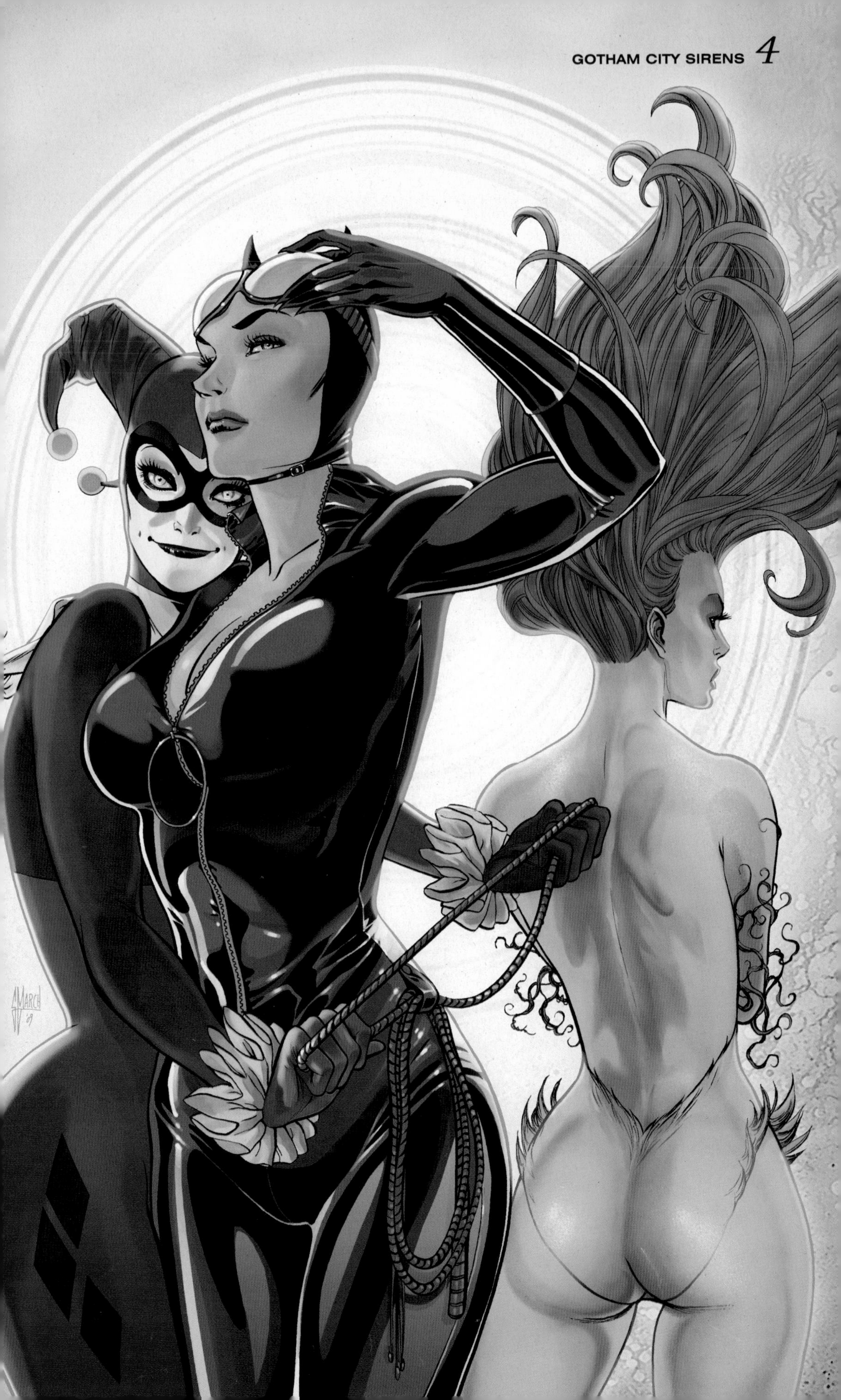
GOTHAM CITY SIRENS 4

SHELTER

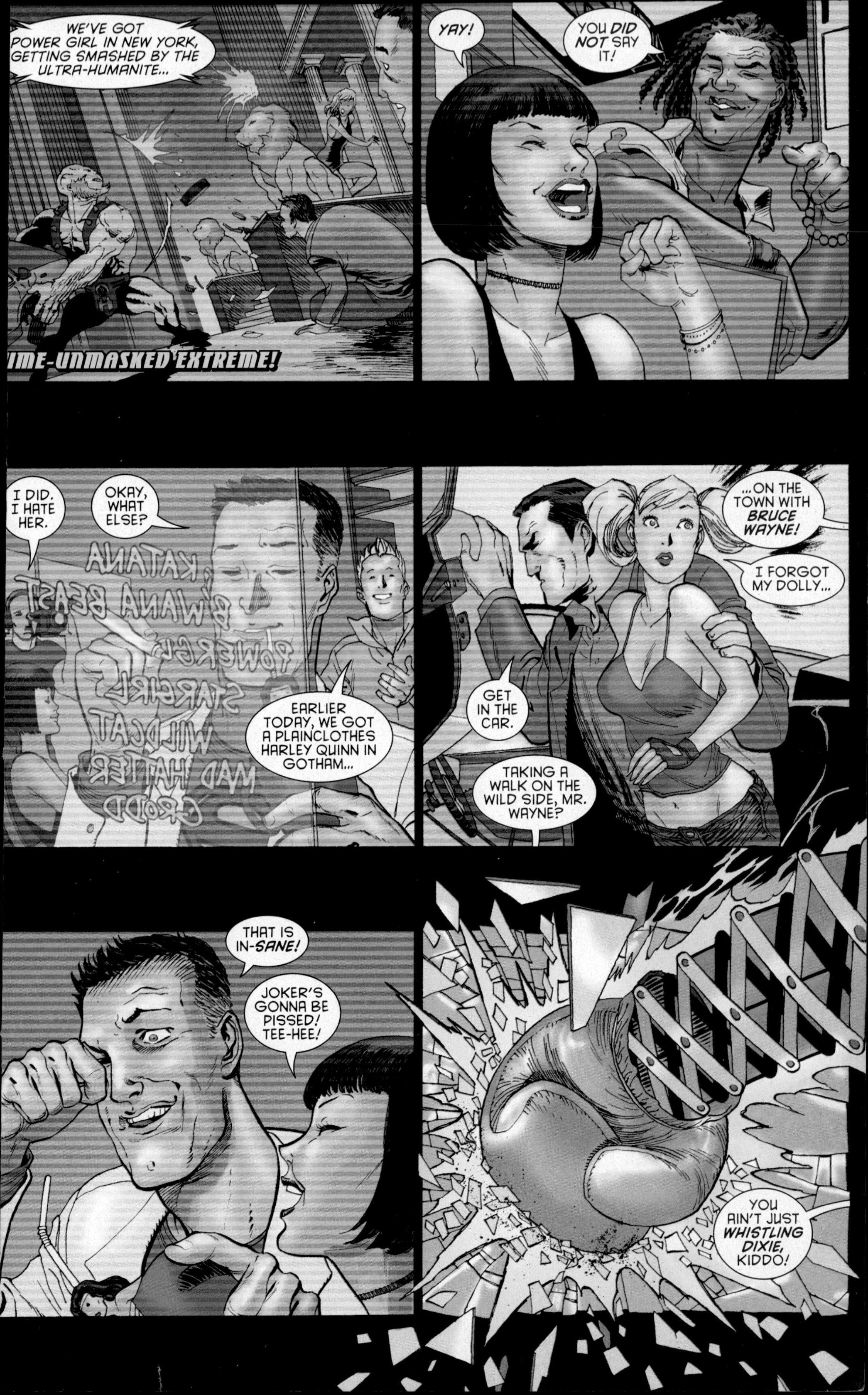
WE'VE GOT POWER GIRL IN NEW YORK, GETTING SMASHED BY THE ULTRA-HUMANITE...
IME-UNMASKED EXTREME!
YAY!
YOU DID NOT SAY IT!
I DID. I HATE HER.
OKAY, WHAT ELSE?
KATANA
B'WANA BEAST
POWERGIRL
STARGIRL
WILDCAT
MAD HATTER
GRODD
EARLIER TODAY, WE GOT A PLAINCLOTHES HARLEY QUINN IN GOTHAM...
...ON THE TOWN WITH BRUCE WAYNE!
I FORGOT MY DOLLY...
GET IN THE CAR.
TAKING A WALK ON THE WILD SIDE, MR. WAYNE?
THAT IS IN-SANE!
JOKER'S GONNA BE PISSED! TEE-HEE!
YOU AIN'T JUST WHISTLING DIXIE, KIDDO!

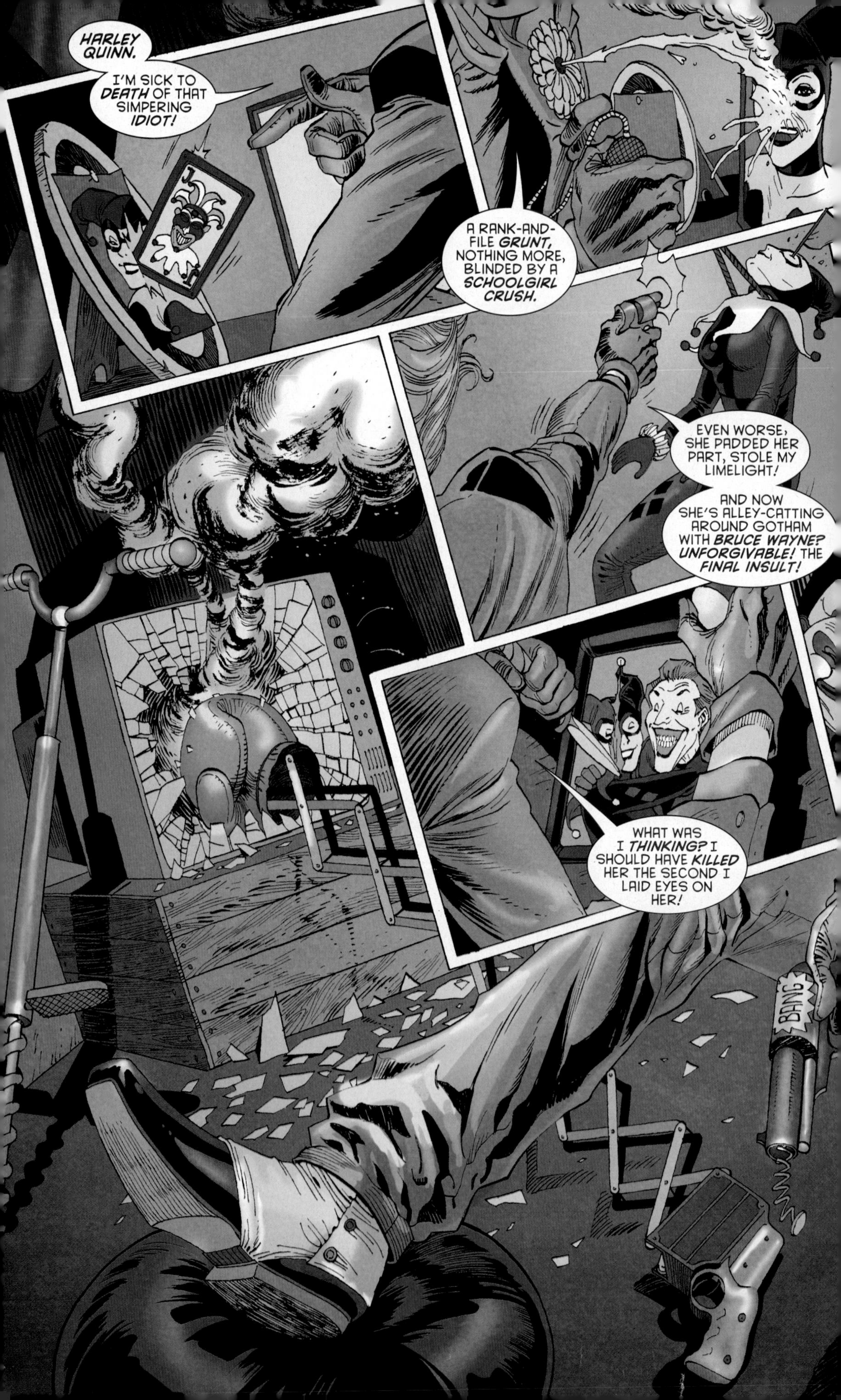
HARLEY QUINN.
I'M SICK TO DEATH OF THAT SIMPERING IDIOT!
A RANK-AND-FILE GRUNT, NOTHING MORE, BLINDED BY A SCHOOLGIRL CRUSH.
EVEN WORSE, SHE PADDED HER PART, STOLE MY LIMELIGHT!
AND NOW SHE'S ALLEY-CATTING AROUND GOTHAM WITH BRUCE WAYNE? UNFORGIVABLE! THE FINAL INSULT!
WHAT WAS I THINKING? I SHOULD HAVE KILLED HER THE SECOND I LAID EYES ON HER!
BANG

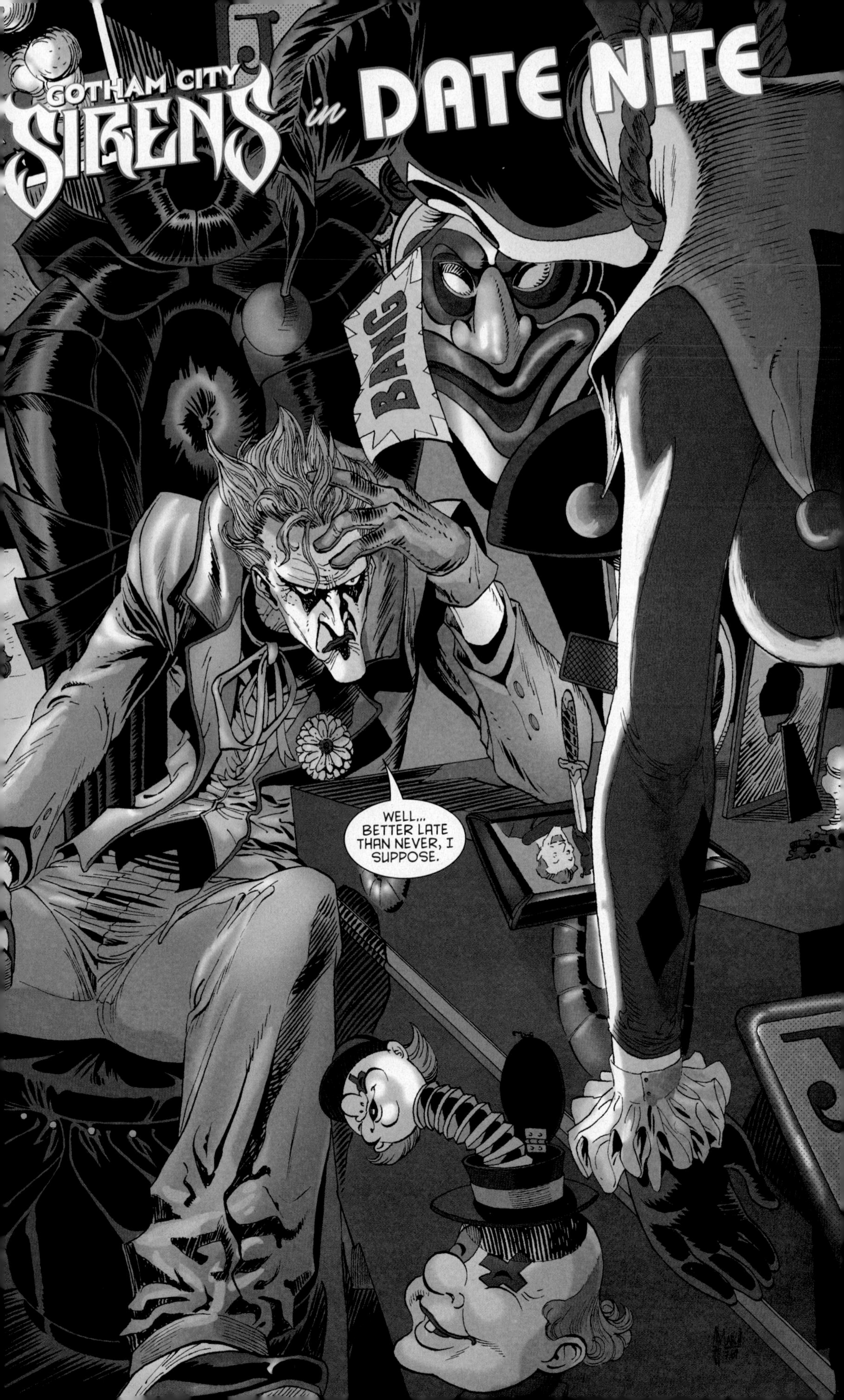
GOTHAM CITY SIRENS in DATE NITE
BANG
WELL... BETTER LATE THAN NEVER, I SUPPOSE.

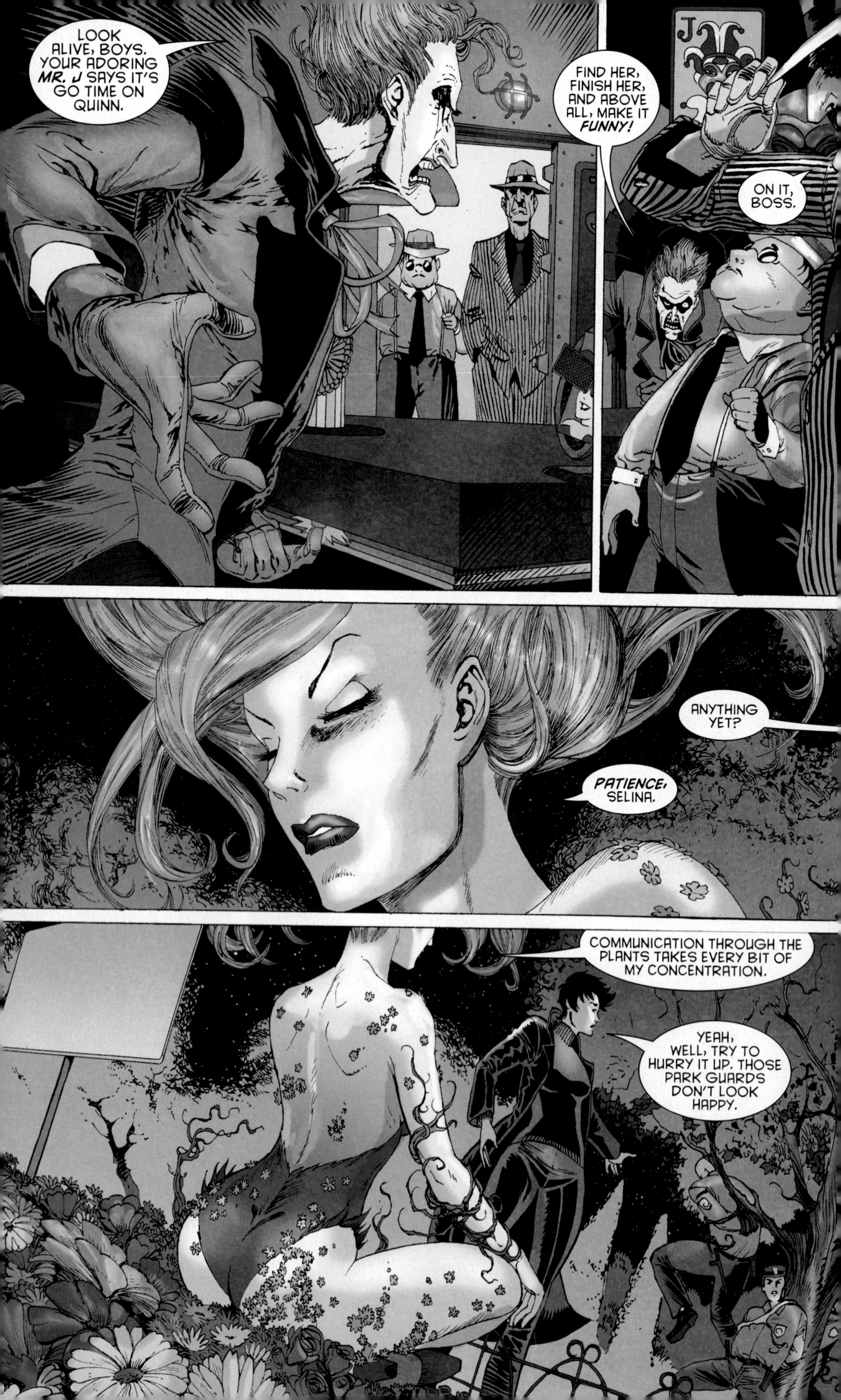

LOOK ALIVE, BOYS. YOUR ADORING *MR. J* SAYS IT'S GO TIME ON QUINN.
FIND HER, FINISH HER, AND ABOVE ALL, MAKE IT *FUNNY!*
ON IT, BOSS.
ANYTHING YET?
*PATIENCE,* SELINA.
COMMUNICATION THROUGH THE PLANTS TAKES EVERY BIT OF MY CONCENTRATION.
YEAH, WELL, TRY TO HURRY IT UP. THOSE PARK GUARDS DON'T LOOK HAPPY.

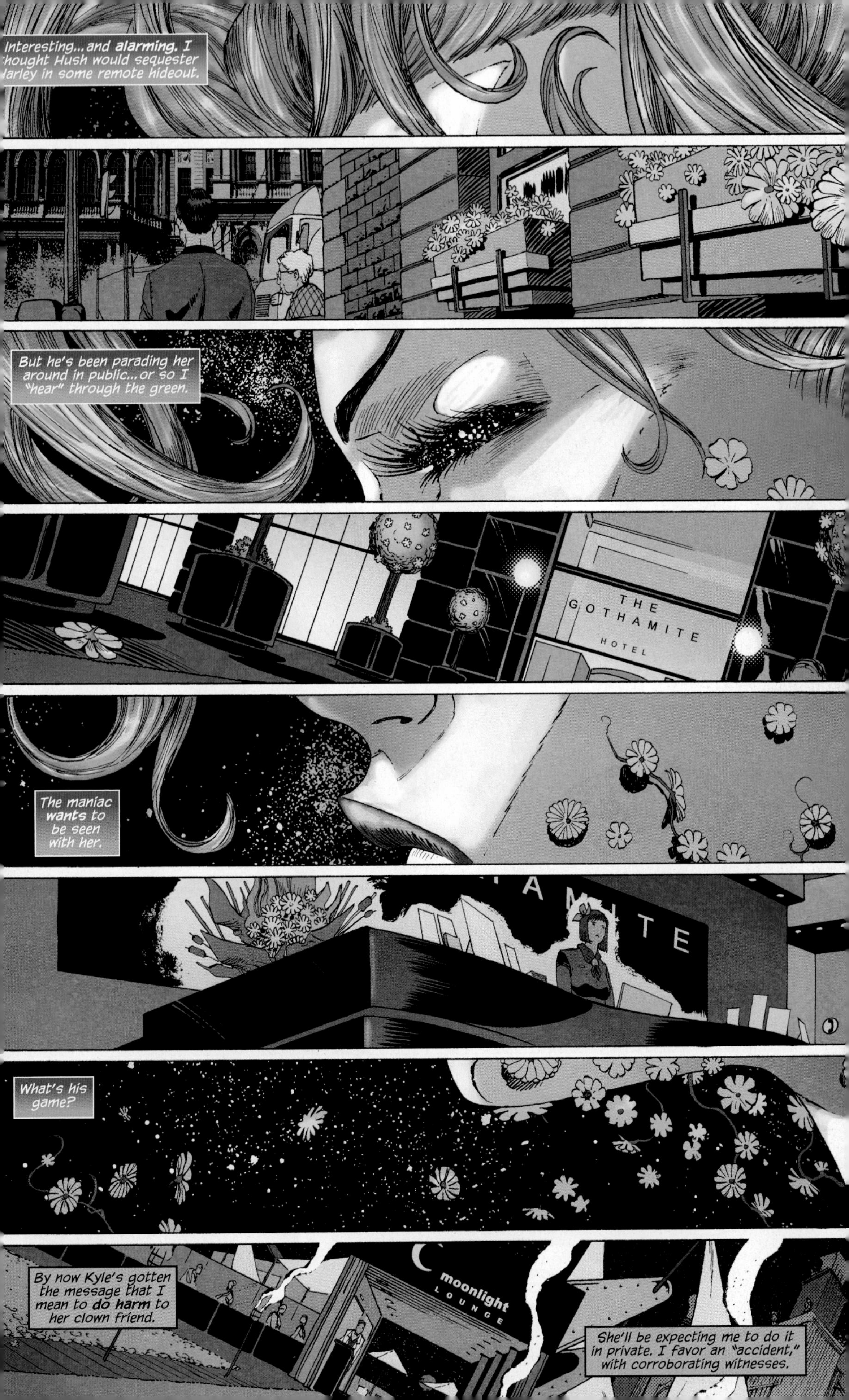

Interesting...and alarming. I thought Hush would sequester Harley in some remote hideout.
But he's been parading her around in public...or so I "hear" through the green.
THE GOTHAMITE HOTEL
The maniac wants to be seen with her.
What's his game?
By now Kyle's gotten the message that I mean to do harm to her clown friend.
moonlight LOUNGE
She'll be expecting me to do it in private. I favor an "accident," with corroborating witnesses.

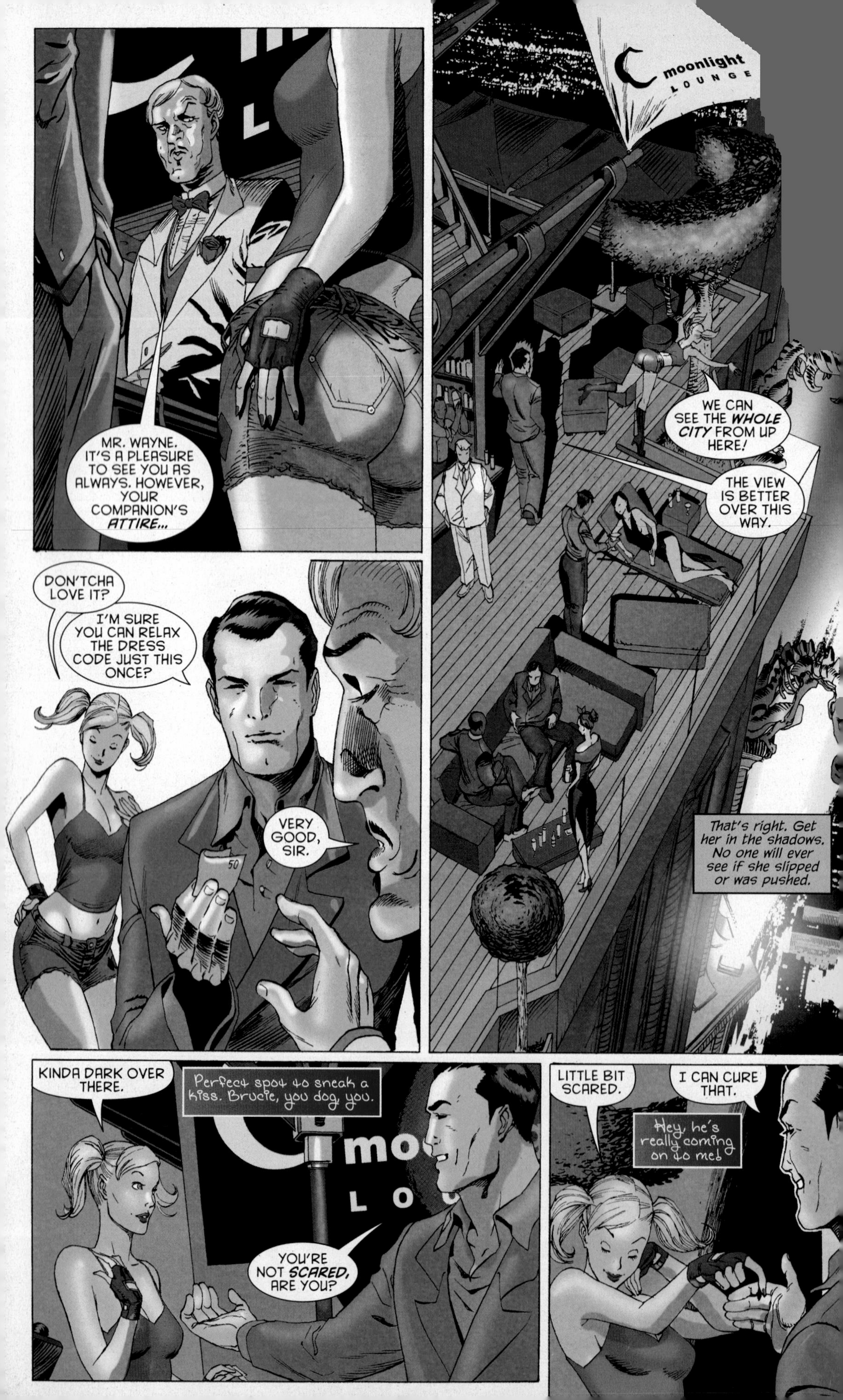
moonlight LOUNGE
MR. WAYNE. IT'S A PLEASURE TO SEE YOU AS ALWAYS. HOWEVER, YOUR COMPANION'S ATTIRE...
DON'TCHA LOVE IT?
I'M SURE YOU CAN RELAX THE DRESS CODE JUST THIS ONCE?
VERY GOOD, SIR.
WE CAN SEE THE WHOLE CITY FROM UP HERE!
THE VIEW IS BETTER OVER THIS WAY.
That's right. Get her in the shadows. No one will ever see if she slipped or was pushed.
KINDA DARK OVER THERE.
Perfect spot to sneak a kiss. Brucie, you dog, you.
YOU'RE NOT SCARED, ARE YOU?
LITTLE BIT SCARED.
I CAN CURE THAT.
Hey, he's really coming on to me!

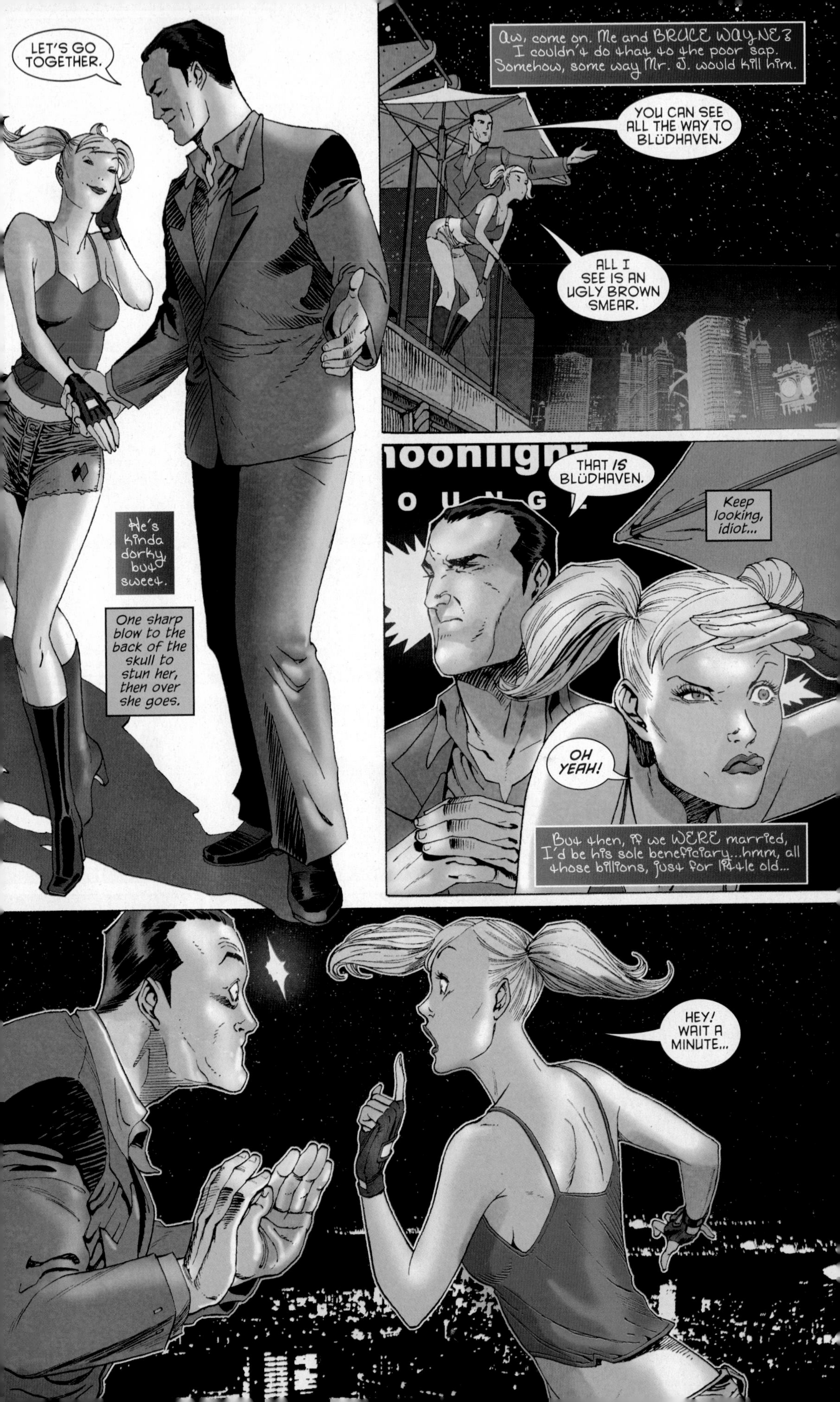
LET'S GO TOGETHER.
He's kinda dorky, but sweet.
One sharp blow to the back of the skull to stun her, then over she goes.
Aw, come on. Me and BRUCE WAYNE? I couldn't do that to the poor sap. Somehow, some way Mr. J. would kill him.
YOU CAN SEE ALL THE WAY TO BLÜDHAVEN.
ALL I SEE IS AN UGLY BROWN SMEAR.
THAT IS BLÜDHAVEN.
Keep looking, idiot...
OH YEAH!
But then, if we WERE married, I'd be his sole beneficiary...hmm, all those billions, just for little old...
HEY! WAIT A MINUTE...

DON'T YOU HAVE A *KID* OR SOMETHING?

*TWO* ACTUALLY, MY ADOPTED SON, TIM AND MY WARD, DICK.

HUH? OH, YES...

*I'm not going to even try to explain* **Damian.** *I can never keep track of who knows about whom.*

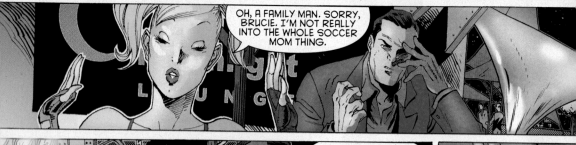

OH, A FAMILY MAN. SORRY, BRUCIE. I'M NOT REALLY INTO THE WHOLE SOCCER MOM THING.

IF SOMEONE TOLD ME I'D SOMEDAY BE FLYING AROUND GOTHAM DRESSED LIKE A REFUGEE FROM "GUYS AND DOLLS" I'D SAY THEY WERE MESSED UP.

THAT'S THE WAY IT IS WHEN YOU WORK FOR THE *JOKER.* HE'S QUIXOTIC.

HE'S WHA...?

YOU KNOW, A DREAMER. BIG PICTURE GUY.

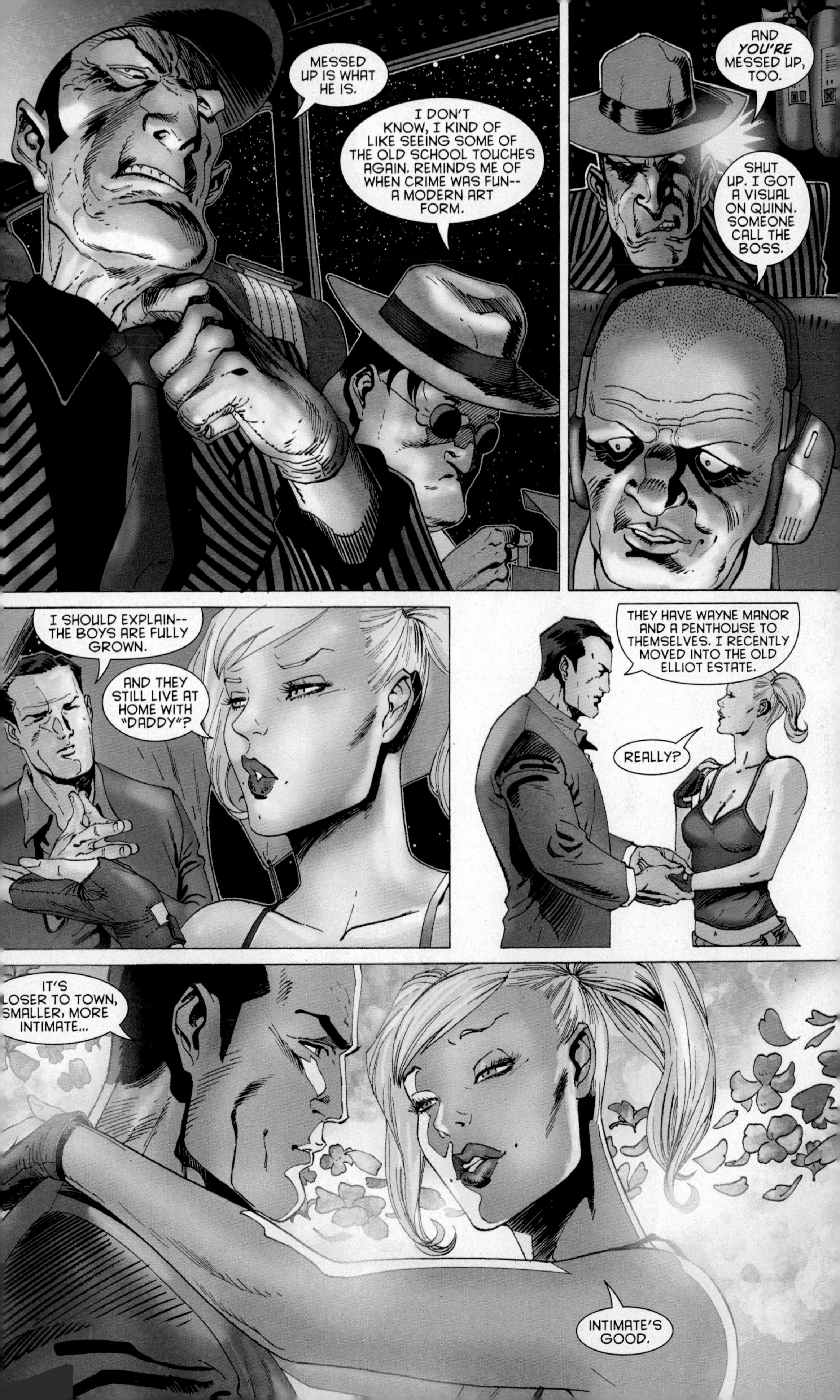
MESSED UP IS WHAT HE IS.
I DON'T KNOW, I KIND OF LIKE SEEING SOME OF THE OLD SCHOOL TOUCHES AGAIN. REMINDS ME OF WHEN CRIME WAS FUN-- A MODERN ART FORM.
AND YOU'RE MESSED UP, TOO.
SHUT UP. I GOT A VISUAL ON QUINN. SOMEONE CALL THE BOSS.
I SHOULD EXPLAIN-- THE BOYS ARE FULLY GROWN.
AND THEY STILL LIVE AT HOME WITH "DADDY"?
THEY HAVE WAYNE MANOR AND A PENTHOUSE TO THEMSELVES. I RECENTLY MOVED INTO THE OLD ELLIOT ESTATE.
REALLY?
IT'S CLOSER TO TOWN, SMALLER, MORE INTIMATE...
INTIMATE'S GOOD.

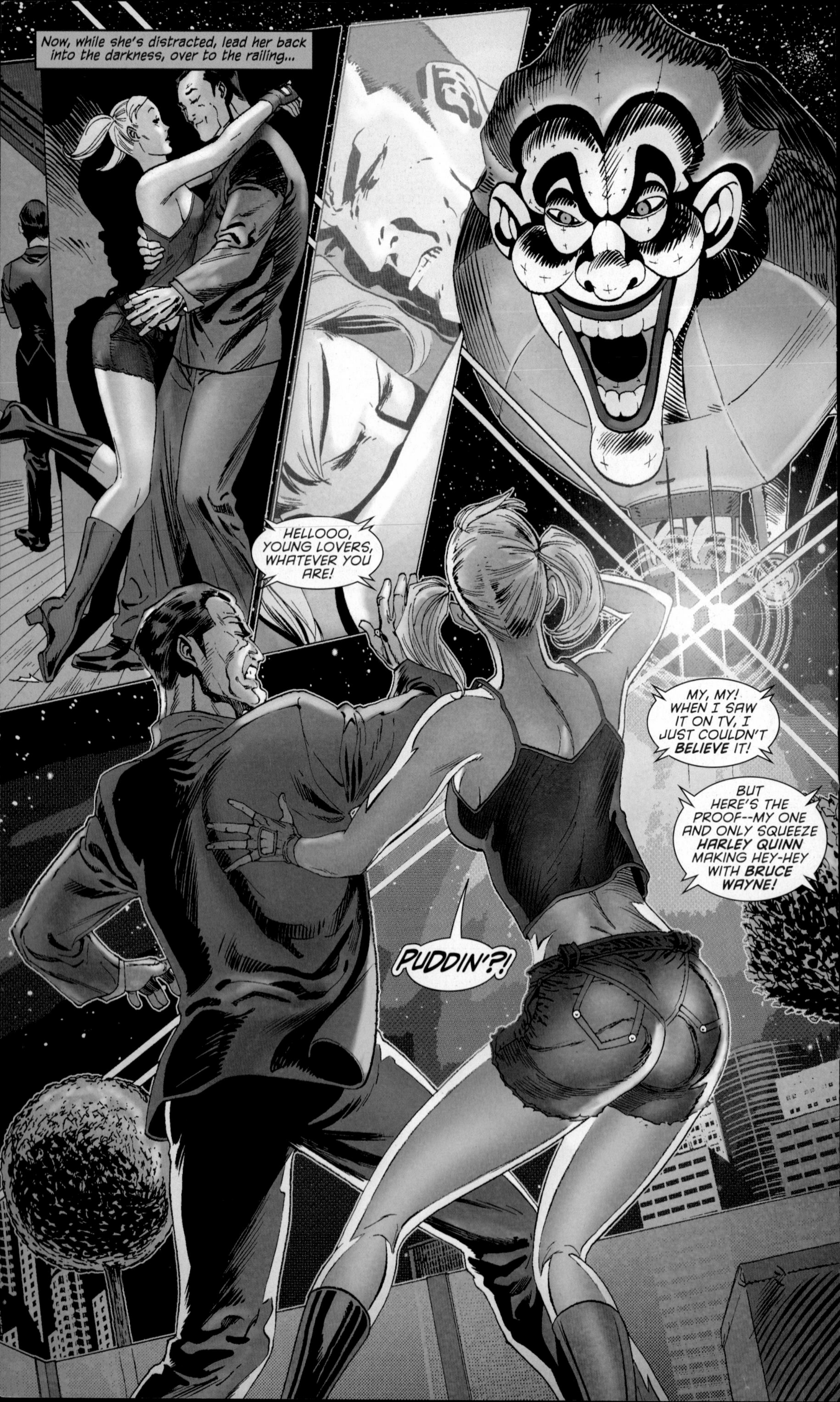
Now, while she's distracted, lead her back into the darkness, over to the railing...
HELLOOO, YOUNG LOVERS, WHATEVER YOU ARE!
MY, MY! WHEN I SAW IT ON TV, I JUST COULDN'T BELIEVE IT!
BUT HERE'S THE PROOF--MY ONE AND ONLY SQUEEZE HARLEY QUINN MAKING HEY-HEY WITH BRUCE WAYNE!
PUDDIN'?!

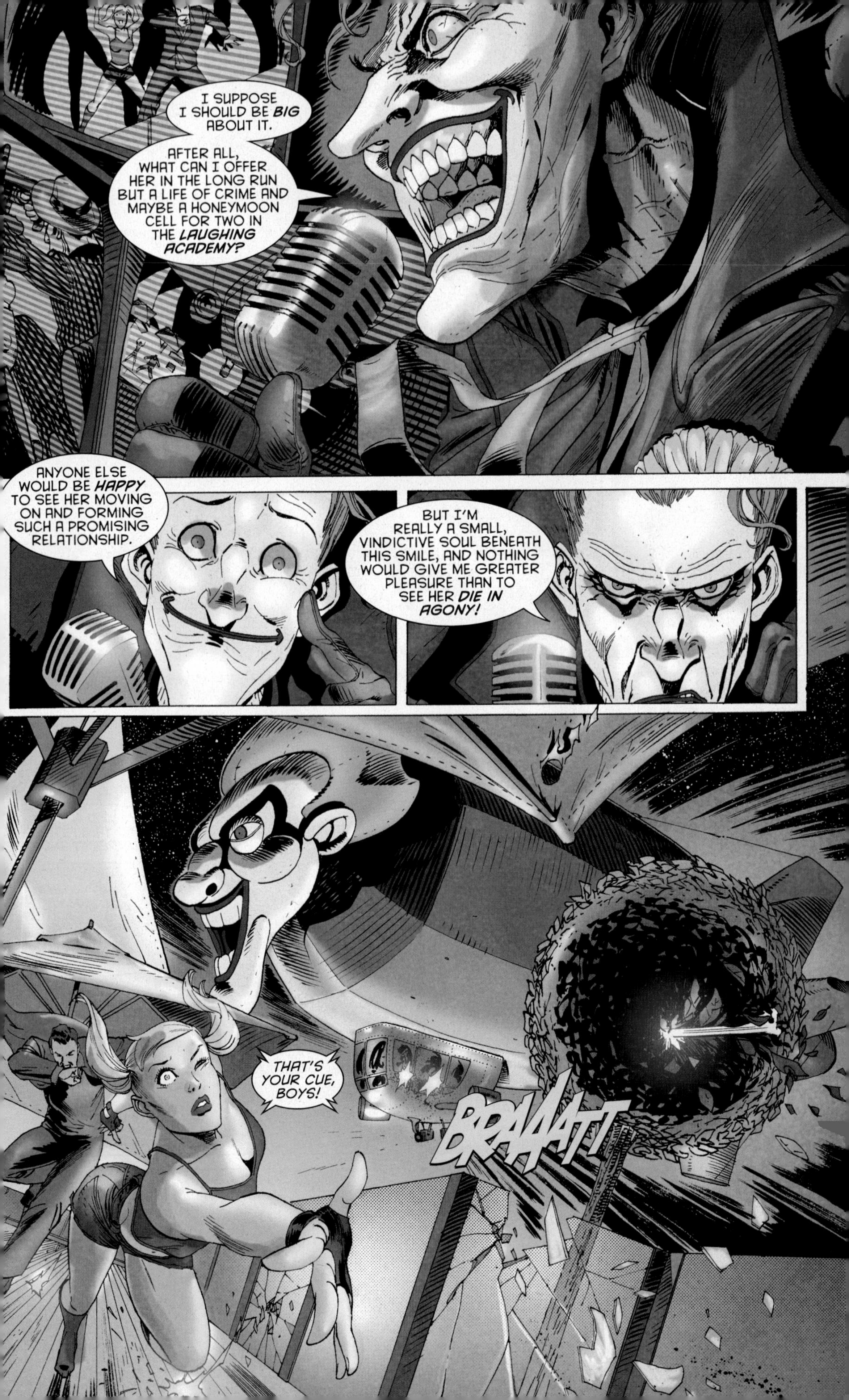

I SUPPOSE I SHOULD BE *BIG* ABOUT IT.
AFTER ALL, WHAT CAN I OFFER HER IN THE LONG RUN BUT A LIFE OF CRIME AND MAYBE A HONEYMOON CELL FOR TWO IN THE *LAUGHING ACADEMY?*
ANYONE ELSE WOULD BE *HAPPY* TO SEE HER MOVING ON AND FORMING SUCH A PROMISING RELATIONSHIP.
BUT I'M REALLY A SMALL, VINDICTIVE SOUL BENEATH THIS SMILE, AND NOTHING WOULD GIVE ME GREATER PLEASURE THAN TO SEE HER *DIE IN AGONY!*
THAT'S YOUR CUE, BOYS!
BRAAATT

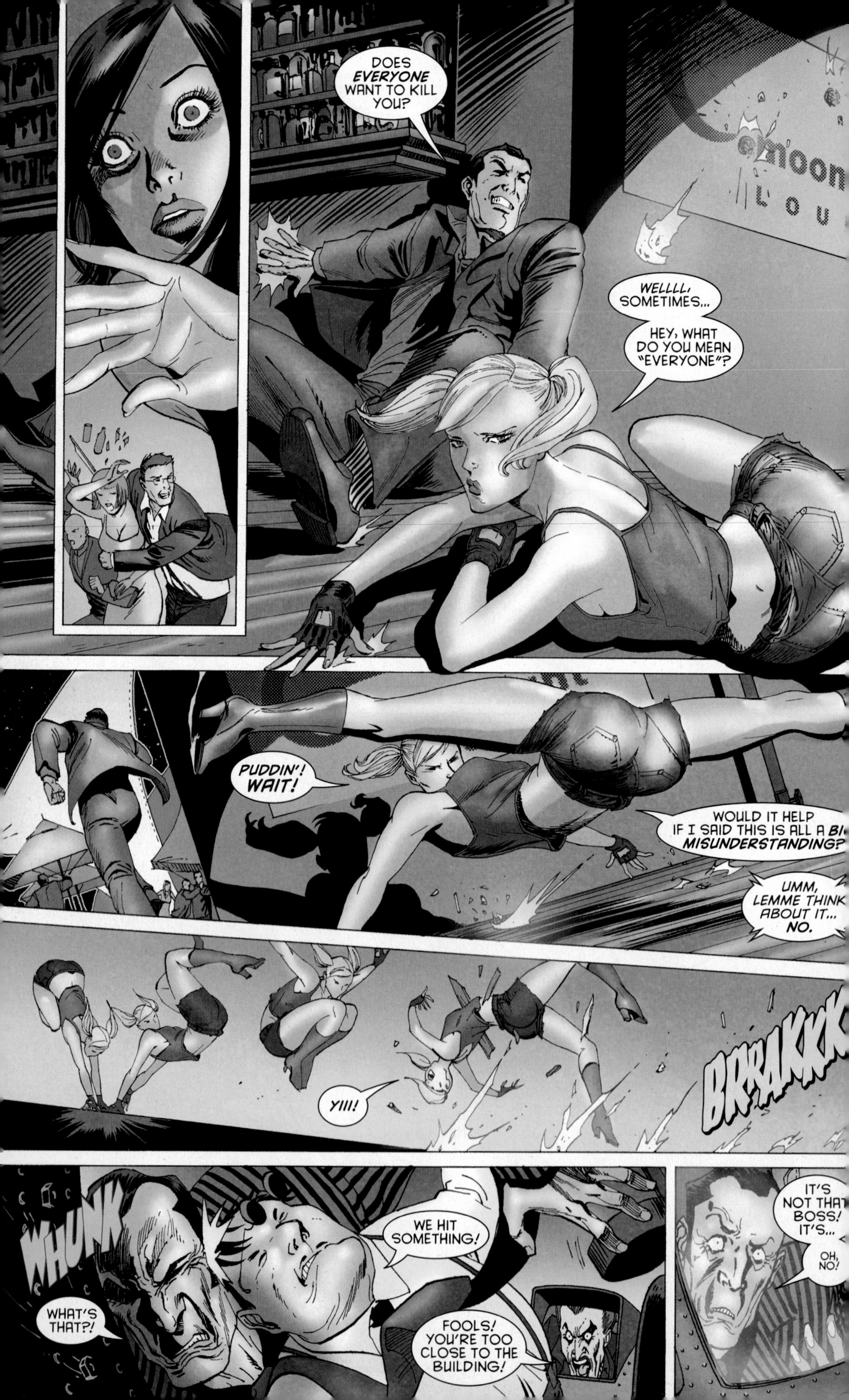

DOES EVERYONE WANT TO KILL YOU?
WELLLL, SOMETIMES...
HEY, WHAT DO YOU MEAN "EVERYONE"?
PUDDIN'! WAIT!
WOULD IT HELP IF I SAID THIS IS ALL A BIG MISUNDERSTANDING?
UMM, LEMME THINK ABOUT IT... NO.
YIII!
BRRAKKK
WHUNK
WE HIT SOMETHING!
WHAT'S THAT?!
FOOLS! YOU'RE TOO CLOSE TO THE BUILDING!
IT'S NOT THAT BOSS! IT'S...
OH, NO!

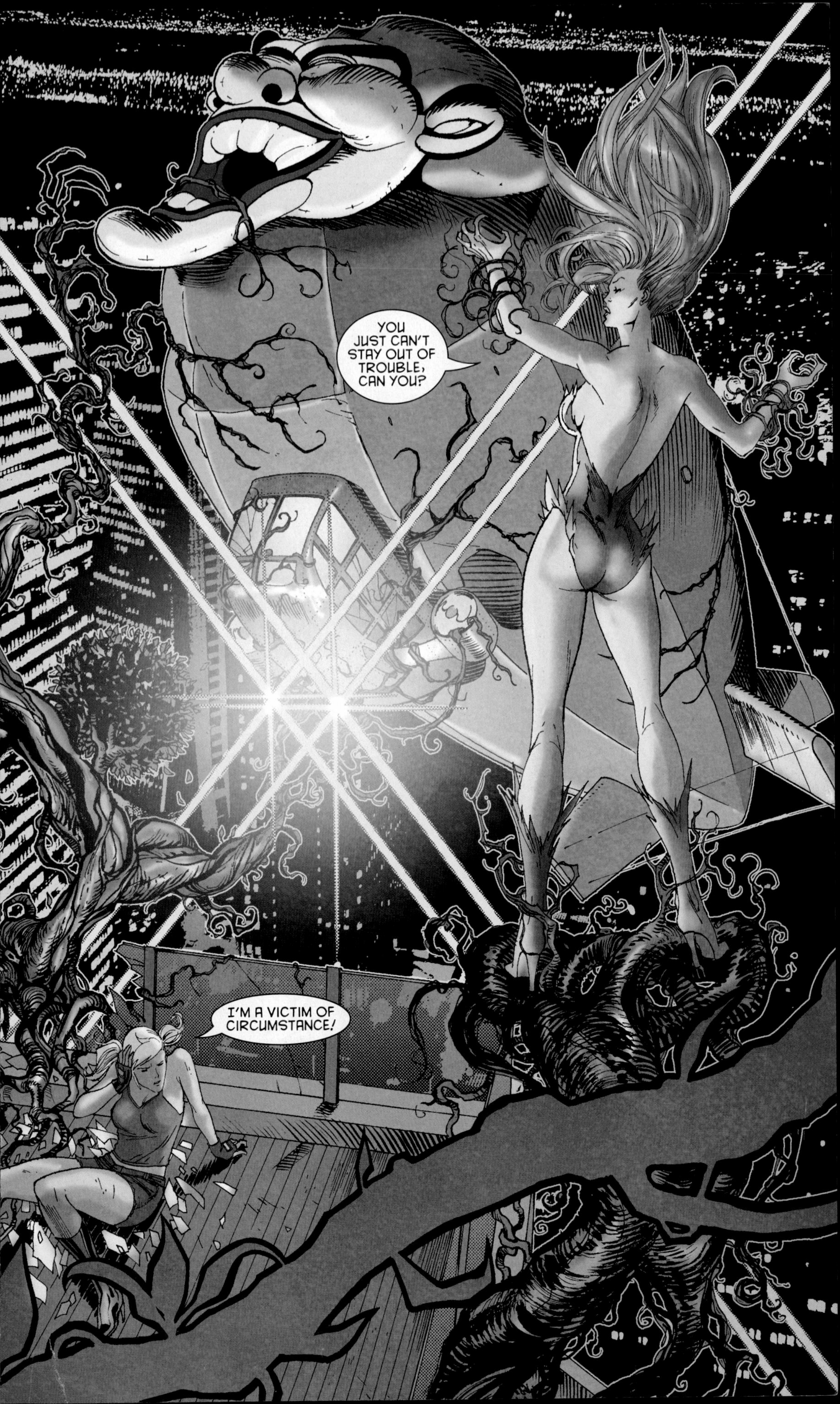
YOU JUST CAN'T STAY OUT OF TROUBLE, CAN YOU?
I'M A VICTIM OF CIRCUMSTANCE!

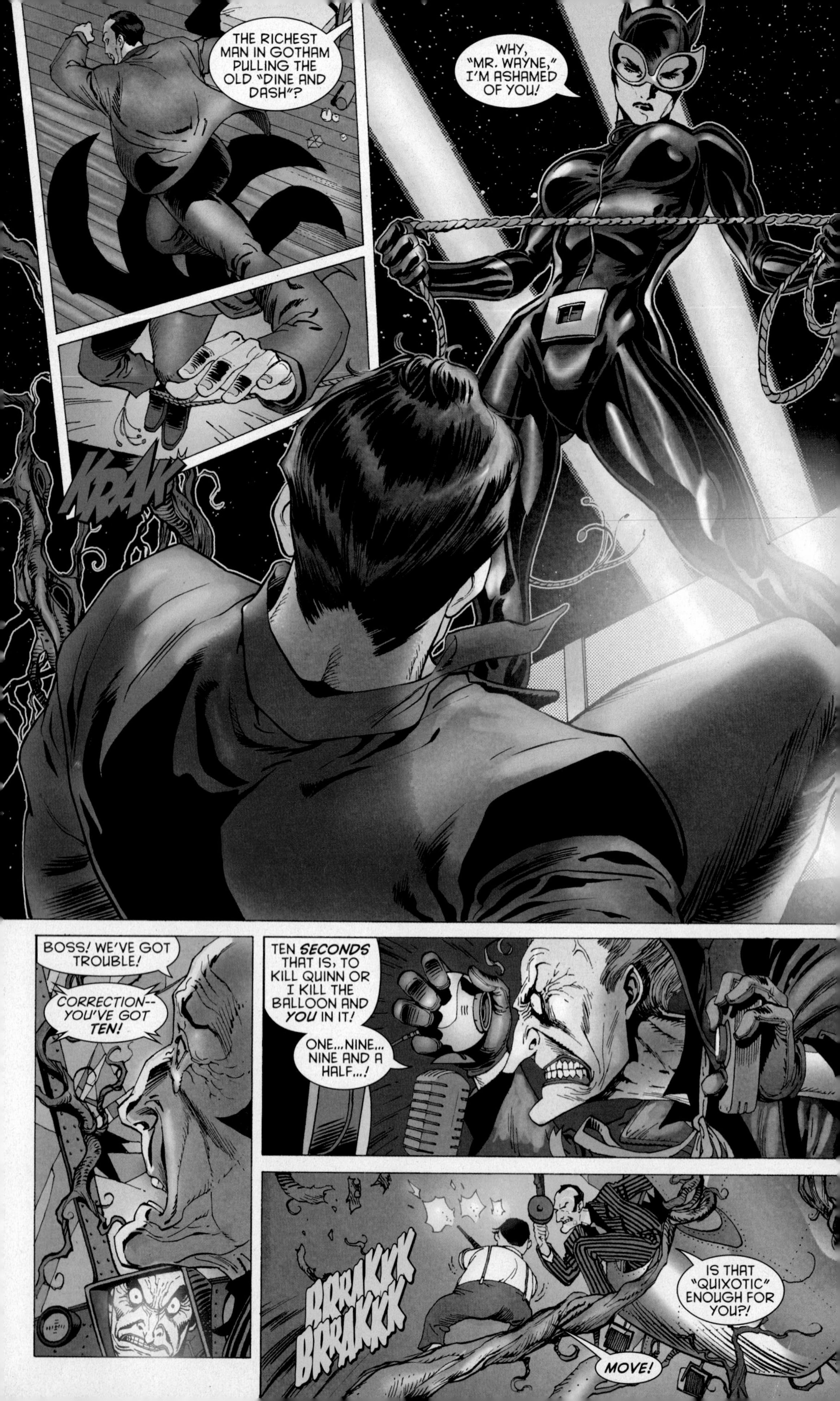
THE RICHEST MAN IN GOTHAM PULLING THE OLD "DINE AND DASH"?
WHY, "MR. WAYNE," I'M ASHAMED OF YOU!
KRAK
BOSS! WE'VE GOT TROUBLE!
CORRECTION-- YOU'VE GOT TEN!
TEN SECONDS THAT IS, TO KILL QUINN OR I KILL THE BALLOON AND YOU IN IT!
ONE...NINE... NINE AND A HALF...!
BRRAKKK BRRAKKK
IS THAT "QUIXOTIC" ENOUGH FOR YOU?!
MOVE!

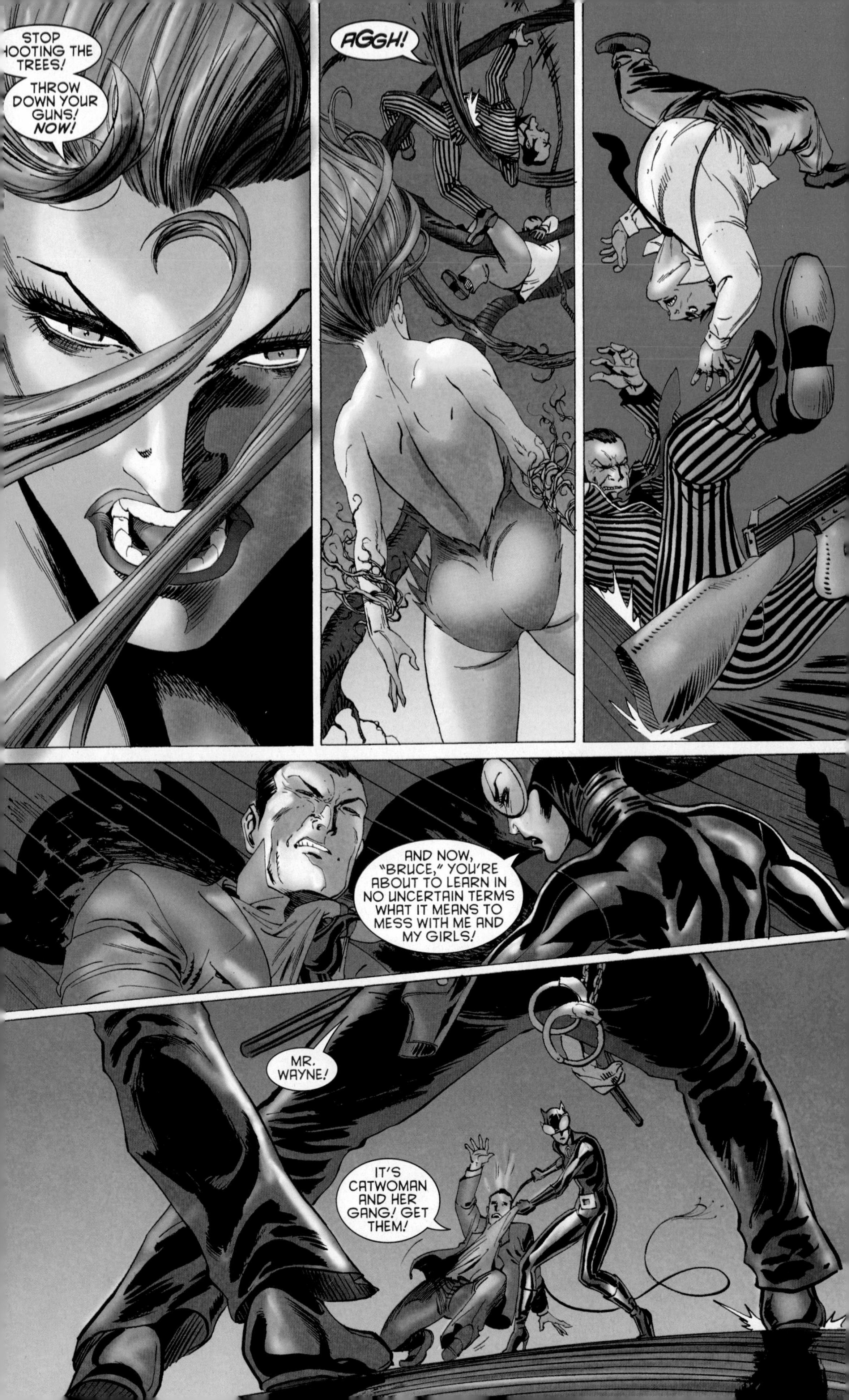
STOP HOOTING THE TREES!
THROW DOWN YOUR GUNS! NOW!
AGGH!
AND NOW, "BRUCE," YOU'RE ABOUT TO LEARN IN NO UNCERTAIN TERMS WHAT IT MEANS TO MESS WITH ME AND MY GIRLS!
MR. WAYNE!
IT'S CATWOMAN AND HER GANG! GET THEM!

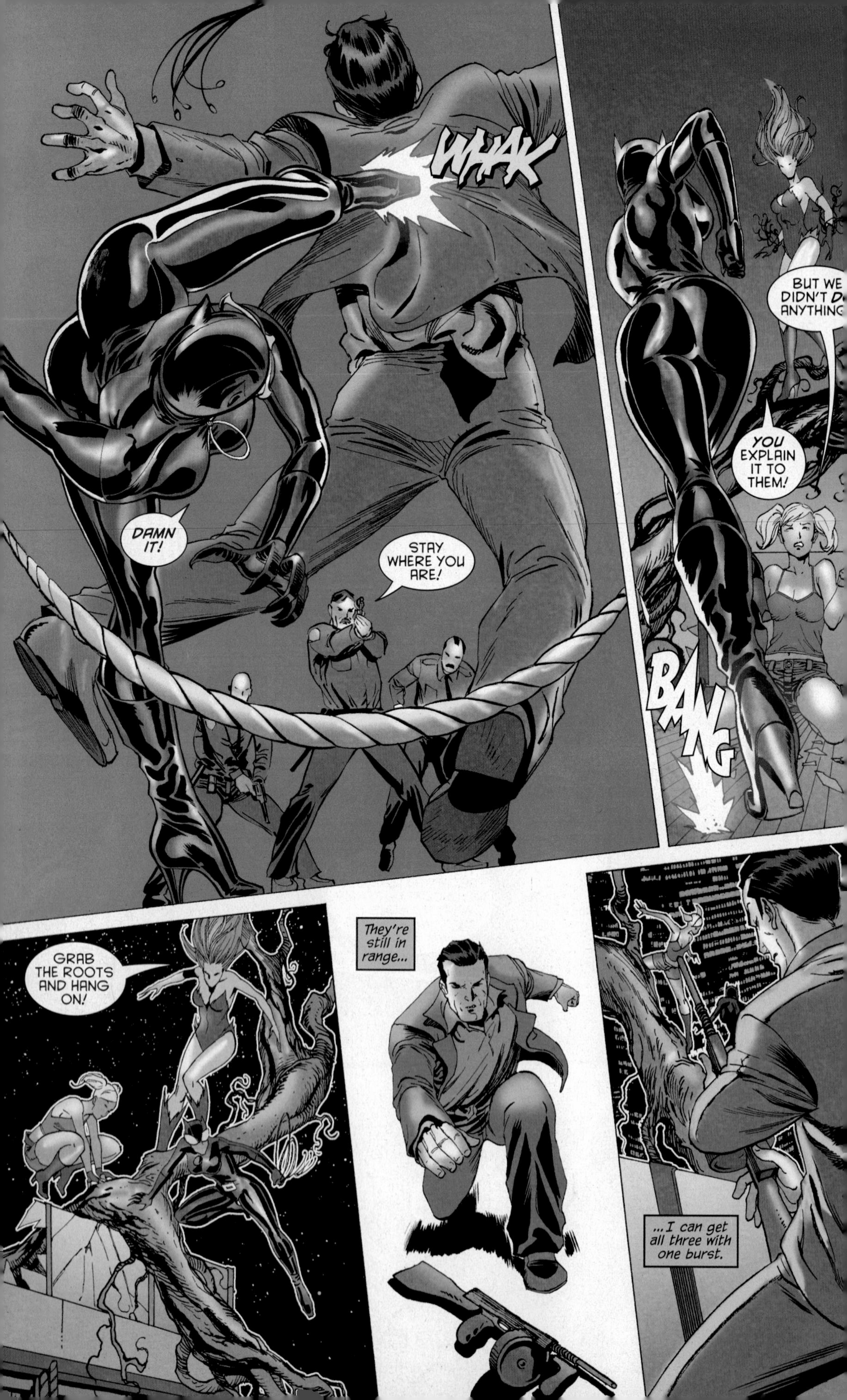
WHAK
DAMN IT!
STAY WHERE YOU ARE!
BUT WE DIDN'T DO ANYTHING
YOU EXPLAIN IT TO THEM!
BANG
GRAB THE ROOTS AND HANG ON!
They're still in range...
...I can get all three with one burst.

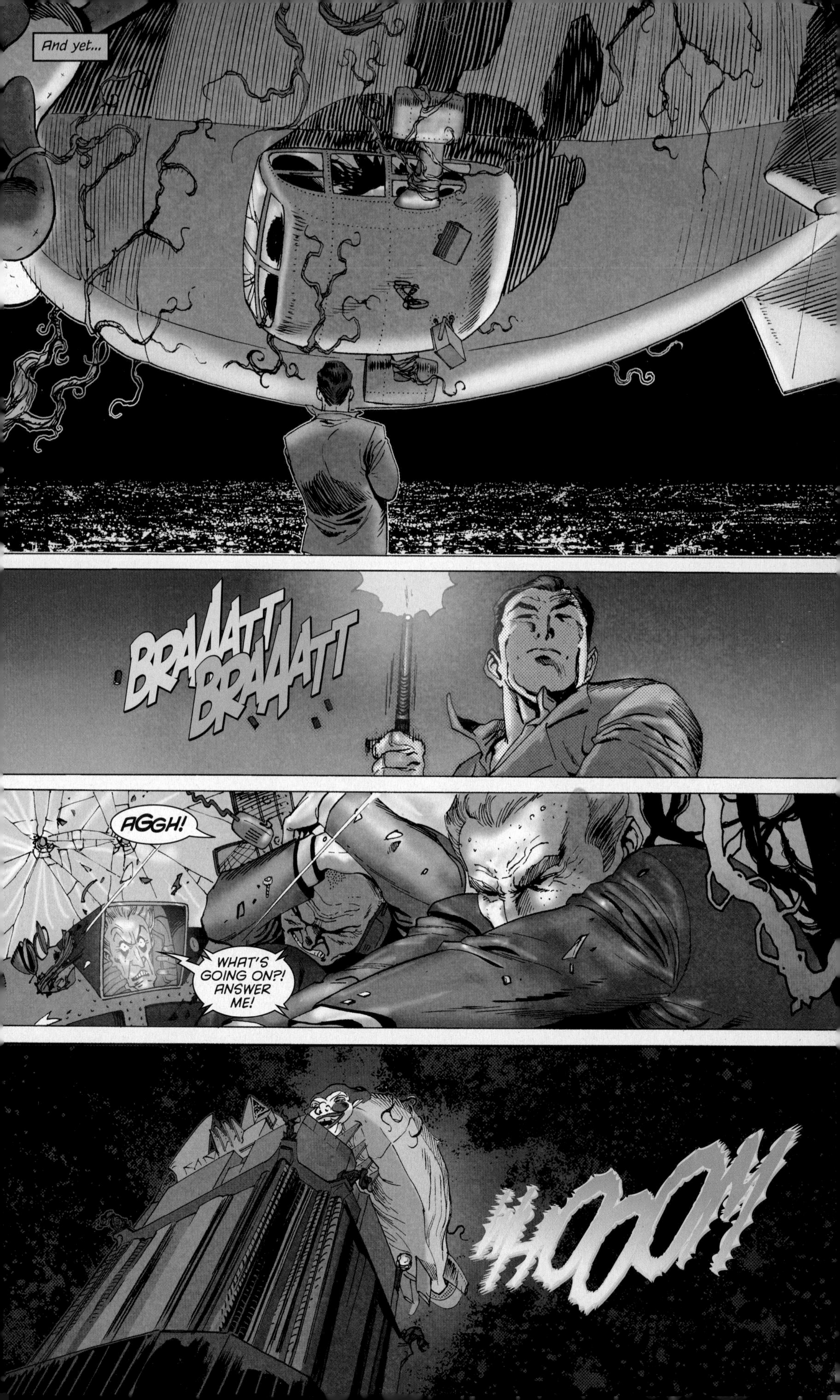
And yet...
BRAAATT BRAAATT
AGGH!
WHAT'S GOING ON?! ANSWER ME!
WOOOM

YOU BROUGHT IT DOWN SINGLE-HANDED, MR. WAYNE!

I COULDN'T LET THE CRIMINALS GET AWAY. FOOLISH OF ME, I KNOW...

*Bruce Wayne shoots three women, he's a cad claiming self-defense. But he brings down a blimp full of the Joker's thugs...*

YOU'RE A HERO!

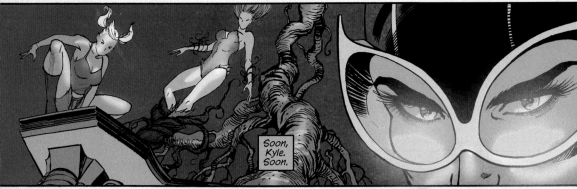

*Soon, Kyle. Soon.*

HUH. BRUCE WAYNE. DIDN'T THINK YOU HAD THE STONES TO MESS WITH MR. J.

WE'LL TAKE THIS UP SOME OTHER TIME.

BUT RIGHT NOW I STILL HAVE UNFINISHED BUSINESS WITH THE KID.

ATOMIC BATTERIES TO POWER, TURBINES TO SPEED...

START

SO I'M NEVER GOING TO BE MRS. BRUCE WAYNE.

DEFINITELY NOT.

AND THAT'S 'CAUSE THE GUY PRETENDING TO [BE] WAYNE IS THE [G]UY WE RIPPED OFF--*HUSH?*

YES, THAT'S WHAT SELINA SAID.

AND BATMAN IS ALLOWING ONE OF HIS WORST ENEMIES TO WALK AROUND FREE FOR *WHAT REASON?*

IT'S... COMPLICATED.

IT HAS SOMETHING TO DO WITH GOTHAM NEEDING A SYMBOL THE PEOPLE CAN TRUST.

'KAY... AND THE REAL BRUCE WAYNE IS... WHERE?

THAT'S COMPLICATED, TOO.

SKIP IT. I DON'T NEED BRUCE WAYNE, ESPECIALLY NOW THAT MR. J. IS BACK!

BUT HE TRIED TO *KILL* YOU!

THAT *PROVES* HE WANTS ME BACK!

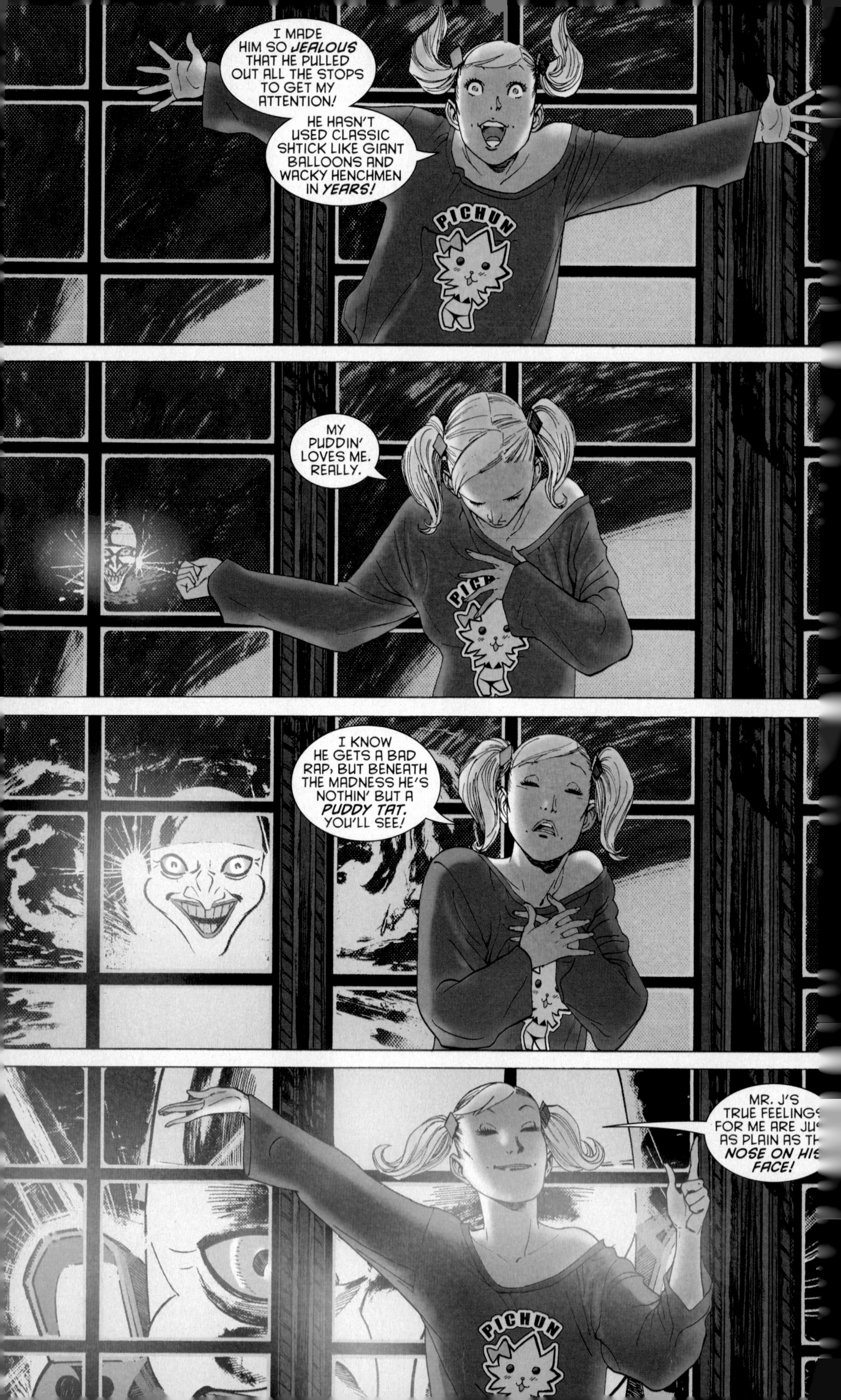
I MADE HIM SO JEALOUS THAT HE PULLED OUT ALL THE STOPS TO GET MY ATTENTION!
HE HASN'T USED CLASSIC SHTICK LIKE GIANT BALLOONS AND WACKY HENCHMEN IN YEARS!
PICHUN
MY PUDDIN' LOVES ME. REALLY.
I KNOW HE GETS A BAD RAP, BUT BENEATH THE MADNESS HE'S NOTHIN' BUT A PUDDY TAT. YOU'LL SEE!
MR. J'S TRUE FEELINGS FOR ME ARE JUS AS PLAIN AS TH NOSE ON HIS FACE!
PICHUN

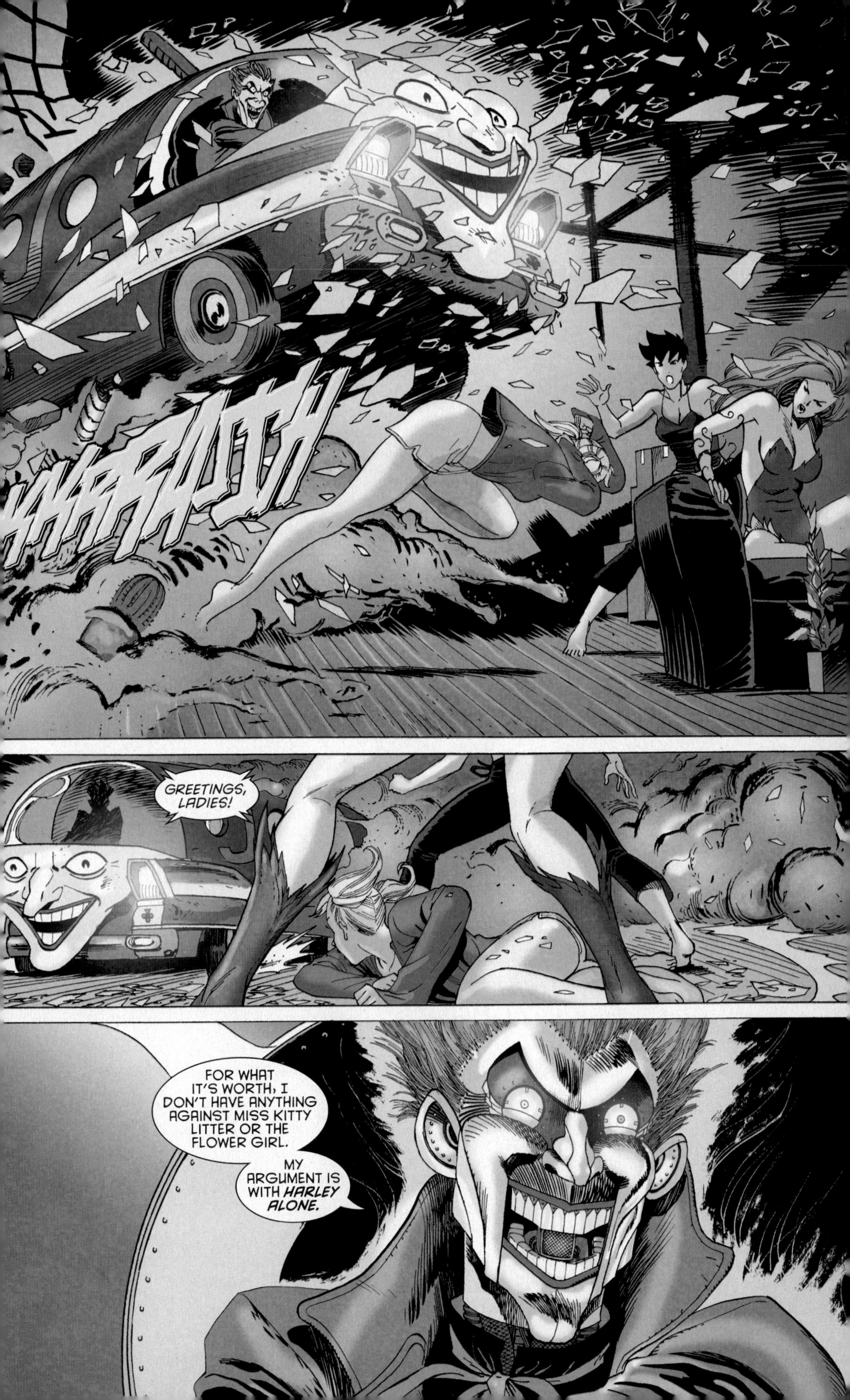
GREETINGS, LADIES!
FOR WHAT IT'S WORTH, I DON'T HAVE ANYTHING AGAINST MISS KITTY LITTER OR THE FLOWER GIRL.
MY ARGUMENT IS WITH HARLEY ALONE.

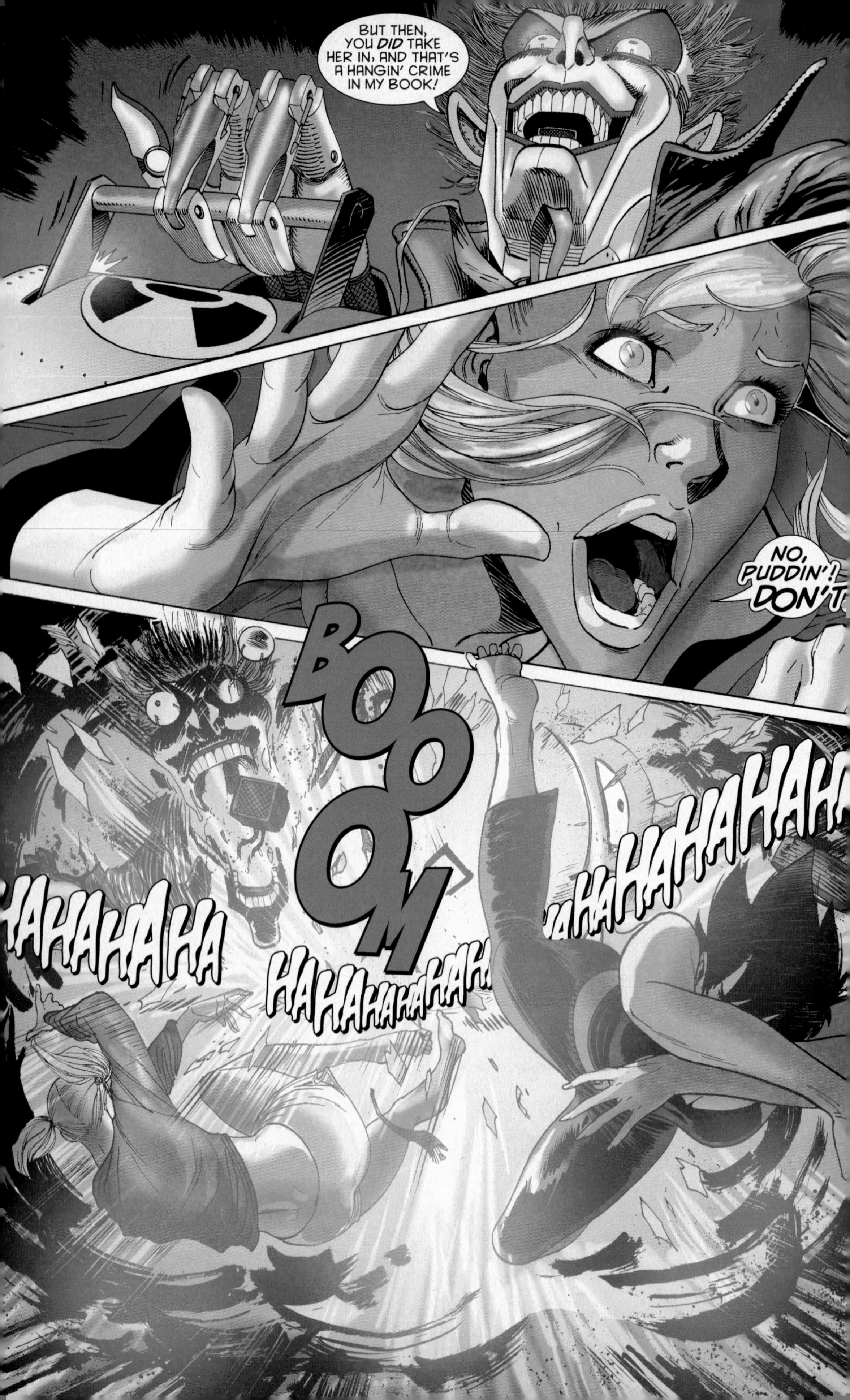
BUT THEN, YOU DID TAKE HER IN, AND THAT'S A HANGIN' CRIME IN MY BOOK!
NO, PUDDIN'! DON'T
BOOOM
HAHAHAHA
HAHAHAHAHAHA
HAHAHAHAHAHAH

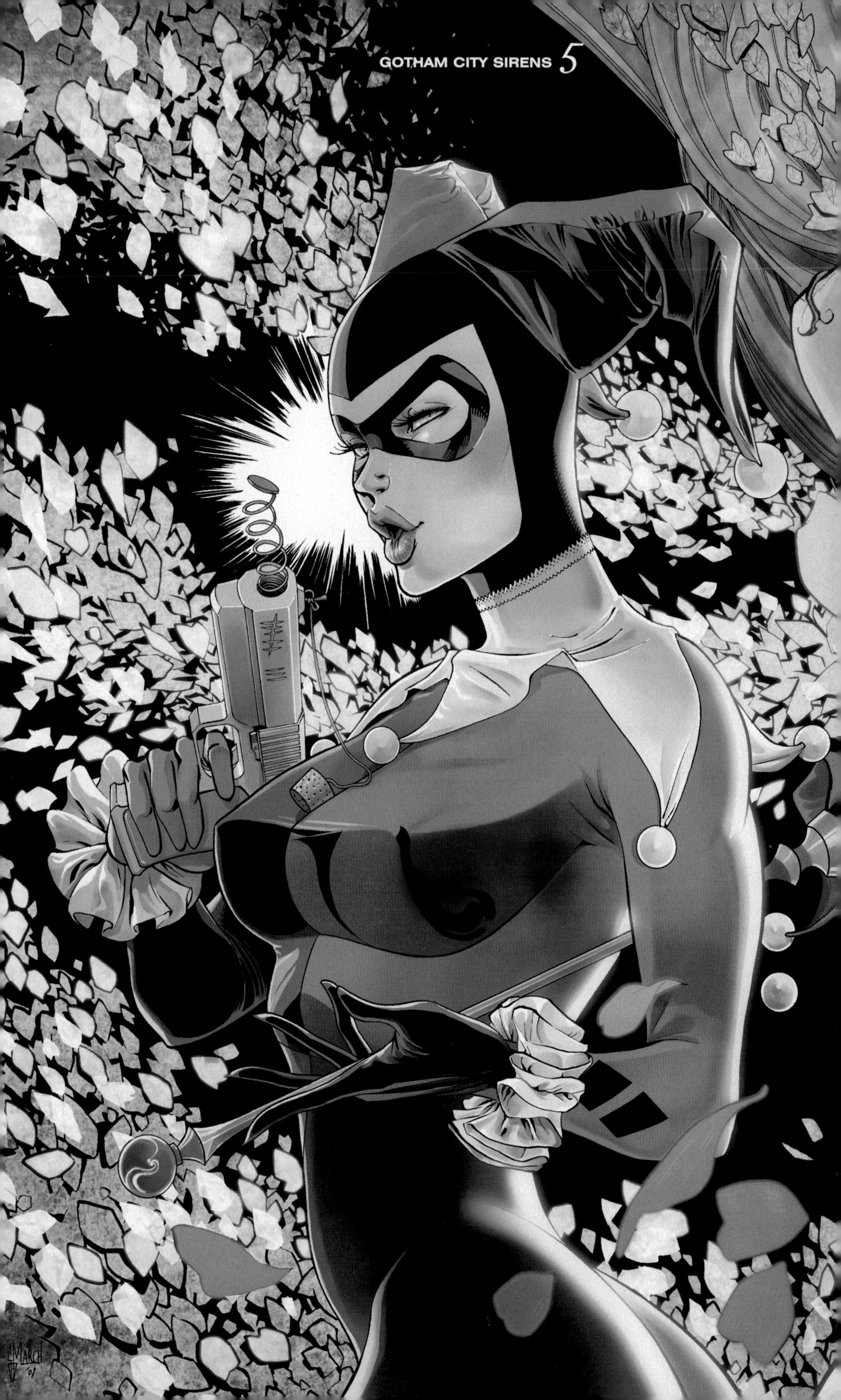
GOTHAM CITY SIRENS 5

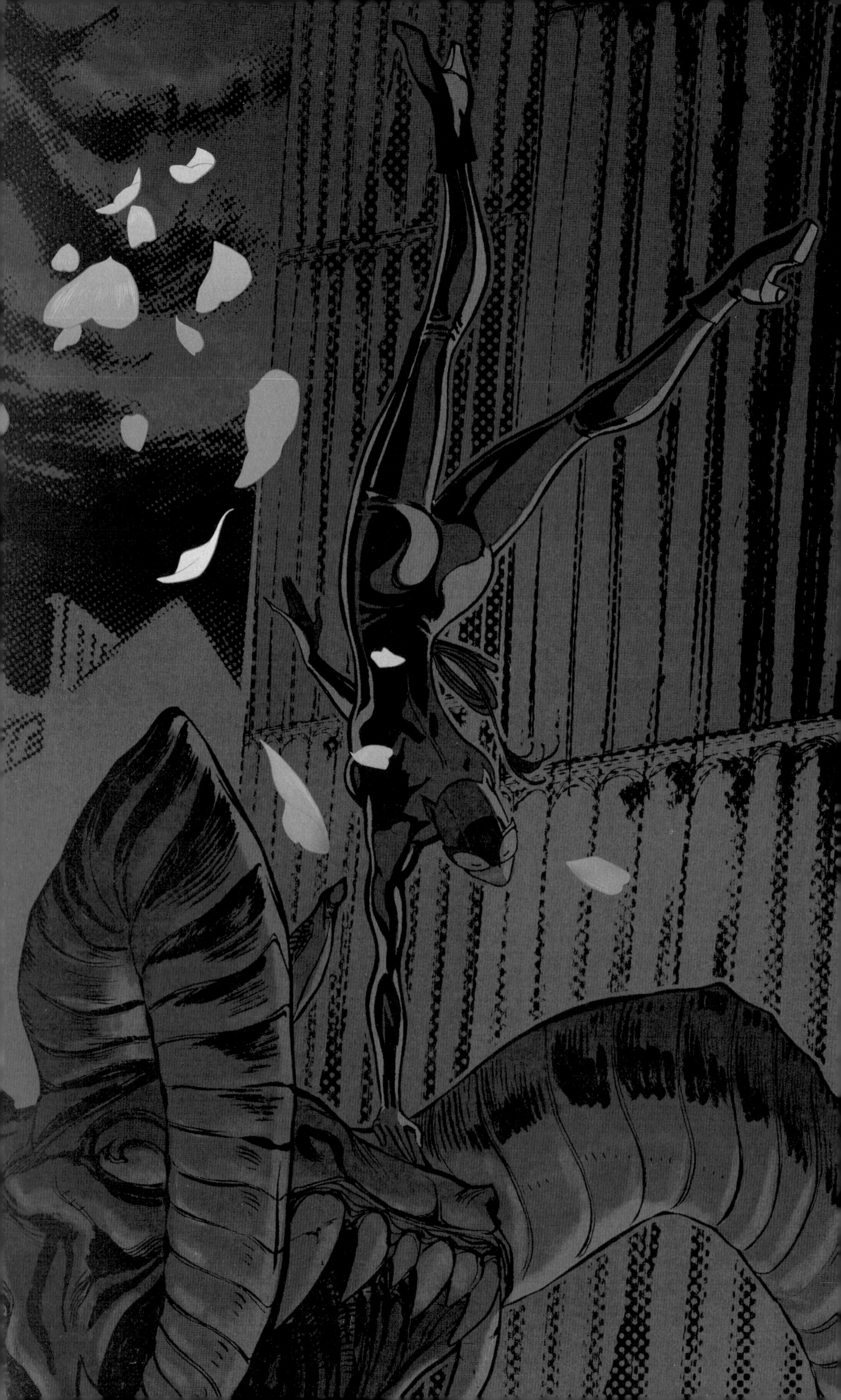

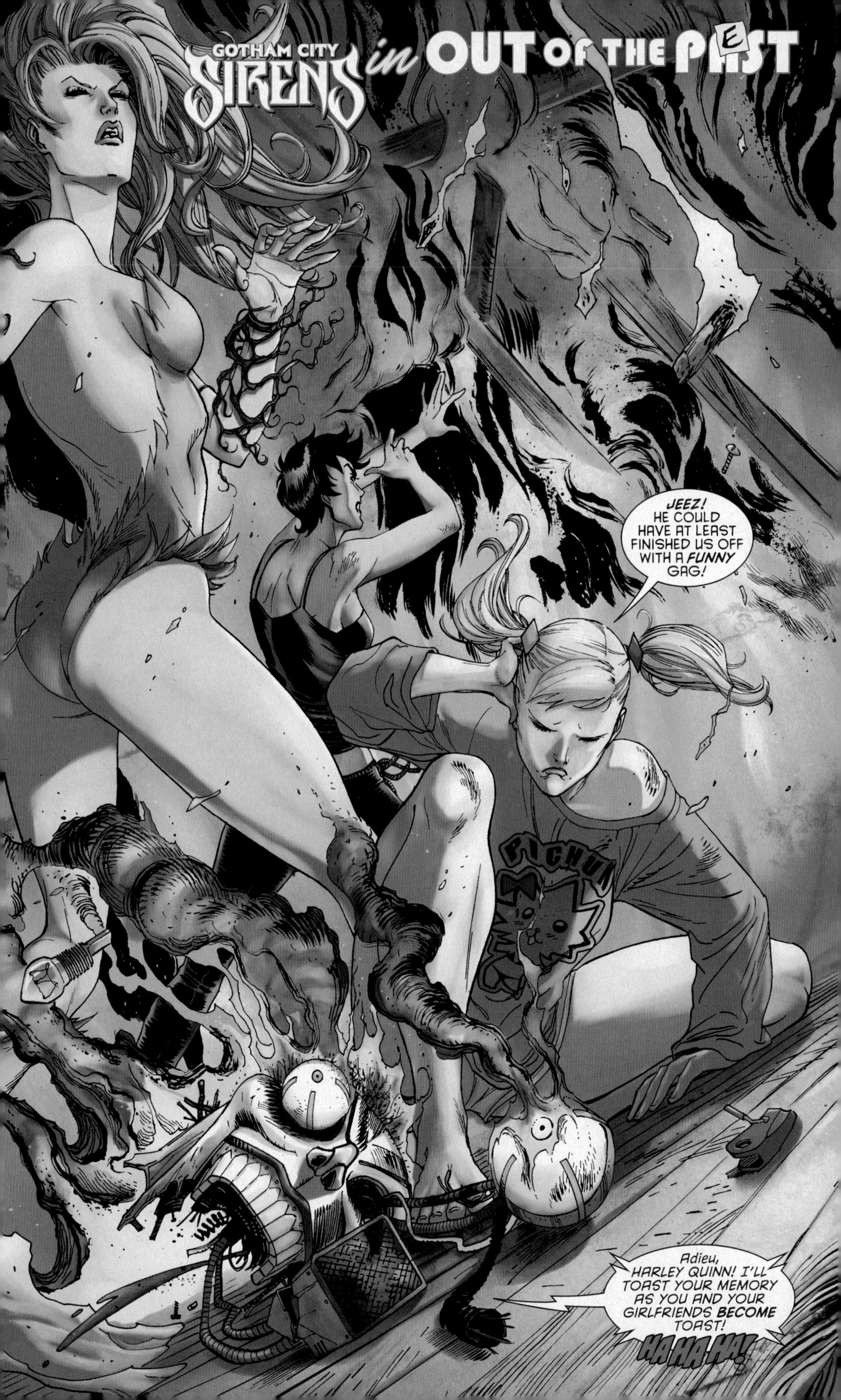
GOTHAM CITY SIRENS in OUT OF THE PAST
JEEZ! HE COULD HAVE AT LEAST FINISHED US OFF WITH A FUNNY GAG!
PICHU
Adieu, HARLEY QUINN! I'LL TOAST YOUR MEMORY AS YOU AND YOUR GIRLFRIENDS BECOME TOAST!
HA HA HA!

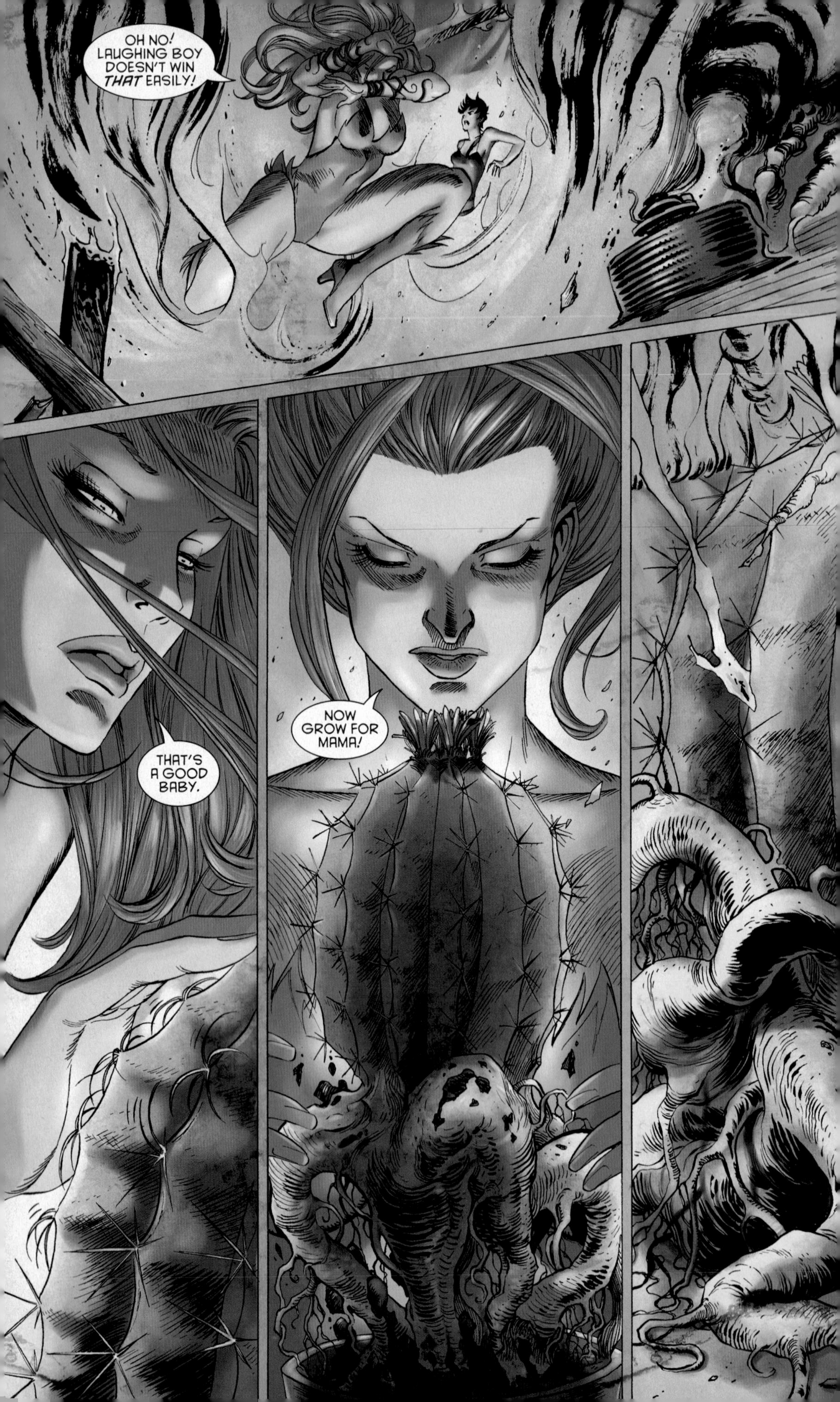
OH NO! LAUGHING BOY DOESN'T WIN *THAT* EASILY!
THAT'S A GOOD BABY.
NOW GROW FOR MAMA!

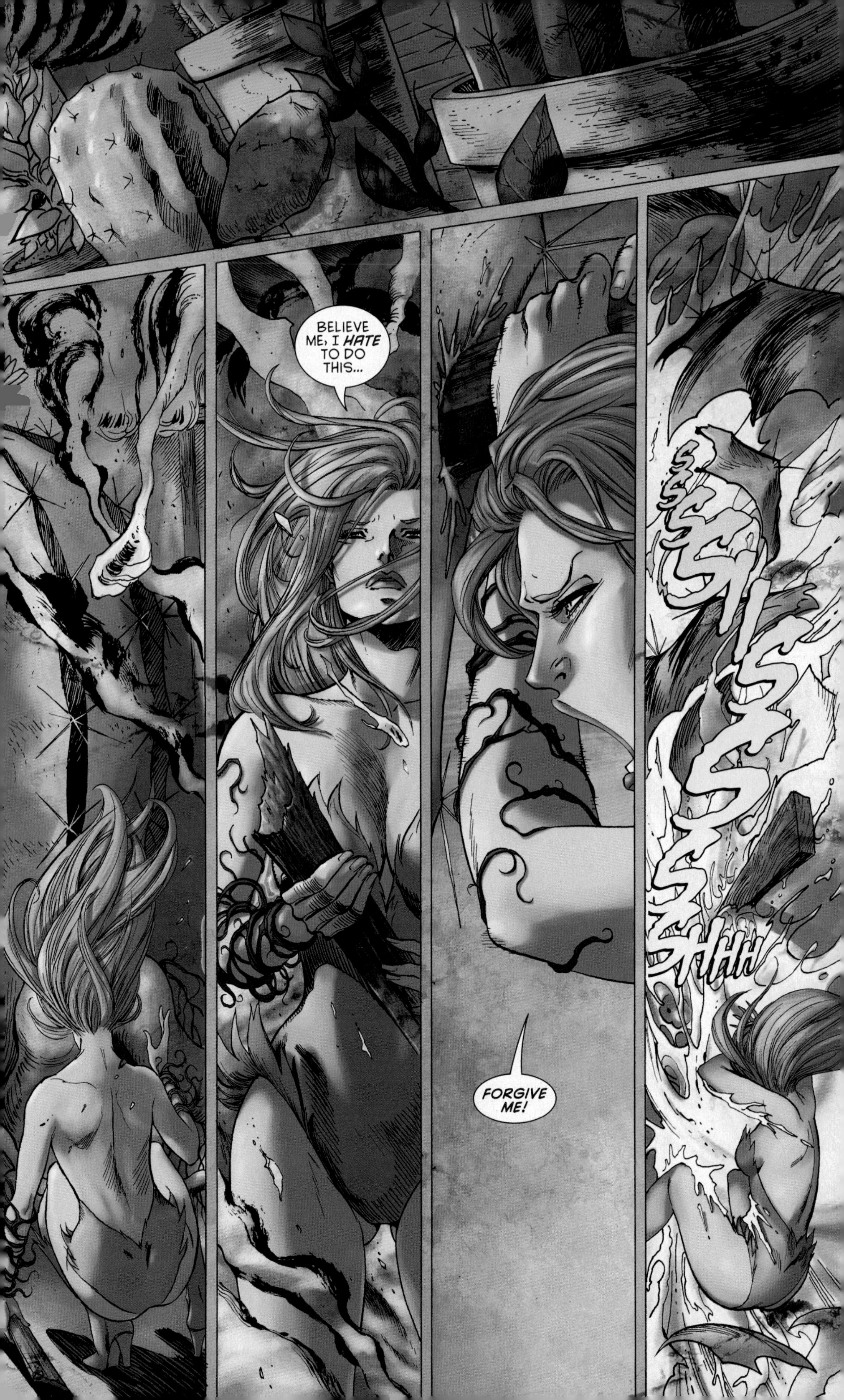
BELIEVE ME, I *HATE* TO DO THIS...
*FORGIVE ME!*

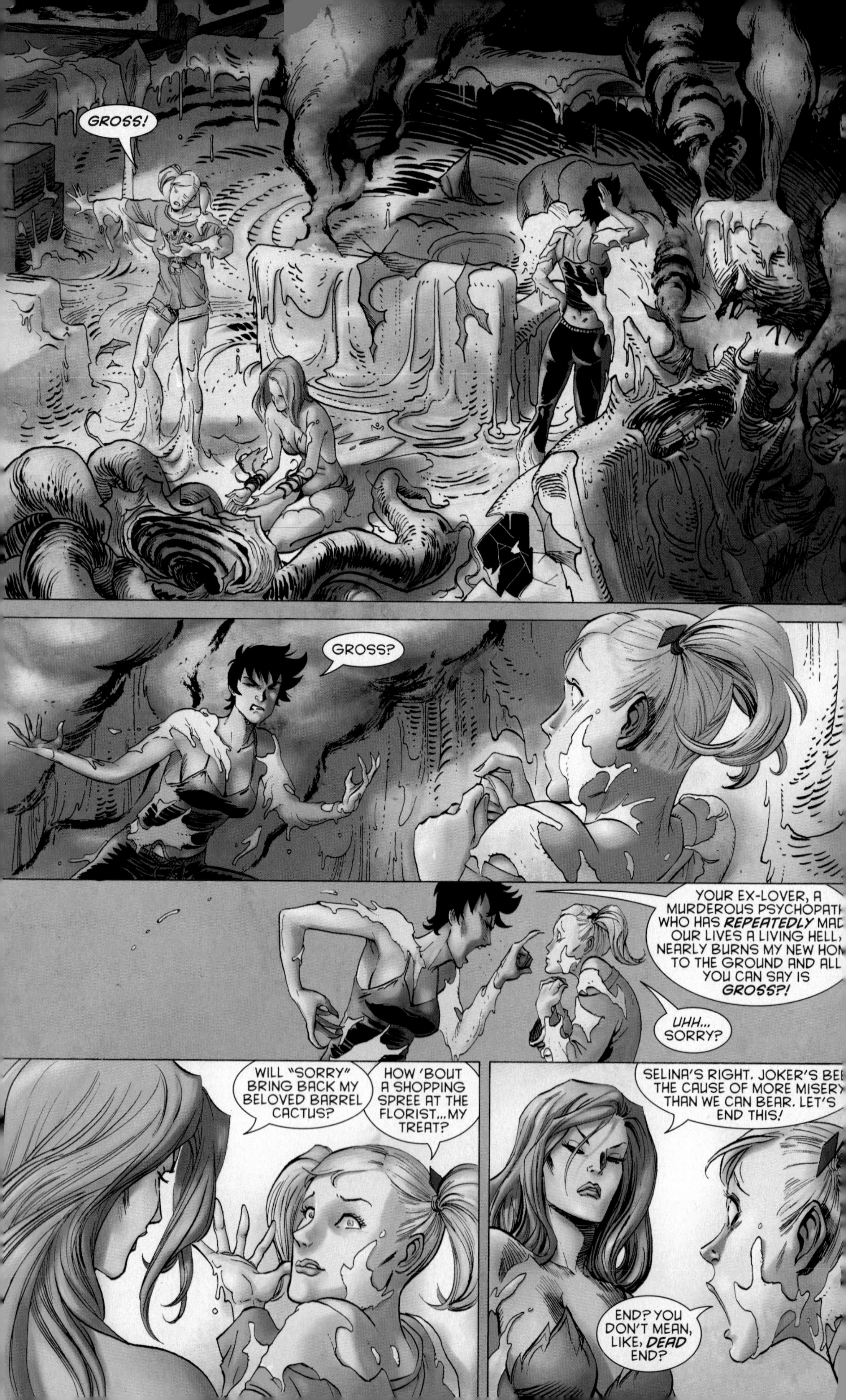

GROSS!
GROSS?
YOUR EX-LOVER, A MURDEROUS PSYCHOPAT WHO HAS *REPEATEDLY* MAD OUR LIVES A LIVING HELL, NEARLY BURNS MY NEW HOM TO THE GROUND AND ALL YOU CAN SAY IS ***GROSS?!***
UHH... SORRY?
WILL "SORRY" BRING BACK MY BELOVED BARREL CACTUS?
HOW 'BOUT A SHOPPING SPREE AT THE FLORIST...MY TREAT?
SELINA'S RIGHT. JOKER'S BEE THE CAUSE OF MORE MISERY THAN WE CAN BEAR. LET'S END THIS!
END? YOU DON'T MEAN, LIKE, *DEAD* END?

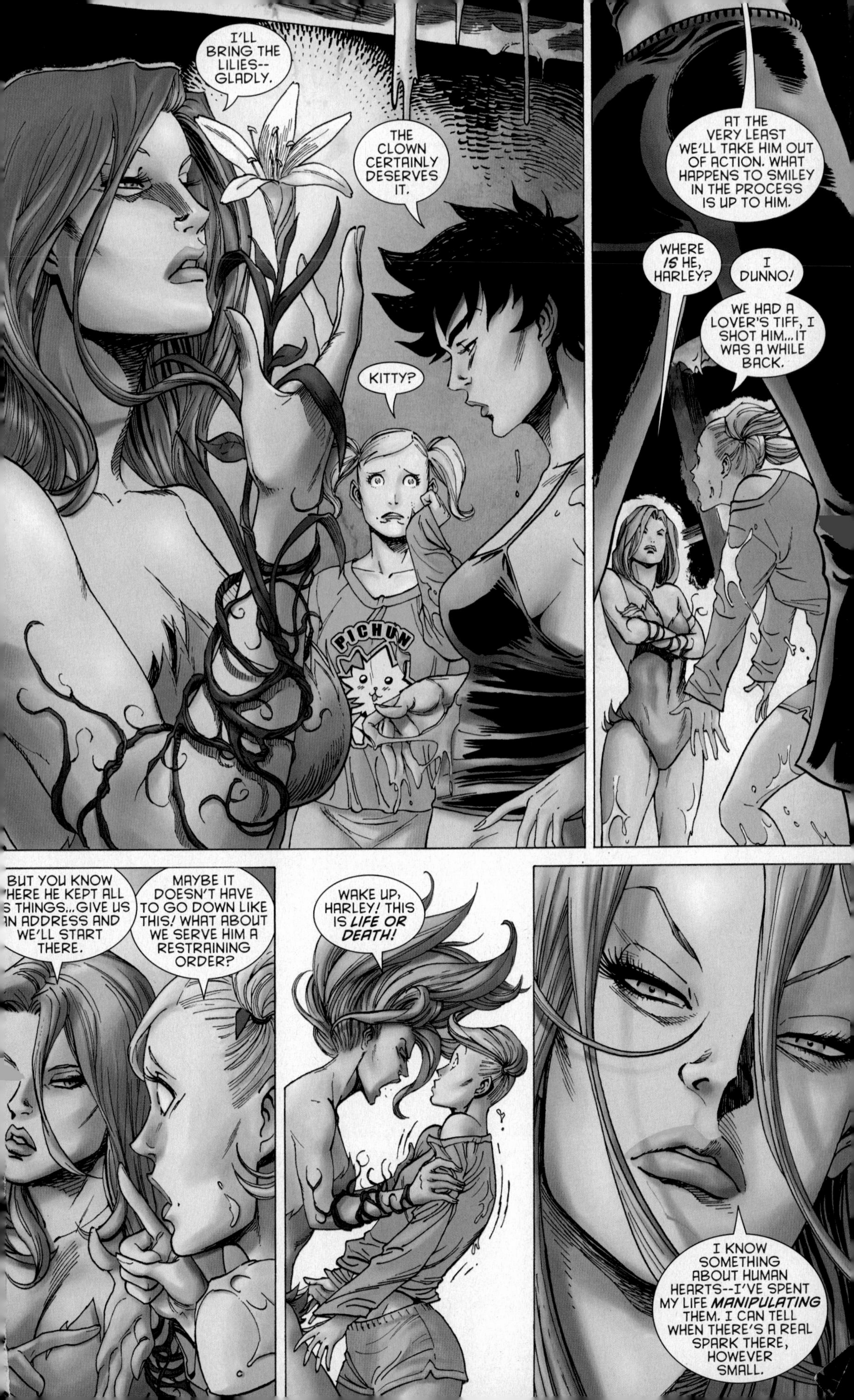
I'LL BRING THE LILIES--GLADLY.
THE CLOWN CERTAINLY DESERVES IT.
KITTY?
PICHUN
AT THE VERY LEAST WE'LL TAKE HIM OUT OF ACTION. WHAT HAPPENS TO SMILEY IN THE PROCESS IS UP TO HIM.
WHERE *IS* HE, HARLEY?
I DUNNO!
WE HAD A LOVER'S TIFF, I SHOT HIM...IT WAS A WHILE BACK.
BUT YOU KNOW HERE HE KEPT ALL S THINGS...GIVE US N ADDRESS AND WE'LL START THERE.
MAYBE IT DOESN'T HAVE TO GO DOWN LIKE THIS! WHAT ABOUT WE SERVE HIM A RESTRAINING ORDER?
WAKE UP, HARLEY! THIS IS ***LIFE OR DEATH!***
I KNOW SOMETHING ABOUT HUMAN HEARTS--I'VE SPENT MY LIFE ***MANIPULATING*** THEM. I CAN TELL WHEN THERE'S A REAL SPARK THERE, HOWEVER SMALL.

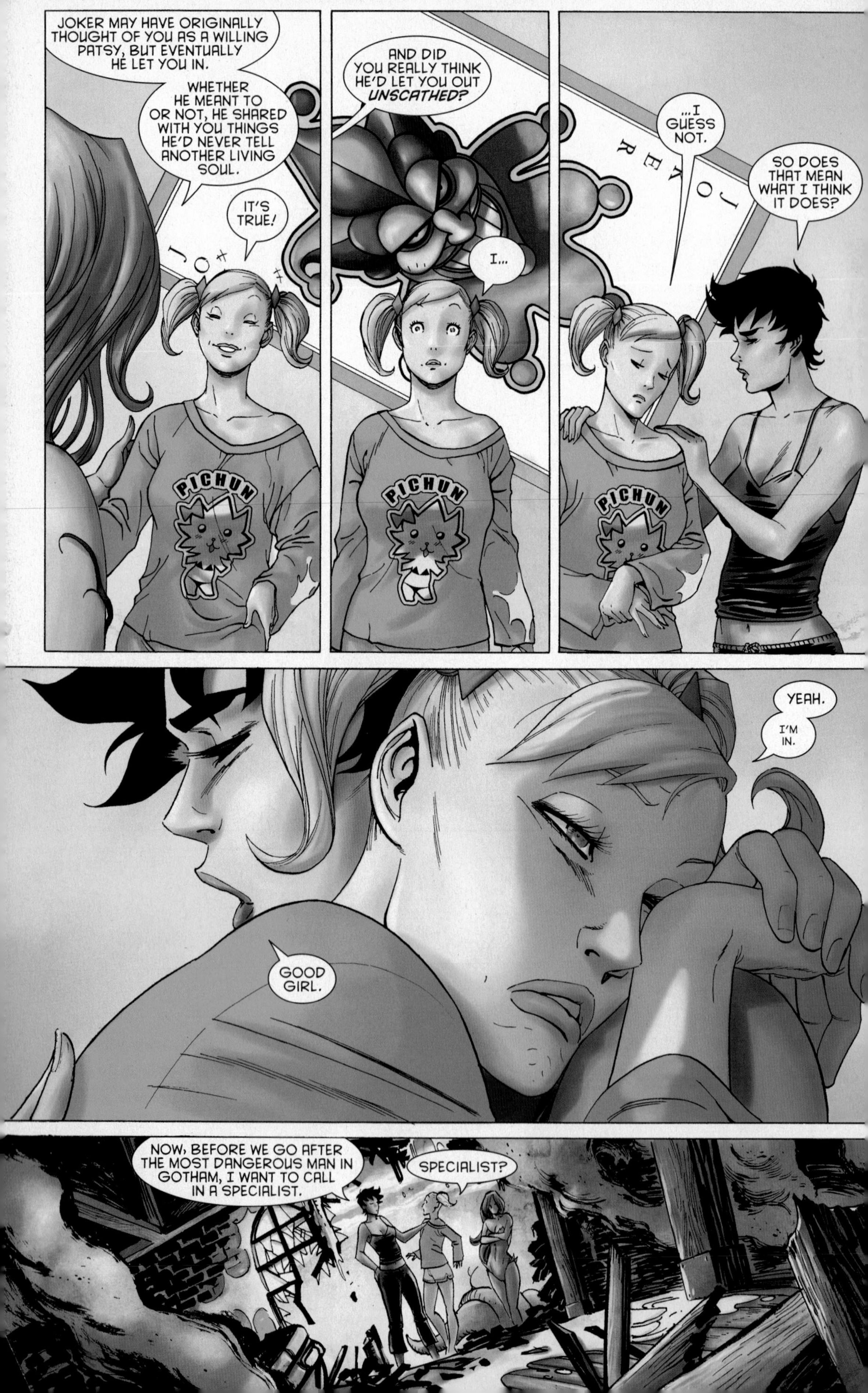
JOKER MAY HAVE ORIGINALLY THOUGHT OF YOU AS A WILLING PATSY, BUT EVENTUALLY HE LET YOU IN.
WHETHER HE MEANT TO OR NOT, HE SHARED WITH YOU THINGS HE'D NEVER TELL ANOTHER LIVING SOUL.
IT'S TRUE!
AND DID YOU REALLY THINK HE'D LET YOU OUT UNSCATHED?
I...
...I GUESS NOT.
SO DOES THAT MEAN WHAT I THINK IT DOES?
PICHUN
YEAH.
I'M IN.
GOOD GIRL.
NOW, BEFORE WE GO AFTER THE MOST DANGEROUS MAN IN GOTHAM, I WANT TO CALL IN A SPECIALIST.
SPECIALIST?

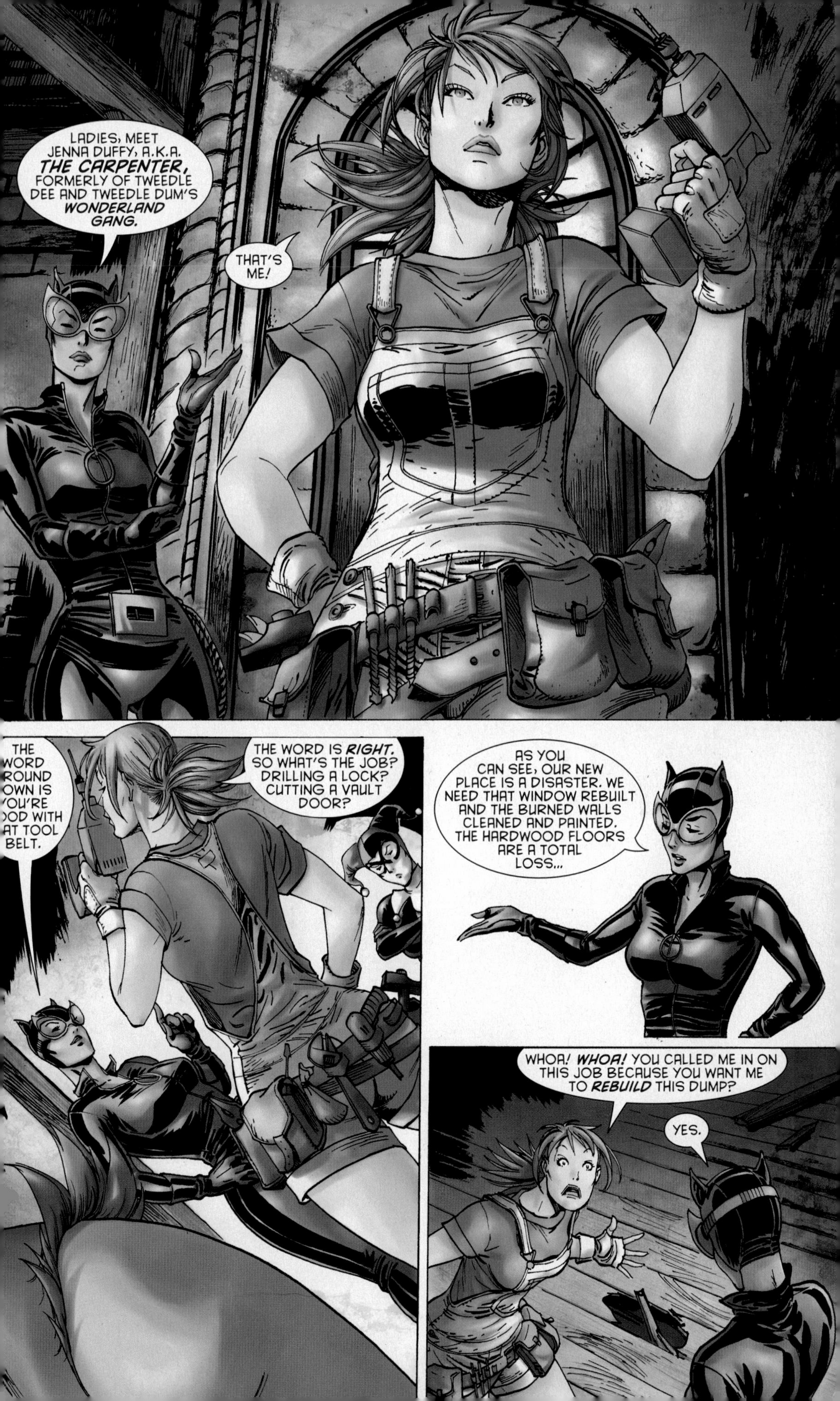

LADIES, MEET JENNA DUFFY, A.K.A. THE CARPENTER, FORMERLY OF TWEEDLE DEE AND TWEEDLE DUM'S WONDERLAND GANG.
THAT'S ME!
THE WORD ROUND OWN IS YOU'RE OOD WITH AT TOOL BELT.
THE WORD IS RIGHT. SO WHAT'S THE JOB? DRILLING A LOCK? CUTTING A VAULT DOOR?
AS YOU CAN SEE, OUR NEW PLACE IS A DISASTER. WE NEED THAT WINDOW REBUILT AND THE BURNED WALLS CLEANED AND PAINTED. THE HARDWOOD FLOORS ARE A TOTAL LOSS...
WHOA! WHOA! YOU CALLED ME IN ON THIS JOB BECAUSE YOU WANT ME TO REBUILD THIS DUMP?
YES.

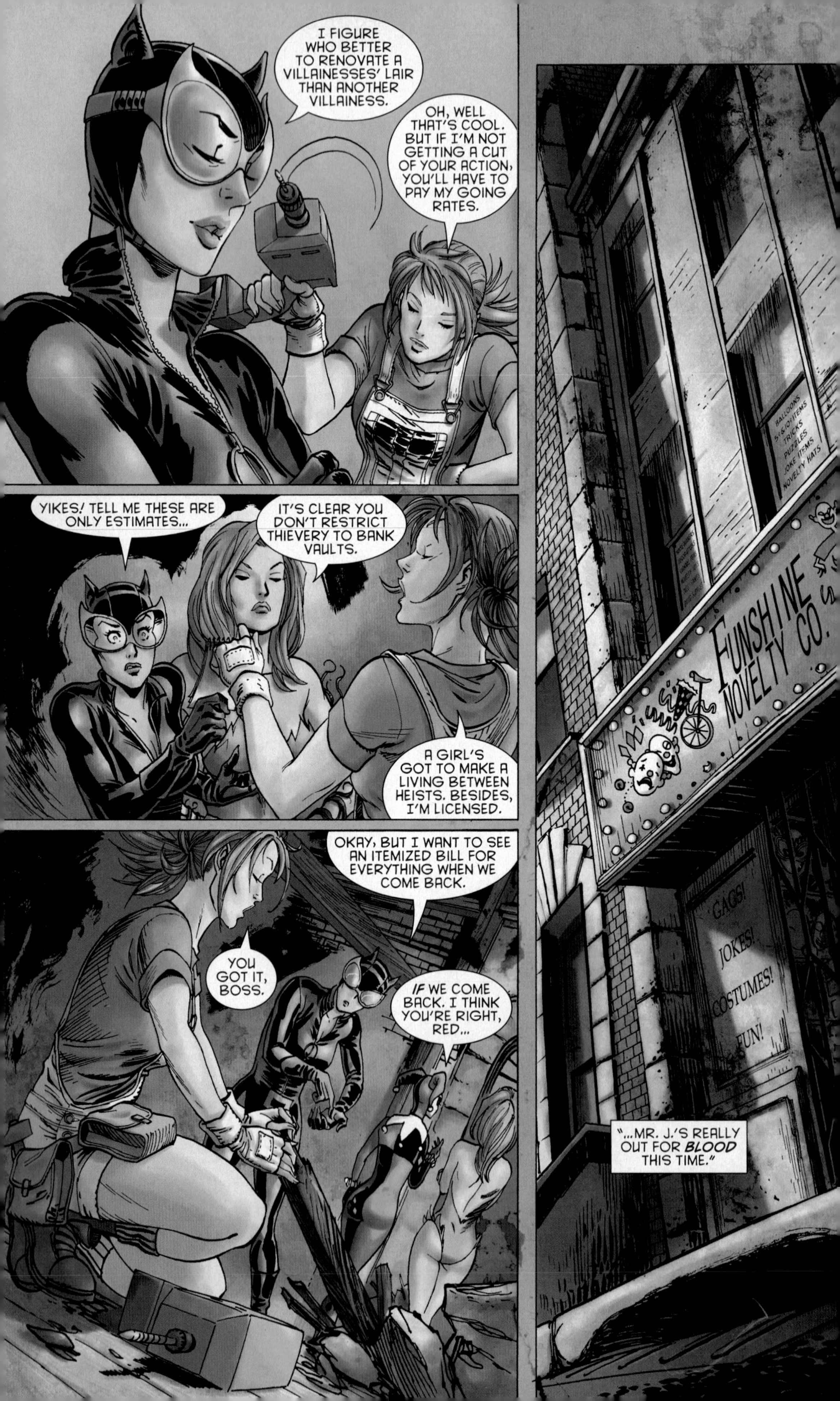
I FIGURE WHO BETTER TO RENOVATE A VILLAINESSES' LAIR THAN ANOTHER VILLAINESS.
OH, WELL THAT'S COOL. BUT IF I'M NOT GETTING A CUT OF YOUR ACTION, YOU'LL HAVE TO PAY MY GOING RATES.
YIKES! TELL ME THESE ARE ONLY ESTIMATES...
IT'S CLEAR YOU DON'T RESTRICT THIEVERY TO BANK VAULTS.
A GIRL'S GOT TO MAKE A LIVING BETWEEN HEISTS. BESIDES, I'M LICENSED.
OKAY, BUT I WANT TO SEE AN ITEMIZED BILL FOR EVERYTHING WHEN WE COME BACK.
YOU GOT IT, BOSS.
*IF* WE COME BACK. I THINK YOU'RE RIGHT, RED...
BALLOONS
5¢ & 10¢ ITEMS
TRICKS
PUZZLES
JOKE ITEMS
NOVELTY HATS
FUNSHINE NOVELTY CO.
GAGS!
JOKES!
COSTUMES!
FUN!
"...MR. J.'S REALLY OUT FOR *BLOOD* THIS TIME."

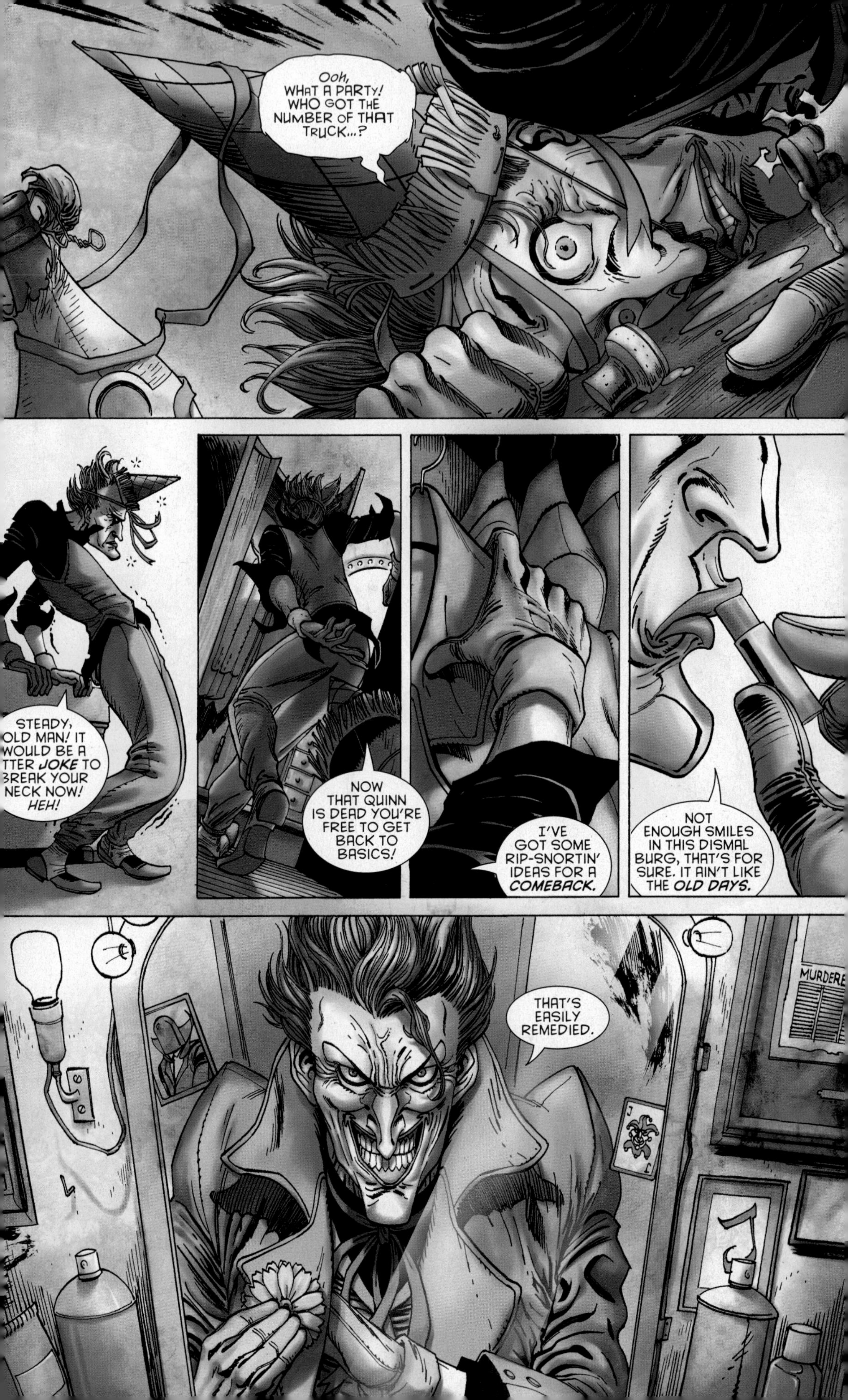

Ooh, WHAT A PARTY! WHO GOT THE NUMBER OF THAT TRUCK...?
STEADY, OLD MAN! IT WOULD BE A TTER *JOKE* TO BREAK YOUR NECK NOW! *HEH!*
NOW THAT QUINN IS DEAD YOU'RE FREE TO GET BACK TO BASICS!
I'VE GOT SOME RIP-SNORTIN' IDEAS FOR A *COMEBACK.*
NOT ENOUGH SMILES IN THIS DISMAL BURG, THAT'S FOR SURE. IT AIN'T LIKE THE *OLD DAYS.*
MURDERE
THAT'S EASILY REMEDIED.

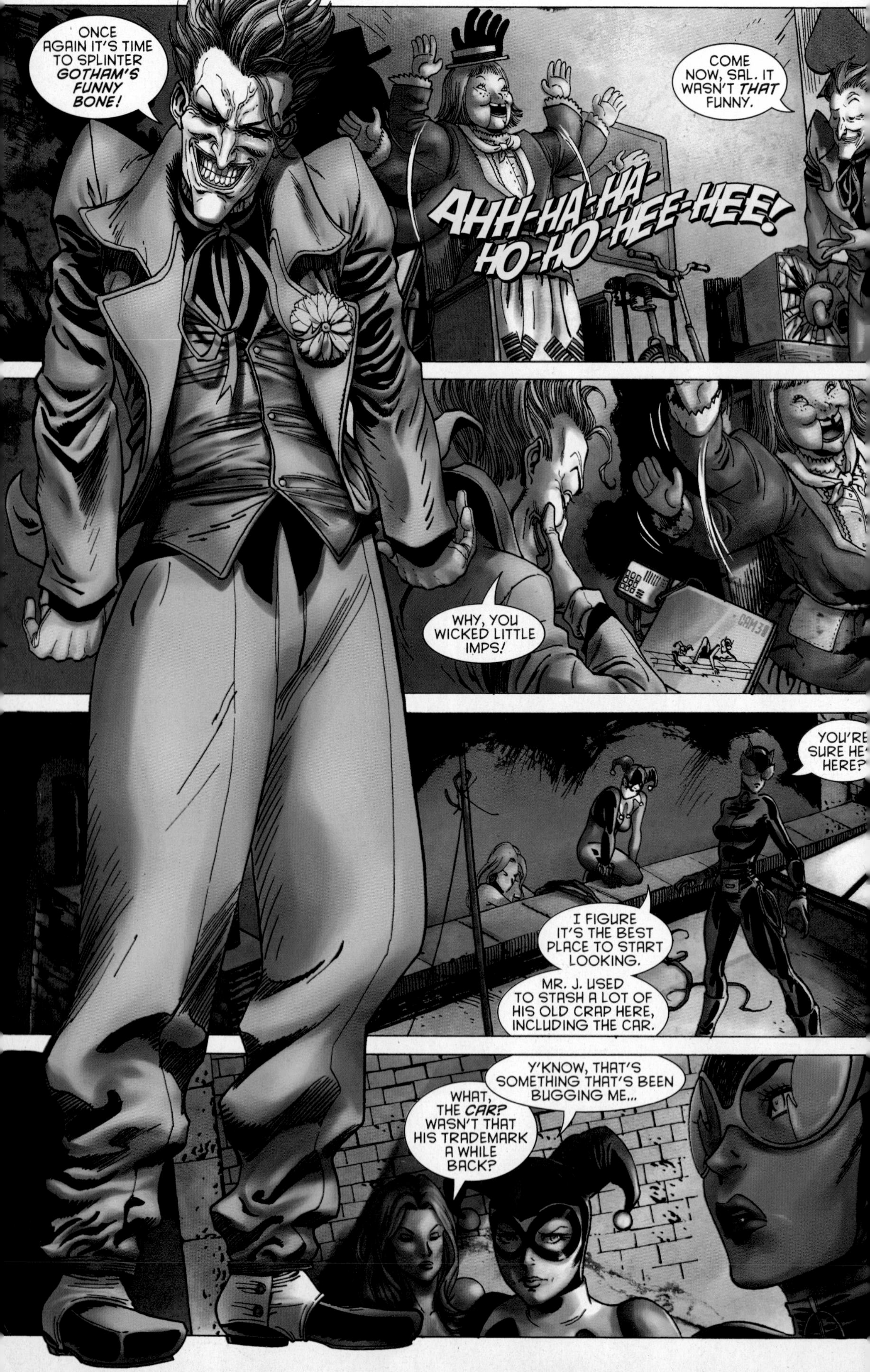
ONCE AGAIN IT'S TIME TO SPLINTER *GOTHAM'S FUNNY BONE!*
AHH-HA-HA-HO-HO-HEE-HEE!
COME NOW, SAL. IT WASN'T *THAT* FUNNY.
WHY, YOU WICKED LITTLE IMPS!
CAM3
YOU'RE SURE HE'S HERE?
I FIGURE IT'S THE BEST PLACE TO START LOOKING.
MR. J. USED TO STASH A LOT OF HIS OLD CRAP HERE, INCLUDING THE CAR.
WHAT, THE *CAR?* WASN'T THAT HIS TRADEMARK A WHILE BACK?
Y'KNOW, THAT'S SOMETHING THAT'S BEEN BUGGING ME...

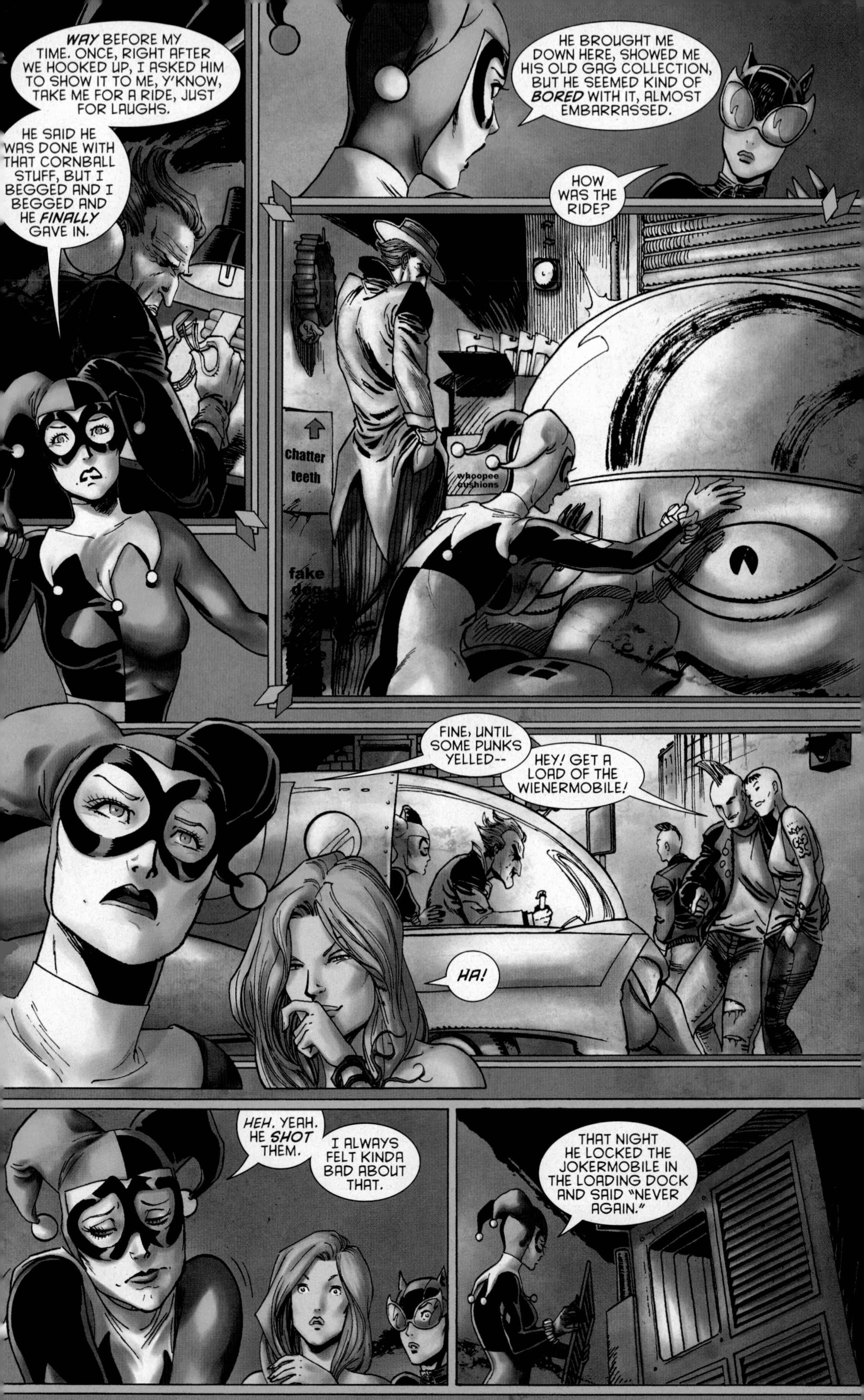

WAY BEFORE MY TIME. ONCE, RIGHT AFTER WE HOOKED UP, I ASKED HIM TO SHOW IT TO ME, Y'KNOW, TAKE ME FOR A RIDE, JUST FOR LAUGHS.
HE SAID HE WAS DONE WITH THAT CORNBALL STUFF, BUT I BEGGED AND I BEGGED AND HE FINALLY GAVE IN.
HE BROUGHT ME DOWN HERE, SHOWED ME HIS OLD GAG COLLECTION, BUT HE SEEMED KIND OF BORED WITH IT, ALMOST EMBARRASSED.
HOW WAS THE RIDE?
chatter teeth
whoopee cushions
fake
FINE, UNTIL SOME PUNKS YELLED--
HEY! GET A LOAD OF THE WIENERMOBILE!
HA!
HEH. YEAH. HE SHOT THEM.
I ALWAYS FELT KINDA BAD ABOUT THAT.
THAT NIGHT HE LOCKED THE JOKERMOBILE IN THE LOADING DOCK AND SAID "NEVER AGAIN."

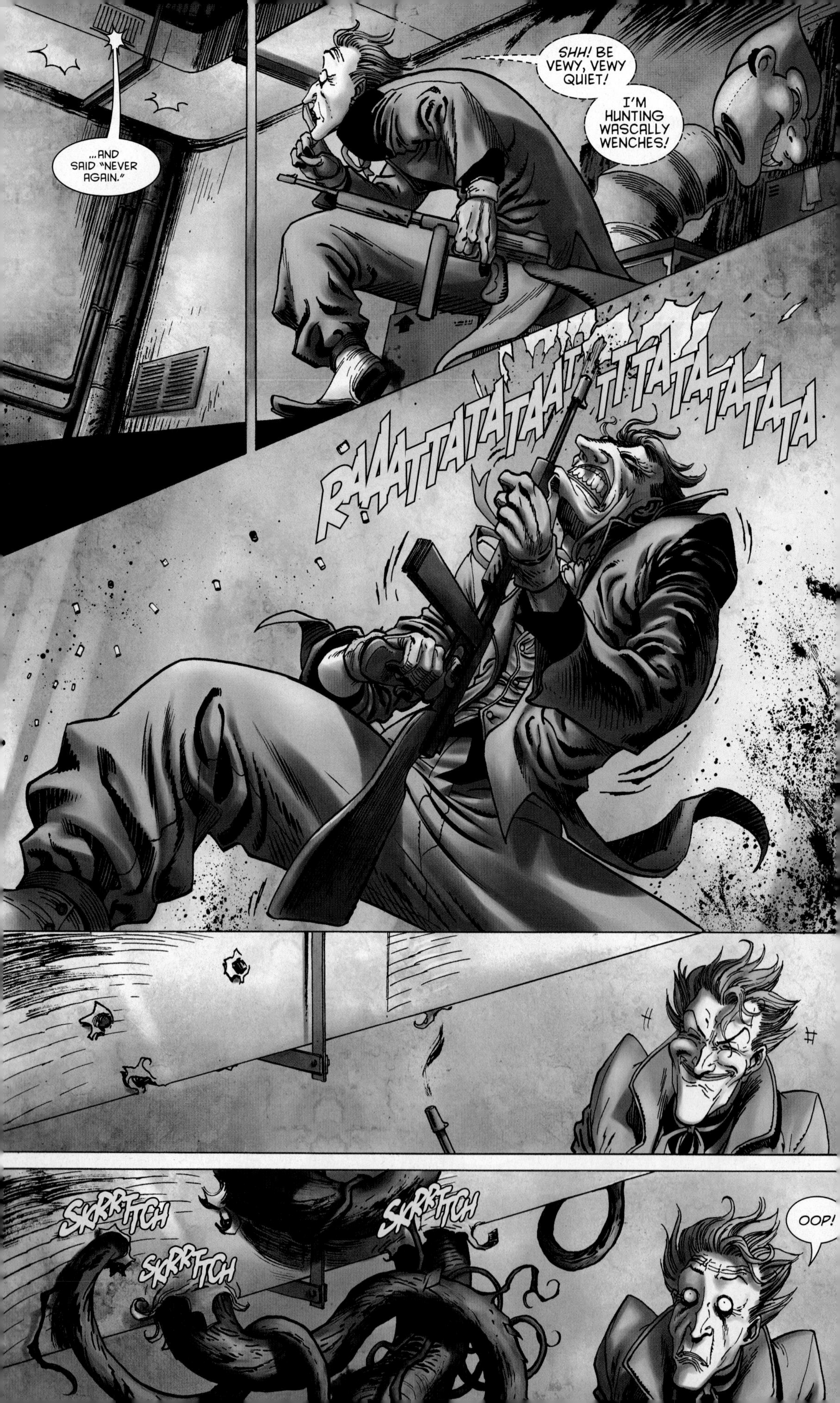
...AND SAID "NEVER AGAIN."
SHH! BE VEWY, VEWY QUIET!
I'M HUNTING WASCALLY WENCHES!
RAAATTATATAAT TTTATATATATATA
SKRRTTCH
SKRRTTCH
SKRRTTCH
OOP!

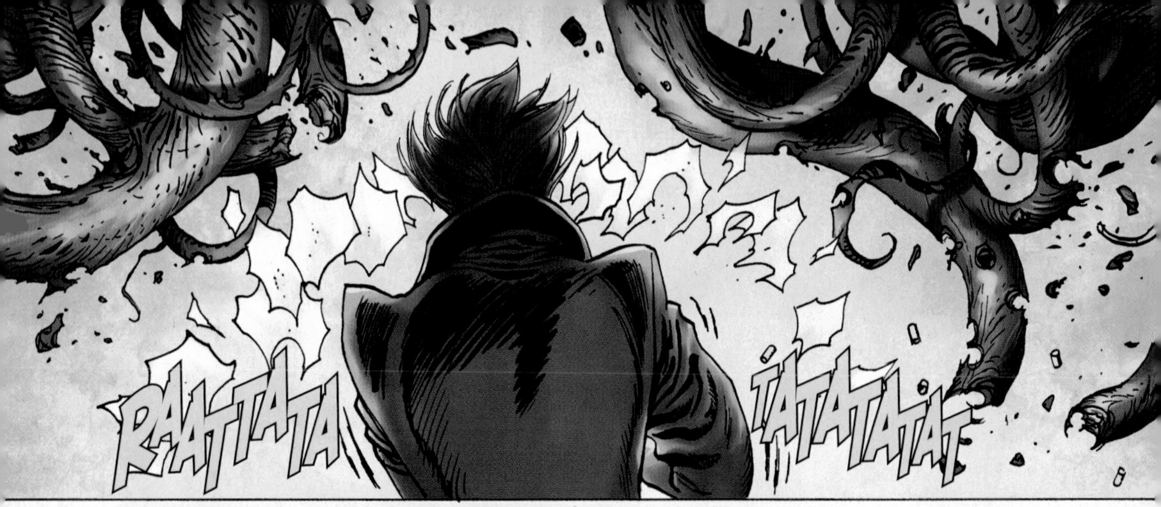
RAATTATA
TATATATAT

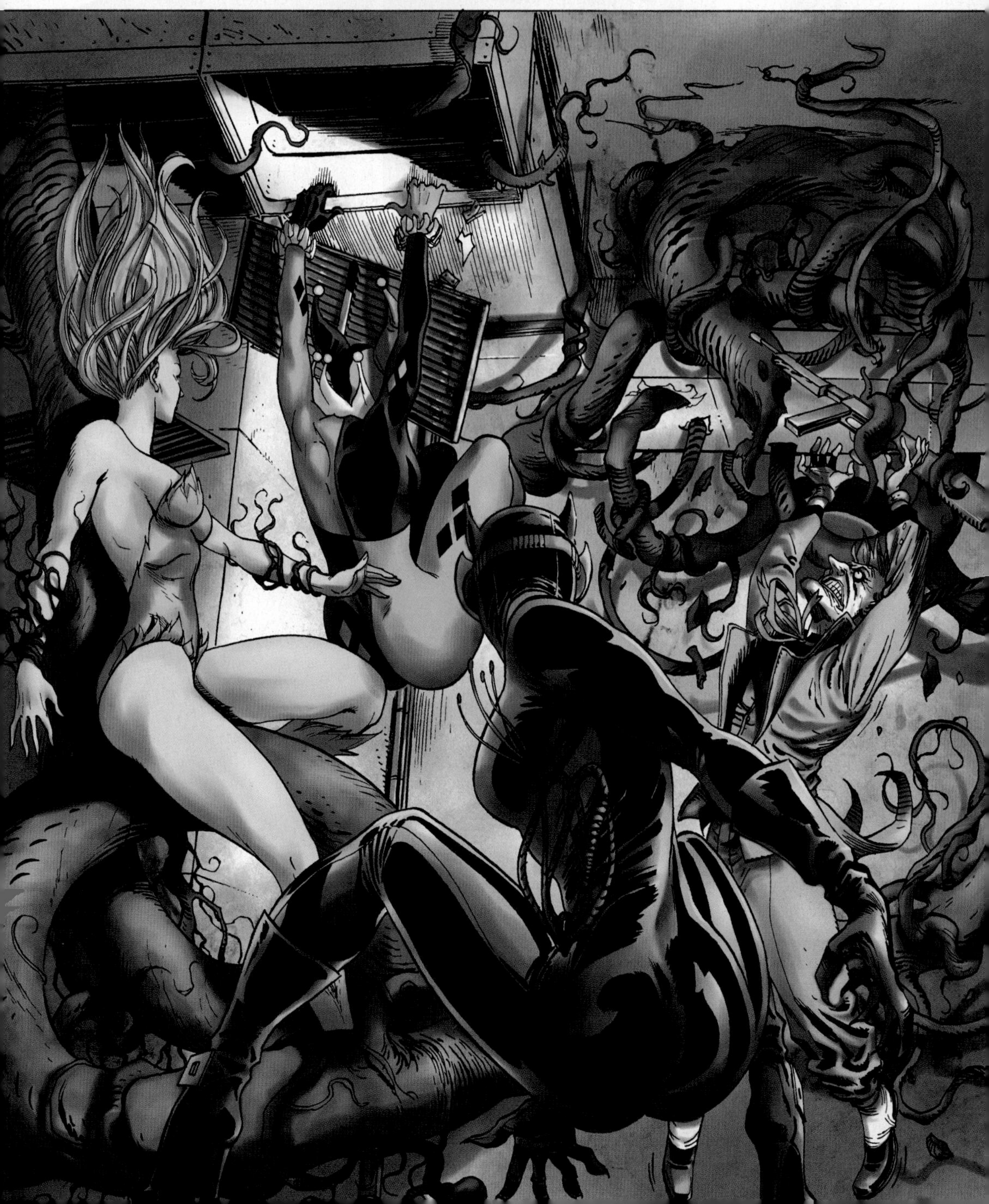

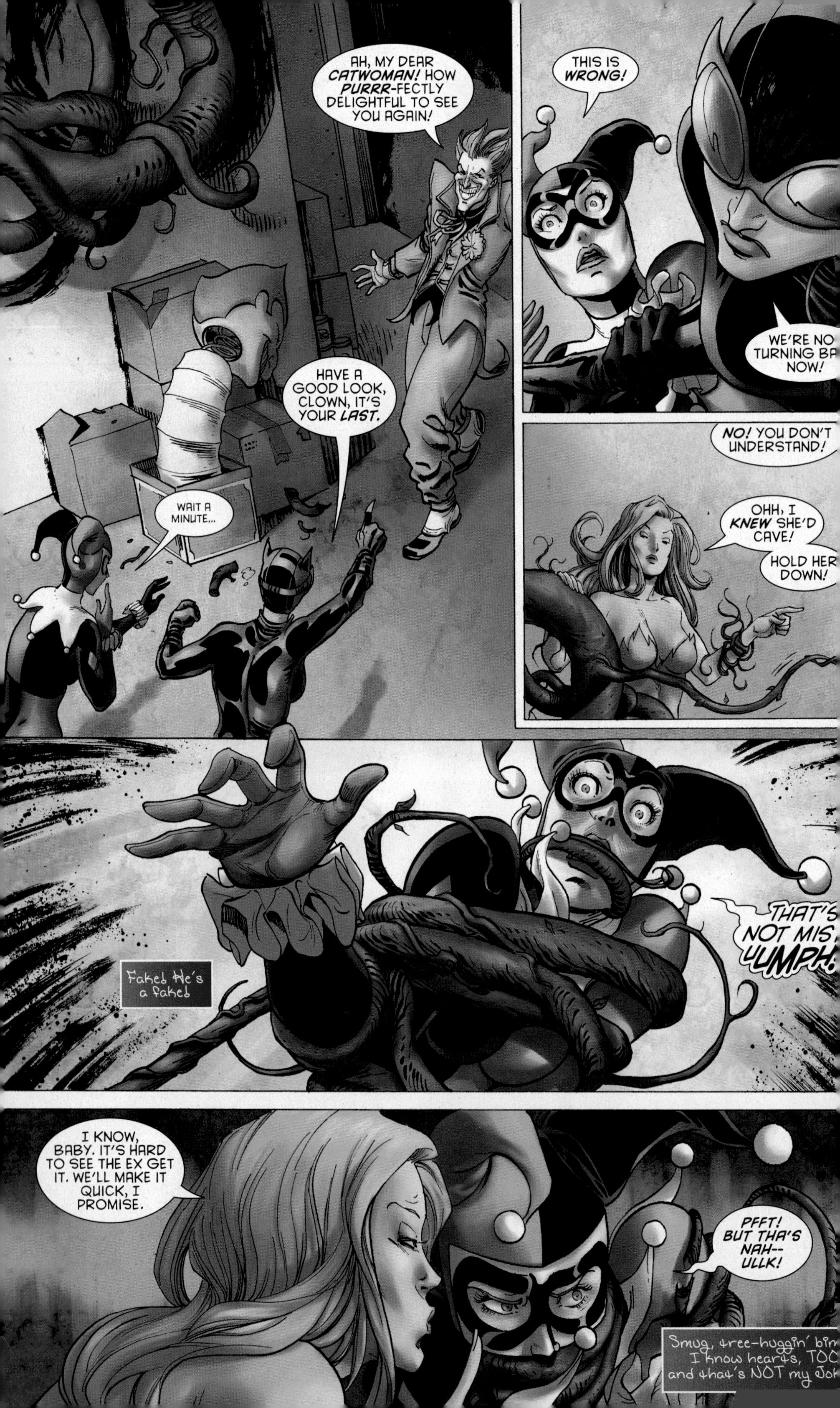
AH, MY DEAR CATWOMAN! HOW PURRR-FECTLY DELIGHTFUL TO SEE YOU AGAIN!
HAVE A GOOD LOOK, CLOWN, IT'S YOUR LAST.
WAIT A MINUTE...
THIS IS WRONG!
WE'RE NO TURNING B NOW!
NO! YOU DON'T UNDERSTAND!
OHH, I KNEW SHE'D CAVE!
HOLD HER DOWN!
Fake! He's a fake!
THAT'S NOT MIS UUMPH!
I KNOW, BABY. IT'S HARD TO SEE THE EX GET IT. WE'LL MAKE IT QUICK, I PROMISE.
PFFT! BUT THA'S NAH-- ULLK!
Smug, tree-huggin' bi I know hearts, TO and that's NOT my Jo

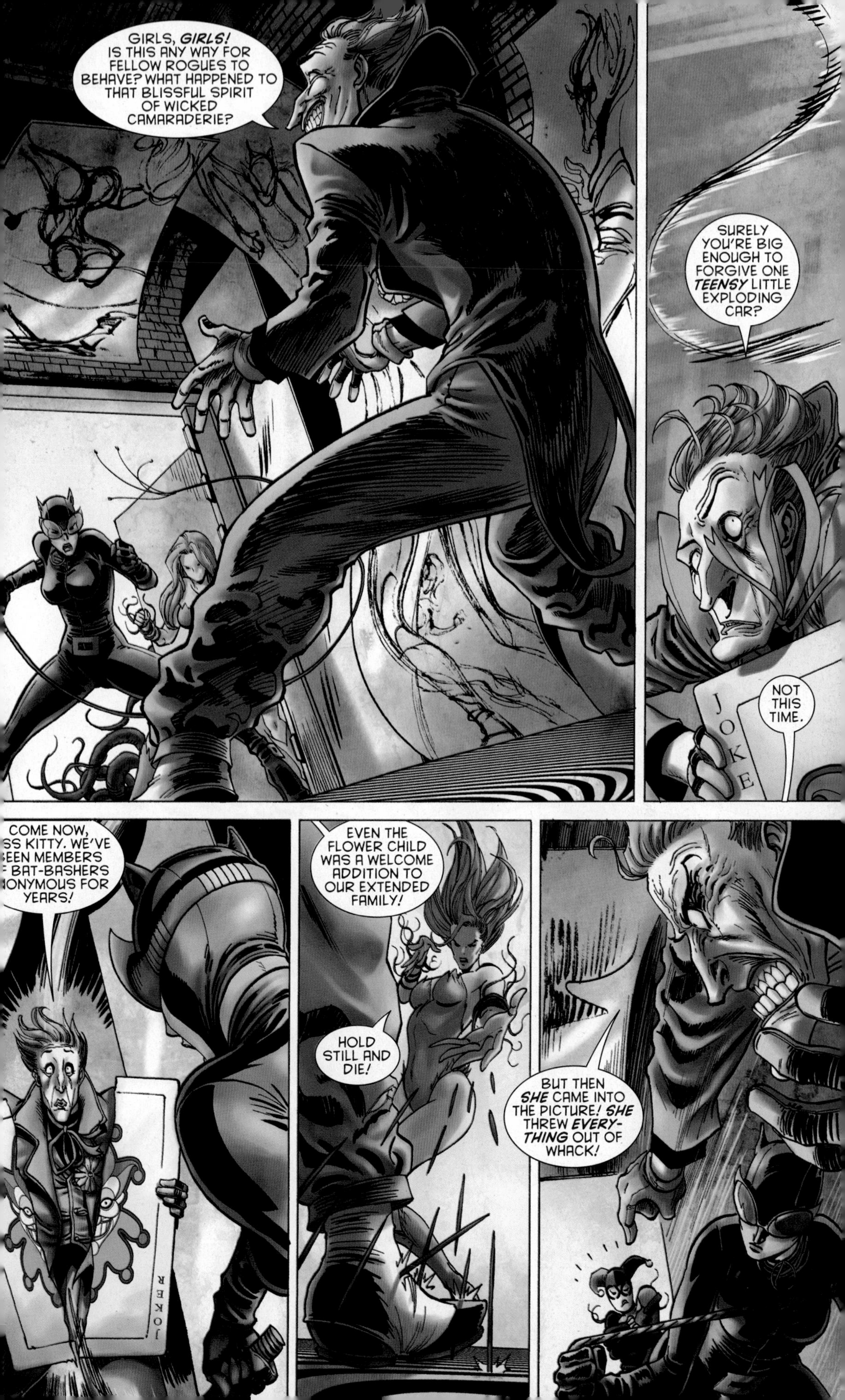
GIRLS, ***GIRLS!*** IS THIS ANY WAY FOR FELLOW ROGUES TO BEHAVE? WHAT HAPPENED TO THAT BLISSFUL SPIRIT OF WICKED CAMARADERIE?
SURELY YOU'RE BIG ENOUGH TO FORGIVE ONE ***TEENSY*** LITTLE EXPLODING CAR?
NOT THIS TIME.
COME NOW, SS KITTY. WE'VE EEN MEMBERS F BAT-BASHERS NONYMOUS FOR YEARS!
EVEN THE FLOWER CHILD WAS A WELCOME ADDITION TO OUR EXTENDED FAMILY!
HOLD STILL AND DIE!
BUT THEN ***SHE*** CAME INTO THE PICTURE! ***SHE*** THREW ***EVERY-THING*** OUT OF WHACK!

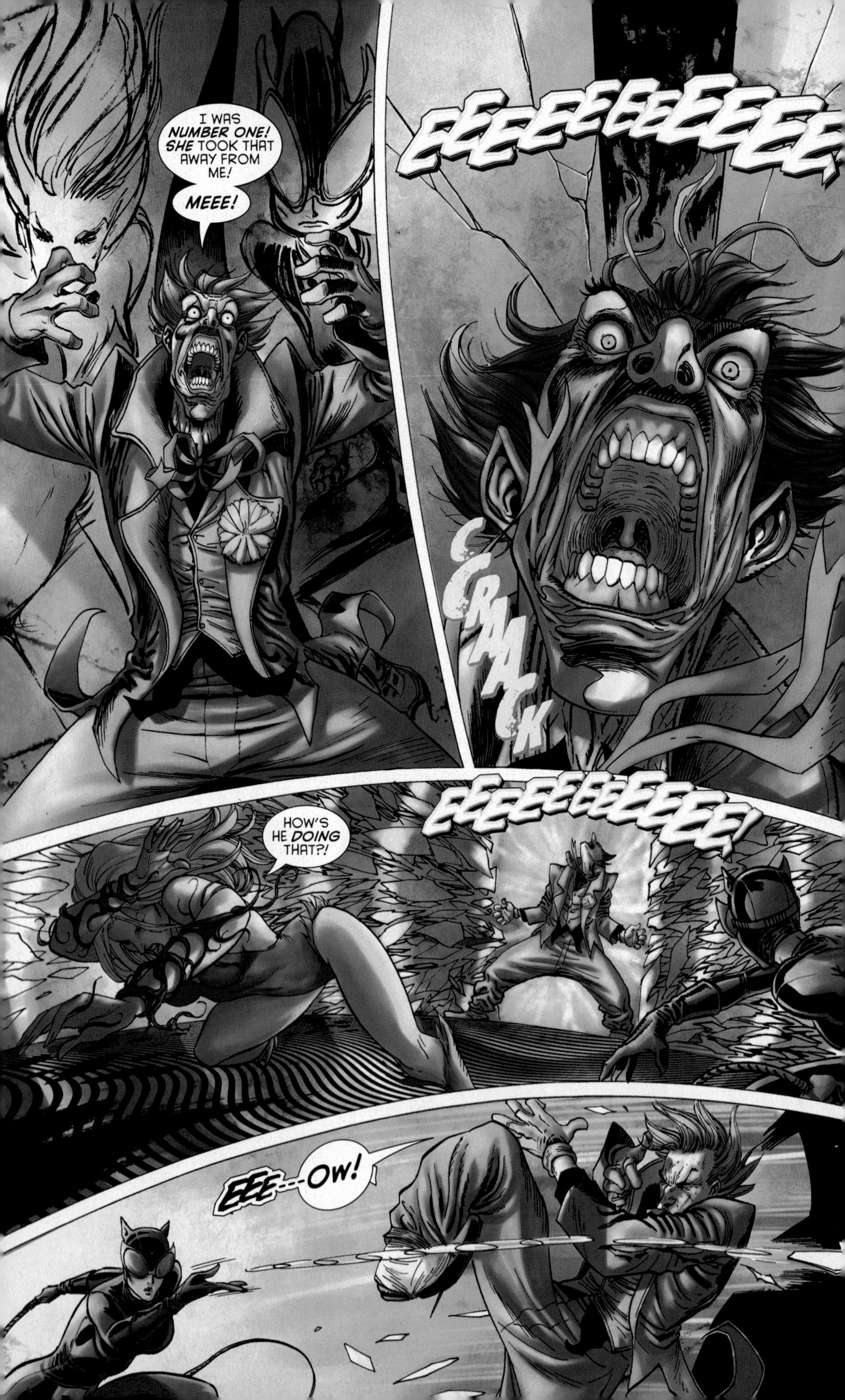
I WAS *NUMBER ONE!* *SHE* TOOK THAT AWAY FROM ME!
*MEEE!*
EEEEEEEEEEEE
CRAAACK
EEEEEEEEEEEEEE!
HOW'S HE *DOING* THAT?!
EEE---OW!

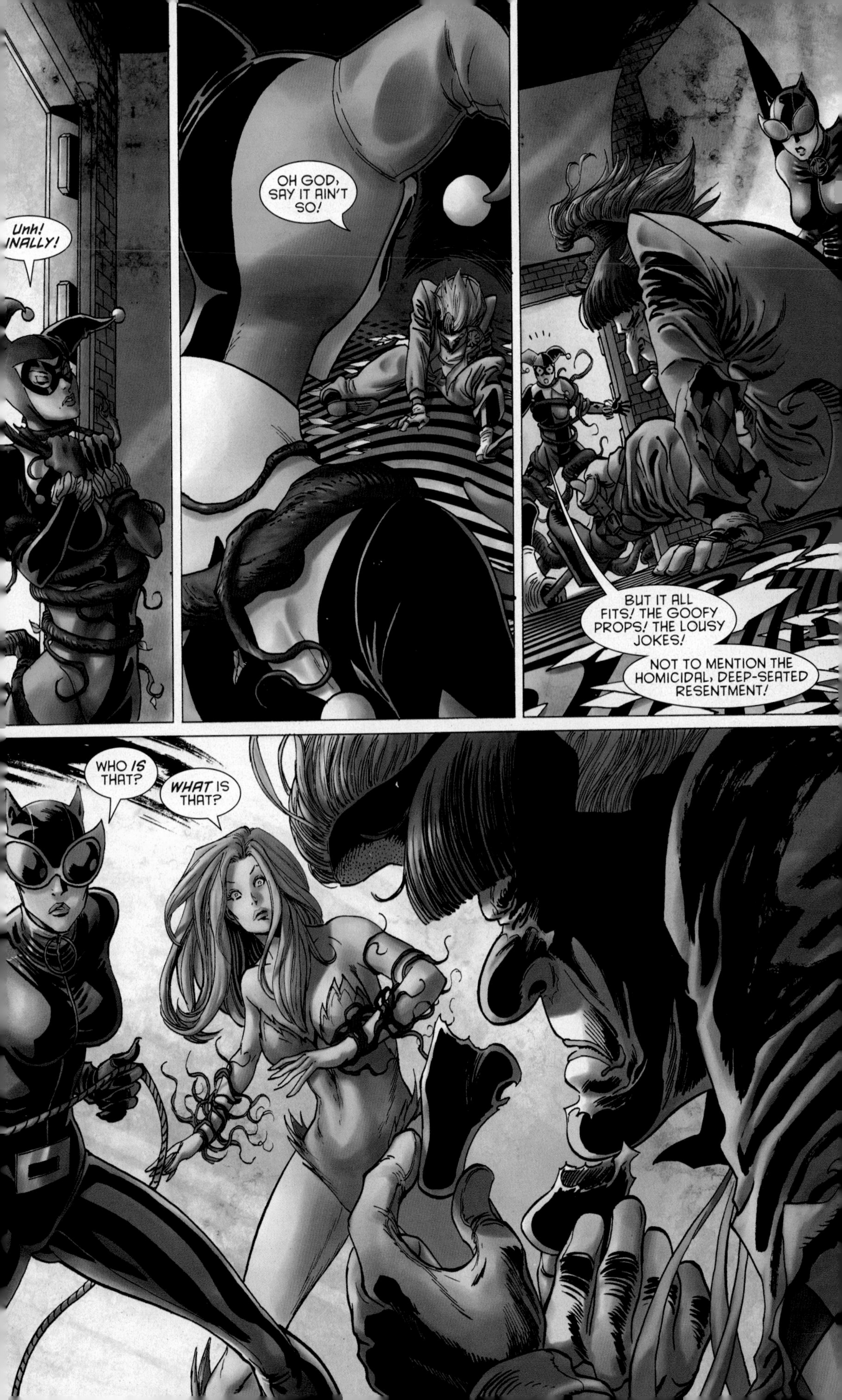

Unh! INALLY!
OH GOD, SAY IT AIN'T SO!
BUT IT ALL FITS! THE GOOFY PROPS! THE LOUSY JOKES!
NOT TO MENTION THE HOMICIDAL, DEEP-SEATED RESENTMENT!
WHO IS THAT?
WHAT IS THAT?

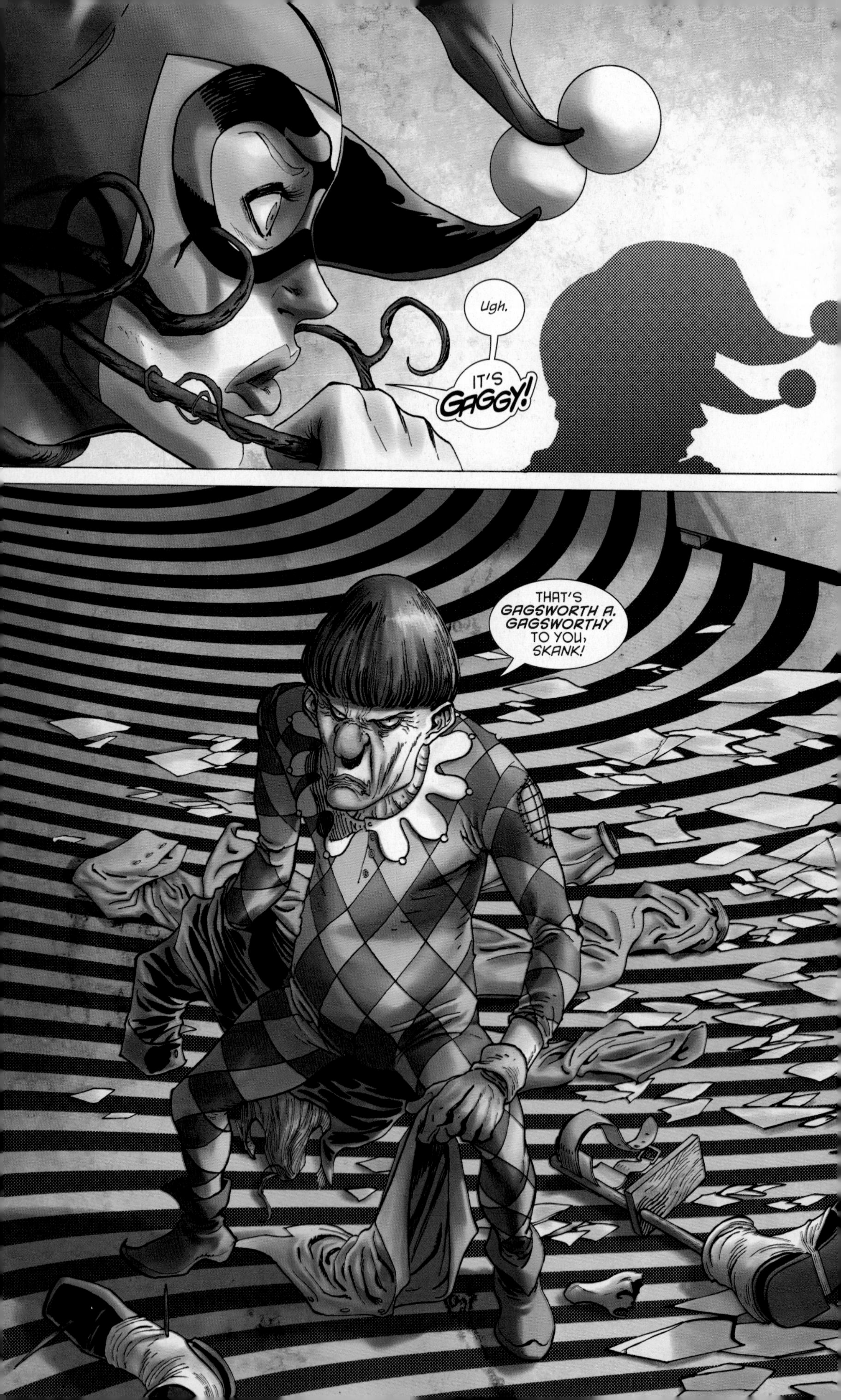

Ugh.
IT'S GAGGY!
THAT'S GAGSWORTH A. GAGSWORTHY TO YOU, SKANK!

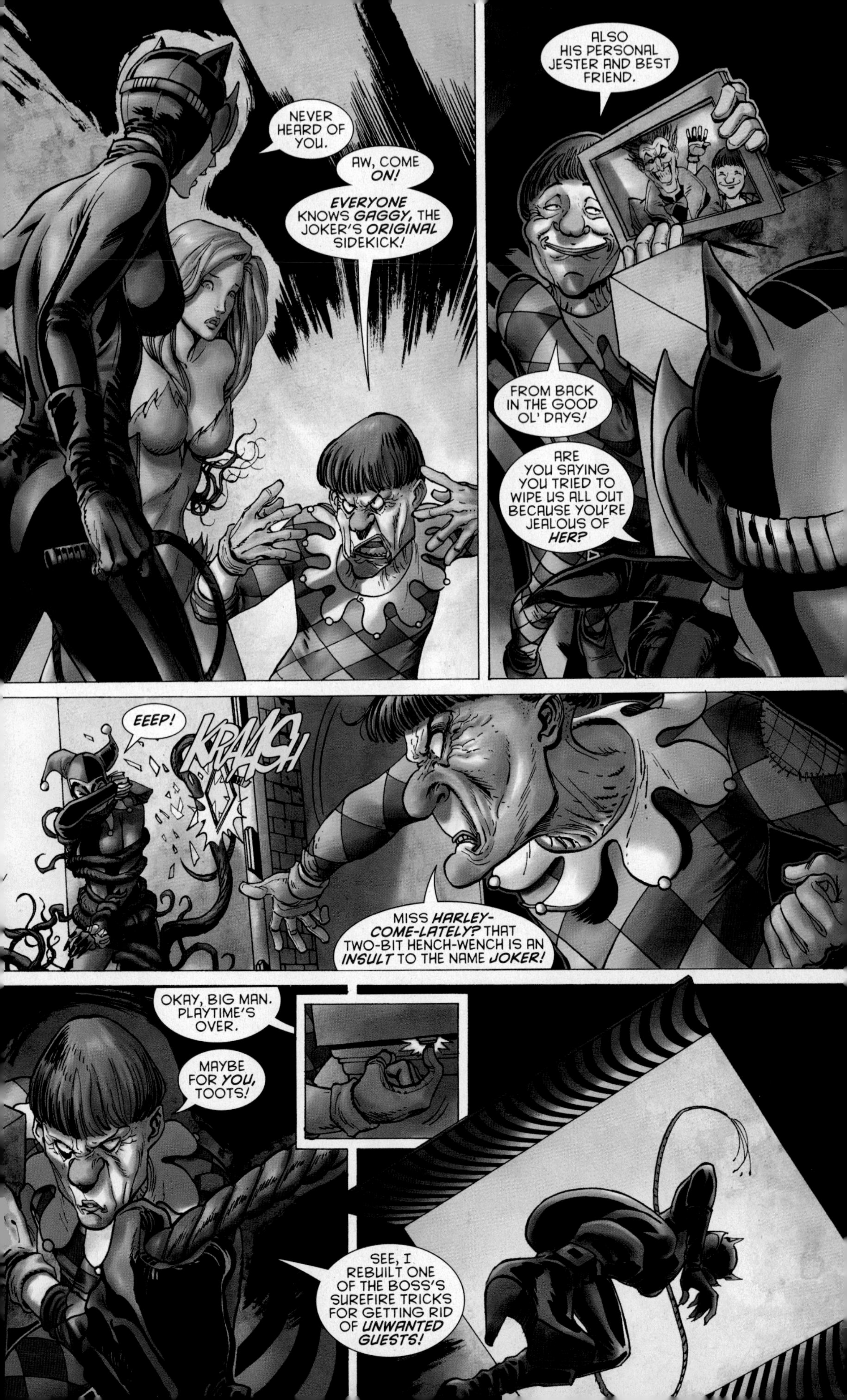
NEVER HEARD OF YOU.
AW, COME ON!
EVERYONE KNOWS GAGGY, THE JOKER'S ORIGINAL SIDEKICK!
ALSO HIS PERSONAL JESTER AND BEST FRIEND.
FROM BACK IN THE GOOD OL' DAYS!
ARE YOU SAYING YOU TRIED TO WIPE US ALL OUT BECAUSE YOU'RE JEALOUS OF HER?
EEEP!
KRAASH
MISS HARLEY-COME-LATELY? THAT TWO-BIT HENCH-WENCH IS AN INSULT TO THE NAME JOKER!
OKAY, BIG MAN. PLAYTIME'S OVER.
MAYBE FOR YOU, TOOTS!
SEE, I REBUILT ONE OF THE BOSS'S SUREFIRE TRICKS FOR GETTING RID OF UNWANTED GUESTS!

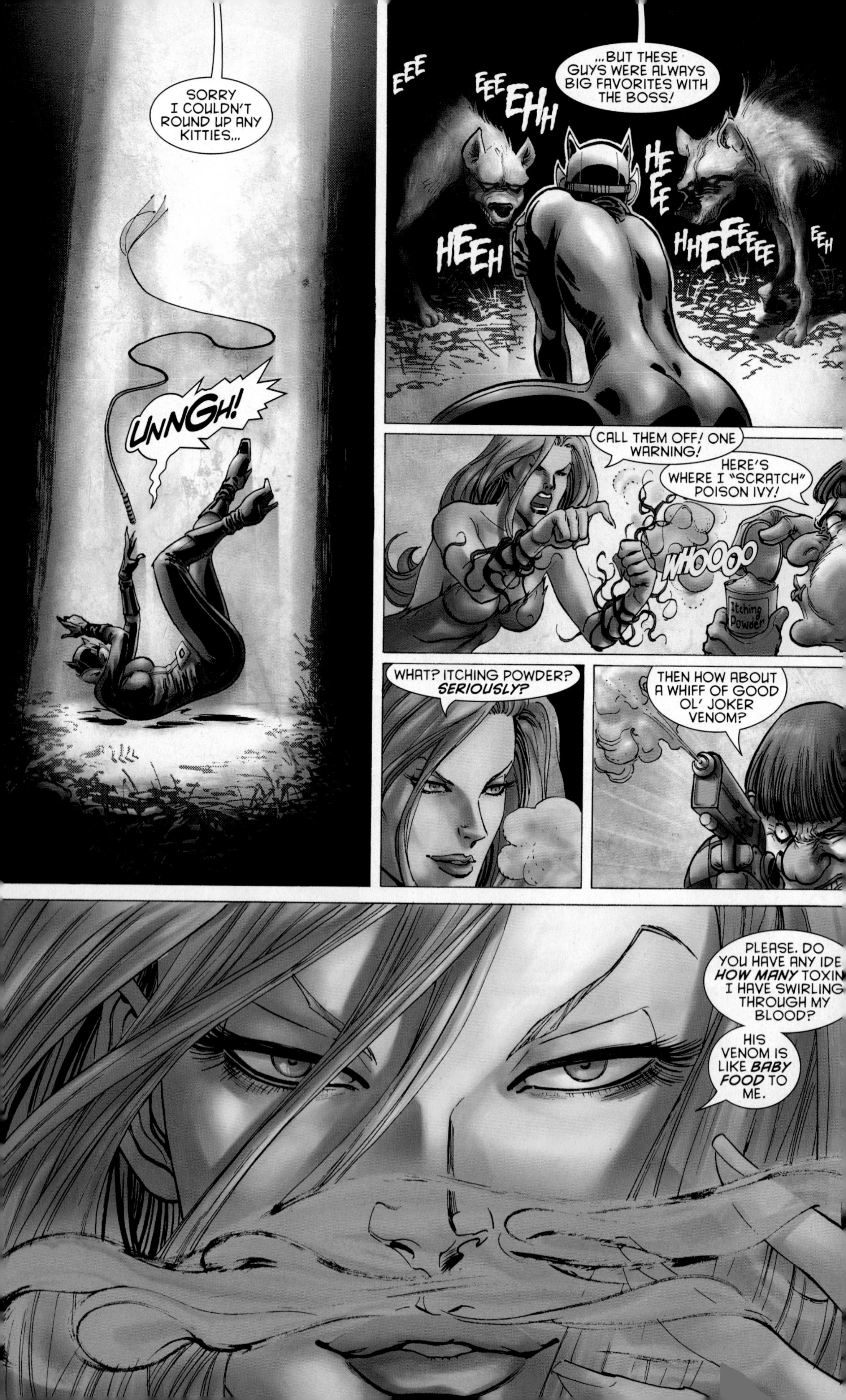
SORRY I COULDN'T ROUND UP ANY KITTIES...
UNNGH!
EEE
EEEEHH
...BUT THESE GUYS WERE ALWAYS BIG FAVORITES WITH THE BOSS!
HEEE
HEEH
HHEEEEEE
EEH
CALL THEM OFF! ONE WARNING!
HERE'S WHERE I "SCRATCH" POISON IVY!
WHOOOO
Itching Powder
WHAT? ITCHING POWDER? SERIOUSLY?
THEN HOW ABOUT A WHIFF OF GOOD OL' JOKER VENOM?
PLEASE. DO YOU HAVE ANY IDE HOW MANY TOXIN I HAVE SWIRLING THROUGH MY BLOOD?
HIS VENOM IS LIKE BABY FOOD TO ME.

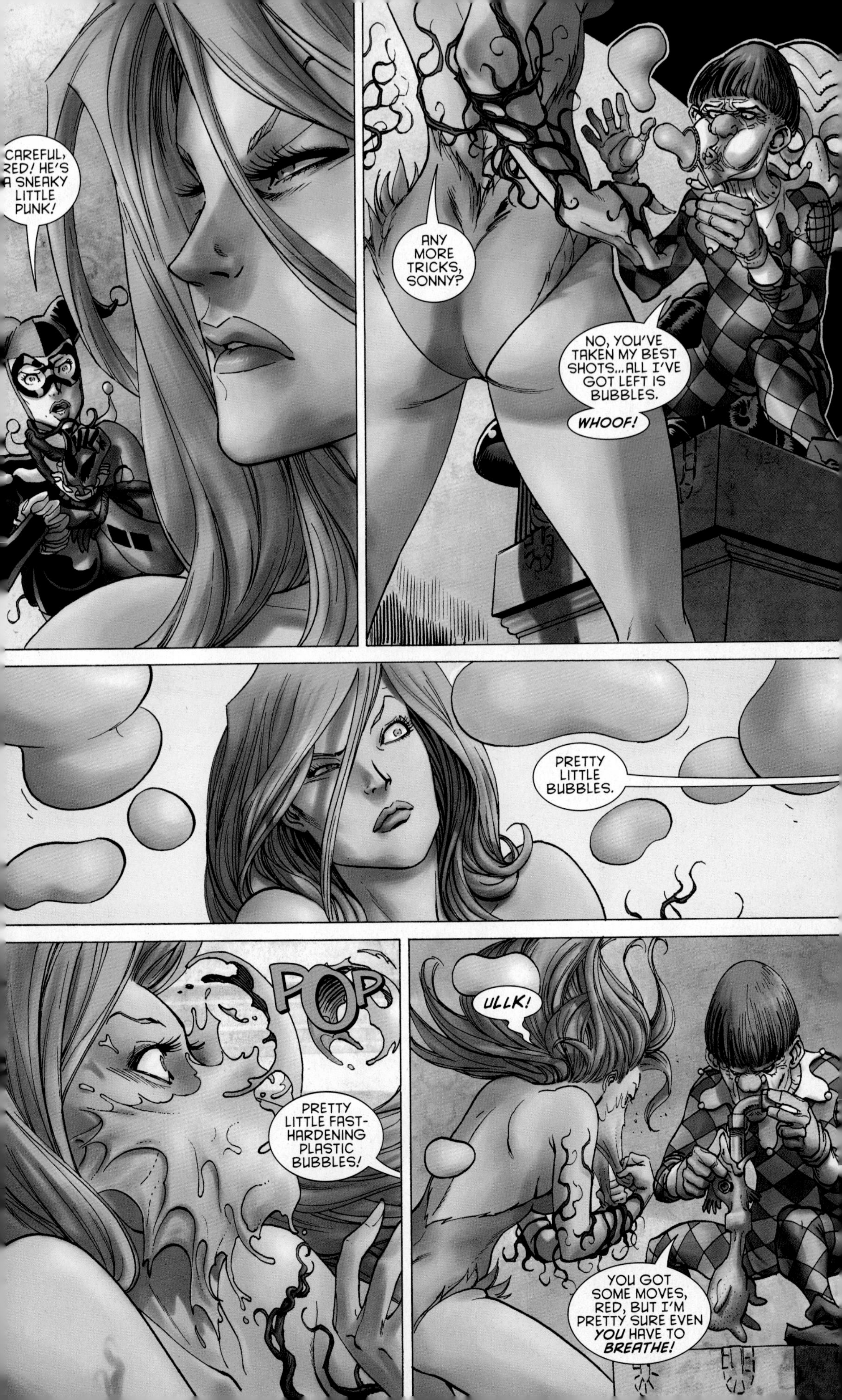
CAREFUL, RED! HE'S A SNEAKY LITTLE PUNK!
ANY MORE TRICKS, SONNY?
NO, YOU'VE TAKEN MY BEST SHOTS...ALL I'VE GOT LEFT IS BUBBLES.
WHOOF!
PRETTY LITTLE BUBBLES.
POP
PRETTY LITTLE FAST-HARDENING PLASTIC BUBBLES!
ULLK!
YOU GOT SOME MOVES, RED, BUT I'M PRETTY SURE EVEN YOU HAVE TO BREATHE!

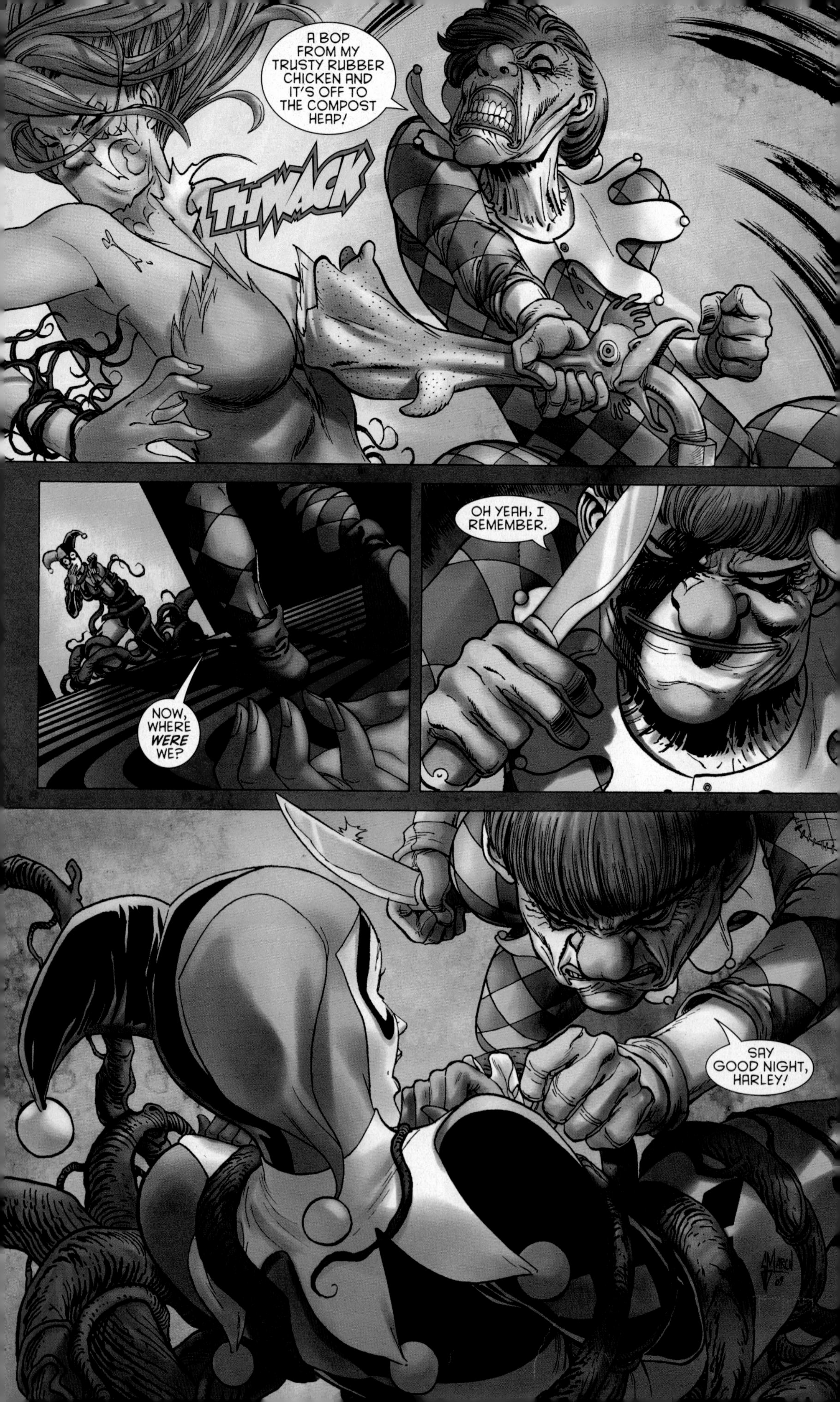

A BOP FROM MY TRUSTY RUBBER CHICKEN AND IT'S OFF TO THE COMPOST HEAP!
THWACK
NOW, WHERE *WERE* WE?
OH YEAH, I REMEMBER.
SAY GOOD NIGHT, HARLEY!

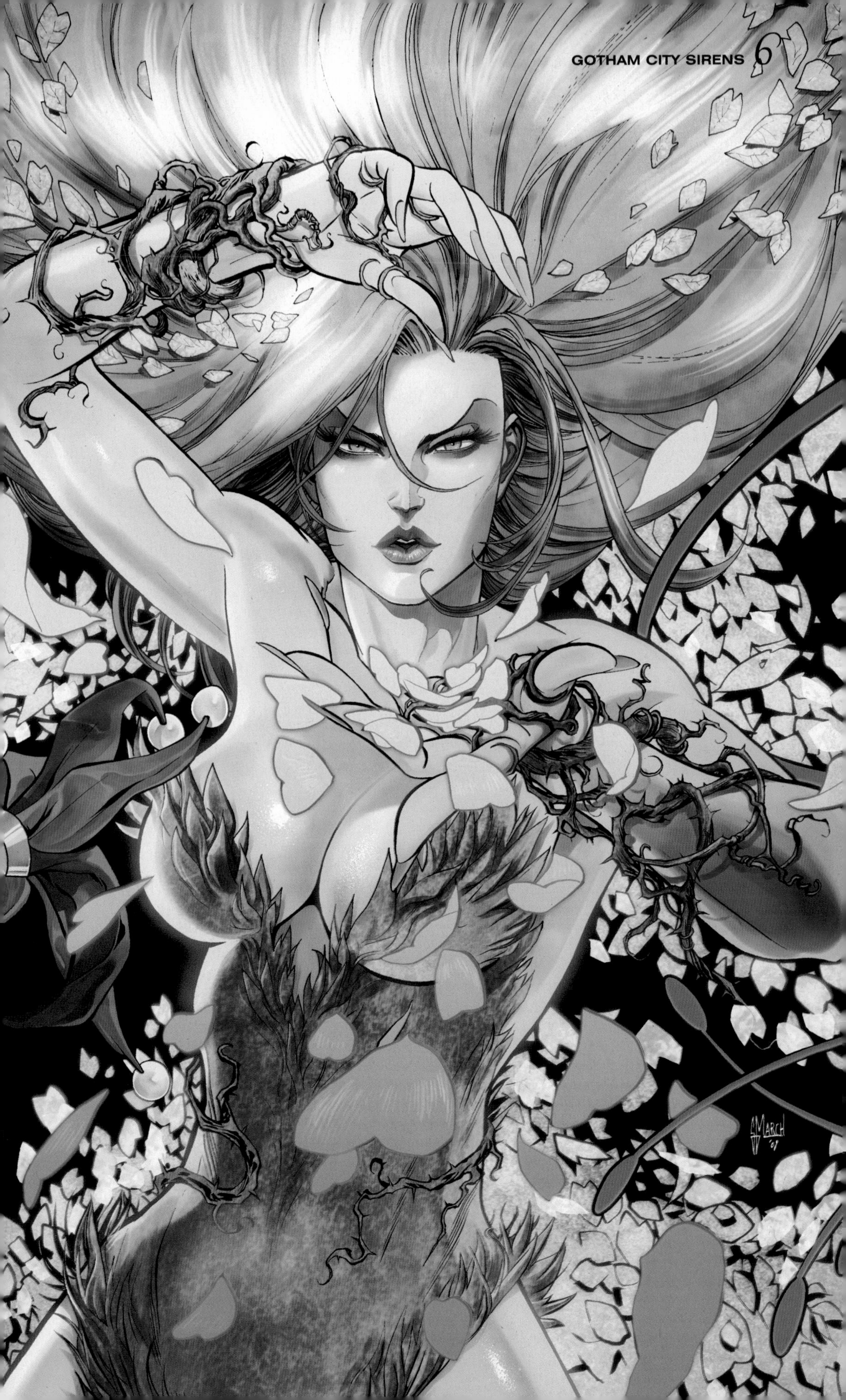
GOTHAM CITY SIRENS 6

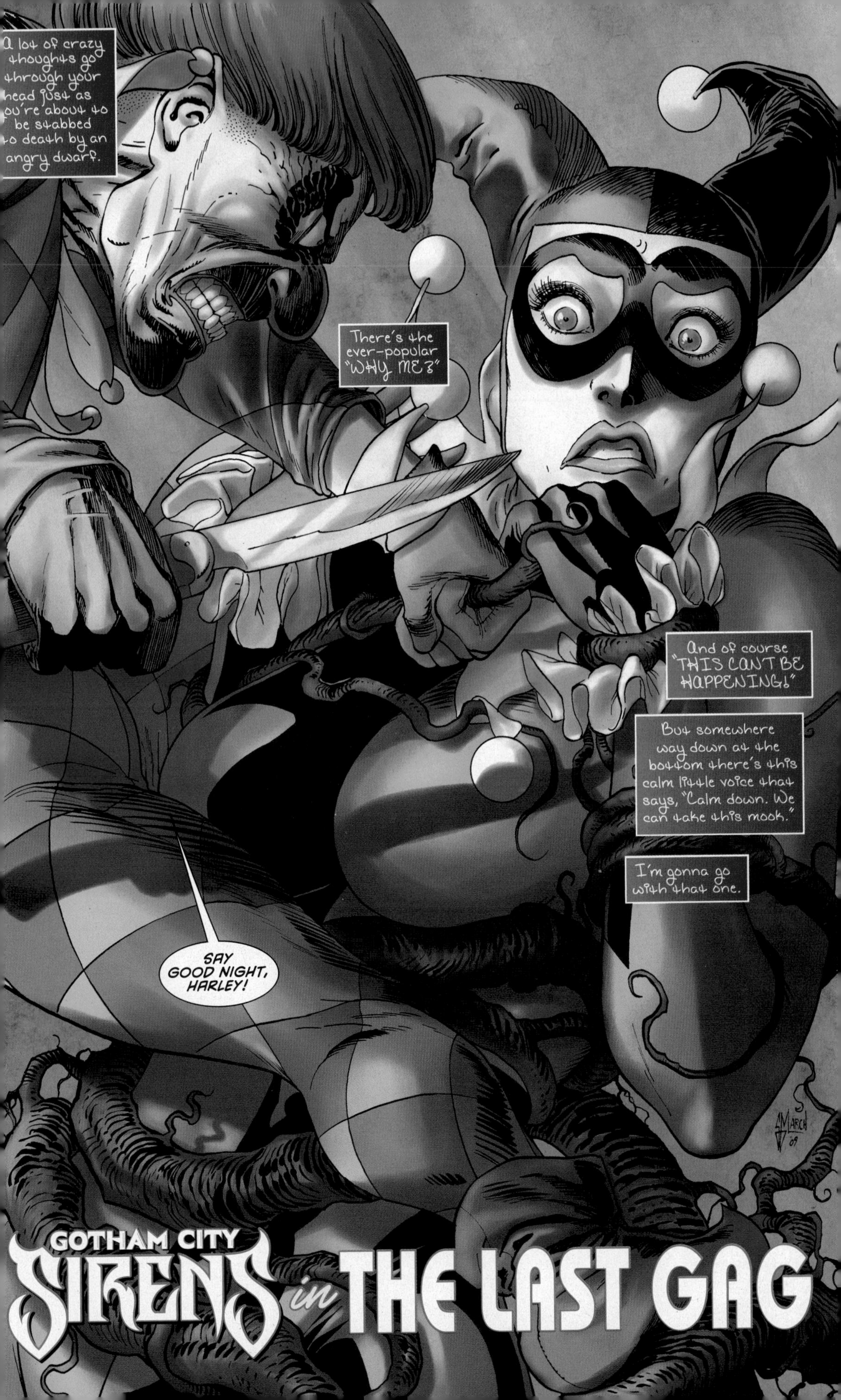

A lot of crazy thoughts go through your head just as you're about to be stabbed to death by an angry dwarf.
There's the ever-popular "WHY ME?"
And of course "THIS CAN'T BE HAPPENING!"
But somewhere way down at the bottom there's this calm little voice that says, "Calm down. We can take this mook."
I'm gonna go with that one.
SAY GOOD NIGHT, HARLEY!
GOTHAM CITY SIRENS in THE LAST GAG

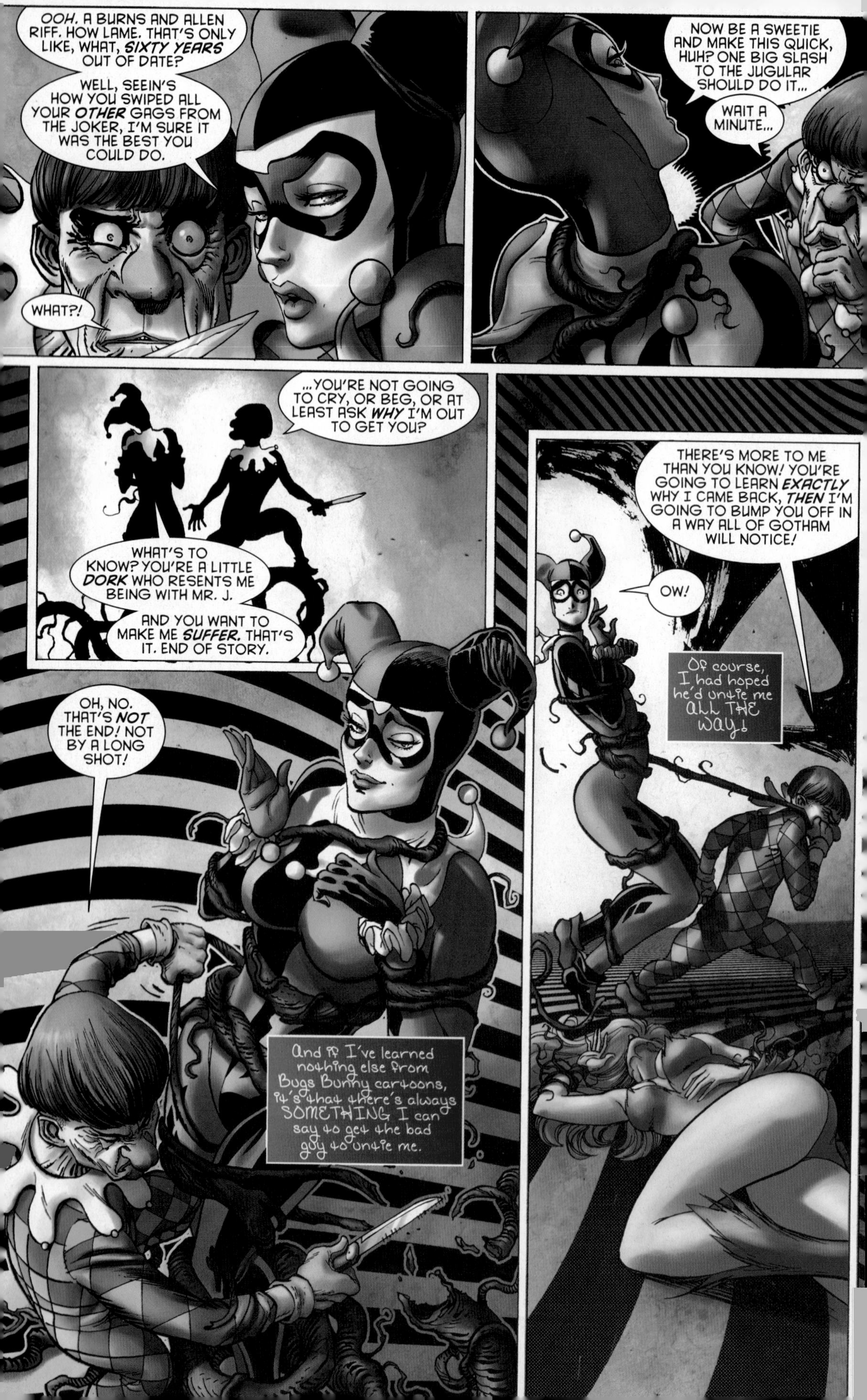
OOH. A BURNS AND ALLEN RIFF. HOW LAME. THAT'S ONLY LIKE, WHAT, SIXTY YEARS OUT OF DATE?
WELL, SEEIN'S HOW YOU SWIPED ALL YOUR OTHER GAGS FROM THE JOKER, I'M SURE IT WAS THE BEST YOU COULD DO.
WHAT?!
NOW BE A SWEETIE AND MAKE THIS QUICK, HUH? ONE BIG SLASH TO THE JUGULAR SHOULD DO IT...
WAIT A MINUTE...
...YOU'RE NOT GOING TO CRY, OR BEG, OR AT LEAST ASK WHY I'M OUT TO GET YOU?
WHAT'S TO KNOW? YOU'RE A LITTLE DORK WHO RESENTS ME BEING WITH MR. J.
AND YOU WANT TO MAKE ME SUFFER. THAT'S IT. END OF STORY.
OH, NO. THAT'S NOT THE END! NOT BY A LONG SHOT!
And if I've learned nothing else from Bugs Bunny cartoons, it's that there's always SOMETHING I can say to get the bad guy to untie me.
THERE'S MORE TO ME THAN YOU KNOW! YOU'RE GOING TO LEARN EXACTLY WHY I CAME BACK, THEN I'M GOING TO BUMP YOU OFF IN A WAY ALL OF GOTHAM WILL NOTICE!
OW!
Of course, I had hoped he'd untie me ALL THE WAY!

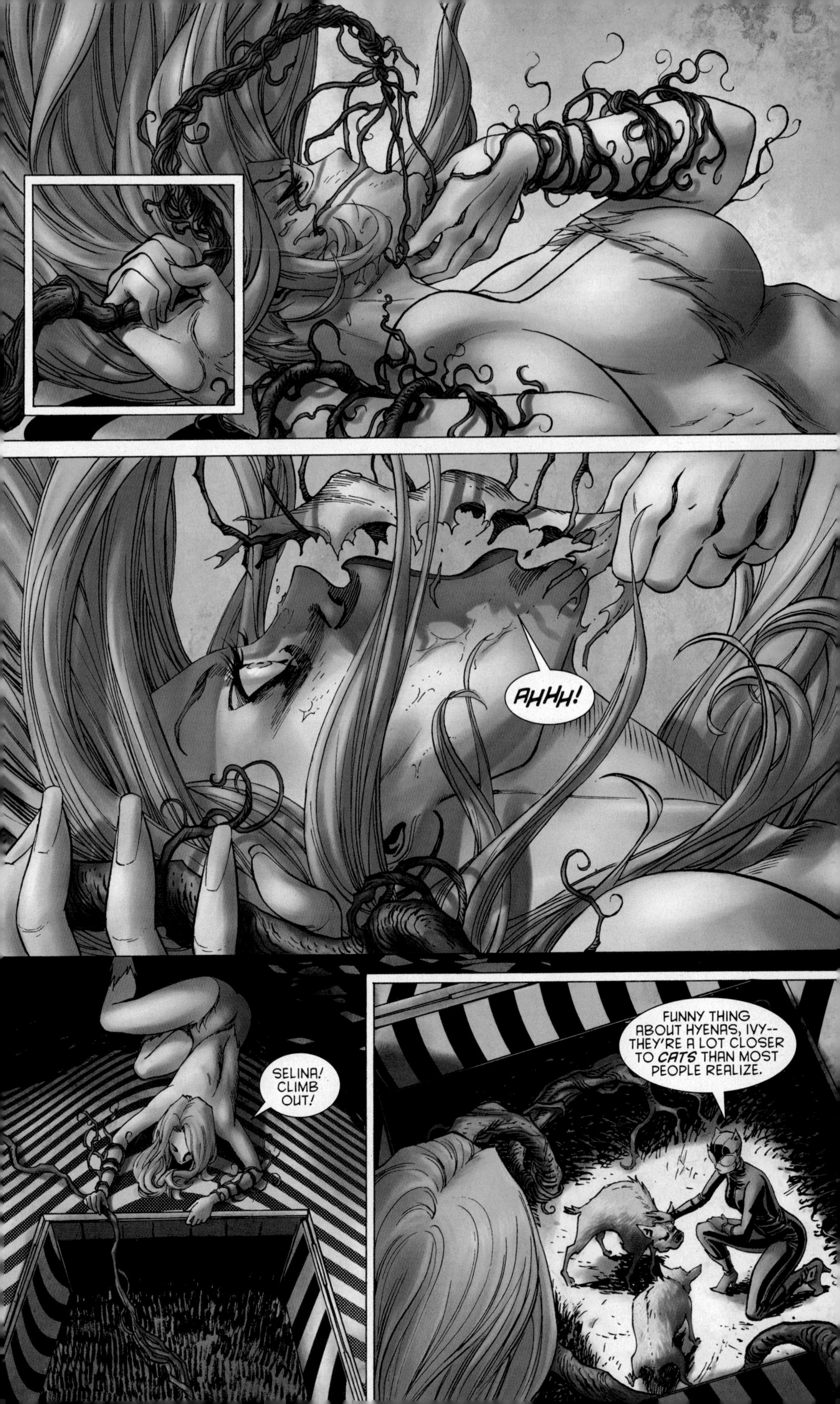
AHHH!
SELINA! CLIMB OUT!
FUNNY THING ABOUT HYENAS, IVY-- THEY'RE A LOT CLOSER TO CATS THAN MOST PEOPLE REALIZE.

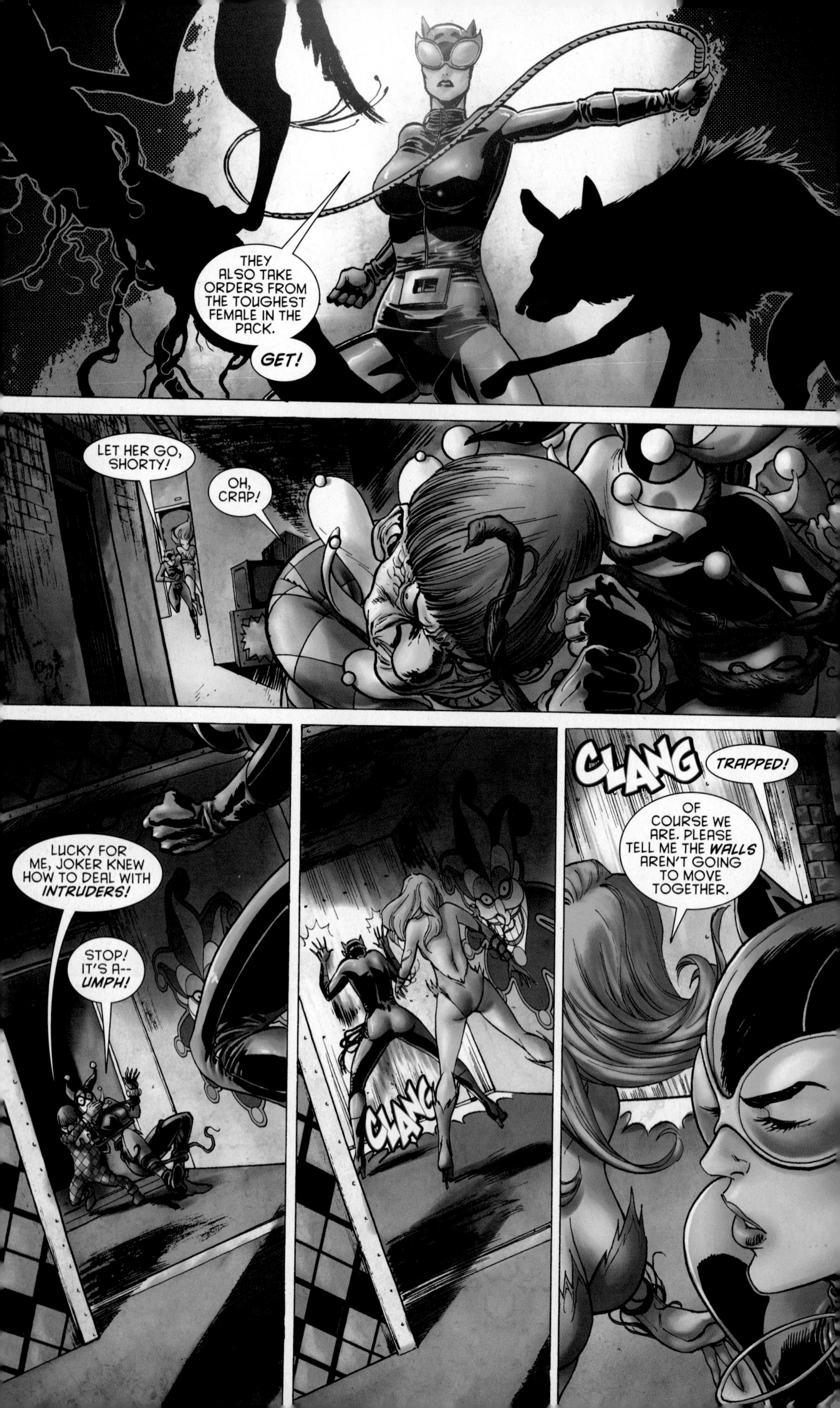
THEY ALSO TAKE ORDERS FROM THE TOUGHEST FEMALE IN THE PACK.
GET!
LET HER GO, SHORTY!
OH, CRAP!
LUCKY FOR ME, JOKER KNEW HOW TO DEAL WITH INTRUDERS!
STOP! IT'S A-- UMPH!
CLANG
CLANG
TRAPPED!
OF COURSE WE ARE. PLEASE TELL ME THE WALLS AREN'T GOING TO MOVE TOGETHER.

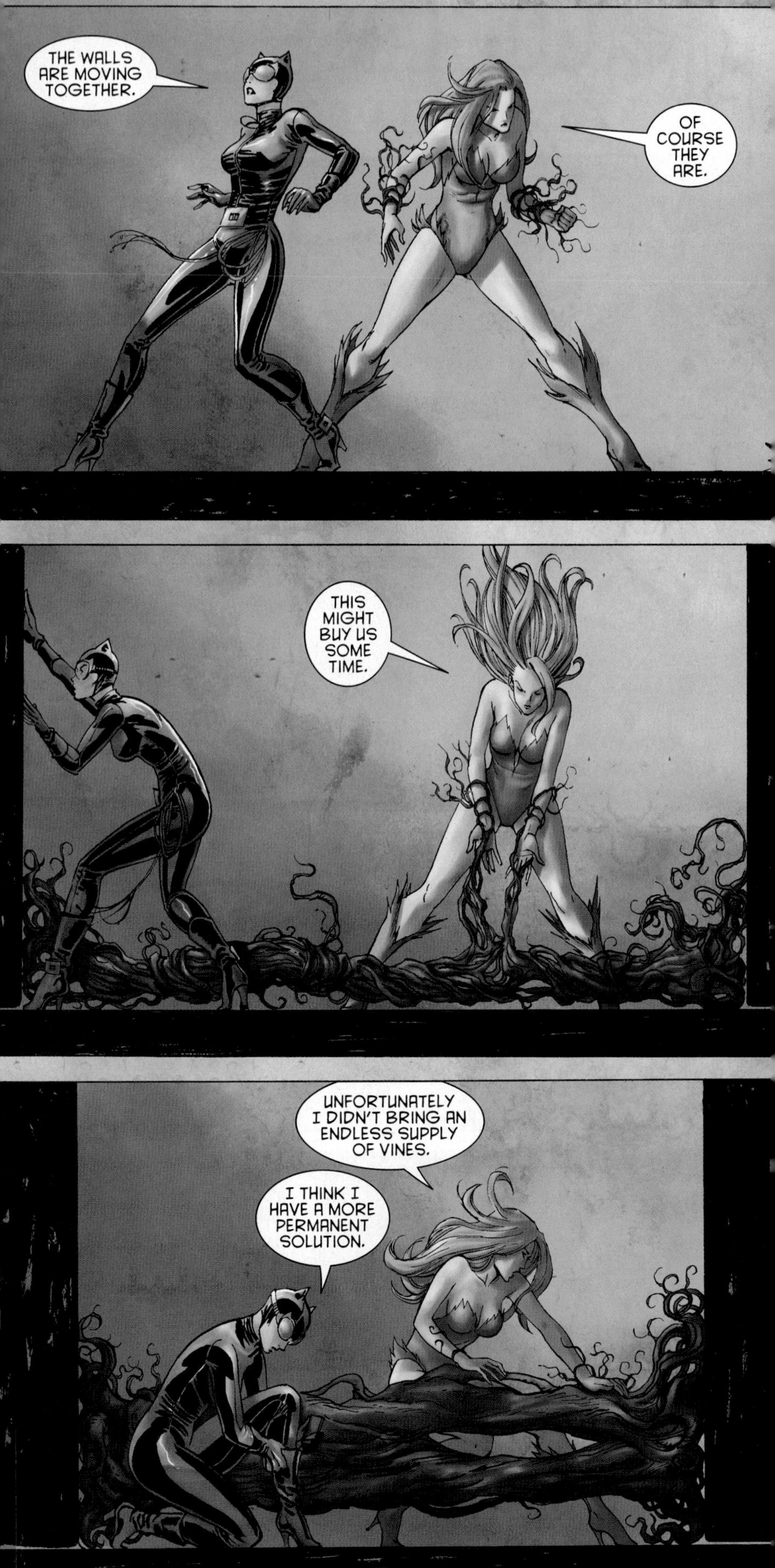
THE WALLS ARE MOVING TOGETHER.
OF COURSE THEY ARE.
THIS MIGHT BUY US SOME TIME.
UNFORTUNATELY I DIDN'T BRING AN ENDLESS SUPPLY OF VINES.
I THINK I HAVE A MORE PERMANENT SOLUTION.

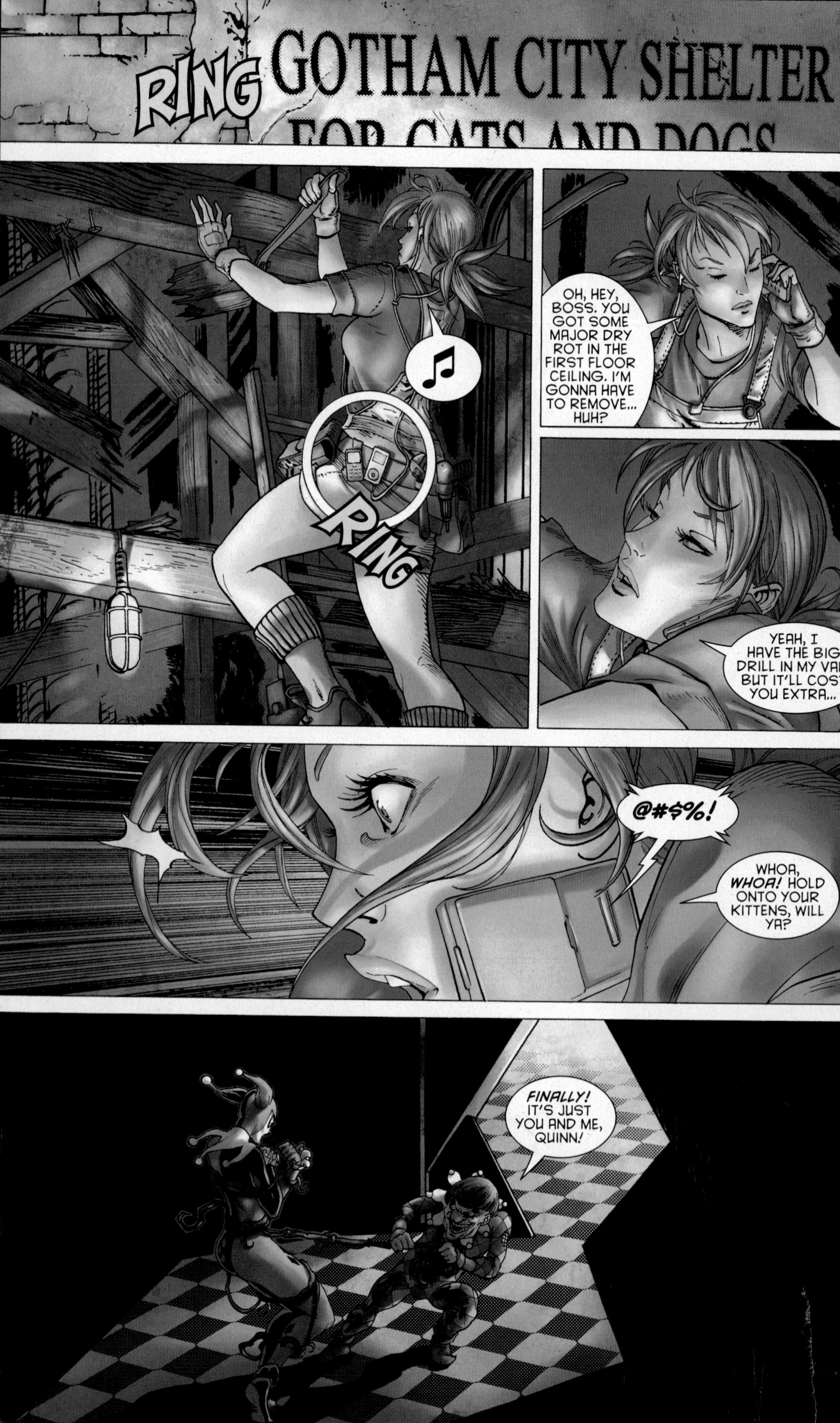
RING
GOTHAM CITY SHELTER
RING
OH, HEY, BOSS. YOU GOT SOME MAJOR DRY ROT IN THE FIRST FLOOR CEILING. I'M GONNA HAVE TO REMOVE... HUH?
YEAH, I HAVE THE BIG DRILL IN MY VA BUT IT'LL COS YOU EXTRA...
@#$%!
WHOA, WHOA! HOLD ONTO YOUR KITTENS, WILL YA?
FINALLY! IT'S JUST YOU AND ME, QUINN!

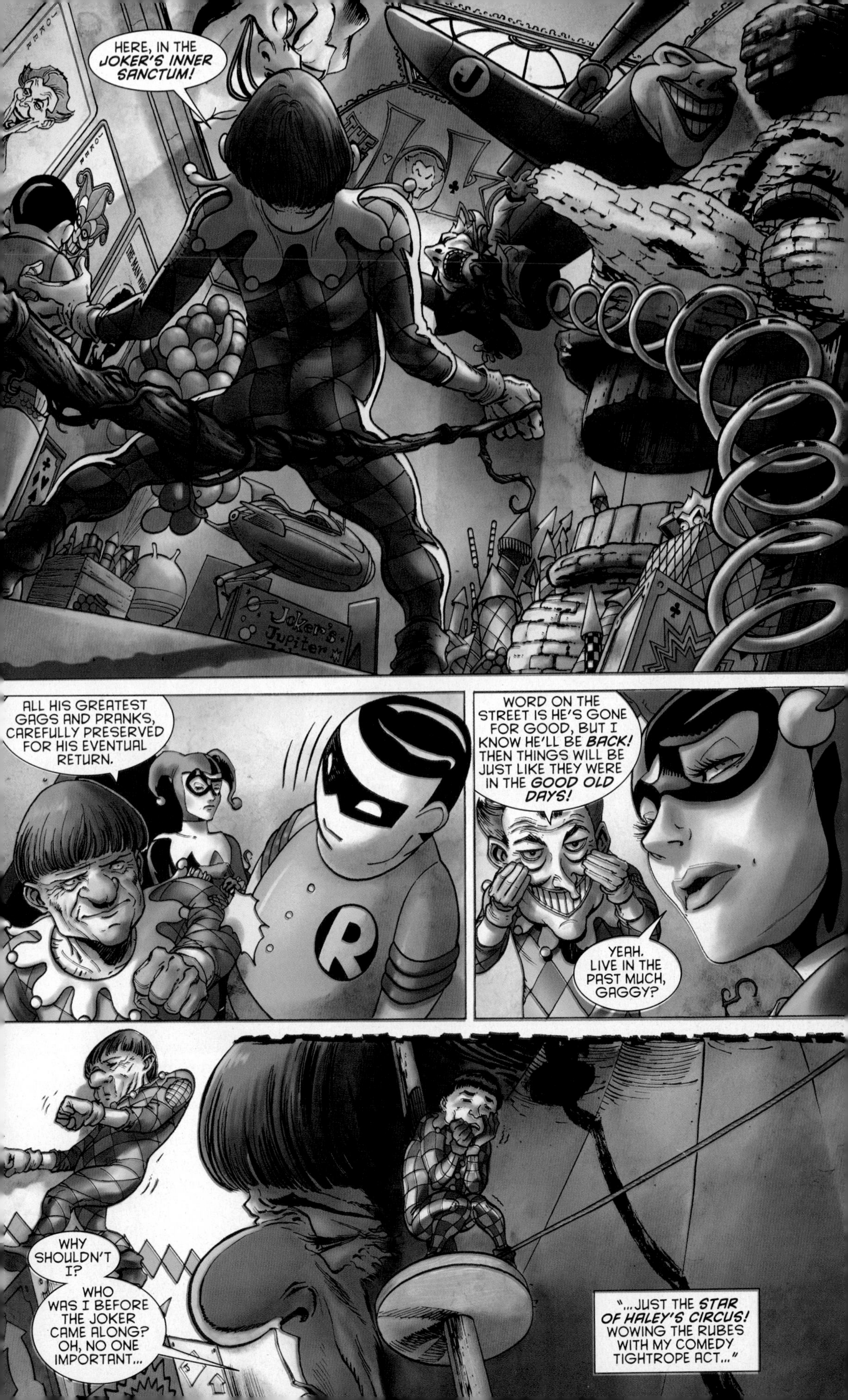
HERE, IN THE JOKER'S INNER SANCTUM!
Joker's Jupiter
ALL HIS GREATEST GAGS AND PRANKS, CAREFULLY PRESERVED FOR HIS EVENTUAL RETURN.
WORD ON THE STREET IS HE'S GONE FOR GOOD, BUT I KNOW HE'LL BE BACK! THEN THINGS WILL BE JUST LIKE THEY WERE IN THE GOOD OLD DAYS!
YEAH. LIVE IN THE PAST MUCH, GAGGY?
WHY SHOULDN'T I?
WHO WAS I BEFORE THE JOKER CAME ALONG? OH, NO ONE IMPORTANT...
"...JUST THE STAR OF HALEY'S CIRCUS! WOWING THE RUBES WITH MY COMEDY TIGHTROPE ACT..."

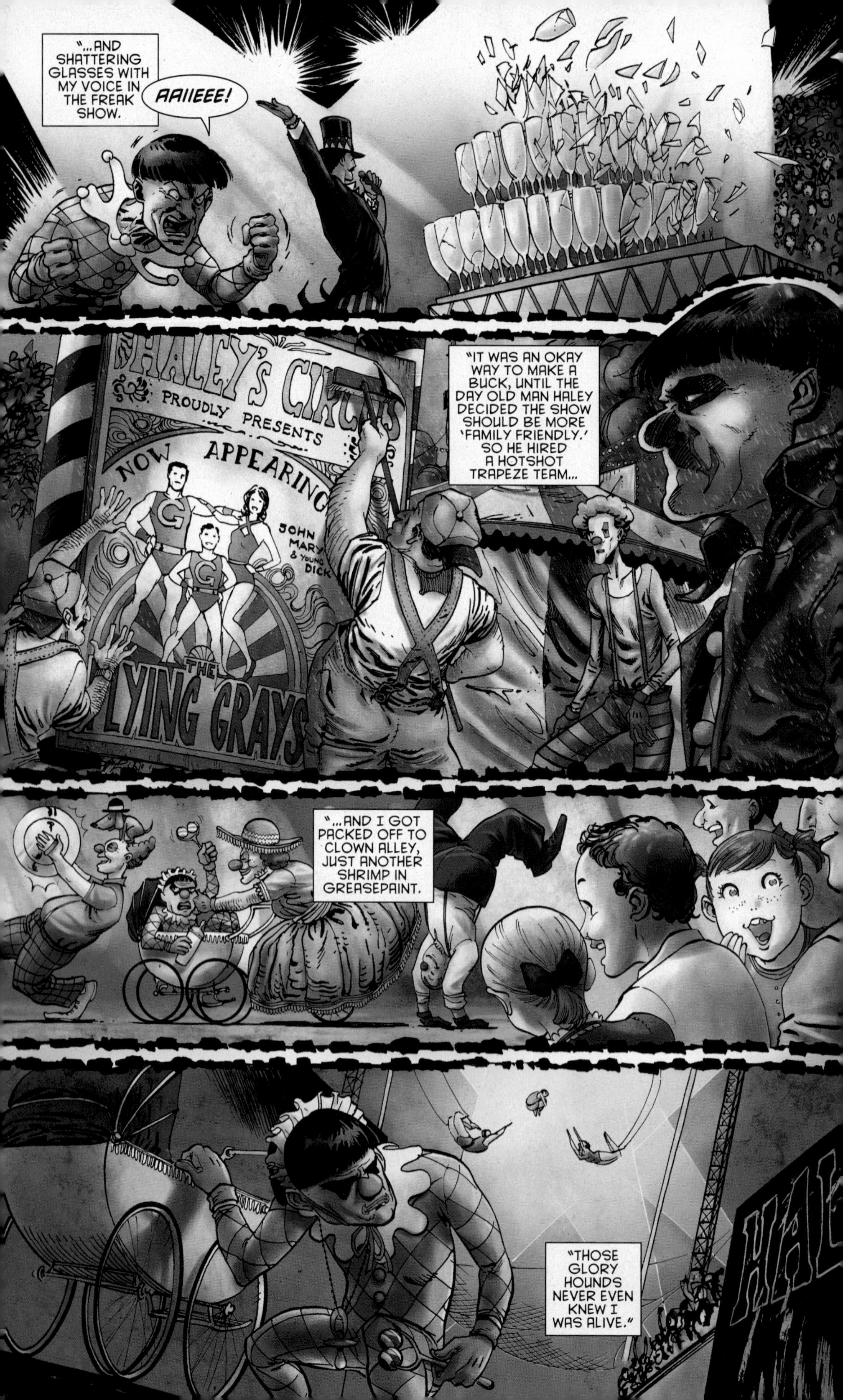
"...AND SHATTERING GLASSES WITH MY VOICE IN THE FREAK SHOW.
AAIIEEE!
HALEY'S CIRCUS PROUDLY PRESENTS
NOW APPEARING
JOHN MARY & YOUNG DICK
THE FLYING GRAYS
"IT WAS AN OKAY WAY TO MAKE A BUCK, UNTIL THE DAY OLD MAN HALEY DECIDED THE SHOW SHOULD BE MORE 'FAMILY FRIENDLY.' SO HE HIRED A HOTSHOT TRAPEZE TEAM...
"...AND I GOT PACKED OFF TO CLOWN ALLEY, JUST ANOTHER SHRIMP IN GREASEPAINT.
"THOSE GLORY HOUNDS NEVER EVEN KNEW I WAS ALIVE."

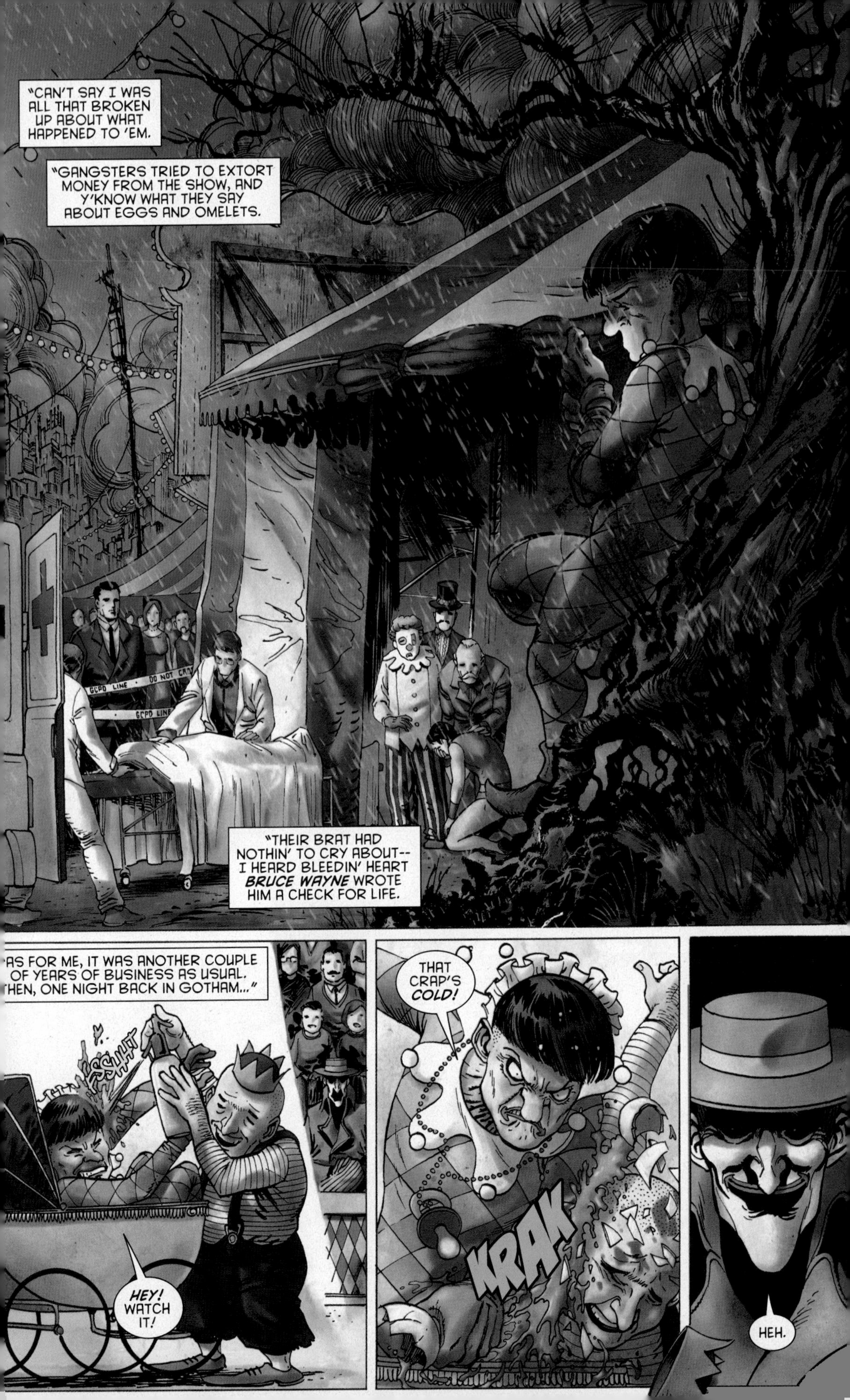
"CAN'T SAY I WAS ALL THAT BROKEN UP ABOUT WHAT HAPPENED TO 'EM.
"GANGSTERS TRIED TO EXTORT MONEY FROM THE SHOW, AND Y'KNOW WHAT THEY SAY ABOUT EGGS AND OMELETS.
GCPD LINE DO NOT CR
GCPD LINE
"THEIR BRAT HAD NOTHIN' TO CRY ABOUT-- I HEARD BLEEDIN' HEART ***BRUCE WAYNE*** WROTE HIM A CHECK FOR LIFE.
AS FOR ME, IT WAS ANOTHER COUPLE OF YEARS OF BUSINESS AS USUAL. THEN, ONE NIGHT BACK IN GOTHAM..."
SSHHT
HEY! WATCH IT!
THAT CRAP'S *COLD!*
KRAK
HEH.

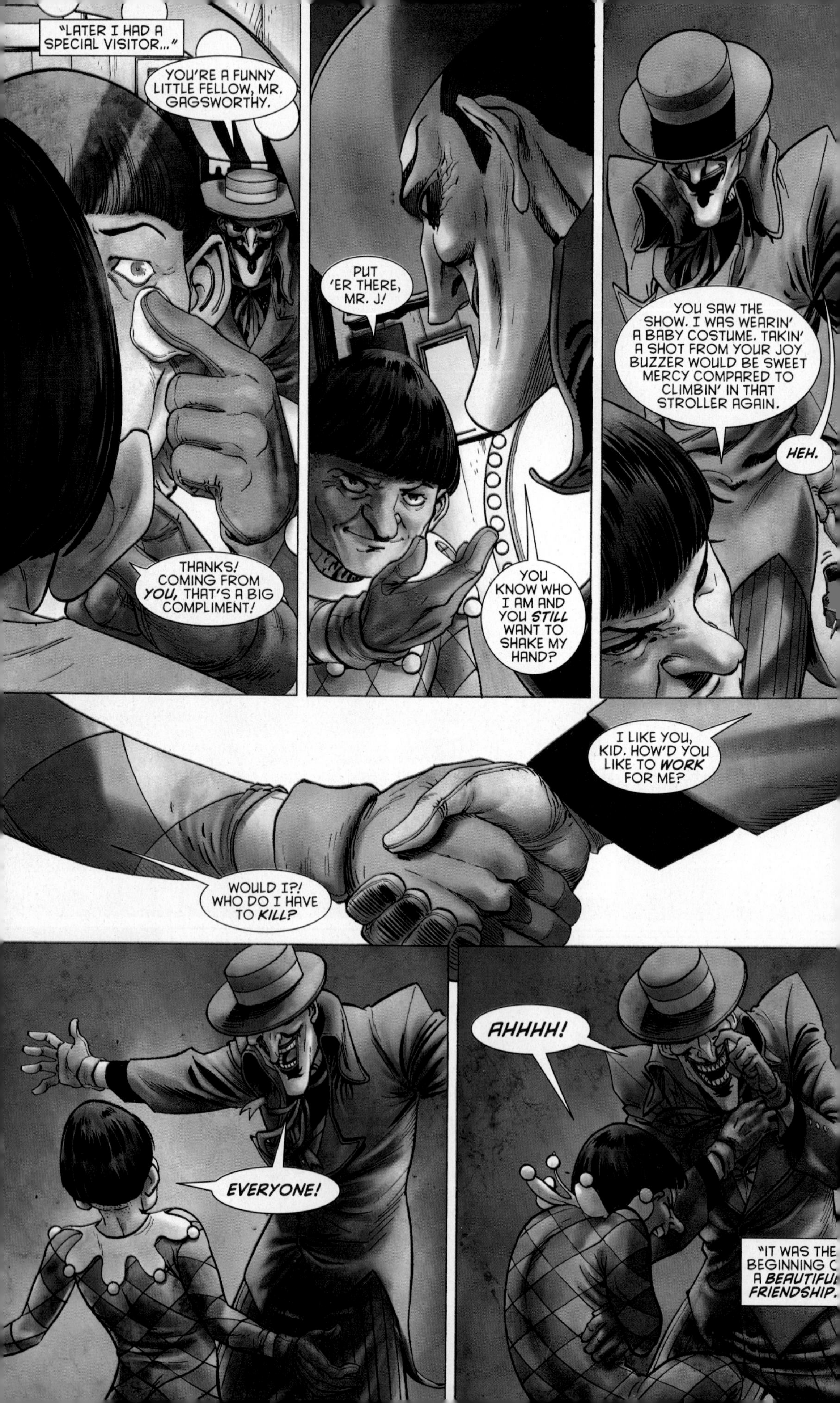
"LATER I HAD A SPECIAL VISITOR..."
YOU'RE A FUNNY LITTLE FELLOW, MR. GAGSWORTHY.
THANKS! COMING FROM *YOU,* THAT'S A BIG COMPLIMENT!
PUT 'ER THERE, MR. J!
YOU KNOW WHO I AM AND YOU *STILL* WANT TO SHAKE MY HAND?
YOU SAW THE SHOW. I WAS WEARIN' A BABY COSTUME. TAKIN' A SHOT FROM YOUR JOY BUZZER WOULD BE SWEET MERCY COMPARED TO CLIMBIN' IN THAT STROLLER AGAIN.
*HEH.*
I LIKE YOU, KID. HOW'D YOU LIKE TO *WORK* FOR ME?
WOULD I?! WHO DO I HAVE TO *KILL?*
*EVERYONE!*
*AHHHH!*
"IT WAS THE BEGINNING O A *BEAUTIFU FRIENDSHIP."*

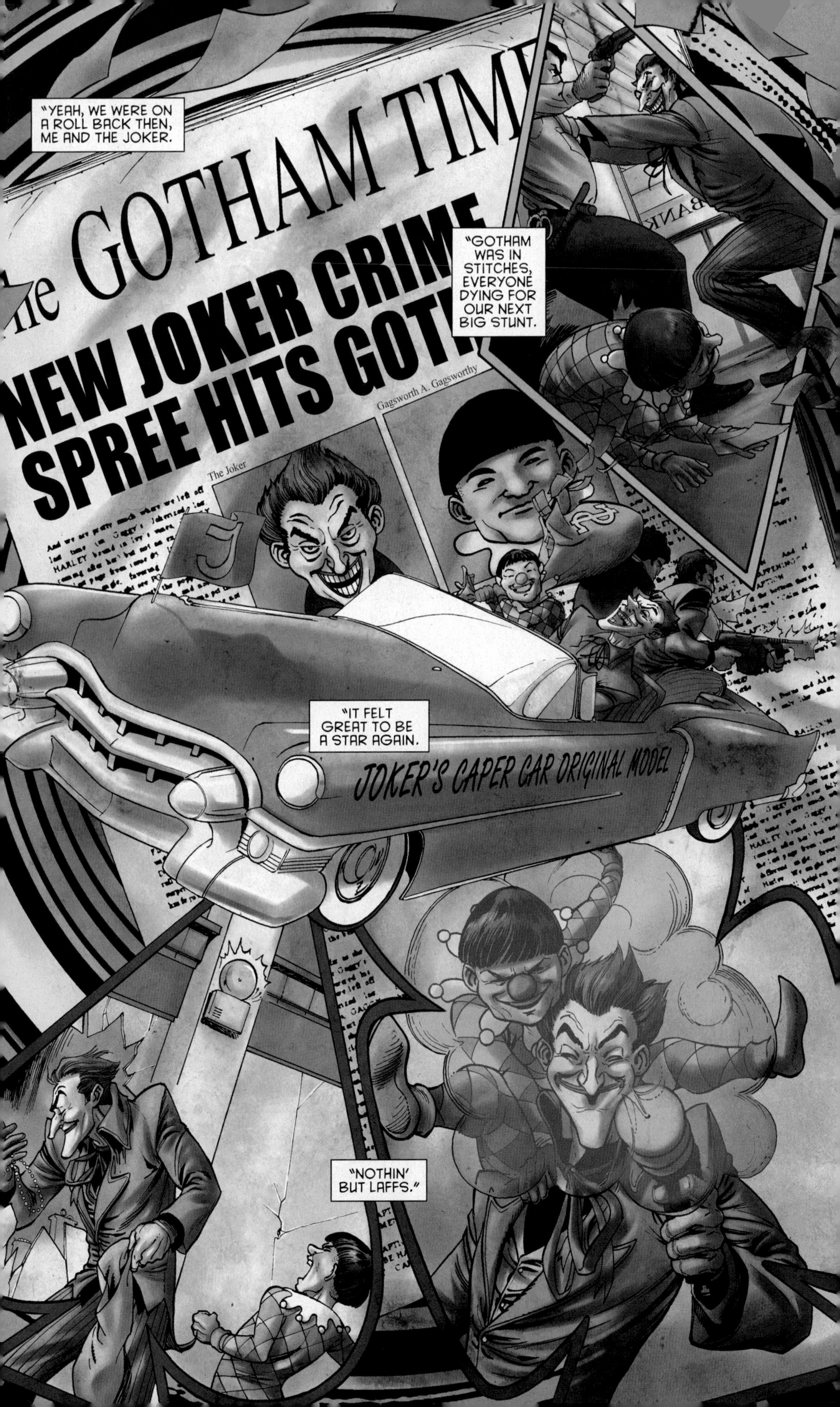
"YEAH, WE WERE ON A ROLL BACK THEN, ME AND THE JOKER.
The GOTHAM TIM
NEW JOKER CRIME SPREE HITS GOTH
Gagsworth A. Gagsworthy
The Joker
"GOTHAM WAS IN STITCHES, EVERYONE DYING FOR OUR NEXT BIG STUNT.
"IT FELT GREAT TO BE A STAR AGAIN.
JOKER'S CAPER CAR ORIGINAL MODEL
"NOTHIN' BUT LAFFS."

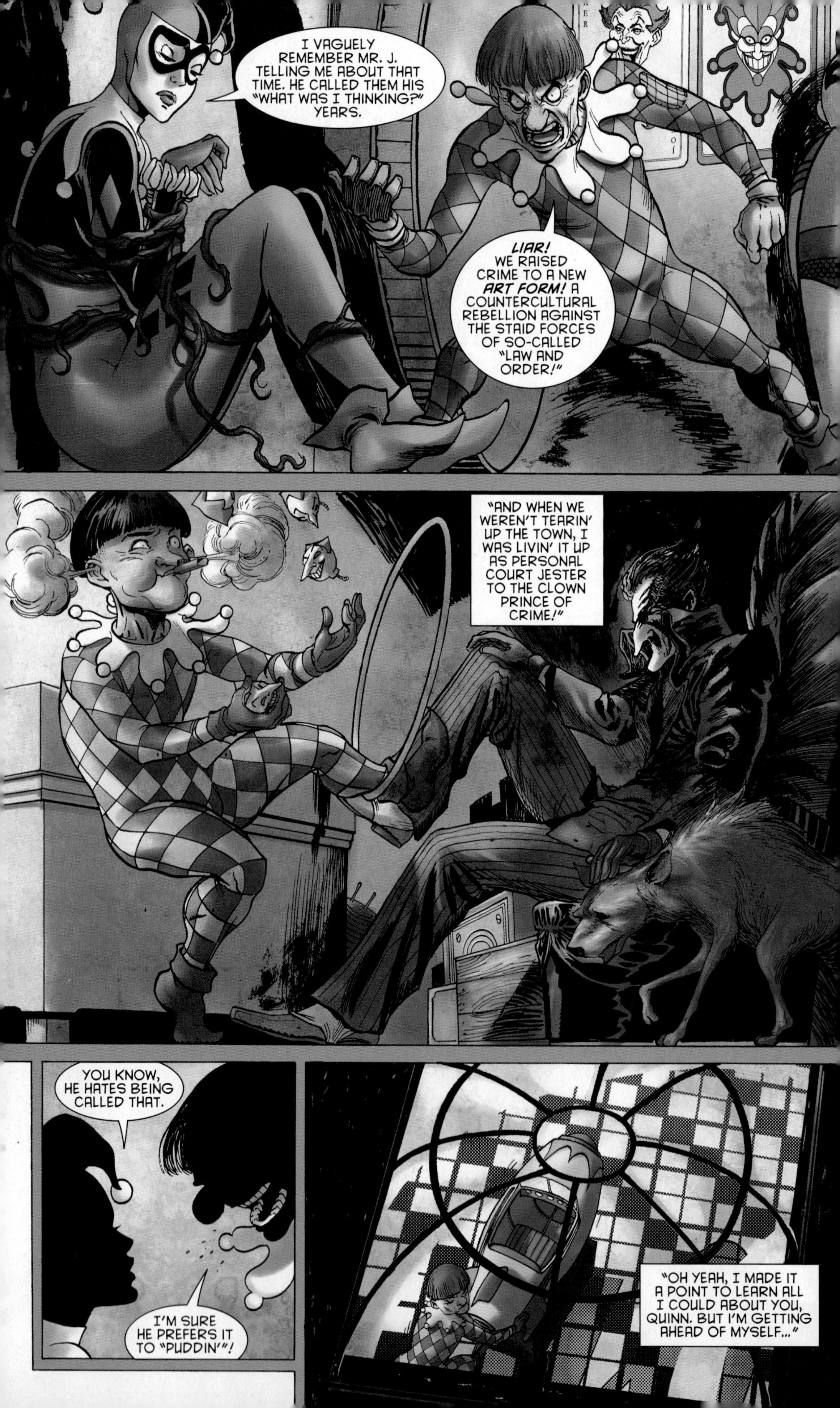

I VAGUELY REMEMBER MR. J. TELLING ME ABOUT THAT TIME. HE CALLED THEM HIS "WHAT WAS I THINKING?" YEARS.
LIAR! WE RAISED CRIME TO A NEW ART FORM! A COUNTERCULTURAL REBELLION AGAINST THE STAID FORCES OF SO-CALLED "LAW AND ORDER!"
"AND WHEN WE WEREN'T TEARIN' UP THE TOWN, I WAS LIVIN' IT UP AS PERSONAL COURT JESTER TO THE CLOWN PRINCE OF CRIME!"
YOU KNOW, HE HATES BEING CALLED THAT.
I'M SURE HE PREFERS IT TO "PUDDIN'"!
"OH YEAH, I MADE IT A POINT TO LEARN ALL I COULD ABOUT YOU, QUINN. BUT I'M GETTING AHEAD OF MYSELF..."

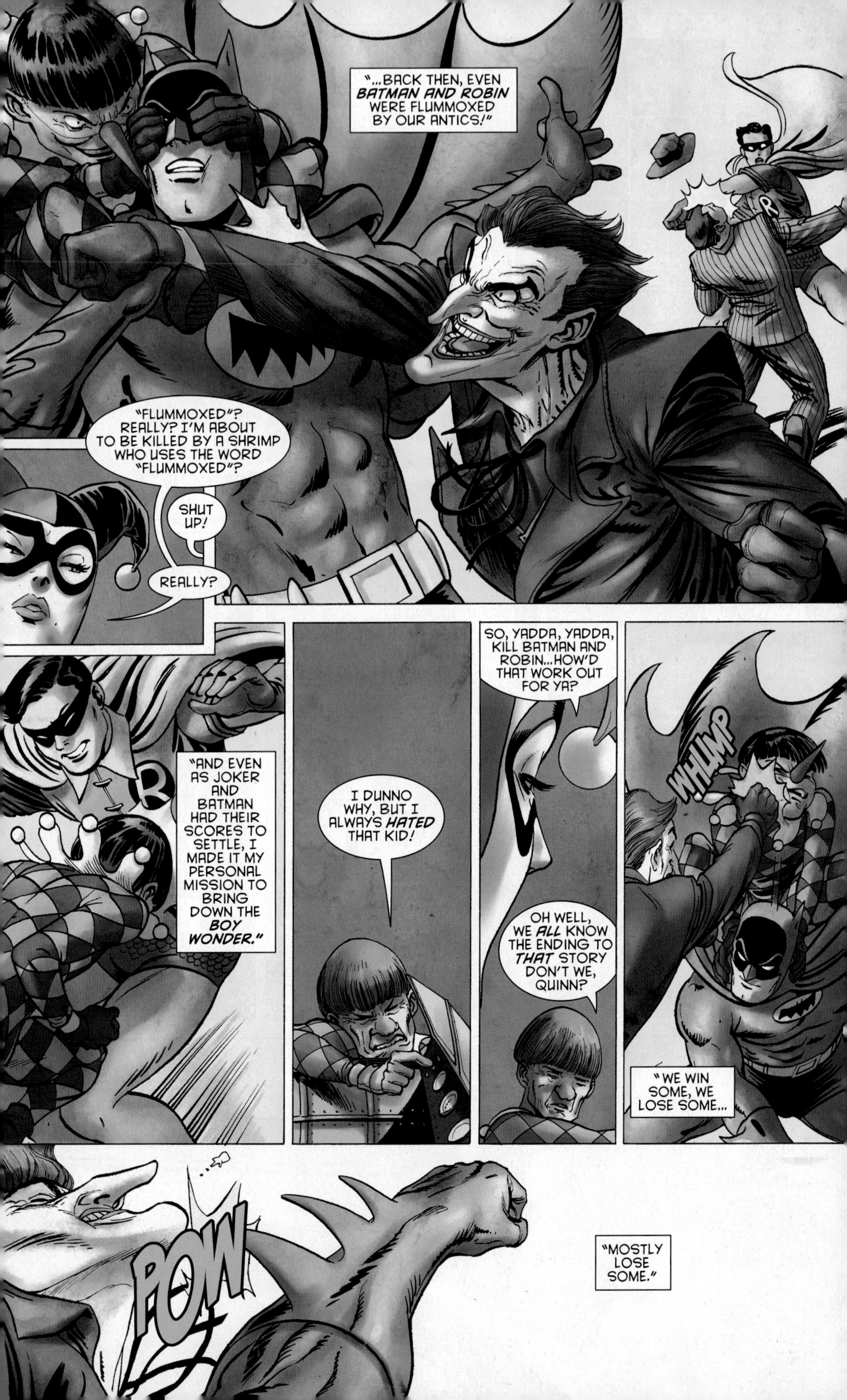
"...BACK THEN, EVEN *BATMAN AND ROBIN* WERE FLUMMOXED BY OUR ANTICS!"
"FLUMMOXED"? REALLY? I'M ABOUT TO BE KILLED BY A SHRIMP WHO USES THE WORD "FLUMMOXED"?
SHUT UP!
REALLY?
"AND EVEN AS JOKER AND BATMAN HAD THEIR SCORES TO SETTLE, I MADE IT MY PERSONAL MISSION TO BRING DOWN THE *BOY WONDER.*"
I DUNNO WHY, BUT I ALWAYS *HATED* THAT KID!
SO, YADDA, YADDA, KILL BATMAN AND ROBIN...HOW'D THAT WORK OUT FOR YA?
OH WELL, WE *ALL* KNOW THE ENDING TO *THAT* STORY DON'T WE, QUINN?
WHUMP
"WE WIN SOME, WE LOSE SOME...
POW
"MOSTLY LOSE SOME."

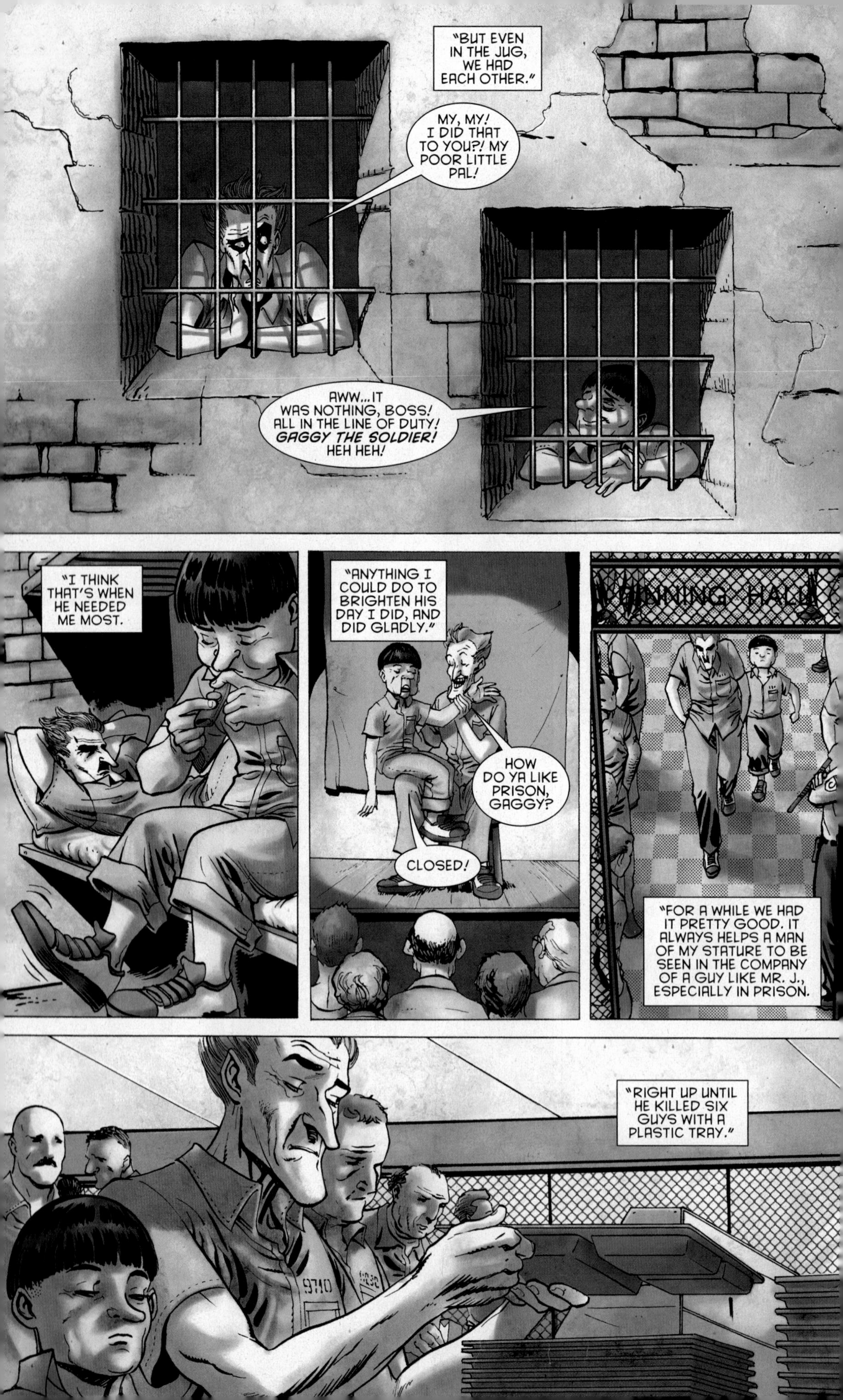
"BUT EVEN IN THE JUG, WE HAD EACH OTHER."
MY, MY! I DID THAT TO YOU?! MY POOR LITTLE PAL!
AWW...IT WAS NOTHING, BOSS! ALL IN THE LINE OF DUTY! GAGGY THE SOLDIER! HEH HEH!
"I THINK THAT'S WHEN HE NEEDED ME MOST.
"ANYTHING I COULD DO TO BRIGHTEN HIS DAY I DID, AND DID GLADLY."
HOW DO YA LIKE PRISON, GAGGY?
CLOSED!
"FOR A WHILE WE HAD IT PRETTY GOOD. IT ALWAYS HELPS A MAN OF MY STATURE TO BE SEEN IN THE COMPANY OF A GUY LIKE MR. J., ESPECIALLY IN PRISON.
"RIGHT UP UNTIL HE KILLED SIX GUYS WITH A PLASTIC TRAY."

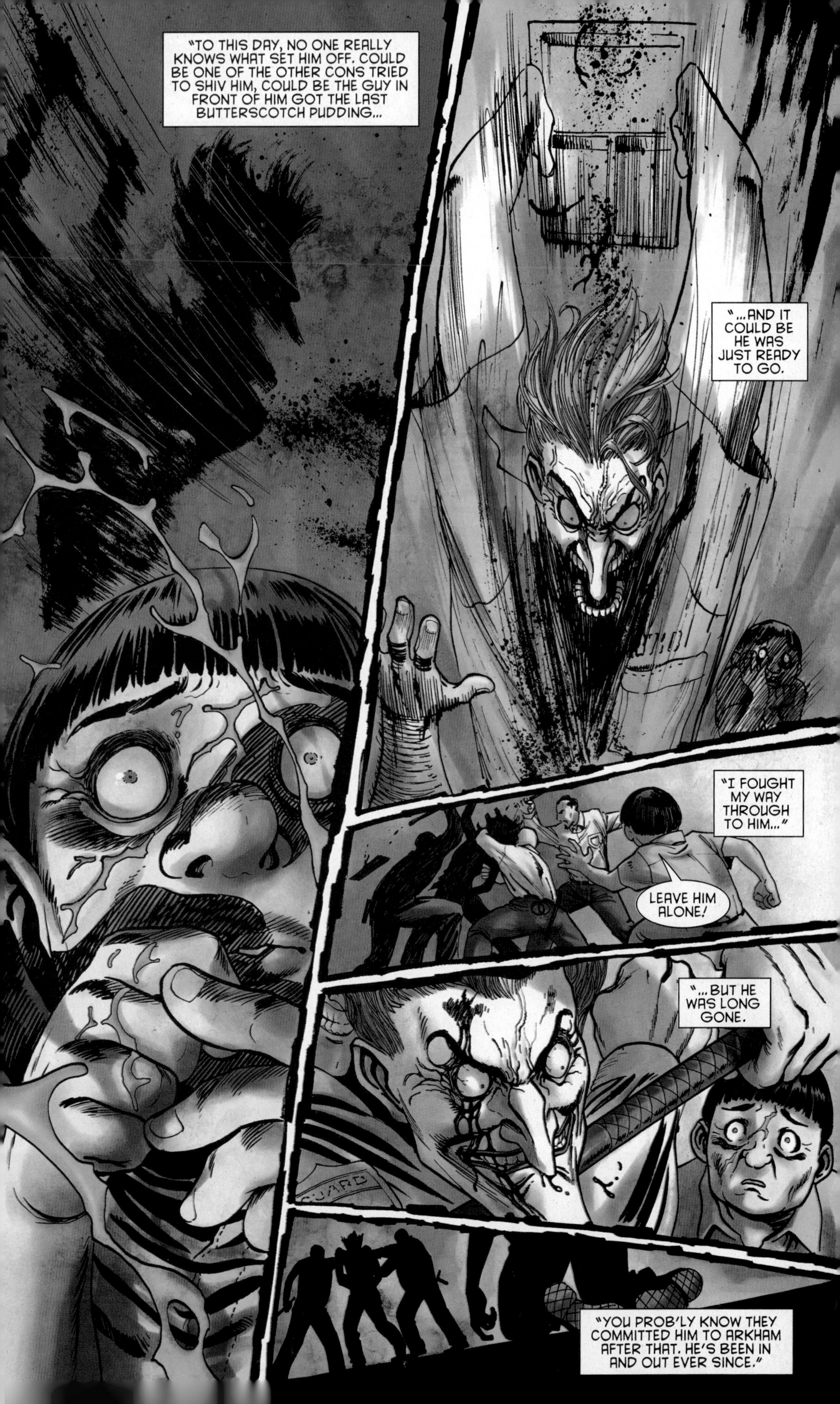
"TO THIS DAY, NO ONE REALLY KNOWS WHAT SET HIM OFF. COULD BE ONE OF THE OTHER CONS TRIED TO SHIV HIM, COULD BE THE GUY IN FRONT OF HIM GOT THE LAST BUTTERSCOTCH PUDDING...
"...AND IT COULD BE HE WAS JUST READY TO GO.
"I FOUGHT MY WAY THROUGH TO HIM..."
LEAVE HIM ALONE!
"...BUT HE WAS LONG GONE.
"YOU PROB'LY KNOW THEY COMMITTED HIM TO ARKHAM AFTER THAT. HE'S BEEN IN AND OUT EVER SINCE."

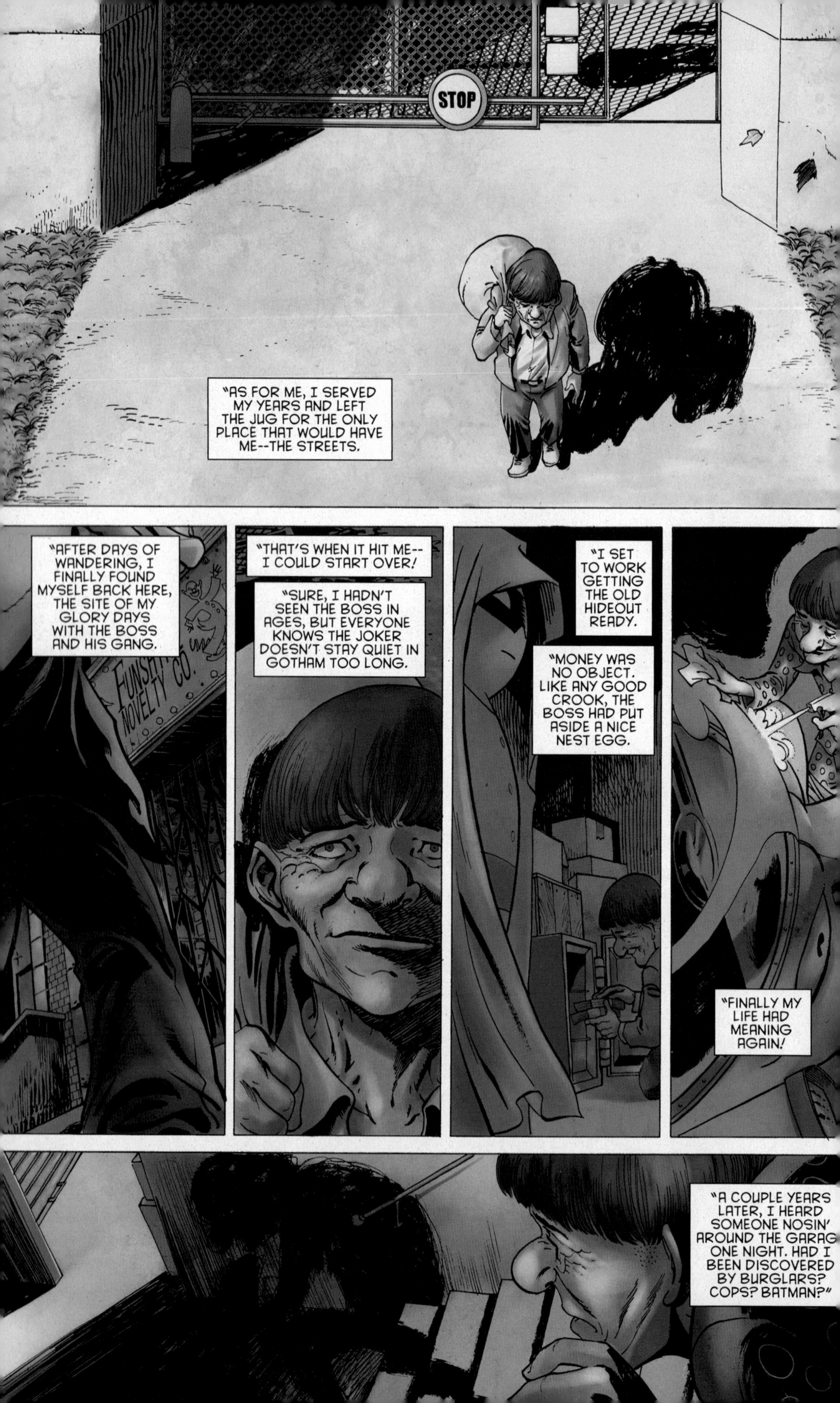

"AS FOR ME, I SERVED MY YEARS AND LEFT THE JUG FOR THE ONLY PLACE THAT WOULD HAVE ME--THE STREETS.
STOP
"AFTER DAYS OF WANDERING, I FINALLY FOUND MYSELF BACK HERE, THE SITE OF MY GLORY DAYS WITH THE BOSS AND HIS GANG.
"THAT'S WHEN IT HIT ME-- I COULD START OVER!
"SURE, I HADN'T SEEN THE BOSS IN AGES, BUT EVERYONE KNOWS THE JOKER DOESN'T STAY QUIET IN GOTHAM TOO LONG.
"I SET TO WORK GETTING THE OLD HIDEOUT READY.
"MONEY WAS NO OBJECT. LIKE ANY GOOD CROOK, THE BOSS HAD PUT ASIDE A NICE NEST EGG.
"FINALLY MY LIFE HAD MEANING AGAIN!
"A COUPLE YEARS LATER, I HEARD SOMEONE NOSIN' AROUND THE GARAG ONE NIGHT. HAD I BEEN DISCOVERED BY BURGLARS? COPS? BATMAN?"

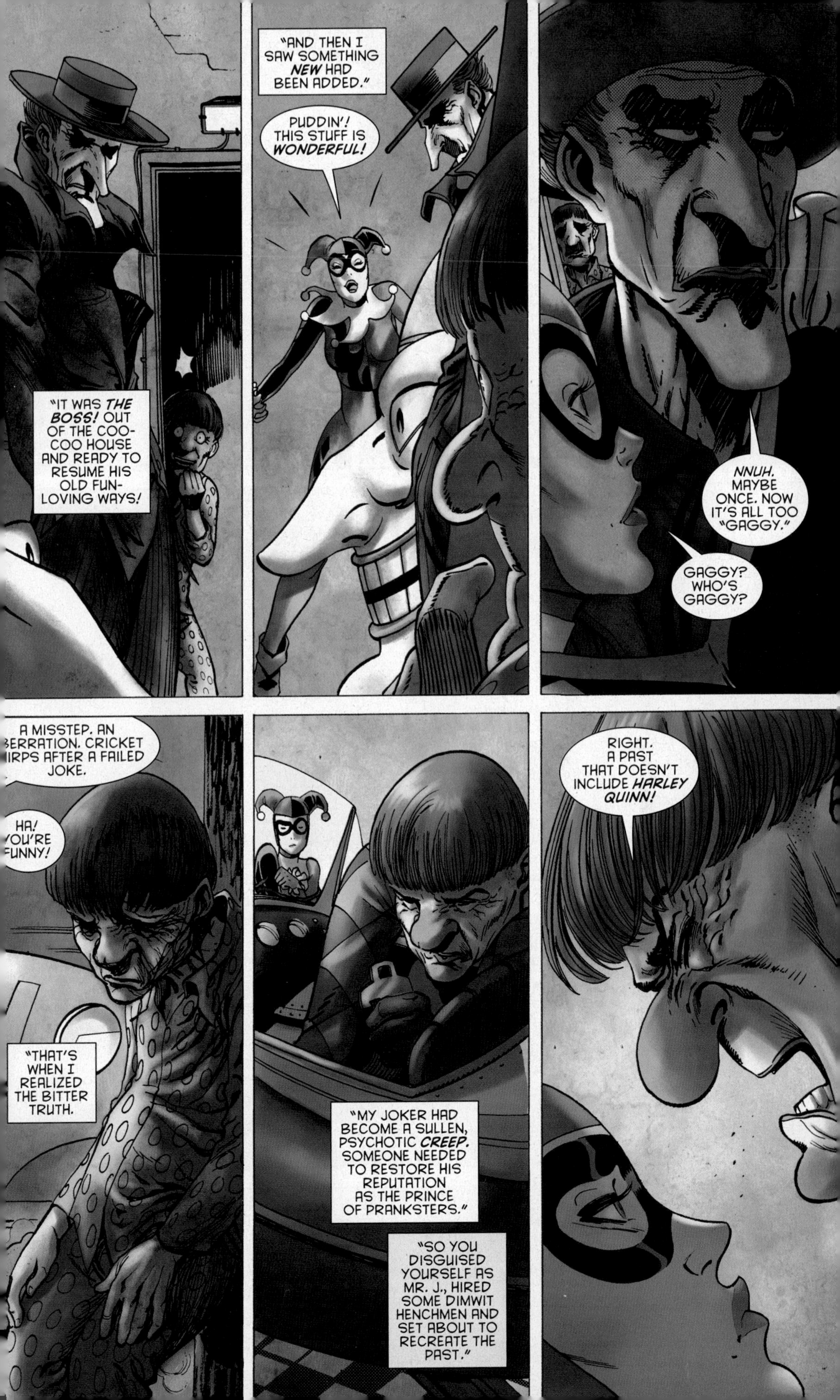
"IT WAS THE BOSS! OUT OF THE COO-COO HOUSE AND READY TO RESUME HIS OLD FUN-LOVING WAYS!
"AND THEN I SAW SOMETHING NEW HAD BEEN ADDED."
PUDDIN'! THIS STUFF IS WONDERFUL!
NNUH. MAYBE ONCE. NOW IT'S ALL TOO "GAGGY."
GAGGY? WHO'S GAGGY?
A MISSTEP. AN BERRATION. CRICKET HIRPS AFTER A FAILED JOKE.
HA! YOU'RE FUNNY!
"THAT'S WHEN I REALIZED THE BITTER TRUTH.
"MY JOKER HAD BECOME A SULLEN, PSYCHOTIC CREEP. SOMEONE NEEDED TO RESTORE HIS REPUTATION AS THE PRINCE OF PRANKSTERS."
"SO YOU DISGUISED YOURSELF AS MR. J., HIRED SOME DIMWIT HENCHMEN AND SET ABOUT TO RECREATE THE PAST."
RIGHT. A PAST THAT DOESN'T INCLUDE HARLEY QUINN!

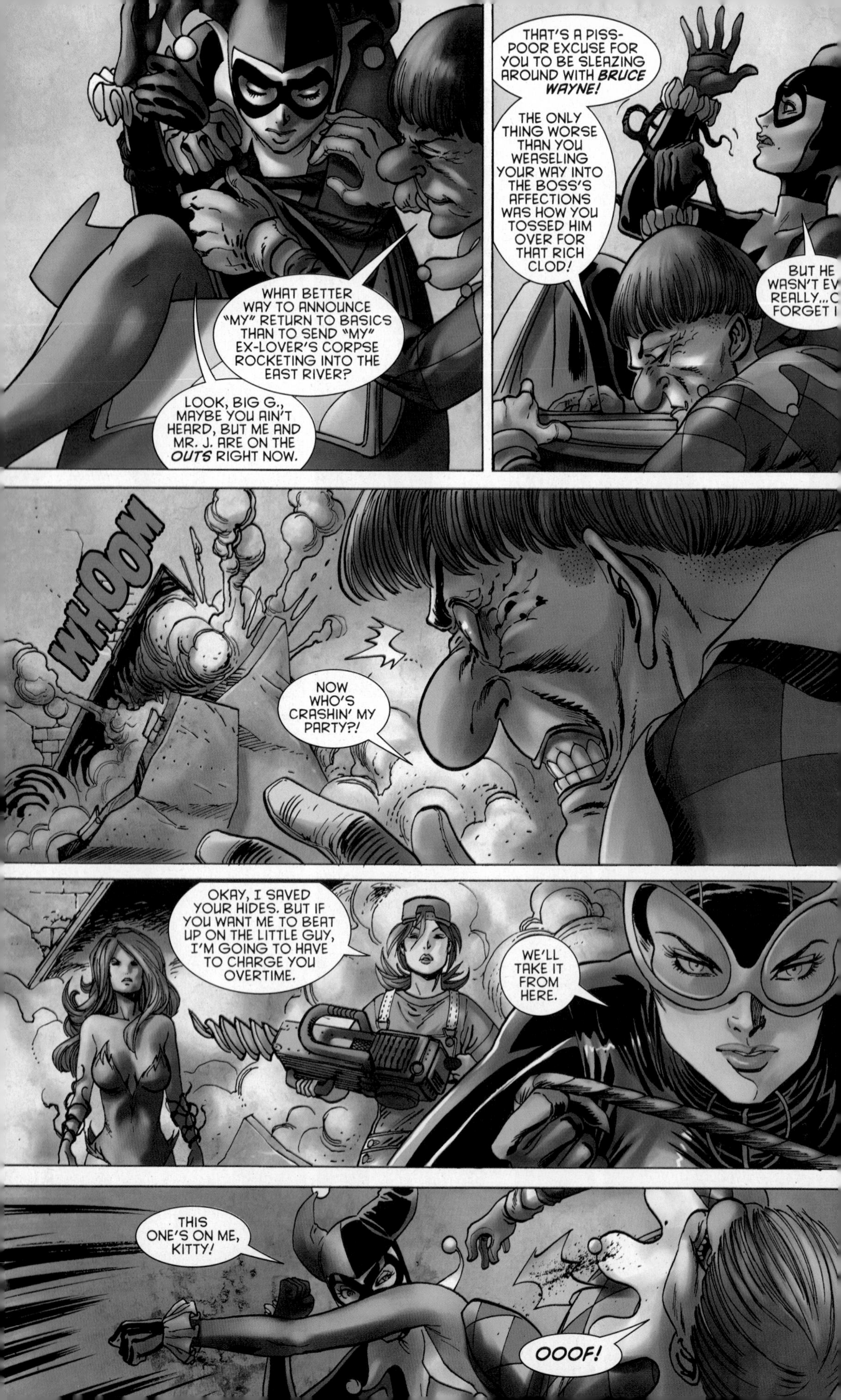
WHAT BETTER WAY TO ANNOUNCE "MY" RETURN TO BASICS THAN TO SEND "MY" EX-LOVER'S CORPSE ROCKETING INTO THE EAST RIVER?
LOOK, BIG G., MAYBE YOU AIN'T HEARD, BUT ME AND MR. J. ARE ON THE OUTS RIGHT NOW.
THAT'S A PISS-POOR EXCUSE FOR YOU TO BE SLEAZING AROUND WITH BRUCE WAYNE!
THE ONLY THING WORSE THAN YOU WEASELING YOUR WAY INTO THE BOSS'S AFFECTIONS WAS HOW YOU TOSSED HIM OVER FOR THAT RICH CLOD!
WHOOM
NOW WHO'S CRASHIN' MY PARTY?!
OKAY, I SAVED YOUR HIDES. BUT IF YOU WANT ME TO BEAT UP ON THE LITTLE GUY, I'M GOING TO HAVE TO CHARGE YOU OVERTIME.
WE'LL TAKE IT FROM HERE.
THIS ONE'S ON ME, KITTY!
OOOF!

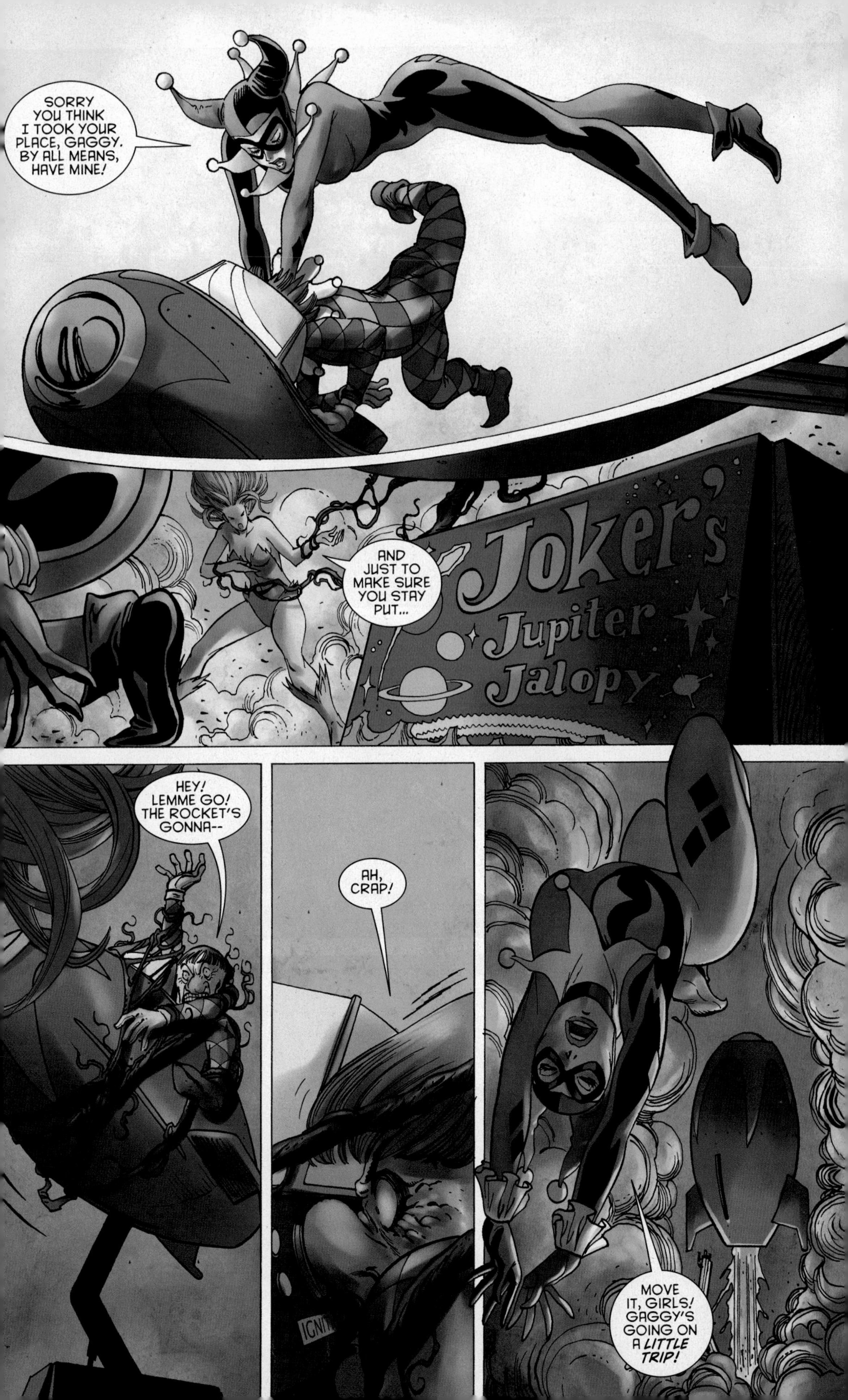
SORRY YOU THINK I TOOK YOUR PLACE, GAGGY. BY ALL MEANS, HAVE MINE!
AND JUST TO MAKE SURE YOU STAY PUT...
Joker's Jupiter Jalopy
HEY! LEMME GO! THE ROCKET'S GONNA--
AH, CRAP!
MOVE IT, GIRLS! GAGGY'S GOING ON A *LITTLE TRIP!*

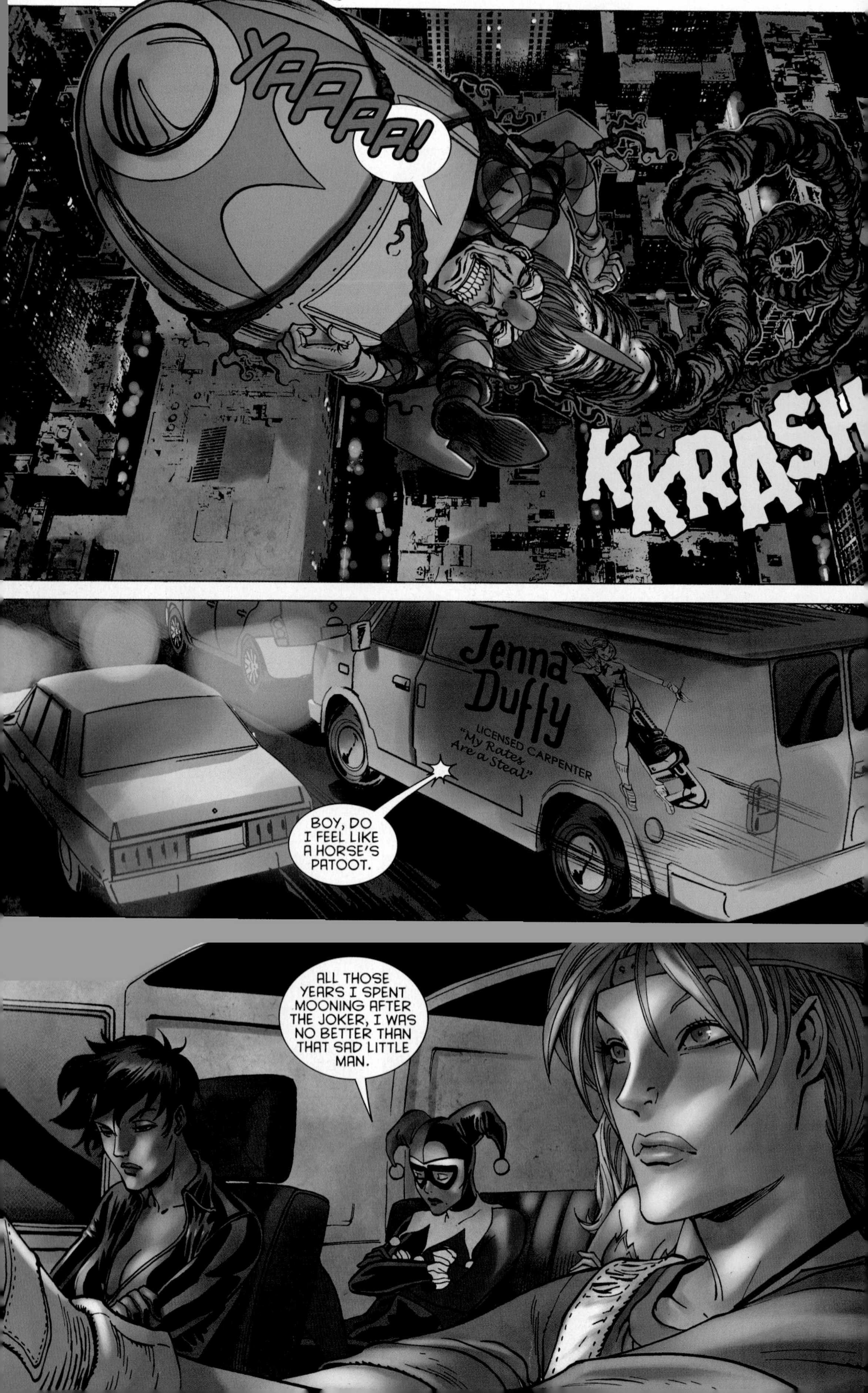
YAAAAA!
KKRASH
Jenna Duffy
LICENSED CARPENTER
"My Rates Are a Steal"
BOY, DO I FEEL LIKE A HORSE'S PATOOT.
ALL THOSE YEARS I SPENT MOONING AFTER THE JOKER, I WAS NO BETTER THAN THAT SAD LITTLE MAN.

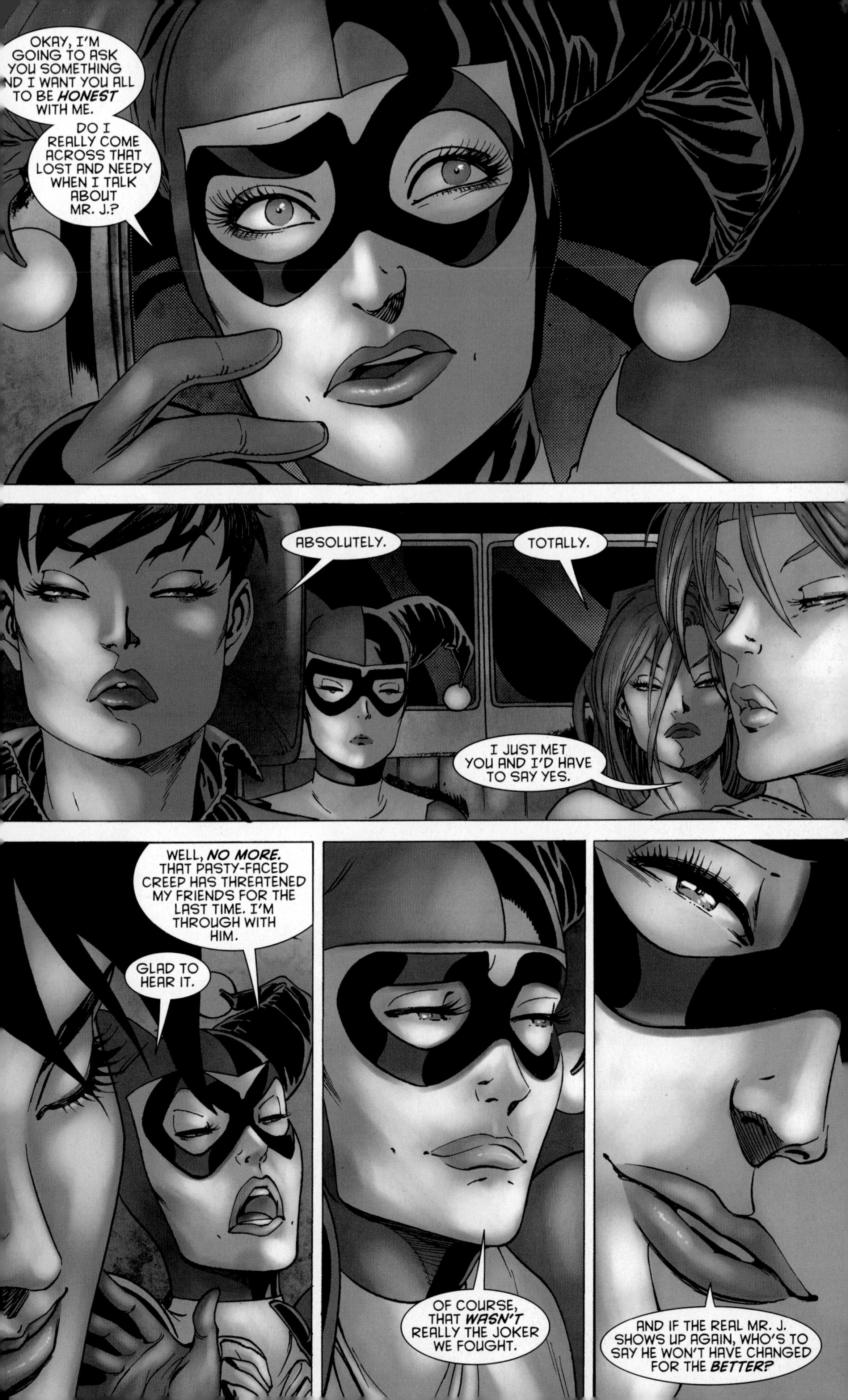

OKAY, I'M GOING TO ASK YOU SOMETHING ND I WANT YOU ALL TO BE *HONEST* WITH ME.
DO I REALLY COME ACROSS THAT LOST AND NEEDY WHEN I TALK ABOUT MR. J.?
ABSOLUTELY.
TOTALLY.
I JUST MET YOU AND I'D HAVE TO SAY YES.
WELL, *NO MORE.* THAT PASTY-FACED CREEP HAS THREATENED MY FRIENDS FOR THE LAST TIME. I'M THROUGH WITH HIM.
GLAD TO HEAR IT.
OF COURSE, THAT *WASN'T* REALLY THE JOKER WE FOUGHT.
AND IF THE REAL MR. J. SHOWS UP AGAIN, WHO'S TO SAY HE WON'T HAVE CHANGED FOR THE *BETTER?*

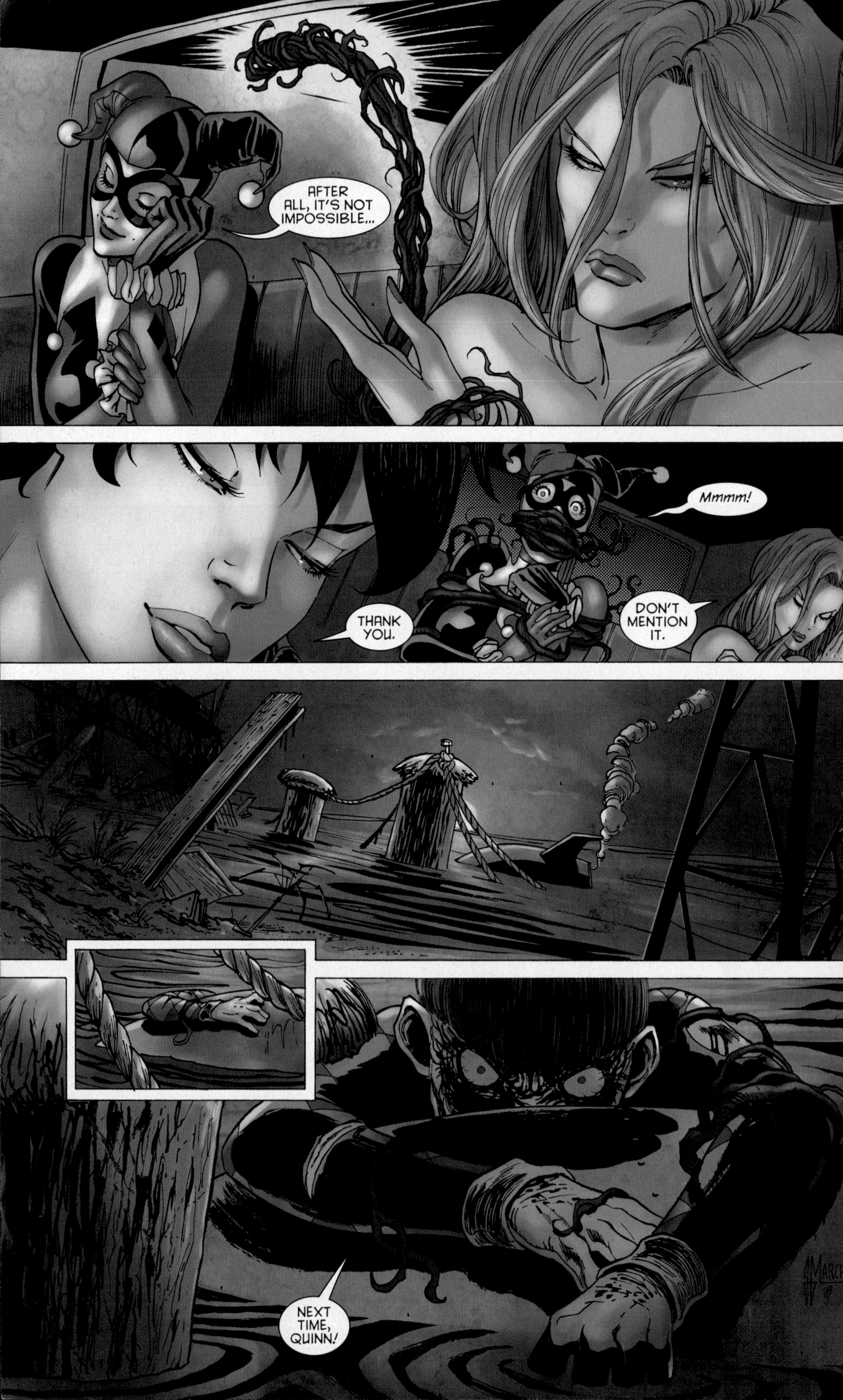
AFTER ALL, IT'S NOT IMPOSSIBLE...
Mmmm!
THANK YOU.
DON'T MENTION IT.
NEXT TIME, QUINN!

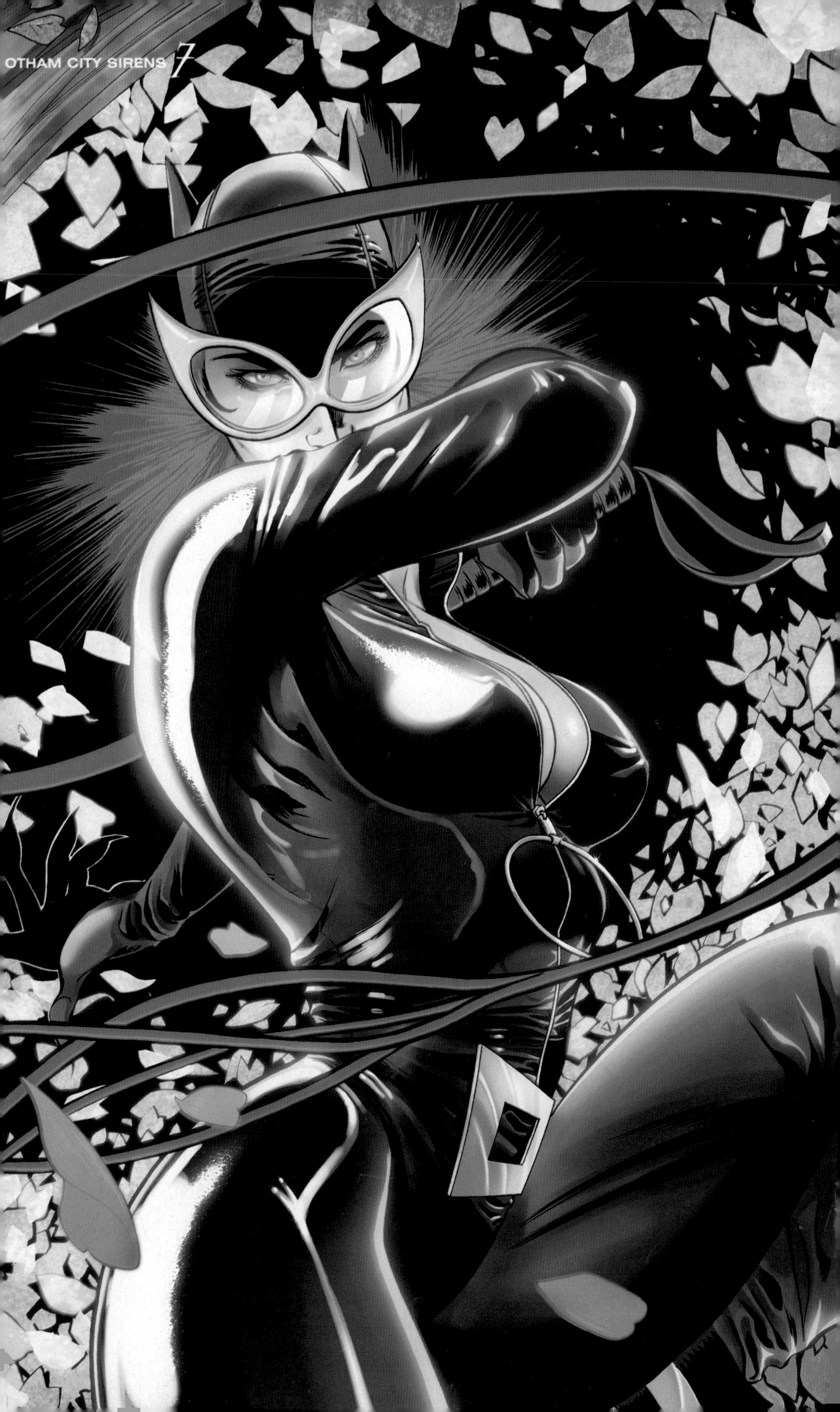
OTHAM CITY SIRENS 7

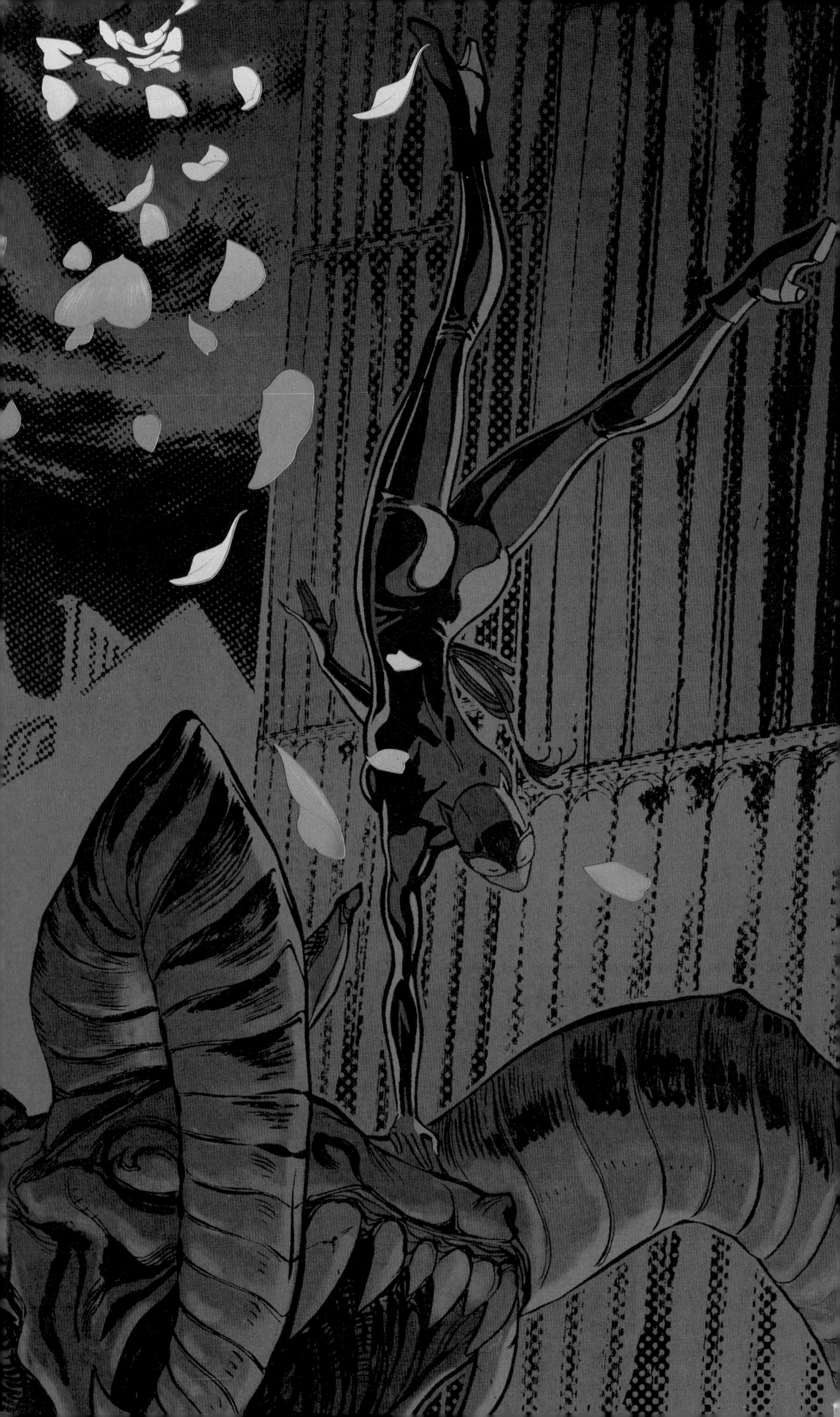

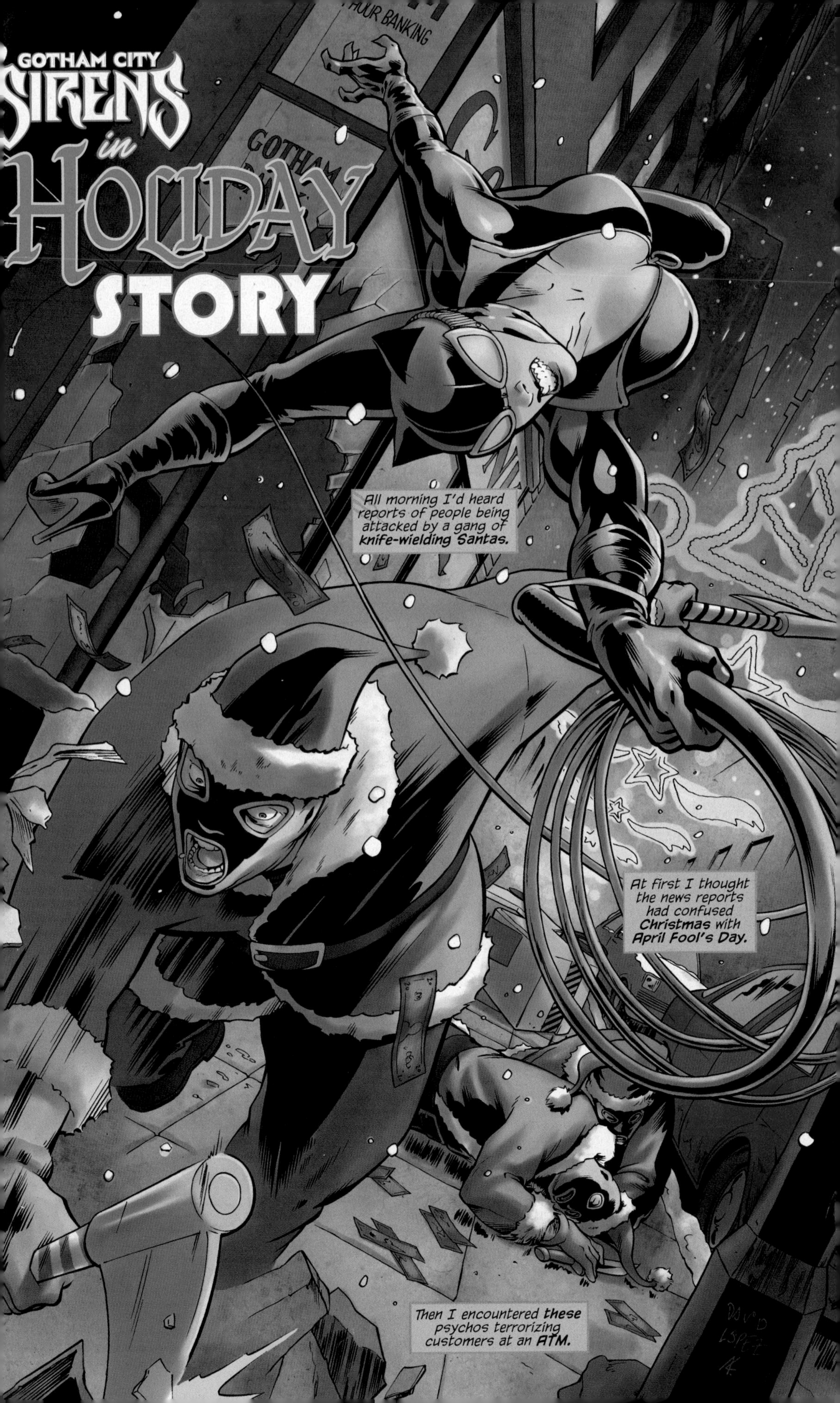

HOUR BANKING
GOTHAM
GOTHAM CITY SIRENS in HOLIDAY STORY
All morning I'd heard reports of people being attacked by a gang of knife-wielding Santas.
At first I thought the news reports had confused Christmas with April Fool's Day.
Then I encountered these psychos terrorizing customers at an ATM.

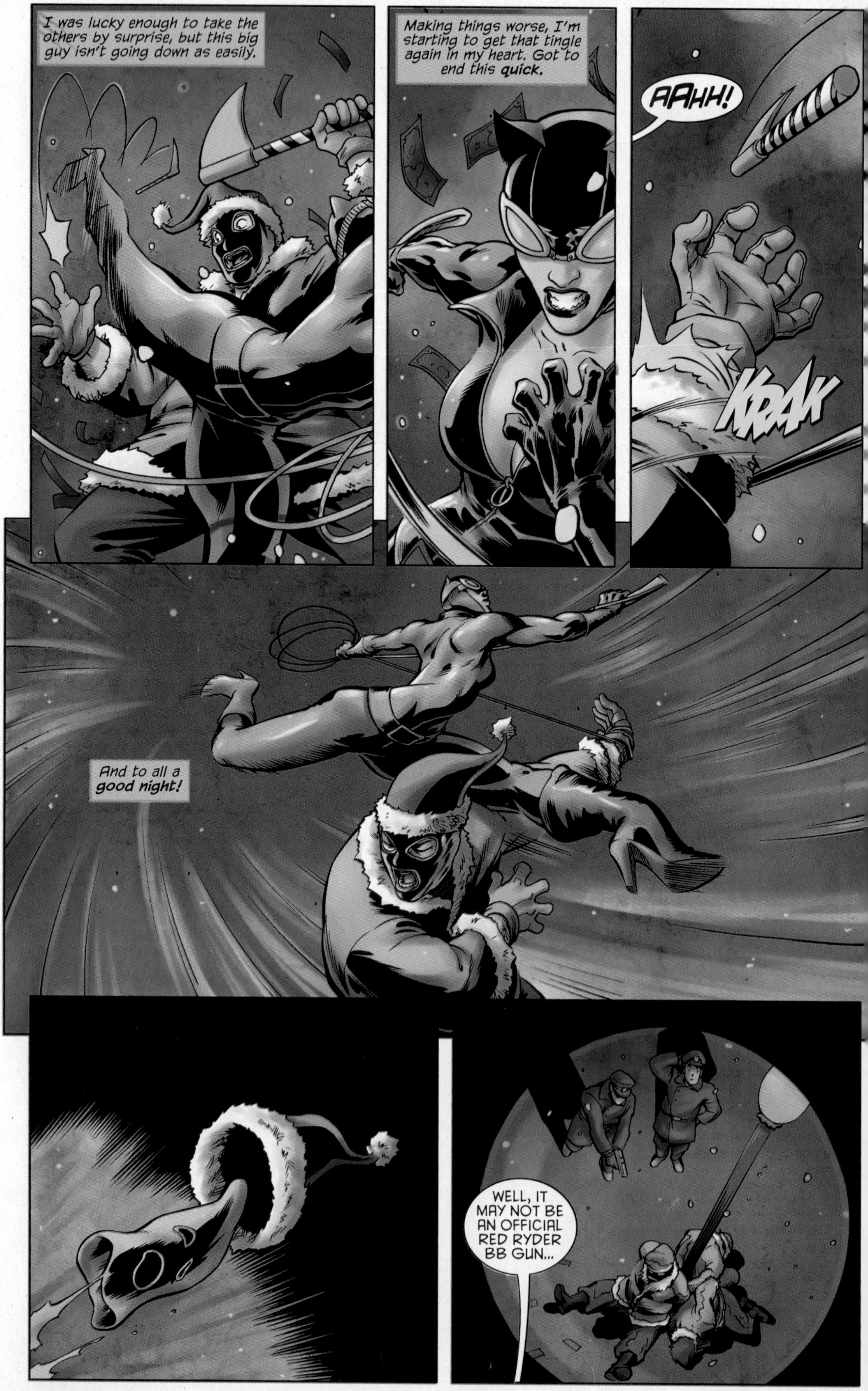
I was lucky enough to take the others by surprise, but this big guy isn't going down as easily.
Making things worse, I'm starting to get that tingle again in my heart. Got to end this **quick.**
AAHH!
KRAK
And to all a **good night!**
WELL, IT MAY NOT BE AN OFFICIAL RED RYDER BB GUN...

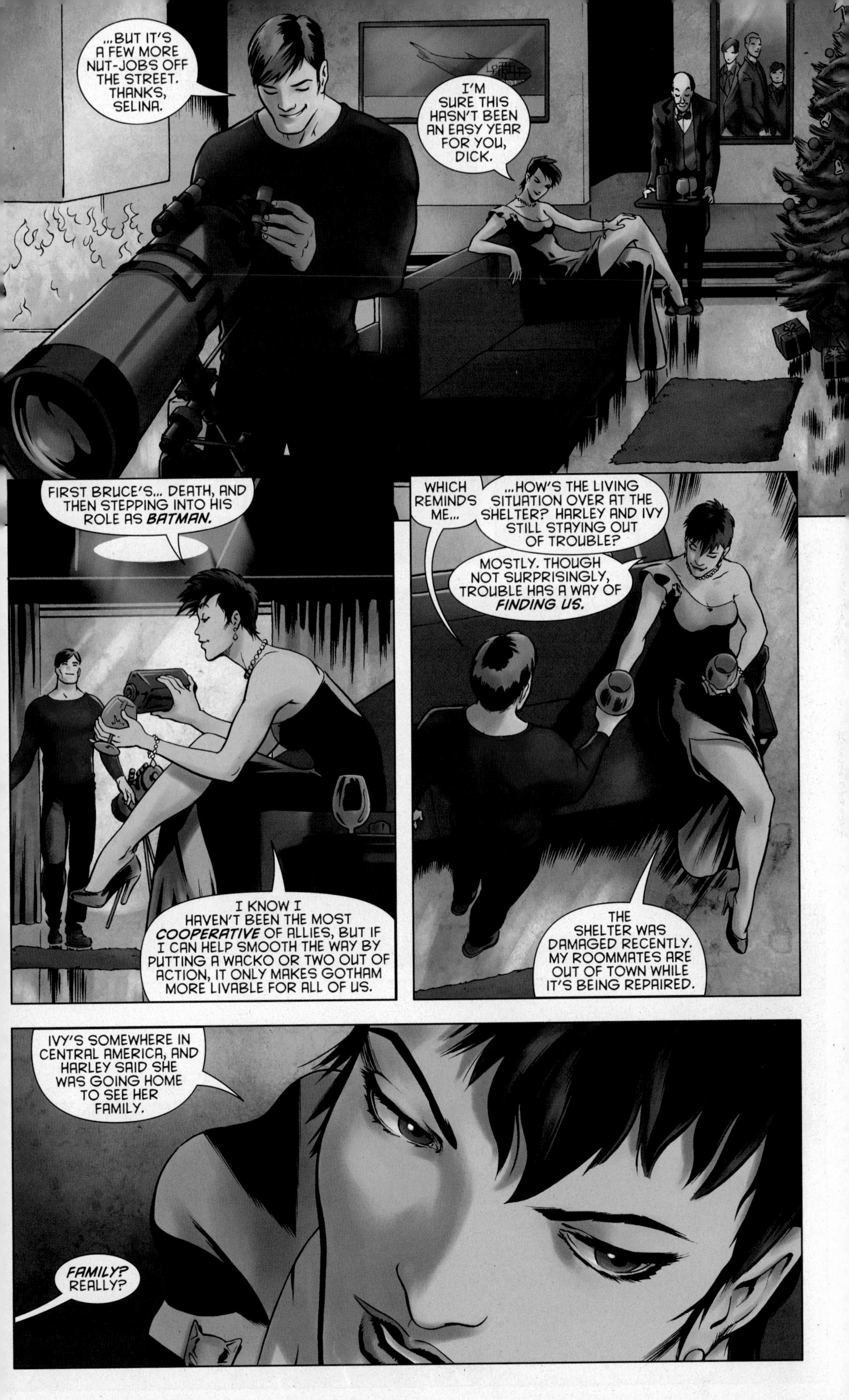

...BUT IT'S A FEW MORE NUT-JOBS OFF THE STREET. THANKS, SELINA.
I'M SURE THIS HASN'T BEEN AN EASY YEAR FOR YOU, DICK.
FIRST BRUCE'S... DEATH, AND THEN STEPPING INTO HIS ROLE AS *BATMAN.*
I KNOW I HAVEN'T BEEN THE MOST *COOPERATIVE* OF ALLIES, BUT IF I CAN HELP SMOOTH THE WAY BY PUTTING A WACKO OR TWO OUT OF ACTION, IT ONLY MAKES GOTHAM MORE LIVABLE FOR ALL OF US.
WHICH REMINDS ME...
...HOW'S THE LIVING SITUATION OVER AT THE SHELTER? HARLEY AND IVY STILL STAYING OUT OF TROUBLE?
MOSTLY. THOUGH NOT SURPRISINGLY, TROUBLE HAS A WAY OF *FINDING US.*
THE SHELTER WAS DAMAGED RECENTLY. MY ROOMMATES ARE OUT OF TOWN WHILE IT'S BEING REPAIRED.
IVY'S SOMEWHERE IN CENTRAL AMERICA, AND HARLEY SAID SHE WAS GOING HOME TO SEE HER FAMILY.
*FAMILY?* REALLY?

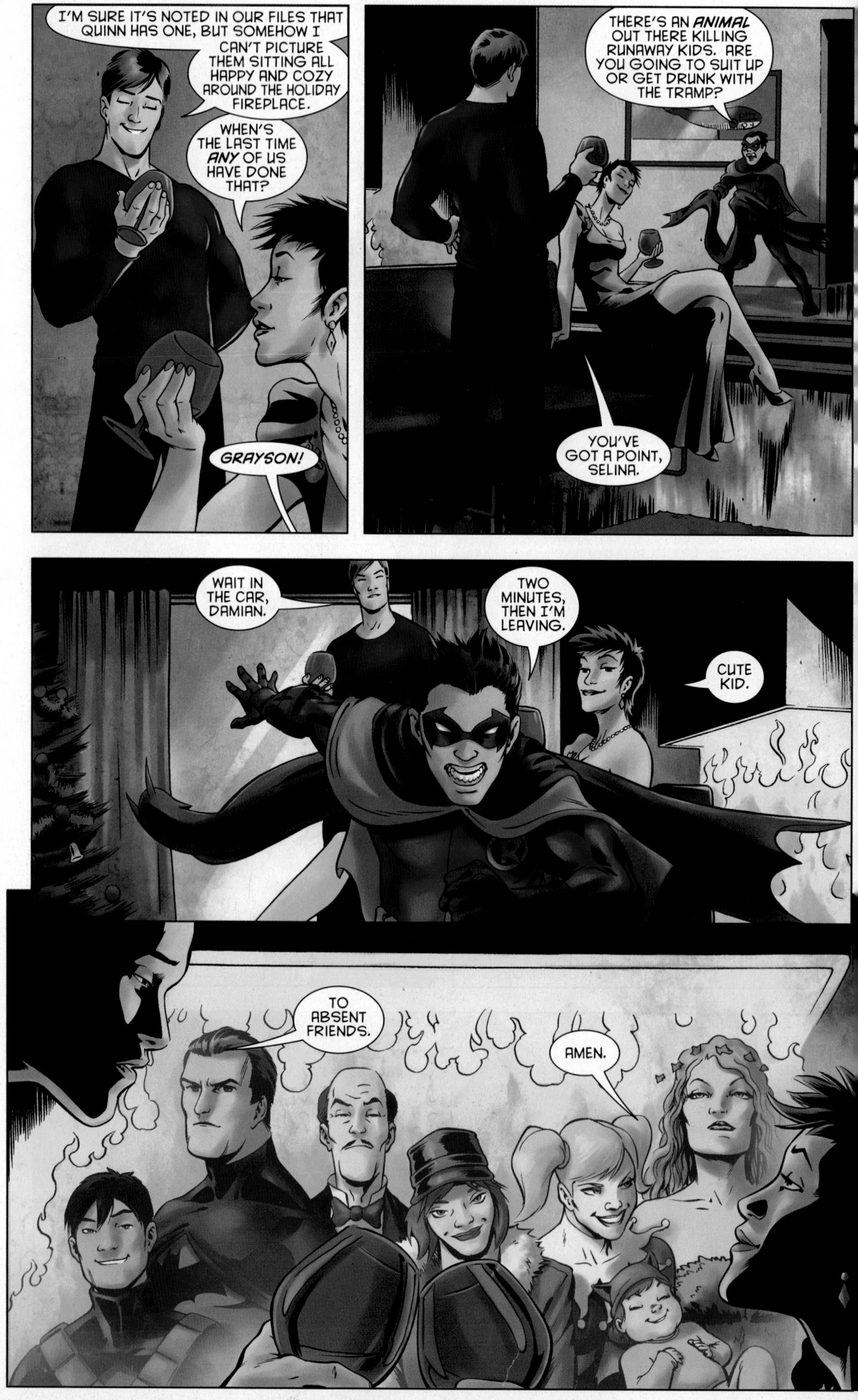
I'M SURE IT'S NOTED IN OUR FILES THAT QUINN HAS ONE, BUT SOMEHOW I CAN'T PICTURE THEM SITTING ALL HAPPY AND COZY AROUND THE HOLIDAY FIREPLACE.
WHEN'S THE LAST TIME ANY OF US HAVE DONE THAT?
GRAYSON!
THERE'S AN ANIMAL OUT THERE KILLING RUNAWAY KIDS. ARE YOU GOING TO SUIT UP OR GET DRUNK WITH THE TRAMP?
YOU'VE GOT A POINT, SELINA.
WAIT IN THE CAR, DAMIAN.
TWO MINUTES, THEN I'M LEAVING.
CUTE KID.
TO ABSENT FRIENDS.
AMEN.

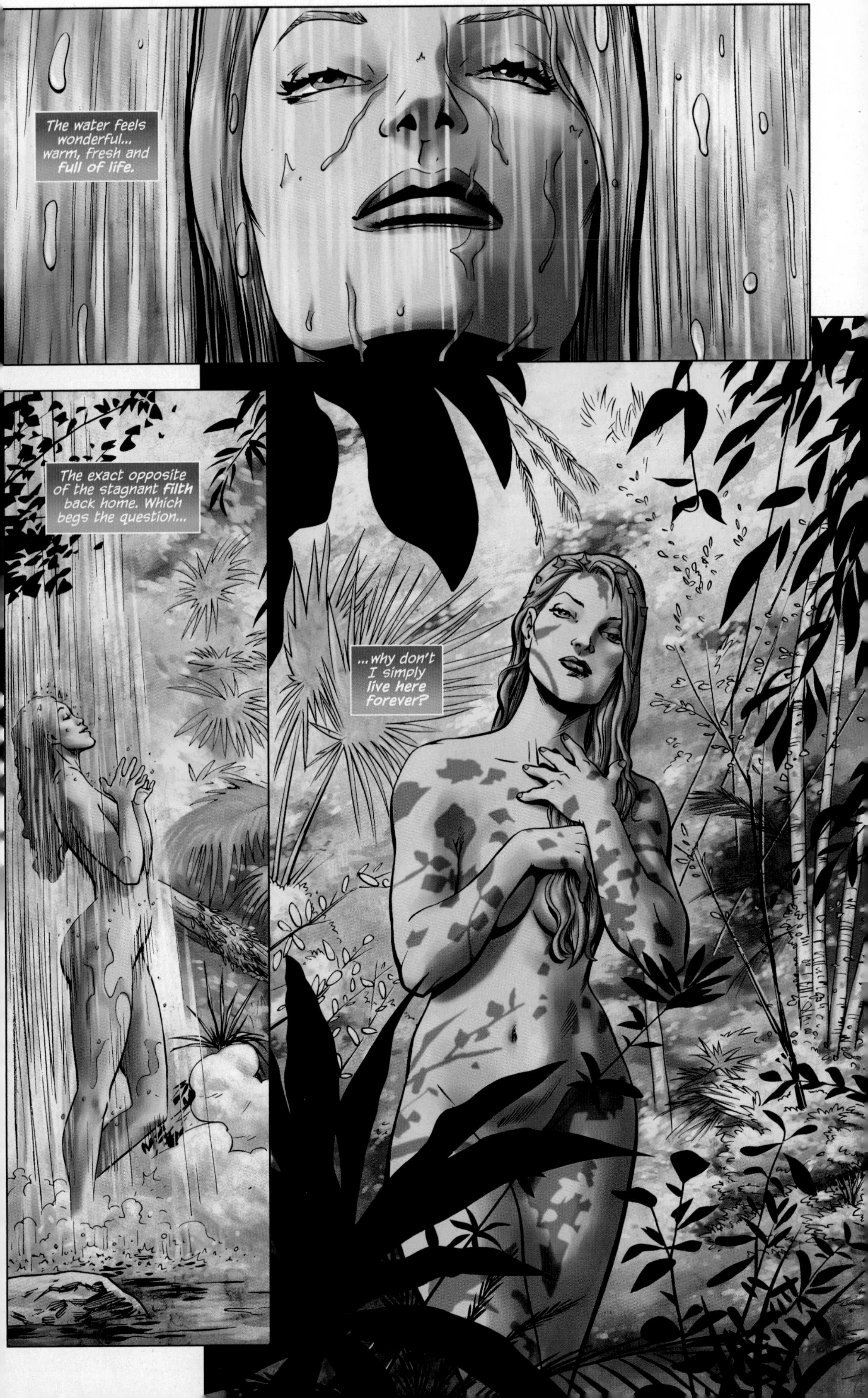
The water feels wonderful... warm, fresh and full of life.
The exact opposite of the stagnant filth back home. Which begs the question...
...why don't I simply live here forever?

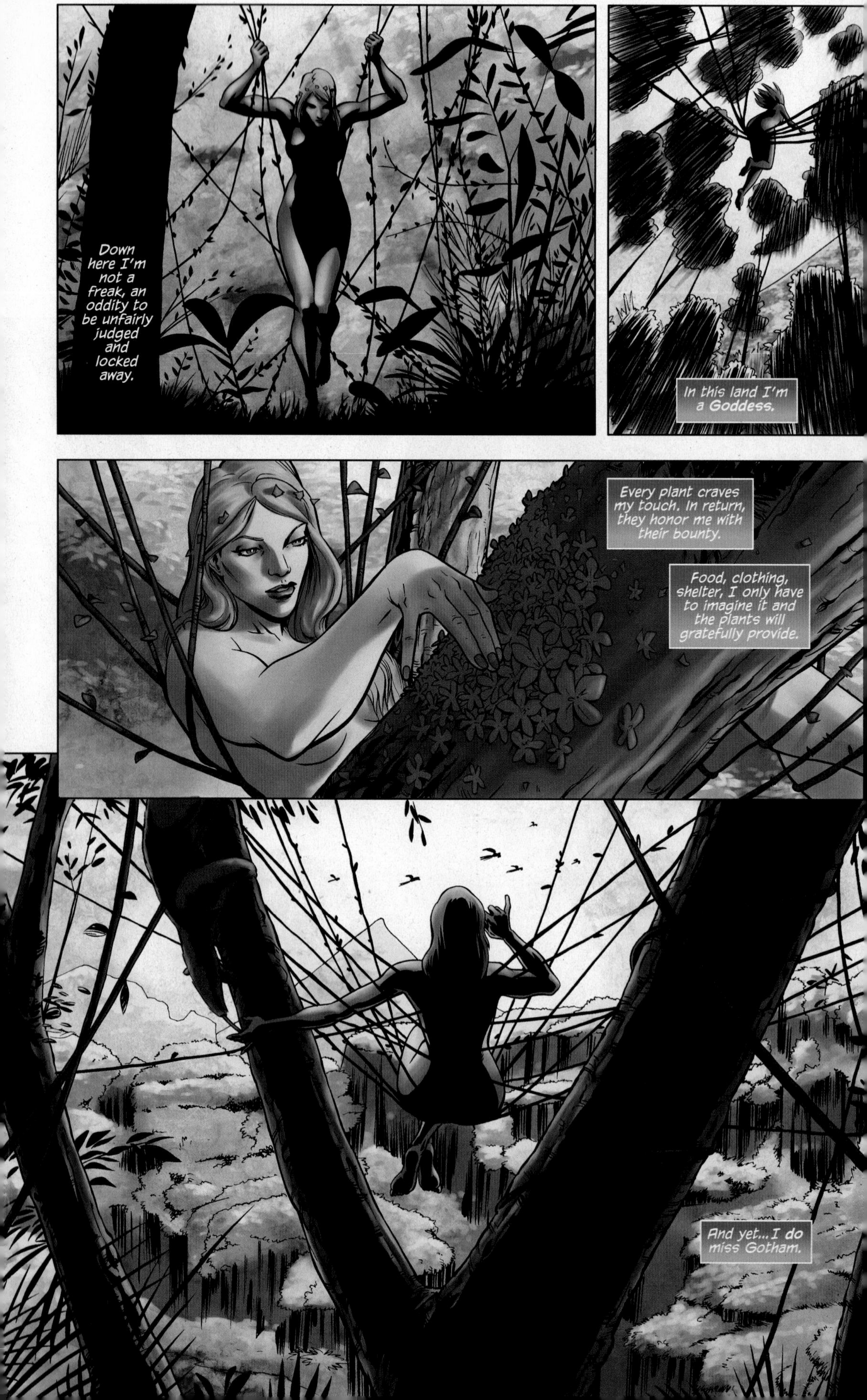
Down here I'm not a freak, an oddity to be unfairly judged and locked away.
In this land I'm a Goddess.
Every plant craves my touch. In return, they honor me with their bounty.
Food, clothing, shelter, I only have to imagine it and the plants will gratefully provide.
And yet...I do miss Gotham.

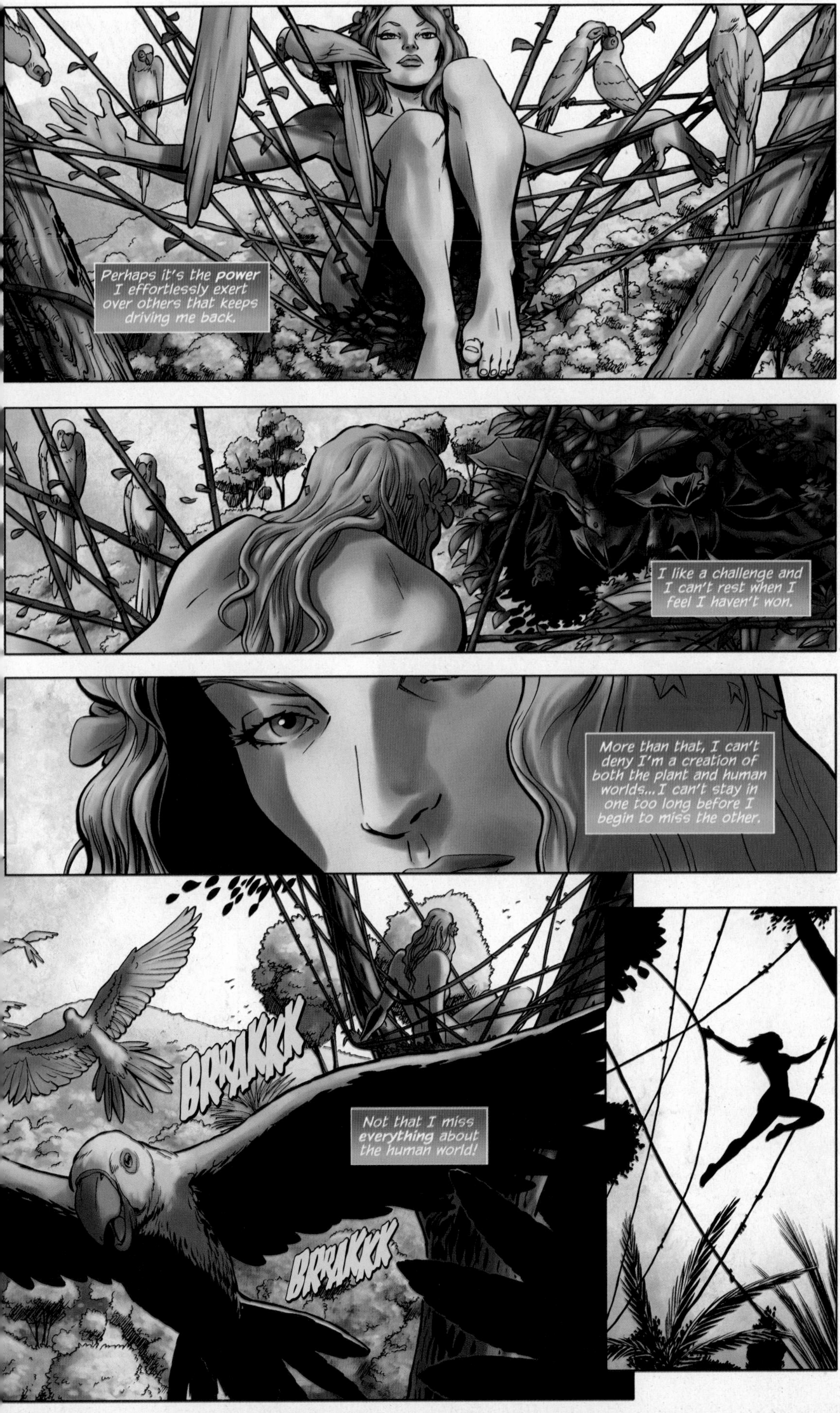
Perhaps it's the **power** I effortlessly exert over others that keeps driving me back.
I like a challenge and I can't rest when I feel I haven't won.
More than that, I can't deny I'm a creation of both the plant and human worlds...I can't stay in one too long before I begin to miss the other.
BRRAKKK
Not that I miss **everything** about the human world!
BRRAKKK

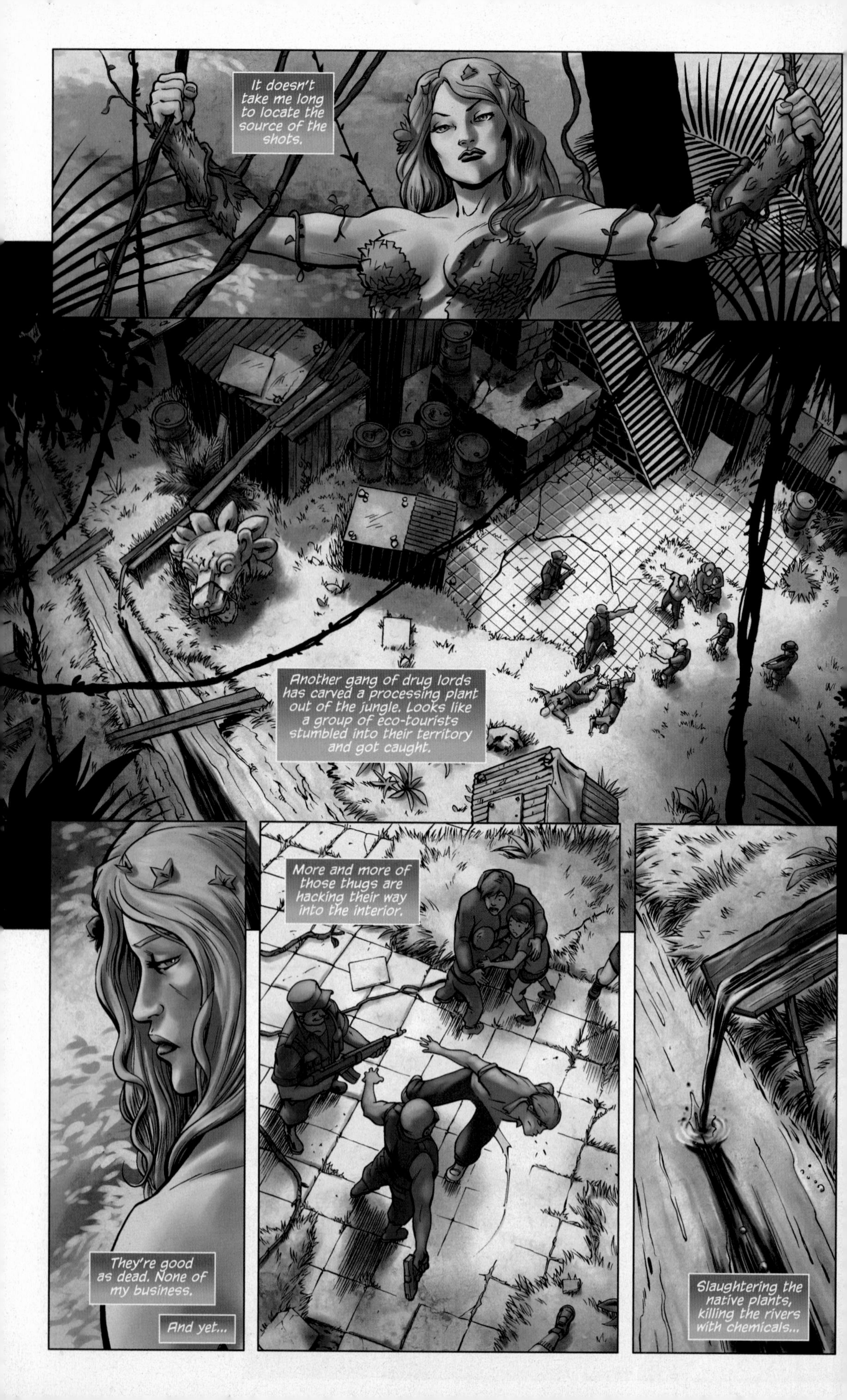
It doesn't take me long to locate the source of the shots.
Another gang of drug lords has carved a processing plant out of the jungle. Looks like a group of eco-tourists stumbled into their territory and got caught.
They're good as dead. None of my business.
And yet...
More and more of those thugs are hacking their way into the interior.
Slaughtering the native plants, killing the rivers with chemicals...

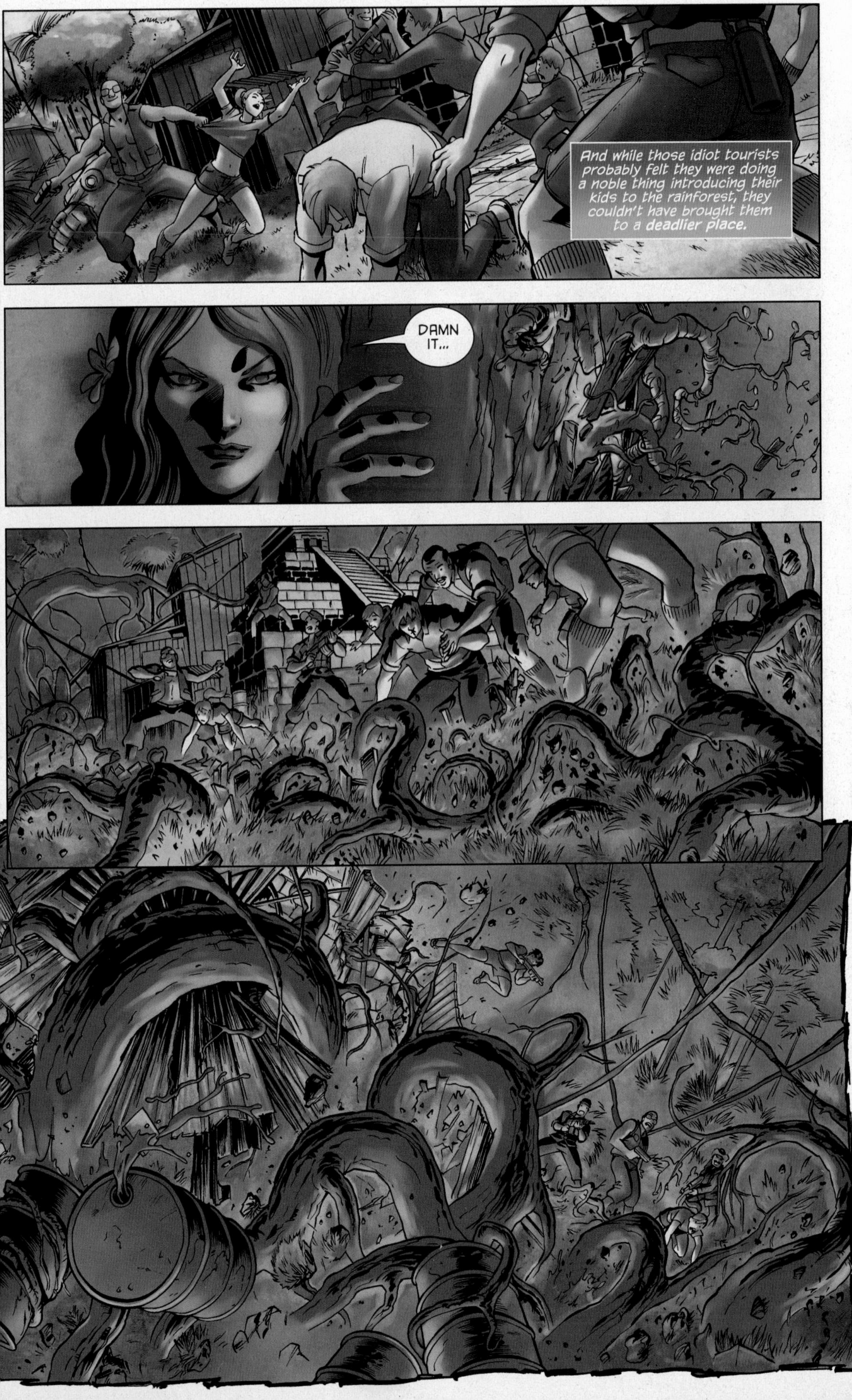

And while those idiot tourists probably felt they were doing a noble thing introducing their kids to the rainforest, they couldn't have brought them to a deadlier place.
DAMN IT...

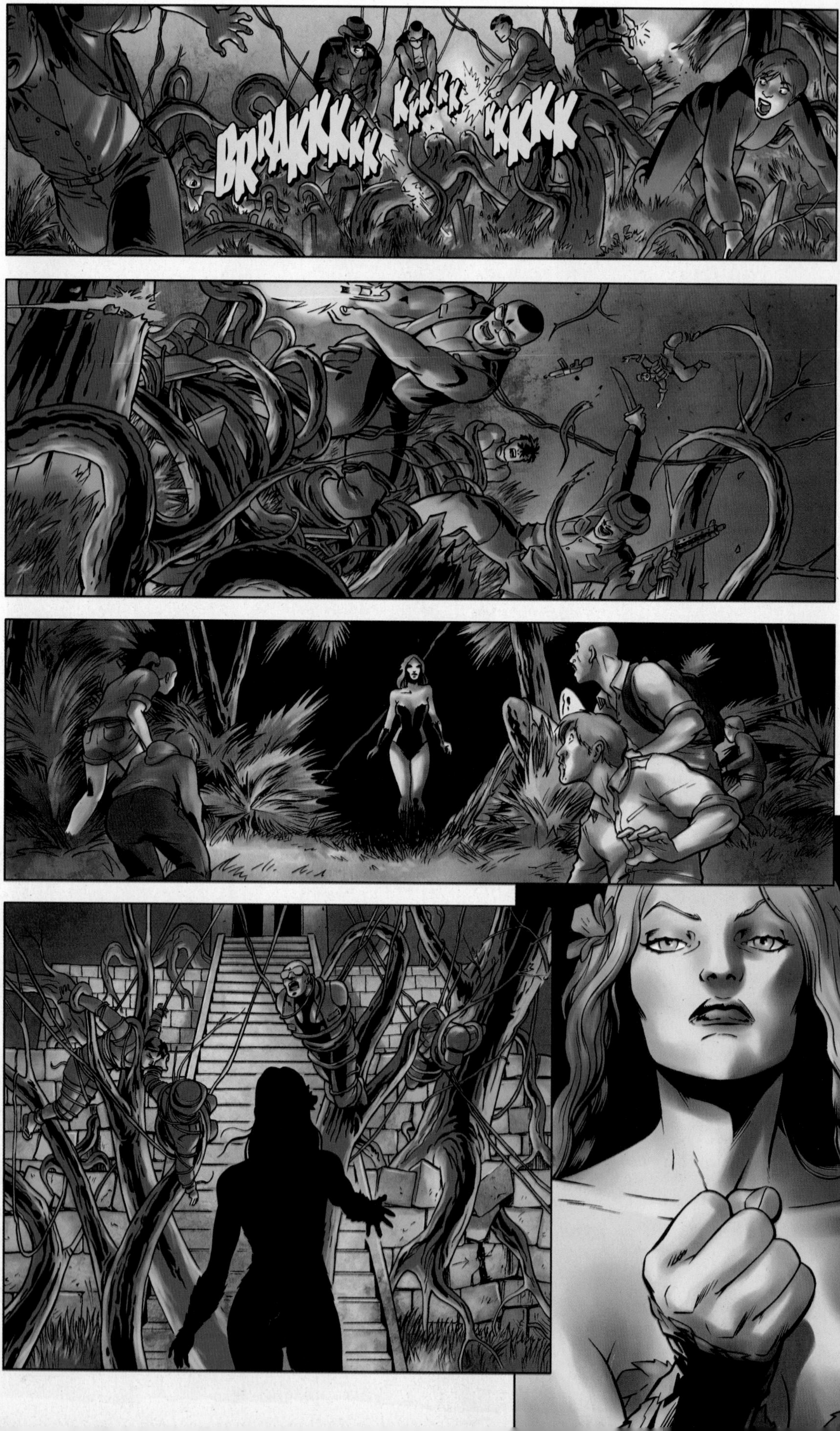
BRRAKKKKKK
KKKKK
KKKK

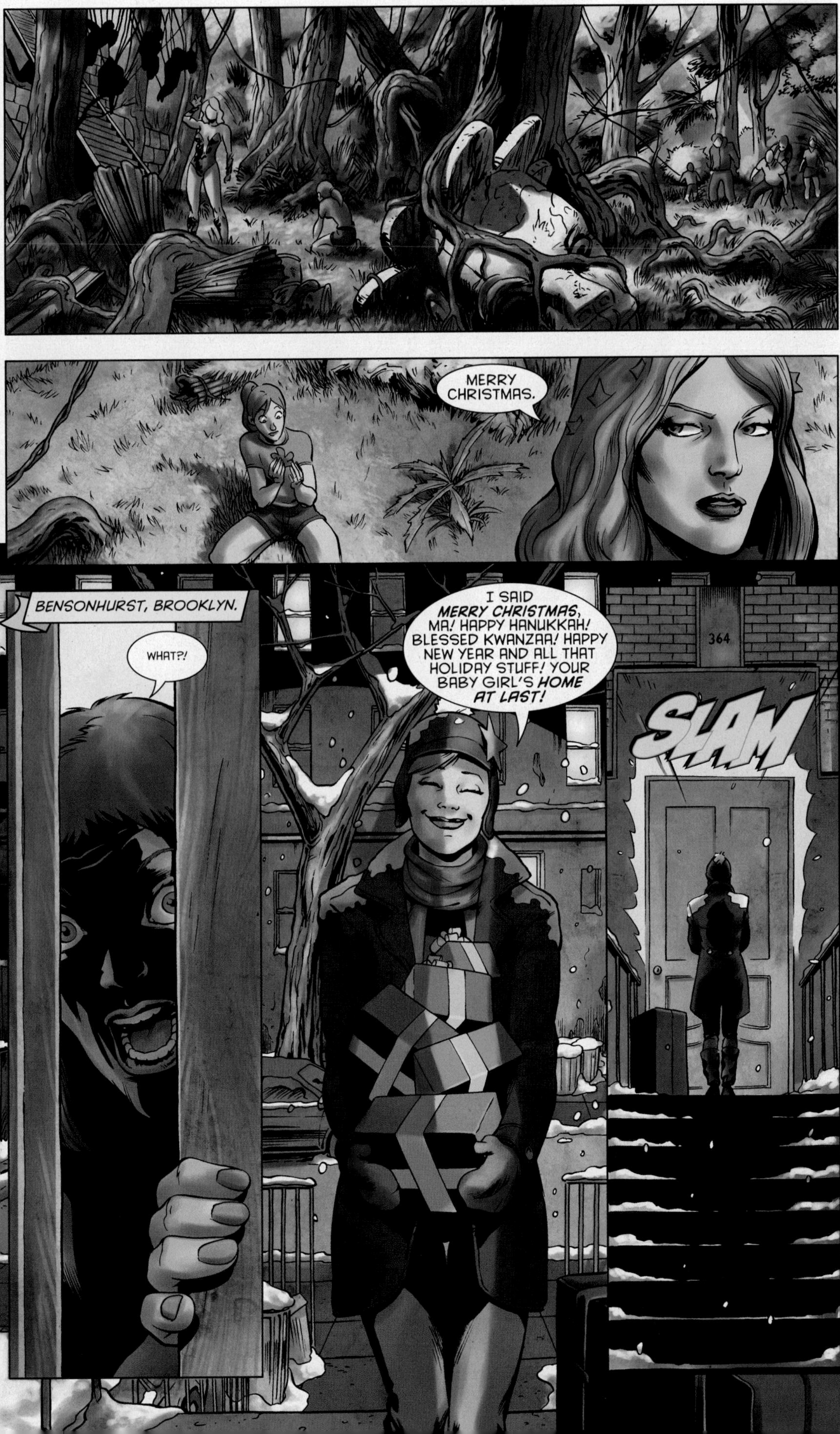
MERRY CHRISTMAS.
BENSONHURST, BROOKLYN.
WHAT?!
I SAID MERRY CHRISTMAS, MA! HAPPY HANUKKAH! BLESSED KWANZAA! HAPPY NEW YEAR AND ALL THAT HOLIDAY STUFF! YOUR BABY GIRL'S HOME AT LAST!
364
SLAM

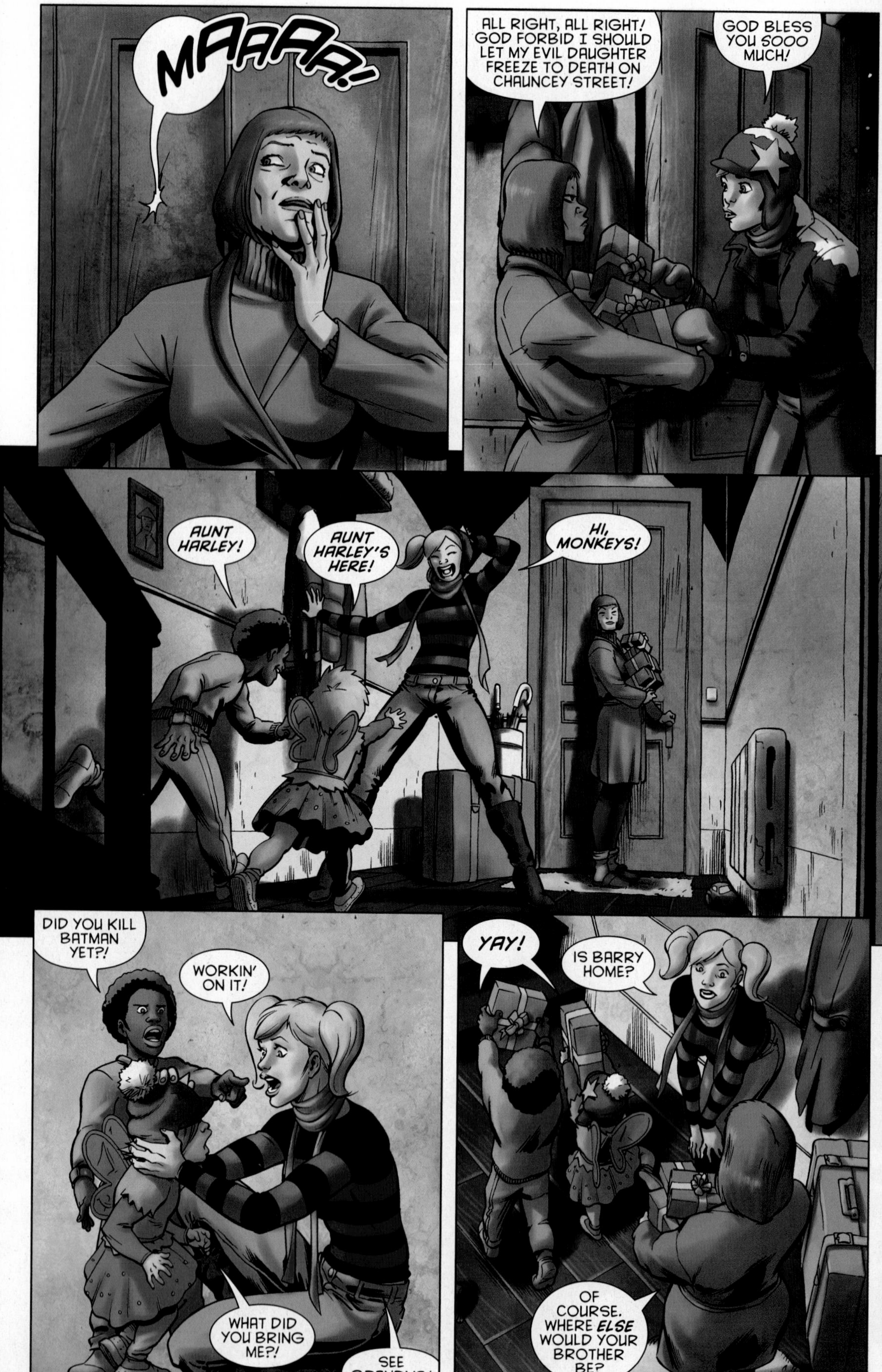
MAAAA!
ALL RIGHT, ALL RIGHT! GOD FORBID I SHOULD LET MY EVIL DAUGHTER FREEZE TO DEATH ON CHAUNCEY STREET!
GOD BLESS YOU SOOO MUCH!
AUNT HARLEY!
AUNT HARLEY'S HERE!
HI, MONKEYS!
DID YOU KILL BATMAN YET?!
WORKIN' ON IT!
WHAT DID YOU BRING ME?!
SEE GRANDMA!
YAY!
IS BARRY HOME?
OF COURSE. WHERE *ELSE* WOULD YOUR BROTHER BE?

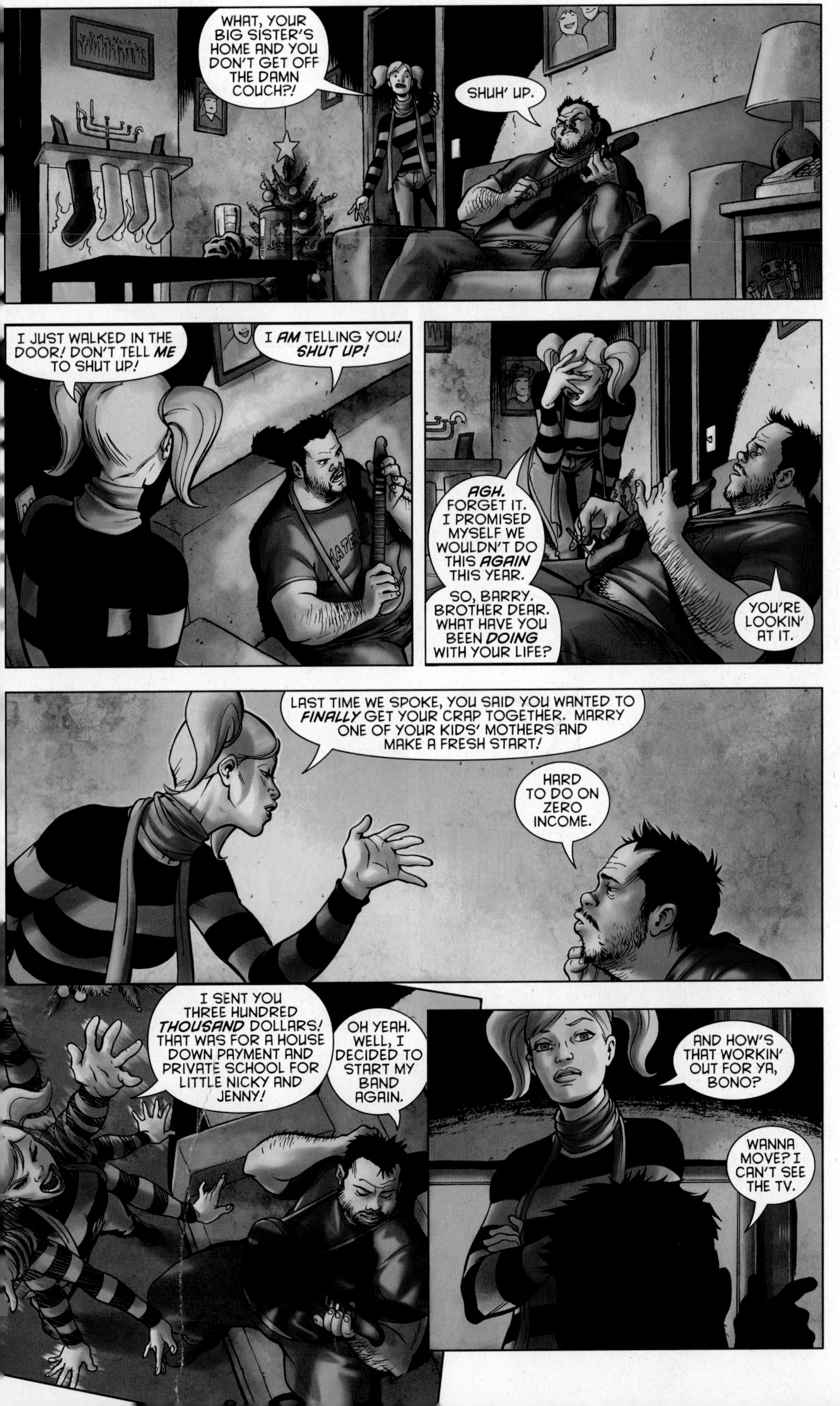
WHAT, YOUR BIG SISTER'S HOME AND YOU DON'T GET OFF THE DAMN COUCH?!
SHUH' UP.
I JUST WALKED IN THE DOOR! DON'T TELL *ME* TO SHUT UP!
I *AM* TELLING YOU! *SHUT UP!*
*AGH.* FORGET IT. I PROMISED MYSELF WE WOULDN'T DO THIS *AGAIN* THIS YEAR.
SO, BARRY. BROTHER DEAR. WHAT HAVE YOU BEEN *DOING* WITH YOUR LIFE?
YOU'RE LOOKIN' AT IT.
LAST TIME WE SPOKE, YOU SAID YOU WANTED TO *FINALLY* GET YOUR CRAP TOGETHER. MARRY ONE OF YOUR KIDS' MOTHERS AND MAKE A FRESH START!
HARD TO DO ON ZERO INCOME.
I SENT YOU THREE HUNDRED *THOUSAND* DOLLARS! THAT WAS FOR A HOUSE DOWN PAYMENT AND PRIVATE SCHOOL FOR LITTLE NICKY AND JENNY!
OH YEAH. WELL, I DECIDED TO START MY BAND AGAIN.
AND HOW'S THAT WORKIN' OUT FOR YA, BONO?
WANNA MOVE? I CAN'T SEE THE TV.

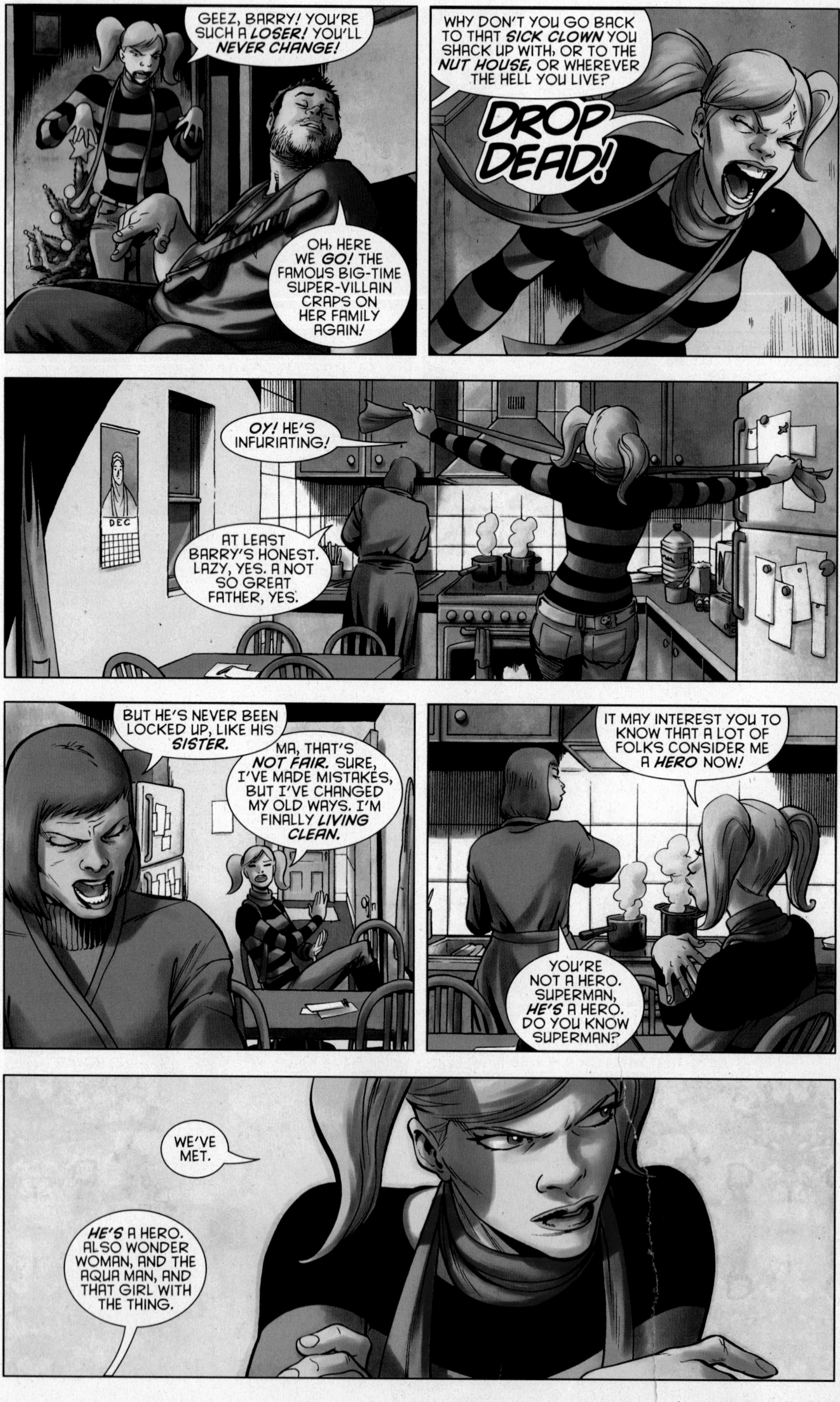
GEEZ, BARRY! YOU'RE SUCH A LOSER! YOU'LL NEVER CHANGE!
OH, HERE WE GO! THE FAMOUS BIG-TIME SUPER-VILLAIN CRAPS ON HER FAMILY AGAIN!
WHY DON'T YOU GO BACK TO THAT SICK CLOWN YOU SHACK UP WITH, OR TO THE NUT HOUSE, OR WHEREVER THE HELL YOU LIVE?
DROP DEAD!
OY! HE'S INFURIATING!
DEC
AT LEAST BARRY'S HONEST. LAZY, YES. A NOT SO GREAT FATHER, YES.
BUT HE'S NEVER BEEN LOCKED UP, LIKE HIS SISTER.
MA, THAT'S NOT FAIR. SURE, I'VE MADE MISTAKES, BUT I'VE CHANGED MY OLD WAYS. I'M FINALLY LIVING CLEAN.
IT MAY INTEREST YOU TO KNOW THAT A LOT OF FOLKS CONSIDER ME A HERO NOW!
YOU'RE NOT A HERO. SUPERMAN, HE'S A HERO. DO YOU KNOW SUPERMAN?
WE'VE MET.
HE'S A HERO. ALSO WONDER WOMAN, AND THE AQUA MAN, AND THAT GIRL WITH THE THING.

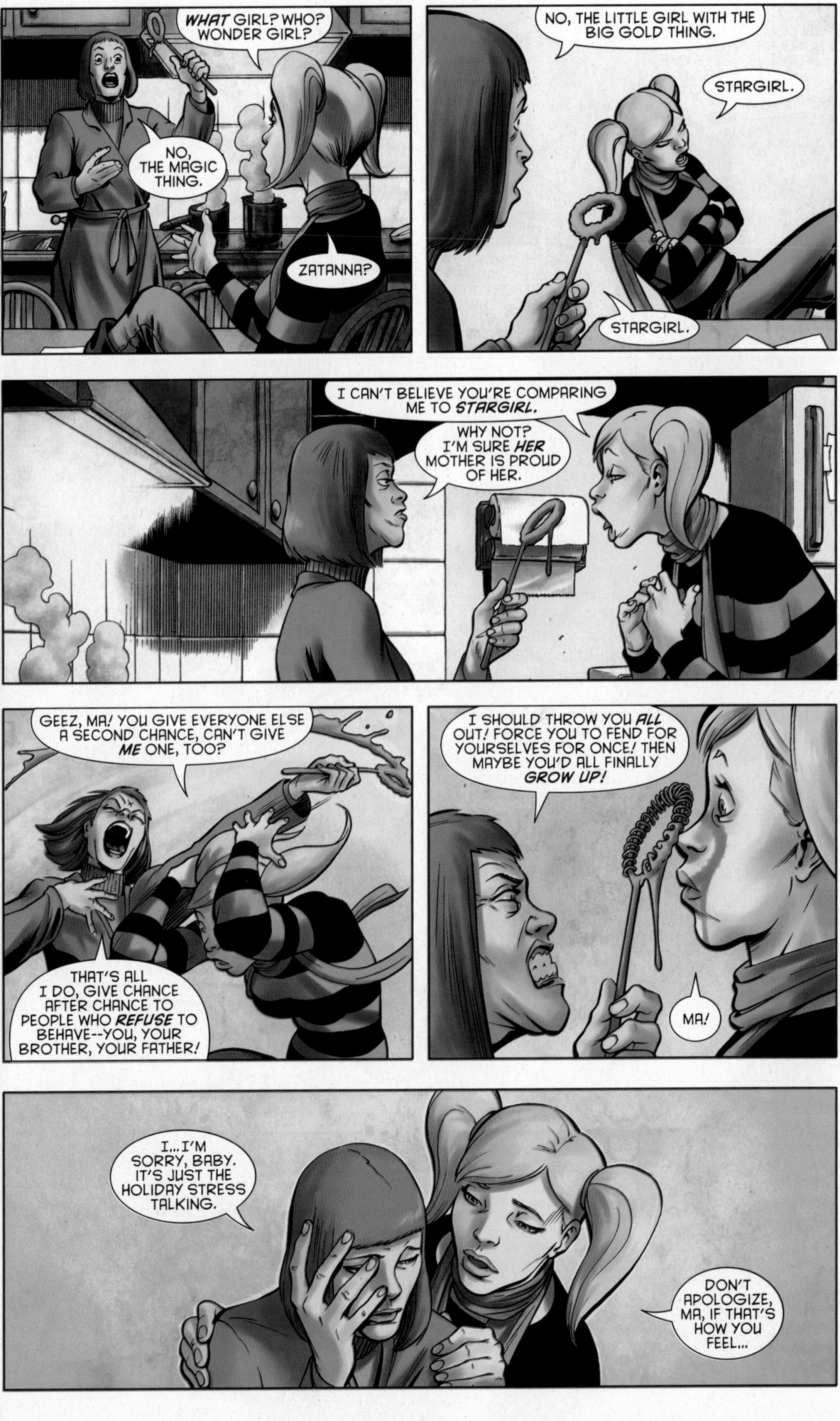

WHAT GIRL? WHO? WONDER GIRL?
NO, THE MAGIC THING.
ZATANNA?
NO, THE LITTLE GIRL WITH THE BIG GOLD THING.
STARGIRL.
STARGIRL.
I CAN'T BELIEVE YOU'RE COMPARING ME TO STARGIRL.
WHY NOT? I'M SURE HER MOTHER IS PROUD OF HER.
GEEZ, MA! YOU GIVE EVERYONE ELSE A SECOND CHANCE, CAN'T GIVE ME ONE, TOO?
THAT'S ALL I DO, GIVE CHANCE AFTER CHANCE TO PEOPLE WHO REFUSE TO BEHAVE--YOU, YOUR BROTHER, YOUR FATHER!
I SHOULD THROW YOU ALL OUT! FORCE YOU TO FEND FOR YOURSELVES FOR ONCE! THEN MAYBE YOU'D ALL FINALLY GROW UP!
MA!
I...I'M SORRY, BABY. IT'S JUST THE HOLIDAY STRESS TALKING.
DON'T APOLOGIZE, MA, IF THAT'S HOW YOU FEEL...

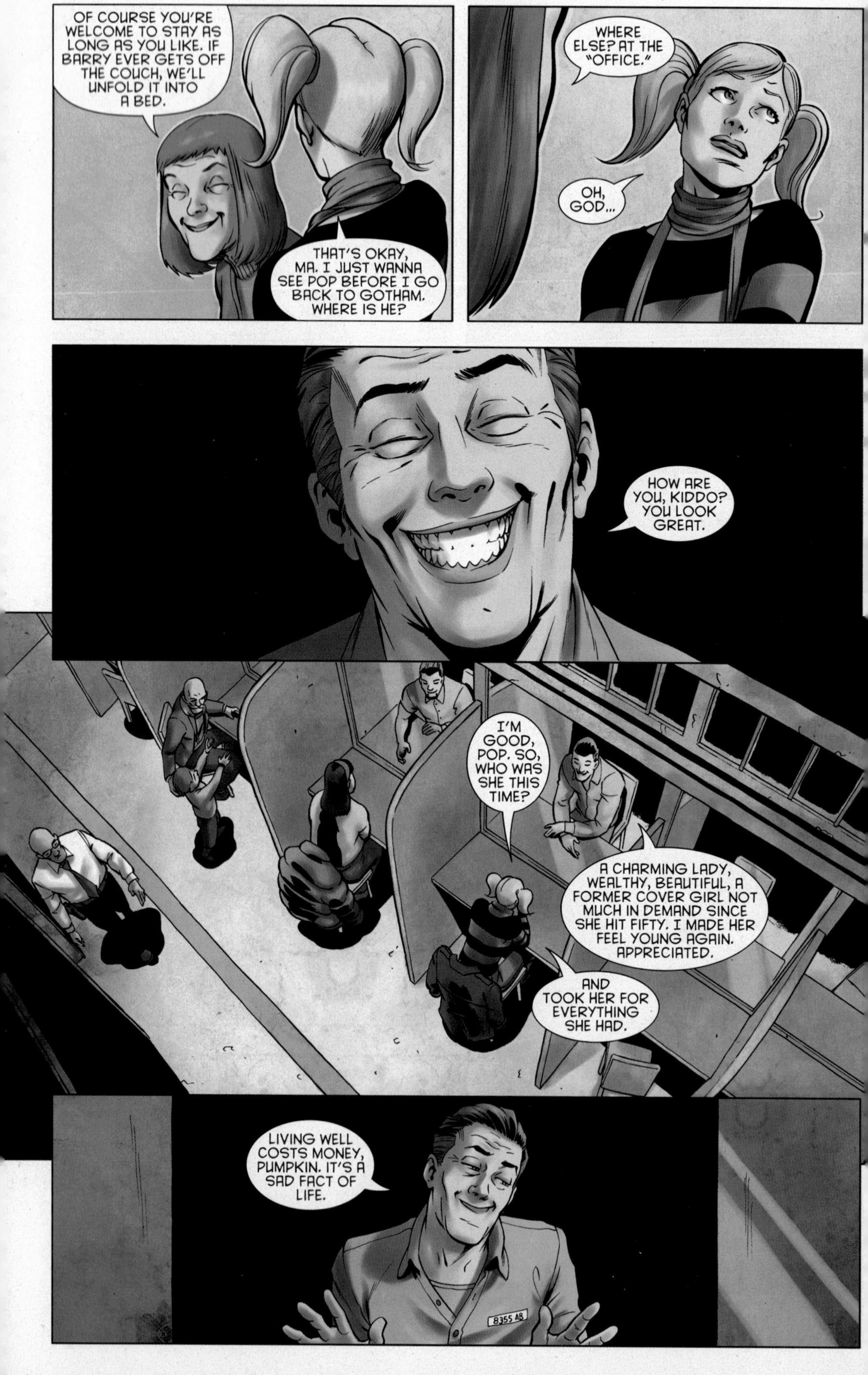

OF COURSE YOU'RE WELCOME TO STAY AS LONG AS YOU LIKE. IF BARRY EVER GETS OFF THE COUCH, WE'LL UNFOLD IT INTO A BED.
THAT'S OKAY, MA. I JUST WANNA SEE POP BEFORE I GO BACK TO GOTHAM. WHERE IS HE?
WHERE ELSE? AT THE "OFFICE."
OH, GOD...
HOW ARE YOU, KIDDO? YOU LOOK GREAT.
I'M GOOD, POP. SO, WHO WAS SHE THIS TIME?
A CHARMING LADY, WEALTHY, BEAUTIFUL, A FORMER COVER GIRL NOT MUCH IN DEMAND SINCE SHE HIT FIFTY. I MADE HER FEEL YOUNG AGAIN. APPRECIATED.
AND TOOK HER FOR EVERYTHING SHE HAD.
LIVING WELL COSTS MONEY, PUMPKIN. IT'S A SAD FACT OF LIFE.
8355 AB

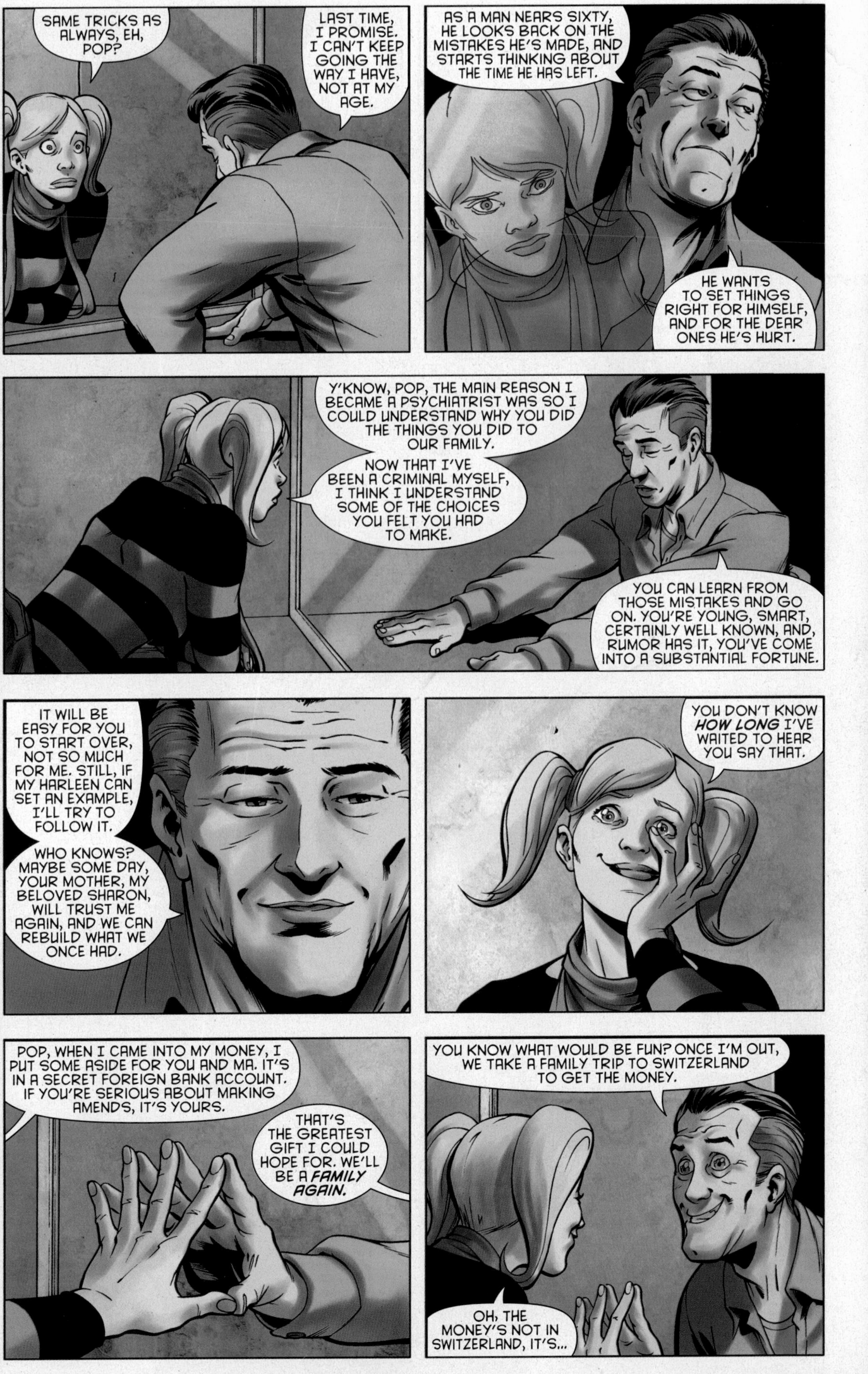
SAME TRICKS AS ALWAYS, EH, POP?
LAST TIME, I PROMISE. I CAN'T KEEP GOING THE WAY I HAVE, NOT AT MY AGE.
AS A MAN NEARS SIXTY, HE LOOKS BACK ON THE MISTAKES HE'S MADE, AND STARTS THINKING ABOUT THE TIME HE HAS LEFT.
HE WANTS TO SET THINGS RIGHT FOR HIMSELF, AND FOR THE DEAR ONES HE'S HURT.
Y'KNOW, POP, THE MAIN REASON I BECAME A PSYCHIATRIST WAS SO I COULD UNDERSTAND WHY YOU DID THE THINGS YOU DID TO OUR FAMILY.
NOW THAT I'VE BEEN A CRIMINAL MYSELF, I THINK I UNDERSTAND SOME OF THE CHOICES YOU FELT YOU HAD TO MAKE.
YOU CAN LEARN FROM THOSE MISTAKES AND GO ON. YOU'RE YOUNG, SMART, CERTAINLY WELL KNOWN, AND, RUMOR HAS IT, YOU'VE COME INTO A SUBSTANTIAL FORTUNE.
IT WILL BE EASY FOR YOU TO START OVER, NOT SO MUCH FOR ME. STILL, IF MY HARLEEN CAN SET AN EXAMPLE, I'LL TRY TO FOLLOW IT.
WHO KNOWS? MAYBE SOME DAY, YOUR MOTHER, MY BELOVED SHARON, WILL TRUST ME AGAIN, AND WE CAN REBUILD WHAT WE ONCE HAD.
YOU DON'T KNOW *HOW LONG* I'VE WAITED TO HEAR YOU SAY THAT.
POP, WHEN I CAME INTO MY MONEY, I PUT SOME ASIDE FOR YOU AND MA. IT'S IN A SECRET FOREIGN BANK ACCOUNT. IF YOU'RE SERIOUS ABOUT MAKING AMENDS, IT'S YOURS.
THAT'S THE GREATEST GIFT I COULD HOPE FOR. WE'LL BE A *FAMILY AGAIN.*
YOU KNOW WHAT WOULD BE FUN? ONCE I'M OUT, WE TAKE A FAMILY TRIP TO SWITZERLAND TO GET THE MONEY.
OH, THE MONEY'S NOT IN SWITZERLAND, IT'S...

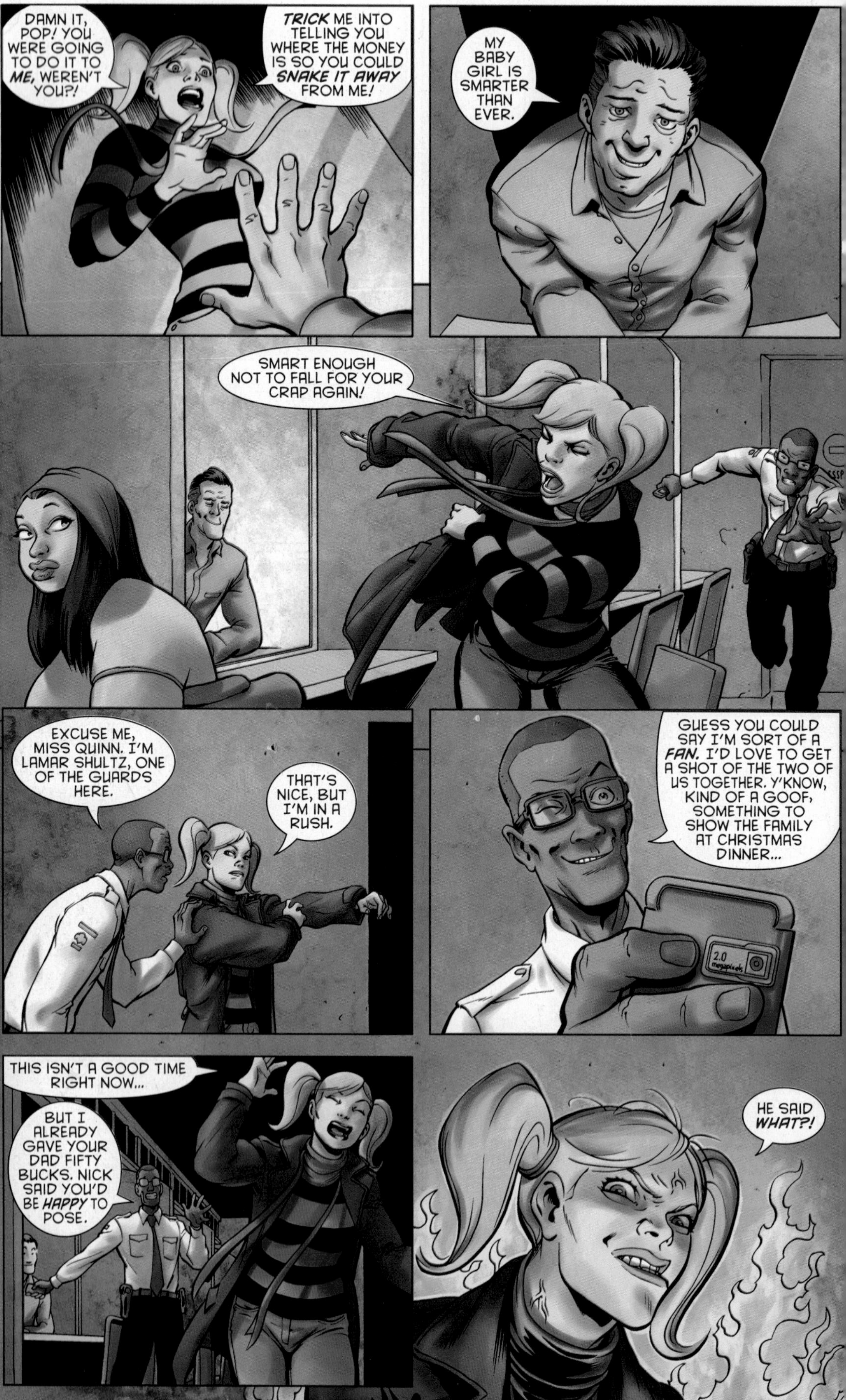
DAMN IT, POP! YOU WERE GOING TO DO IT TO *ME*, WEREN'T YOU?!
*TRICK* ME INTO TELLING YOU WHERE THE MONEY IS SO YOU COULD *SNAKE IT AWAY* FROM ME!
MY BABY GIRL IS SMARTER THAN EVER.
SMART ENOUGH NOT TO FALL FOR YOUR CRAP AGAIN!
EXCUSE ME, MISS QUINN. I'M LAMAR SHULTZ, ONE OF THE GUARDS HERE.
THAT'S NICE, BUT I'M IN A RUSH.
GUESS YOU COULD SAY I'M SORT OF A *FAN.* I'D LOVE TO GET A SHOT OF THE TWO OF US TOGETHER. Y'KNOW, KIND OF A GOOF, SOMETHING TO SHOW THE FAMILY AT CHRISTMAS DINNER...
2.0 megapixels
THIS ISN'T A GOOD TIME RIGHT NOW...
BUT I ALREADY GAVE YOUR DAD FIFTY BUCKS. NICK SAID YOU'D BE *HAPPY* TO POSE.
HE SAID *WHAT?!*

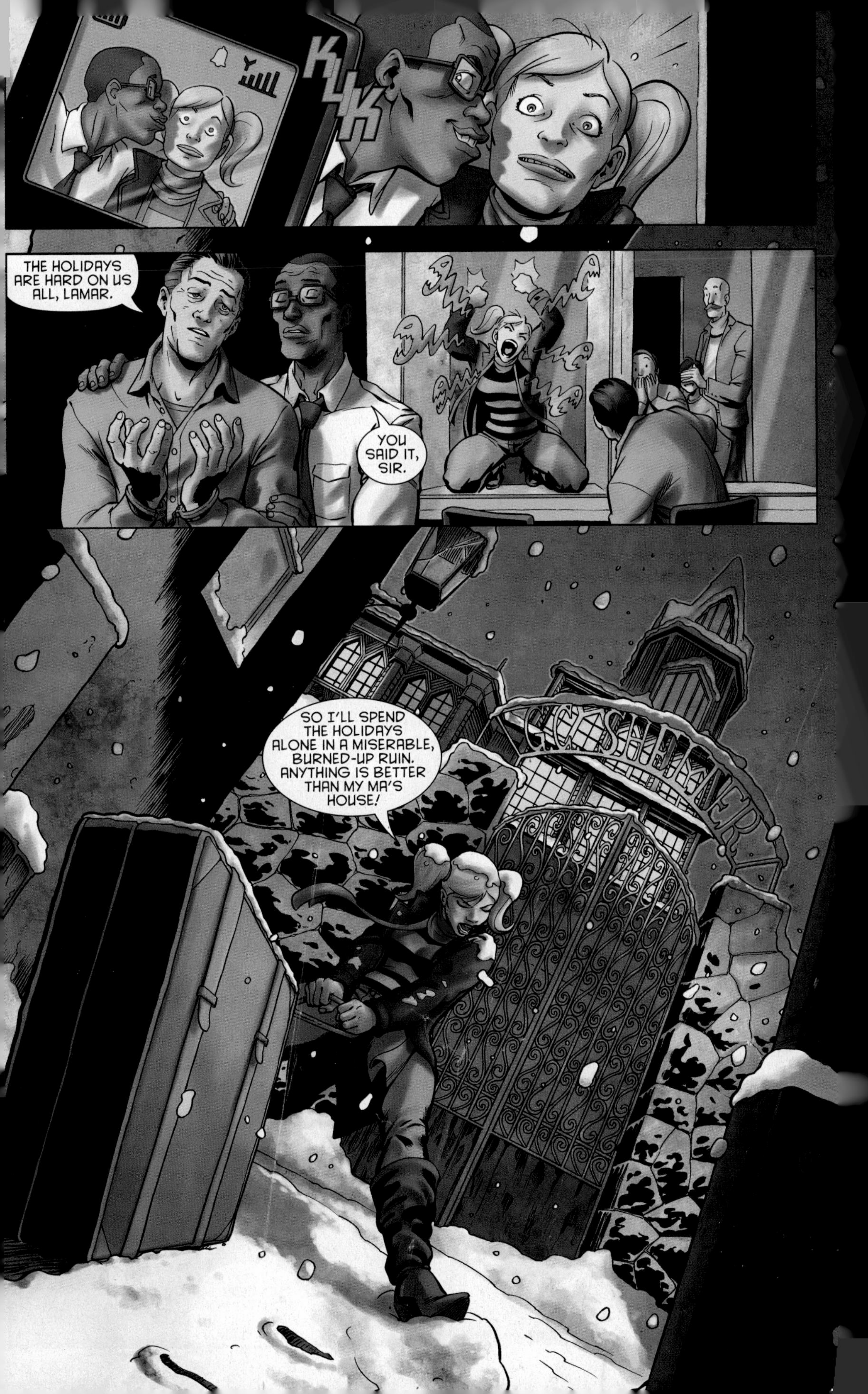
KLIK
THE HOLIDAYS ARE HARD ON US ALL, LAMAR.
YOU SAID IT, SIR.
SO I'LL SPEND THE HOLIDAYS ALONE IN A MISERABLE, BURNED-UP RUIN. ANYTHING IS BETTER THAN MY MA'S HOUSE!

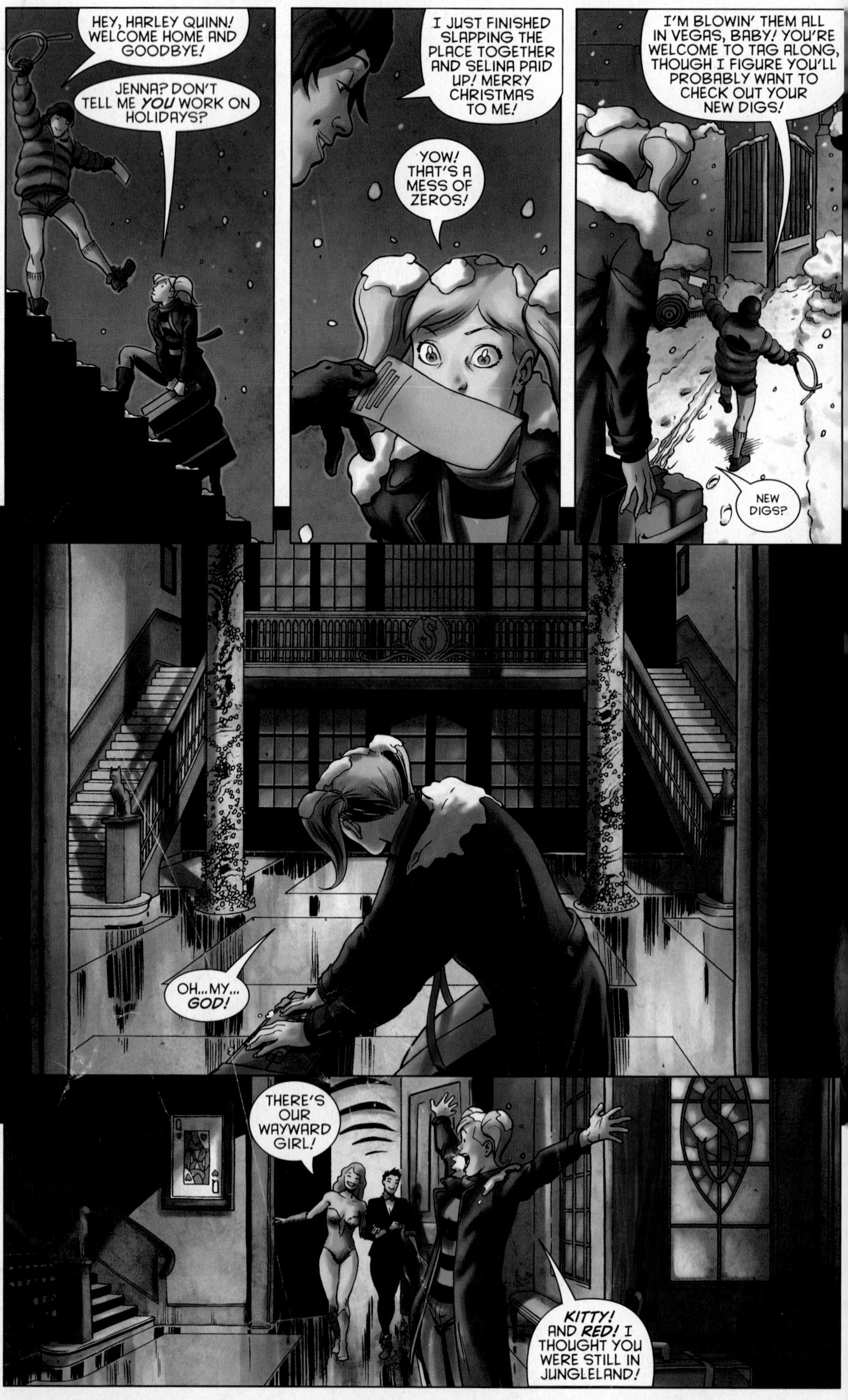
HEY, HARLEY QUINN! WELCOME HOME AND GOODBYE!
JENNA? DON'T TELL ME *YOU* WORK ON HOLIDAYS?
I JUST FINISHED SLAPPING THE PLACE TOGETHER AND SELINA PAID UP! MERRY CHRISTMAS TO ME!
YOW! THAT'S A MESS OF ZEROS!
I'M BLOWIN' THEM ALL IN VEGAS, BABY! YOU'RE WELCOME TO TAG ALONG, THOUGH I FIGURE YOU'LL PROBABLY WANT TO CHECK OUT YOUR NEW DIGS!
NEW DIGS?
OH... MY... *GOD!*
THERE'S OUR WAYWARD GIRL!
*KITTY!* AND *RED!* I THOUGHT YOU WERE STILL IN JUNGLELAND!

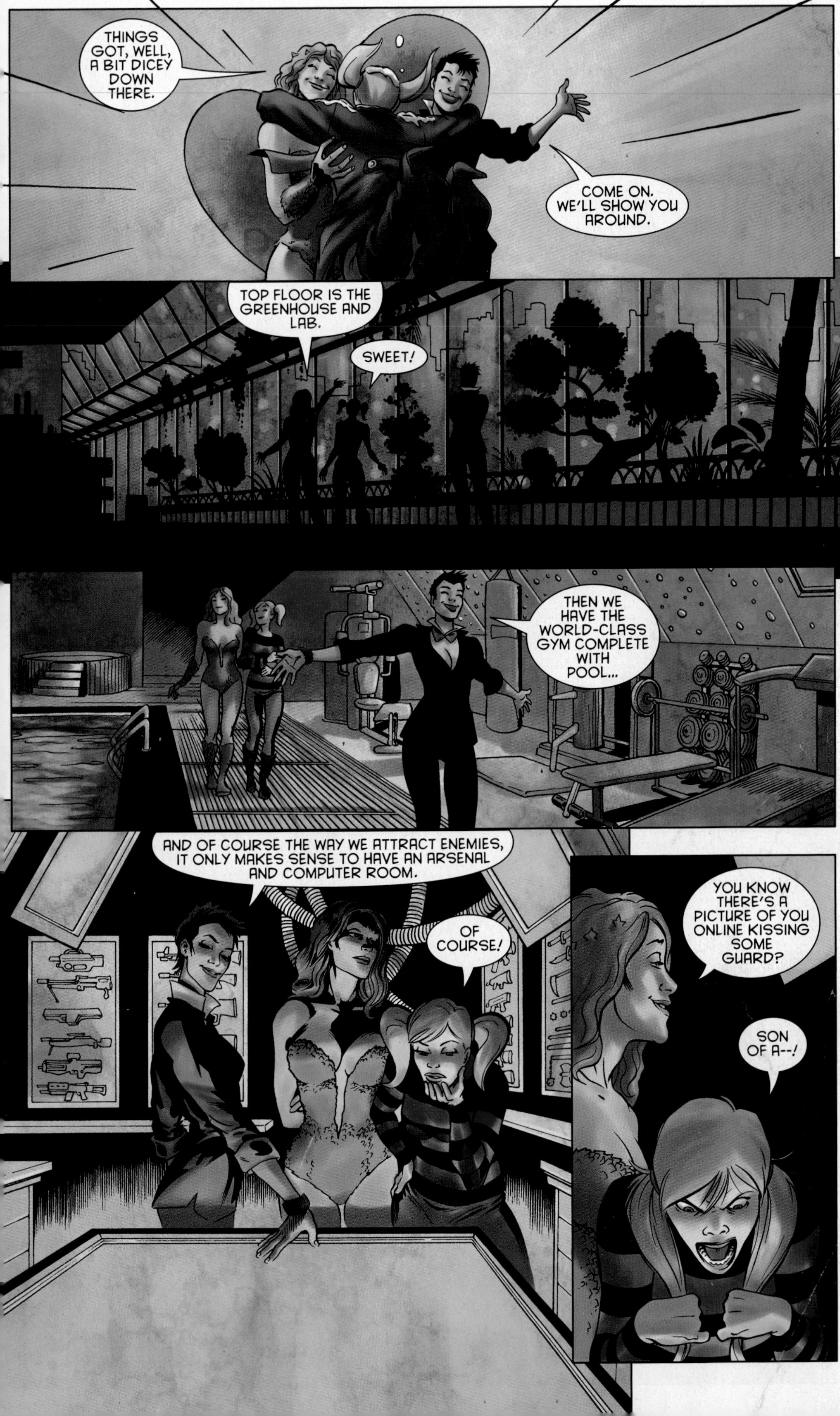
THINGS GOT, WELL, A BIT DICEY DOWN THERE.
COME ON. WE'LL SHOW YOU AROUND.
TOP FLOOR IS THE GREENHOUSE AND LAB.
SWEET!
THEN WE HAVE THE WORLD-CLASS GYM COMPLETE WITH POOL...
AND OF COURSE THE WAY WE ATTRACT ENEMIES, IT ONLY MAKES SENSE TO HAVE AN ARSENAL AND COMPUTER ROOM.
OF COURSE!
YOU KNOW THERE'S A PICTURE OF YOU ONLINE KISSING SOME GUARD?
SON OF A--!

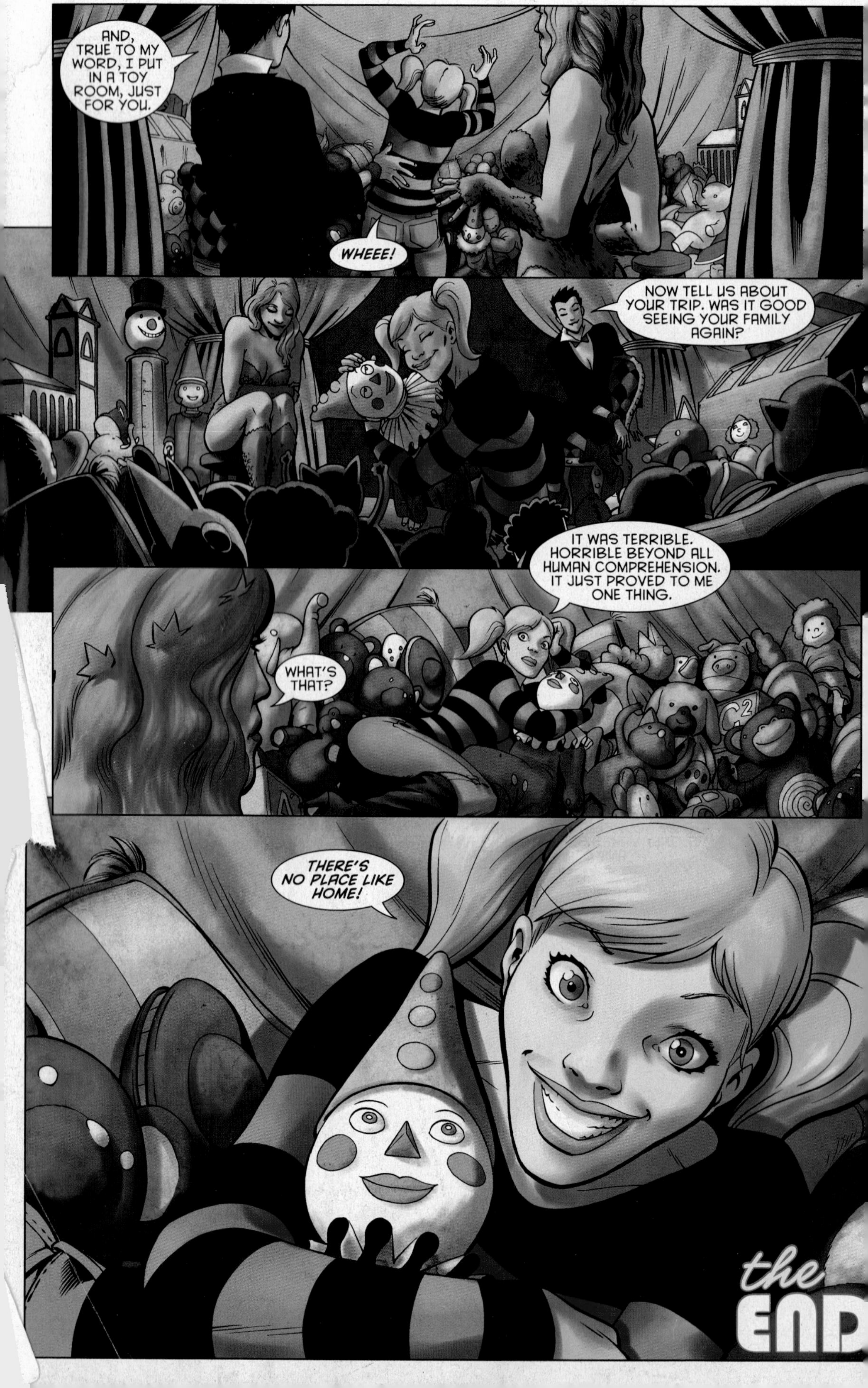
AND, TRUE TO MY WORD, I PUT IN A TOY ROOM, JUST FOR YOU.
WHEEE!
NOW TELL US ABOUT YOUR TRIP. WAS IT GOOD SEEING YOUR FAMILY AGAIN?
IT WAS TERRIBLE. HORRIBLE BEYOND ALL HUMAN COMPREHENSION. IT JUST PROVED TO ME ONE THING.
WHAT'S THAT?
THERE'S NO PLACE LIKE HOME!
the END